Taoism

FOR

DUMMIES®

A Wiley Brand

by Jonathan R. Herman, PhD

FOR

DUMMIES®

A Wiley Brand

Taoism For Dummies®

Published by
John Wiley & Sons Canada, Ltd.
6045 Freemont Blvd.
Mississauga, ON L5R 4J3
www.wiley.com

For general information on John Wiley & Sons Canada, Ltd., including all books published by Wiley, please call our warehouse, Tel 1-800-567-4797. For reseller information, including discounts and premium sales, please call our sales department, Tel 416-646-7992. For press review copies, author interviews, or other publicity information, please contact our marketing department, Tel 416-646-4584, Fax 416-236-4448.

For technical support, please visit www.wiley.com/techsupport.

Wiley publishes in a variety of print and electronic formats and by print-on-demand. Some material included with standard print versions of this book may not be included in e-books or in print-on-demand. If this book refers to media such as a CD or DVD that is not included in the version you purchased, you may download this material at http://booksupport.wiley.com. For more information about Wiley products, visit www.wiley.com.

Library and Archives Canada Cataloguing in Publication Data

Herman, Jonathan R., 1957–

Taoism for dummies / Jonathan Herman.

Includes index.

Issued also in electronic format.

ISBN 978-1-118-42396-7 (pbk); 978-1-118-42397-4 (ebk); 978-1-118-42398-1 (ebk); 978-1-118-42665-4 (ebk)

1. Taoism. I. Title.

BL1920.S48 2013   299.5'14   C2013-900865-9

Printed in the United States

1 2 3 4 5 RRD 17 16 15 14 13

About the Author

Jonathan R. Herman received his PhD in Chinese Religion from Harvard University in 1992. He is currently the Director of Undergraduate Studies and Associate Professor of Religious Studies at Georgia State University in Atlanta, where he teaches courses on Taoism, Confucianism, Buddhism, Shinto, world religions, comparative mysticism, and critical theory in the study of religion. He has also taught at Harvard University, Boston College, Tufts University, the University of Vermont, and Lewis & Clark College, and served for 12 years as an officer in the Society for the Study of Chinese Religions.

Jon is the author of *I and Tao: Martin Buber's Encounter with Chuang Tzu* (State University of New York Press) and has written extensively on a range of Chinese religion topics, including American and European transmissions of Taoism, Taoist environmentalism, Confucian hermeneutics, and Neo-Confucian mysticism. He also writes about a number of contemporary issues in the study of religion, including interfaith dialogue, mysticism and postmodernism, the relationship between religion and spirituality, religion and public discourse, and character education in the public schools.

Dedication

To my mother, Mae, who loved to teach and who continues to teach me how to teach out of love.

Author's Acknowledgments

Thanks to my catcher and copy editor, Elizabeth Kuball; my acquisitions editor at Wiley, Anam Ahmed; my research assistant, Randall Knighton; and my GSU department chair, Kathryn McClymond, who supported this departure from the usual "publish or perish" scholarship. Thanks to my many friends, colleagues, and mentors in Taoist studies and the academic study of religion for all they've taught me over the years, with a special thanks to Norman Girardot for his critical eye and enthusiastic support.

Most of all, I thank my family — Carly, Molly, and Ellen — for giving me the space and time to work on this book . . . and just for being my family.

Publisher's Acknowledgments

We're proud of this book; please send us your comments at http://dummies.custhelp.com. For other comments, please contact our Customer Care Department within the U.S. at 877-762-2974, outside the U.S. at 317-572-3993, or fax 317-572-4002.

Some of the people who helped bring this book to market include the following:

Acquisitions and Editorial

Project Editor: Elizabeth Kuball

Acquiring Editor: Anam Ahmed

Copy Editor: Elizabeth Kuball

Technical Editor: Norman Girardot, PhD

Production Editor: Lindsay Humphreys

Editorial Assistant: Kathy Deady

Cover Photos: © iStockphoto.com / me4o

Cartoons: Rich Tennant (www.the5thwave.com)

Composition Services

Senior Project Coordinator: Kristie Rees

Layout and Graphics: Jennifer Creasey

Proofreaders: Melissa D. Buddendeck, Jessica Kramer

Indexer: Slivoskey Indexing Services

John Wiley & Sons Canada, Ltd.

Deborah Barton, Vice President and Director of Operations

Jennifer Smith, Publisher, Professional Development

Alison Maclean, Managing Editor, Professional Development

Publishing and Editorial for Consumer Dummies

Kathleen Nebenhaus, Vice President and Executive Publisher

David Palmer, Associate Publisher

Kristin Ferguson-Wagstaffe, Product Development Director

Publishing for Technology Dummies

Andy Cummings, Vice President and Publisher

Composition Services

Debbie Stailey, Director of Composition Services

Contents at a Glance

Table of Contents

Introduction

● ●

*T*aoism is one of China's "Three Teachings," a religious tradition that traces back to a mythic sage named Lao Tzu and flourishes today in modern China, as well as other parts of East Asia. In recent years, it has even begun to make some headway into Western Europe and North America. Almost every basic world religions textbook has a chapter on it, and many bookstores carry a smattering of Taoist texts or books about some aspect of Taoism.

But if you want to start learning something about Taoism, how do you know where to begin? Some books barely whet your appetite with a brief historical summary and provocative quotations from a handful of classical texts, while others overwhelm you with technical language and microscopic analysis. Some encourage you to adopt Taoist philosophy in your own life, or package Taoism as the latest in "self-help" — but you never really know whether they're just making it all up!

Fortunately, your troubles are over.

About This Book

This book introduces Taoism in a way that makes it easy to grasp, while at the same time giving you a clear sense of parts of the tradition that can get a little complicated. You can follow the development of Taoism from its origins in ancient China, through the specific sects that have survived in a rapidly changing contemporary Chinese society, all the way to organizations that have popped up in New York, San Francisco, and other North American cities. And you can find out about Taoist ideas, texts, and practices — everything from "non-doing" and *yin-yang* philosophy to *ch'i-kung* and rituals of cosmic renewal.

We're talking here about a religious tradition that has undergone more than two millennia of history, transformed over time, given rise to multiple sects and lineages, and played a role in the lives of literally *billions* of people, so it would be pretty hard to dig into every single detail with the depth that each one deserves. But that doesn't mean that a book like this can't touch as many bases as possible and have some fun while doing so. You can count on this book being broad (it covers a wide spectrum of Taoist information), accurate (it doesn't tell you anything that isn't true), and understandable (it never tries to dazzle you with fancy language or dense philosophical banter). And mostly, you can count on it being an enjoyable and entertaining read.

Conventions Used in This Book

Because this book presents its subjects in a straightforward, easy-to-digest style, you don't have to memorize a bunch of specialized conventions before you even get started, but I do want to let you know about a few standard practices that this book follows:

- ✔ The book assigns dates using B.C.E. (Before the Common Era) and C.E. (Common Era) instead of B.C. (Before Christ) and A.D. (*Anno Domini,* or "In the Year of the Lord"), because the newer designations are more religiously neutral. But this isn't a big deal, because they're referring to the same calendar.

- ✔ I don't talk about Taoism as a "religion" as much as a "religious tradition" or simply a "tradition." This helps break the habit of thinking of Taoism (or any *–ism,* for that matter) as one fixed, unchanging entity that exists apart from the way human beings construct it, employ it, and transform it. Somehow, a "tradition" gives the impression of being more fluid and internally diverse than a "religion."

- ✔ Finally, and this is the big one, although I don't want to overwhelm you with long lists of hard-to-pronounce Chinese words, there are enough important people in Taoist history that you really need to pick up some rudimentary ground rules for how to read *Romanized* (that is, English-language versions of) Chinese words and names. And this will probably come in handy well beyond *Taoism For Dummies.* The system of Romanization this book uses is the Wade–Giles system, which is covered in Appendix C.

  When you read Chinese words and names, try saying them out loud (using the pronunciation guide in Appendix C). People learn words and names better when they actually hear them, instead of just reading the letters on the printed page, and I promise you it'll be a whole lot easier to keep track of them when you try it this way.

These are the biggest conventions to keep in mind. But in addition to these, my editor wanted me to let you know that I *italicize* new terms when they're first used (and define them shortly thereafter, often in parentheses), and I use `monofont` for web addresses.

Note: When this book was printed, some web addresses may have needed to break across two lines of text. If that happened, rest assured that we haven't put in any extra characters (such as hyphens) to indicate the break. So, when using one of these web addresses, just type in exactly what you see in this book, pretending as though the line break doesn't exist.

Foolish Assumptions

No, I'm not going to knock whatever assumptions you may have about Taoism — that wouldn't be fair. But I am going to come clean about some of the assumptions that I have about *you:*

✔ You're probably not a Taoist, but you have some interest in this particular tradition, in China more generally, or in any religious tradition that's not your own.

✔ You take seriously the religious beliefs and practices of other people, and you want to become familiar with Taoism as one way to understand your friends, neighbors, or colleagues a little better.

✔ You don't necessarily know a lot about Taoism, and you probably don't know all the technical vocabulary when it comes to religion, but you're interested in the subject and a quick-enough study that you'll pick up a lot, as long as I don't talk down to you and just explain things in a straightforward way.

How This Book Is Organized

Regardless of websites that tell you Taoism is nothing more than adopting a philosophy of simplicity and "going with the flow," the historical Taoist religious tradition is actually tremendously complex, with distinct lineages and sects, an extensive pantheon of deities, a hierarchical priesthood, and texts that are intelligible only to those who've been initiated into certain teachings.

To make your journey into Taoism a little less intimidating, this book is organized into distinct parts, each of which is built around a broad theme. These parts don't follow any standard formula, or correspond to any official Taoist "orthodoxy" — they're just presented in a way that makes the subject more approachable and lets you look into the areas you find most interesting.

Part 1: Navigating the World of Taoism

This part lets you tiptoe into the world of Taoism by introducing you to its Chinese religious background and presenting an overview of the tradition. It straightens out some common misconceptions, points out the ambiguity of the word *Taoism,* and gives you some important distinctions to help you navigate the rest of the book.

Part II: Looking At the Development of Taoism

Every story starts at the beginning, and the story of Taoism is no exception. But this story doesn't just give you a dry "names and dates" version of history; instead, it takes you through a remarkable journey of narrative twists and turns. You see how the tradition begins with a handful of classical texts, produces communitarian organizations and self-cultivation groups, evolves into the liturgical and monastic sects you can find in China today, and is developing a Western identity as we speak.

Part III: Examining Important Taoist Concepts

Here's a chance to take a look at some enduring Taoist ideas and themes, including the concepts of *Tao,* "non-doing," and *yin* and *yang.* It's also a chance to discover some important aspects of Taoism that don't always make it into the world religion textbooks, like the belief in a "new age" or the scriptural canon that includes well over a thousand texts.

Part IV: Exploring Taoist Practices

Religion is more than a collection of beliefs, doctrines, or texts; it involves how people *live* and what traditions they practice. This section takes a look at some important aspects of Taoist practice, including meditation, alchemy, self-cultivation, martial arts, and ritual.

Part V: The Part of Tens

In a hurry? Just want some quick bedside reading? Or maybe you like your Taoism straight, with no chaser? Here's Taoism condensed into bite-size portions, a trio of top-ten lists that give you a *very* brief summary of basic entry points into Taoism. Here, you can redress the most common misconceptions, get a road map for seeing some Taoism in action, and even pick up pointers for acquiring Taoist wisdom and applying it to your life.

Part VI: Appendixes

Doctors say that the human appendix is useless, something that may have once served a purpose but is now just taking up space. But the appendixes in this book actually contain some pretty useful information, and you may want to turn to them from time to time as you read the book.

Appendix A contains a glossary of important Taoist figures, key Taoist terminology, and other technical terms. These can jog your memory if you read the chapters out of sequence, pick up the book only once in a while, or just want a quick way to review a critical mass of material. Appendix B contains some recommendations for other resources you can consult if you'd like to delve deeper into any of the subjects discussed here. And Appendix C is a pronunciation guide, giving you pointers on how to pronounce all the difficult Chinese names and terms you encounter throughout this book. It also includes a chart that compares the Wade–Giles system used in this book with the *pinyin* system that many other sources use.

Icons Used in This Book

A handful of cute icons show up periodically throughout this book, in part to give you a "goose" to break up the "duck-duck-duck" rhythm of each chapter, but mainly to draw your attention to points that are especially important, interesting, or just worth repeating. Here are the icons you'll find:

The Remember icon points out things to keep in mind as you read a particular chapter or move on to the next one. Often, this contains a surprising bit of information or corrects common misconceptions about Taoism, China, or both.

The Tip icon alerts you to strategies for sorting things out, or for making sense of things that could seem confusing. It may suggest to you *how* you can read or think about a particular section.

The Warning icon gives you a heads-up about places where the subject could start to get more complicated, or topics that not all Taoists agree on or do the same way.

The Technical Stuff icon points out information — background history, complex explanations, problems in interpretation — that is certainly important, but that may be harder to keep track of on your first reading. Feel free either to skim these tidbits or read them extra-carefully, whichever suits you better.

Where to Go from Here

Think of this book as an educational buffet on Taoism, a smorgasbord of resources that are here for only one purpose: to help you understand Taoism better. Depending on which plate you pick up, or where you dip your ladle, you can engage the classical philosophers, meet the medieval alchemists, locate Taoist practice groups in America, hit your head against the counterintuitive idea of "actionless action," explore the Taoist practice of "sitting and forgetting," get a look at cults of immortality, and find out how Taoist priests perform rituals from time to time that serve to renew the entire cosmos.

Read this book the way that works best for you. Feel free to read it in order from beginning to end, poke through the Table of Contents to find the themes that most attract you, or just use the Index to chase down a particular text or historical period you'd most like to explore in more detail. Whichever you choose, make sure you have some fun, because Taoism promises you an exciting world of learning. Or to give just a sniff of the Taoist cork, perhaps I should say that Taoism promises you the even more exciting world of *unlearning* — and what could be more fun than that?

Part I
Navigating the World of Taoism

The 5th Wave   By Rich Tennant

ARTHUR'S JOURNEY DOWN THE PATH OF TAOISM IS BRIEFLY INTERRUPTED

In this part . . .

When you take your first steps into the world of Taoism, be prepared for some basic questions to come fast and furious. Is Taoism a philosophy or a religion? What's the relationship between Taoism and other Chinese traditions, like Confucianism, Buddhism, or folk religion? What are the different types of Taoism? What are the most common misconceptions about Taoism? How is Taoism different from Western traditions?

Sit back, and get ready to participate in a great adventure. Or better yet, lean forward and prepare to devour every word, because Taoism can be fascinating, sophisticated, and inspiring, and it can also surprise you at every turn.

Chapter 1

An Introduction to Taoism

*N*ot much more than a half-century ago, many Americans had their main exposure to Chinese people and things Chinese from an exotic meal at the local Chinese restaurant, a touristy adventure in a big-city Chinatown, or even a Charlie Chan movie. Today, things have certainly changed, and the Chinese presence in America (and in the world) has come a long way from pu-pu platters, isolated ethnic enclaves, and cinematic sages speaking fortune-cookie dialogue in broken English. Today nearly 4 million Chinese people (or people of at least partial Chinese descent) live in the United States, and Chinese people may make up close to 5 percent of the Canadian population. What's more, Chinese people now participate in pretty much every aspect of modern American culture — their contributions to schools, neighborhoods, businesses, and local communities are as important and as visible as those of any other American. And, by the way, you just may have heard somewhere that China is now an important global economic and political power, too!

So, what could possibly be a better time for picking up a few pointers on Taoism, one of China's oldest (and most interesting) indigenous religious traditions? If you're not Chinese, learning about Taoism could help you gain some insight into Chinese religious, philosophical, and cultural sensibilities. If you are Chinese, it's a chance to get to know your own background and history a little better. But the funny thing is that even though Taoism has informed much of Chinese identity, it isn't the easiest thing to find. Very few Chinese people in America identify themselves specifically as Taoists, and most communities don't have Taoist temples. And when you do find a Taoist temple or teaching center, you may find that the staff and students consist entirely of non-Chinese people. In other words, despite the unprecedented integration of Chinese in the West, and even with the deluge of "Tao of" readers on bookstore shelves, Taoism is still pretty much a mystery to many people.

Taoism or Daoism?

Maybe you already know that the first syllable of Taoism is pronounced *dow* (as in the Dow Jones Industrial Average), or that some books spell it *Daoism* rather than *Taoism*. Maybe you've noticed that the capital of China used to be called "Peking" but today is called "Beijing" (even though you still order Peking duck at Chinese restaurants). And textbooks used to call the longtime leader of China "Mao Tse-tung," but today they call him "Mao Zedong." What's going on here?

Part of it is the difference in regional dialects, but the bigger issue is that the sources that regularly deal with things Chinese — texts, newspapers, websites — use two different Romanization systems, which are sometimes in a kind of competition with each other. The Wade–Giles system, which spells *Tao* with a *T*, took hold in the early 1900s and dominated almost all publications for most of the 20th century. However, the Chinese were never nuts about the system and eventually developed *Hanyu Pinyin,* the system with the *D,* in the late 1950s. This one started to pick up international recognition by the early 1980s, though Taiwan initially resisted it, and many areas with large Chinese populations — like American Chinatowns — have been slow to adopt it. In some circles, choosing one system over another could be perceived as making a political statement, but none of that is figuring into the choice for this book. We've gone with *Taoism* for this book because the publisher judged that more readers would recognize *Taoism* than *Daoism*. So, this book uses the older Wade–Giles system, except when referring to place names (like Beijing or Xi'an) where a different spelling will probably be more familiar to most readers.

So, why does the Wade–Giles system spell things with a *T* even though they're pronounced like a *D?* Is this some bizarre code that only nerdy polyglots can understand? There are actually a few reasons:

✔ **There's no Chinese alphabet.** Each character has a specific pronunciation (including a particular tone) that you can only know if someone else (like your parents) teaches it to you; you can't just read the letters and know the exact pronunciation.

✔ **There are lots of sounds in Chinese that don't have exact parallels in English.** Every time you read a Romanized Chinese word or name, it's really just an approximation of that word.

✔ **Although there is no Chinese alphabet, many characters do have certain phonetic characteristics — calligraphic hints as to how they could be pronounced — and usually, words that are etymologically related sound similar.** For example, some characters that are pronounced *tao* (with a *t* sound) are related and look similar to some that are pronounced *dao* (with a *d* sound). So, the creators of the Wade–Giles system asked a question that would only matter to specialists: How on Earth can we put all the *taos* and all the *daos* close to each other in Chinese-English dictionaries that are arranged alphabetically?

Their solution was ingenious . . . or kind of crazy, depending on how you look at it. Try the following exercise: Hold the open palm of your hand right in front of your face — up close to your lips, but not touching them — and say the English word *tie*. Do you notice that you get a breath of air blowing against your palm? Now say the word *die*. Do you notice that your lips, teeth, and tongue seem to be doing the exact same thing as when you said *tie,* but without the breath of air on your palm? That's because *tie* and *die* are essentially the same words, but one is *aspirated* (that is, breathed with a burst of air), and the other is not. And so, the Wade–Giles architects decided that *t'ao* (with the apostrophe) would be read as written, with the aspirated *t* sound, while *tao* (without the apostrophe) would be read with the unaspirated *d* sound. And — *voilà!* — *tao* is pronounced like *dow!* And that's why *pao* is pronounced like *bow* and *kao* is pronounced like *cow*. You can check out Appendix C for a complete pronunciation guide to the Wade–Giles system used in this book.

Getting the Lay of the Taoist Land

As you get oriented to Taoism, you quickly find out that there seem to be lots of different kinds of Taoism and Taoists, and that it's often hard to figure out how any one of these "Taoisms" relates to any other. Part of this is that the Chinese aren't always consistent in how they use the terms, and they may even apply them to people and practices that technically aren't really Taoist. It's especially common for people to call various nondenominational family or community customs "popular Taoism" or "folk Taoism," just because they're clearly not Buddhist and no one's quite sure what category to put them in. Certainly, a big part of navigating Taoism is the process of sorting one strain from another.

Along these same lines, Taoism (like every other one of the world's major traditions) changes over time, and not always in a linear fashion that you can chronicle with a nice, neat, century-by-century timeline. If you try to imagine a Taoist family tree, you need to be prepared for lots of gnarled branches, limbs that snap suddenly and then somehow seem to regrow again in some other location, roots that entangle with those of other trees and then become indistinguishable from each other, and oddly shaped fruits that look and taste completely different from other fruits growing on different vines on the very same tree. It is, to put it mildly, a tangled family tree.

The first step to keeping all the Taoisms straight in your mind is to develop a certain working vocabulary for classifying Taoism. This often involves examining the categories you hear most often online and in textbooks — like "philosophical Taoism" and "religious Taoism" — and then moving on to more careful and more nuanced language and divisions. You can find a discussion about all this in Chapter 2.

But nothing makes Taoism harder to understand than approaching the subject with misconceptions — either about Chinese religion in general or about Taoism in particular — and then finding that the stuff you read doesn't make any sense. If you heard somewhere that Taoism is atheistic or agnostic, you'll certainly get confused when you start finding huge collections of deities enshrined at Taoist temples. If you've found inspiration in the *Tao Te Ching*, one of the most frequently translated books in human history, you'll probably be disappointed to learn that it often doesn't have much to do with actual Taoist practice. If you have the idea that Lao Tzu and Chuang Tzu taught a spiritual path, it'll no doubt shake you up a bit to discover that the whole concept of *spirituality* is actually a Western (and recent) invention. The good news, of course, is that once you understand the odd confluence of events, the intellectual chain reactions that cemented most of these misconceptions in the Western imagination, you'll get not only new eyes for "real" Chinese Taoism, but also a new perspective on the shape and flavor of the Taoism that's catching on in the West.

Tossing out these types of misconceptions about Taoism opens things up for you to see Taoism on its own terms, and to situate it in its broader context as one ingredient of Chinese religion and culture. Fortunately, Chinese religion is not some alien or wholly other prospect — we're not dealing with Martians or anything like that here — but it does contain some unexpected surprises. For the most part, the Chinese religious worldview is very pragmatic in its concerns; the Chinese have historically given much more attention to matters of day-to-day living than abstract speculation about the nature of God or the human soul. This involves a strong emphasis on family and regional identity, where family relationships serve as a model for most ethical norms. Chinese religious practitioners ordinarily engage a range of gods and other spirits — irrespective of whether they originate in one tradition or another — who have various specialties, functions, and most important, the ability to influence human affairs. And a number of religious "experts" — priests, diviners, exorcists, and so on — help mediate the interactions between humans and spirits, and officiate at various public and private events. I discuss this in more detail in Chapter 3.

Delving into the Evolution of Taoism

If you have an idea that history is a lot of dull stuff — names, dates, facts, and figures — you're not alone. And trying to memorize a collage of uncoordinated details can be about as snooze-worthy as it gets. Fortunately, you'll find it hard to nap through the story of Taoism. Colorful characters, dramatic innovations, and unexpected augmentations to the tradition show up at just about every turn! And the more you can fill in the historical background, the more things start to make sense.

Taoist origins and development

The assorted texts, practices, and cultural traditions that we call Taoism had their earliest rumblings close to 2,500 years ago, even though it took several hundred years before any people thought of themselves as Taoists or developed any sense of shared Taoist identity. The tradition more or less began during a period of tremendous intellectual ferment in China, an extended time when numerous philosophical schools contended with one another for intellectual supremacy and political power. The Taoist texts from this period, including Lao Tzu's *Tao Te Ching* and the *Chuang Tzu,* still rank among the most stimulating and entertaining works in all of Chinese literature. These authors failed to "win" the debates from the Hundred Schools Period (as it is now known), in the sense that they never convinced the political leaders of the time to adopt their teachings, but they did briefly influence the ruling ideology of the early Han Dynasty (206 B.C.E.–220 C.E.) in a short-lived movement called Huang-Lao Taoism, and leave a permanent mark on later Chinese religion and culture (see Chapter 4).

The first documented record of anything we can call a Taoist community or institution took shape a few hundred years after that, and it represents the first sharp right-angle turn in Taoism's history. This all began with the emergence of a charismatic teacher and healer named Chang Tao-ling, who founded a tightly knit society called, alternatively, the Way of the Celestial Masters, the Five Pecks or Rice Sect, or somewhat later, the Way of Orthodox Unity. This group

✔ Worshiped Lao Tzu as a divine figure (along with many other deities)

✔ Publicly recited the *Tao Te Ching*

✔ Believed in the coming of a "new age"

✔ Developed both a hierarchical priesthood and series of secretive rituals that continue to shape Taoism today

The community didn't last, but its forms and surviving members mixed and mingled with other people in different regions, and over the next several hundred years the tradition eventually accumulated many new sacred texts (like the Highest Purity and Numinous Treasure revelations), practices (like alchemy), and deities (like the Heavenly Worthy of the Primordial Beginning). By the 12th and 13th centuries, many new Taoist sects — like the Correct Method of the Celestial Heart, and the Perfect Great Way — were in competition with one another. I discuss these developments in Chapter 5.

Tao now (brown cow)

Taoism in China suffered terribly during large swaths of the 20th century, to the point that Mao Tse-tung and his ill-conceived Cultural Revolution nearly wiped it out altogether by the mid-1970s. But since then, Taoism has mounted a vigorous comeback, including the restoration of many temples, the resumption of priestly ordination, and the performance of public ceremonies. Although a wide range of people claim various Taoist affiliations — some more legitimately than others — most Chinese Taoism today falls into two distinct denominations or lineages:

✔ **The Way of Orthodox Unity:** The liturgical and ritualistic branch that is more common in southern China and Taiwan

✔ **The Way of Complete Perfection:** The monastic branch that is more common in northern China

Although these divisions pretty much define Taoism in modern China, the vast majority of Westerners — even those who've read the *Tao Te Ching* for years and fancy themselves enthusiasts of Taoist philosophy — have never heard of either sect. I discuss these sects and compare them with each other in Chapter 6.

Speaking of the West, the history of Taoism isn't limited to China — it has begun to sprout legs and start walking around North American countries as well. The face of American Taoism is very different from that of China, which leads (some) people to debate whether it even "counts" as Taoism. For many years, Taoism's main presence in the West was through texts, including the many (if not always accurate) translations of the *Tao Te Ching* and *Chuang Tzu* and creative popular writings like Benjamin Hoff's *The Tao of Pooh,* though Taoist temples, study centers, and online marketplaces have begun popping up over the last few decades. For the most part, these American venues focus on historically marginal Taoist practices like *t'ai-chi* and *ch'i-kung,* and have found some unanticipated alliances with many of those involved in the New Age Movement. American Taoism often includes other Chinese resources, like meditation, acupuncture, traditional herbal medicine, and even sexual techniques. You can find out about the Western *Tao* in Chapter 7.

Considering Taoist Ideas

Taoists do think about a lot of interesting things, and many Taoist texts contain some of the most philosophically rich thinking you'll find in any tradition. For the most part, Taoist ideas don't involve litanies of doctrinal formulations that people have to say they believe in order to be good Taoists, as much as observations and interpretations of the world that translate into specific ways that people should act, whether out of their own enlightened self-interest or out of interpersonal obligation. And just as Taoism changes over time and produces contending lineages, the ideas also change over time and vary in accord with the different lineages. You'll always be better off if you make peace with Taoism's internal diversity instead of trying to get everything to fit together into one "essence."

It all begins with the Tao

You probably already have an idea that Taoism has to do with the *Tao,* just as Christianity has to do with Christ and Buddhism has to do with the Buddha. But Taoism isn't really about a belief in the *Tao* or anything like that. That's because the term *Tao* simply means "the Way," and it was already part of the Chinese worldview well before Taoism came into existence. What's more, other non-Taoist Chinese traditions lay equal claim to ownership of the term, because almost all expressions of Chinese religion and philosophy in one manner or another have something to do with figuring out the "ways" of the universe (possibly including deities) and what "ways" human beings should follow. And Chinese frequently think of various other "ways" that don't have much to do with religion or philosophy either. In other words, the term *Tao* extends well beyond Taoism, well beyond Chinese religion.

But *Tao* is an especially loaded term in the Taoist context, and discussions of it in the *Tao Te Ching* and *Chuang Tzu* waste no time letting you know something funny's going on. First, they tell us that conventional language isn't sufficient for describing it, that those who claim to understand it couldn't possibly have it right, and that dim-witted people who hear about it won't be able to do much more than laugh. And then, they illustrate it through colorful, often paradoxical, figures of speech, and continually remind us how difficult it is to comprehend its mystery. It's as though the authors are in on some secret joke, and they keep redirecting you someplace else every time they think you're getting too close to the punchline. If you're not in a hurry, you may end up hitting your head against the *Tao* for a *very* long time.

Even with all the paradoxes and apparent narrative dead ends, some fairly clear characteristics of the Taoist concept of the *Tao* do come through in the texts:

- ✔ It represents a creative principle, and the authors frequently allude to it through the metaphor of a procreative mother and other feminine imagery.

- ✔ It somehow owes its creative power to being empty, which explains why so much Taoist philosophy deals with discussions of "non-being" or the relationship between "being" and "non-being."

- ✔ Whatever the *Tao* may be, human beings habitually lose sight of it and need to recover it through a process of *returning* (a process that many people are convinced involves some type of mysticism).

You can get your *Tao* on in Chapter 8.

The Taoist process of following the Way can't really be reduced to one or two things; it's no exaggeration to suggest that every aspect of the Taoist tradition in some measure addresses following the Way, whether it involves praying to deities or engaging in the smelting of metals in a laboratory. But in the *Tao Te Ching* and *Chuang Tzu* especially, the concept of *Tao* attaches very closely to a truly mind-boggling principle for moral action: that of *wu-wei,* which people alternately translate as "non-doing," "doing nothing," "actionless action," and dozens of similar phrases. The basic idea here is that although the creative power of the *Tao* lies in its emptiness, humans can only "plug in" to the *Tao* by taking on that very quality of emptiness. This translates into acting in a way that comes not from personal desire or affect, but by emulating the empty, impartial qualities of the *Tao* itself, so you don't even feel like you're the agent of your own action. And to boot, this non-doing is utterly effective — so both the *Tao* and the person who correctly follows the *Tao* "do nothing, yet nothing remains undone."

The discussions of non-doing introduce a roster of memorable metaphors for accomplishing such a state. The "uncarved block" refers to an object that exists in a natural state of simplicity and perfection, not yet structured (and limited) by human intervention. Bending along the "hinge of the Way" refers to the ability to adapt flexibly and fluidly to the constantly shifting circumstances of existence. And the "mind as a mirror" (which also gets a lot of mileage in

Zen Buddhism) alludes to reflecting and responding to reality as it is, without superimposing any of your own interpretations or motivations onto it. I discuss all this in Chapter 9.

The expansion of the Tao

Although the concept of the *Tao* and the principle of non-doing are profound, provocative innovations, it would be hard to imagine enduring religious communities based entirely on those ideals. First-time readers of the *Tao Te Ching* may be disappointed to learn not only that *wu-wei* in isolation isn't really viable as universal public morality, but also that the text never really functioned as a Taoist "Bible," providing a social blueprint for how people should live their day-to-day lives. To understand Taoism in Chinese culture over the last 2,000 years, you need to look at different ideas and resources.

One development that fits somewhat congenially with the original ideas of *Tao* and non-doing is the integration of *yin-yang* and "five phases" (or "five elements") theory into almost all forms of Taoism. By explaining the function of the *Tao* in terms of interactions of *yin* and *yang,* or more complexly as the cycles of five active "agents" — wood, fire, earth, metal, and water — Taoists eventually came to understand everything from imperial history to medical science through elaborate systems of correspondence and resonance. In Chapter 10, I talk about the nuances of *yin-yang* theory and how that creates the basis for many Taoist practices, including various forms of physical self-cultivation.

The first actual Taoist community believed in a coming "new age" (see Chapter 11), and although the new millennium may never have actually come, Taoists over the next several centuries wrote (or received revelations through) hundreds of new texts. This may come as a surprise if you think the only significant Taoist texts are the *Tao Te Ching,* the *Chuang Tzu,* and *The Tao of Pooh.* In fact, there are nearly 1,500 volumes in the Taoist Canon, the comprehensive collection of books used by various Taoists from different time periods, most of which have never seen the light of day in English translation. The vast majority of these texts don't discuss philosophical matters like the *Tao* — in fact, most of them don't actually *discuss* anything. Instead, they include guides to performing rituals, formulas meant to be recited or chanted, aids to meditation, alchemical manuals, and documents covering a variety of disciplines (like numerology, geography, and medicine). You can find out about the history, contents, and ways of accessing the Canon in Chapter 12.

Looking at the Practice of Taoism

You're probably getting the idea that if there are well over a thousand texts dealing with Taoist practice that most Westerners don't know, it stands to reason that most Westerners don't know much about Taoist practice! In fact, many people are mistakenly convinced that Taoists have no practices (and no doctrines, no deities, and no clergy, for that matter) of any kind, apart from the vague goal of non-doing. In fact, there's probably no greater "undiscovered country" in Taoism, no territory where scholars are still learning more every day, than the world of Taoist practice. And not coincidentally, there's probably no aspect of Taoism that can be any more difficult to understand.

Methods of personal cultivation

It's hard to tell exactly when something we can categorically recognize as Taoist practice first began, but regardless, it's still pretty clear that many of the earliest Taoist practices took the form of applying techniques of physical and spiritual self-cultivation. Some of these techniques resembled meditation, in that they involved a prescribed posture, emphasis on the development of mental discipline, and sometimes even the familiar Buddhist focus on your own breath. Two practices in particular, both described briefly in the *Chuang Tzu,* involve the systematic de-conditioning of all your cognitive and intellectual machinery, the undoing of destructive mental habits in order to return to the original *Tao.* One of these, "sitting and forgetting," is just what it sounds like: gradually peeling away what you already know through an introspective quiet sitting. A related practice, the "fasting of the mind and heart," involves "starving" your ordinary forms of perception until you can develop an entirely different type of immediately, intuitive perception. I talk about these practices in Chapter 13.

Many of the techniques of Taoist self-cultivation involve training of the physical body, and some of these have goals ranging from basic physical health and longevity to attaining an "immortal" status after death. Taoists haven't always spoken with one voice on matters of life and death, and they almost certainly imported their first immortality practices (and generous amounts of related folklore) from a number of non-Taoist sources, which you can read about in Chapter 14.

Over time, the most important immortality practices had to do with variations on *alchemy* (the concocting and combining of various substances in the laboratory), which adepts believed they could use to cure illnesses, gain the protection of spirits, and, of course, transform their own postmortem status. There have been many kinds of alchemical practices in Taoism, but they fall roughly into two categories:

- ✔ **Exterior alchemy:** The literal alchemy involving preparing and ingesting substances
- ✔ **Interior alchemy:** A practice in which alchemical formulas and instructions serve as metaphors for techniques of cultivating and transforming your body's internal energies

If you're especially interested in Taoist alchemy, check out Chapter 15.

Among the many physical practices in Taoism, a handful that have functioned somewhat on the periphery of the tradition have caught on big time in the West. Practices like *t'ai-chi, ch'i-kung,* and a range of other techniques that combine martial arts and spiritual teachings all had loose connections to Taoism in China, but they have, in many ways, become the primary faces of Western Taoism. And because of this, they get their own chunk of this book devoted specifically to them (see Chapter 16).

The ritual process

Thinking about Taoist ritual may seem a little odd if you remember a passage in the *Tao Te Ching* where Lao Tzu seems to be trashing the performance of ritual. But ever since the beginnings of the Way of the Celestial Masters, various forms of ritual — atonement of sins, purification rites, ceremonies on behalf of the dead — have been hugely important in Taoism. When Taoist initiates achieve ordination or advance in priestly rank, they effectively receive authorization to participate in or conduct specific rituals, which almost always involve gaining access to esoteric ritual secrets. Many of the texts in the Taoist Canon actually function as guides or companions to these ritual performances, which is why they're virtually impossible to understand if you just "cold-call" them, but also why they're such a valuable (and under-studied) resource for understanding the realities of Taoist practice.

Although most of the rituals have an esoteric component, many are dramatic and colorful, even if you don't understand what's going on. This is particularly true of rites of "cosmic renewal," some of which occur only once every several years, take days to perform, and include the participation of dozens (or hundreds) of priests. In Chapter 17, I try to make some of these impenetrable ritual processes a little easier to understand.

Chapter 2

What Is Taoism?

*I*n some ways, the answer to the question, "What is Taoism?" is quite simple. Taoism is a religious tradition that is native to China. It's about 2,000 years old (though many of the sources that inspired and influenced it go back at least several hundred years before that, so it's also okay to think of Taoism as about 2,500 years old). Taoism has spread to other parts of Asia, including Japan, Korea, Malaysia, the Philippines, Singapore, and Vietnam. In recent years, it has found its way into European and North American countries as well.

And yet, Taoism is probably the most poorly understood of all the world's major religions. This doesn't mean that you can't easily find out a lot about Taoism through books, videos, and websites. It means that most of what you *can* find in those places is, unfortunately, confusing, misleading, or just not presented with the necessary background information. This can be incredibly frustrating — you may not always know what sources you can trust for reliable information, you may find different accounts of Taoism that seem to contradict each other, or you may discover that things you already knew about Taoism actually paint a somewhat distorted picture of the tradition.

There is a lot of inaccurate or contradictory information out there about Taoism. Part of the challenge is getting a handle on what information is reliable and figuring out how to make sense of what you learn.

Your first exposure to Taoism may seem a little intimidating, so in this chapter, I offer some pointers to help you navigate the tradition a lot more smoothly. Here, you discover exactly why Taoist resources can initially come off as misleading or confusing, and you pick up some important vocabulary and categories for keeping track of things.

Your First Encounter with Taoism

You may have already had your first encounter with Taoism. Maybe you read the *Tao Te Ching* in a world religion class or came across it while browsing in a bookstore. Or perhaps you've heard someone spin fortune-cookie aphorisms like "He who knows does not speak; he who speaks does not know." Maybe you've taken a few *t'ai-chi* lessons or you have a friend who redecorated after practicing the Chinese art of *feng-shui*. Or maybe you've seen some Hong Kong martial arts movies or read *The Tao of Pooh* or any of the dozens of other books that talk about the *Tao* of one thing or another.

But you may also have seen videos online of hundreds of Taoist priests participating in a ritual of "cosmic renewal," or seen pictures of Taoist deities in a book of Chinese art, or heard somewhere that Taoism has something to do with alchemy, acupuncture, the search for immortality, or even quantum physics, whatever that is. And you may be wondering how these all fit together, how these could all be different parts of one religion. Or do they even fit together at all? Could it be that Taoism is one chaotic hodgepodge of beliefs and practices that all just "go with their own flow"?

Part of the problem is simply that a lot of what people say and write about Taoism contains overgeneralizations, personal impressions, and preformed assumptions about the tradition, Chinese religion, and religion in general. But believe it or not, you can blame a huge chunk of the apparent chaos on the term *Taoism,* which is itself ambiguous and which people tend not to use very carefully, even in China.

In this section, I run through an exercise to help you become more attentive to difficulties with the word *Taoism* and illustrate what can go wrong when people aren't attentive to those difficulties. You learn to recognize overgeneralizations and ambiguous language, and maybe even develop some healthy skepticism about things you hear about Taoism.

Seeing how Taoists are like Yankees

You'll probably be happy to know that I don't really want to convince you that Taoists are anything like Yankees, but I do want to show you how the terms *Taoist* and *Taoism* are an awful lot like the term *Yankee.*

If someone were to ask you what a Yankee is or what the word *Yankee* means, your answer would probably depend on a few things, including where you live and whether you like sports:

✔ **If you live in the southeastern part of the United States,** a Yankee is a "northerner," but you almost certainly wouldn't mean people from Oregon or Montana. More likely, you'd mean people who live in or come from the northeastern part of the country, especially people in or originally from states north of the Mason–Dixon Line, or states that aligned with the Union during the Civil War.

✔ **If you're Mexican or European, or you live in any country that has an unwelcome U.S. military presence,** a Yankee is someone from anywhere in the United States. You can be sure there are plenty of people in Georgia and Alabama who aren't crazy about being called Yankees!

✔ **If you live in New England,** the term *Yankee* may be reserved for people who come from old, established, northeastern families, especially those descended from colonial English settlers. This is the origin of the term *Connecticut Yankees.*

✔ **If you live anywhere in the United States (except probably the southeast),** you can use *Yankee* as an adjective to describe a way to prepare food ("Yankee pot roast"), to solve problems ("Yankee ingenuity"), or even to manage money ("Yankee frugality").

✔ **If you're a sports fan,** the term *Yankee* can really only mean those guys who play baseball and make a lot of money doing so! Babe Ruth was one real Yankee who probably ate a lot of Yankee pot roast but didn't practice Yankee frugality.

In other words, the term *Yankee* can mean very different things, sometimes because of specific political or social concerns — things that may end up being only slightly related to each other. And if you hear someone use the term one way when you don't know that usage or think he means something else, you're sure to stumble into a comedy of errors. Imagine what would happen if you heard someone say that the Yankees walked a dozen Tigers, when you thought that person was talking about the Civil War! Or if you were in a baseball frame of mind and heard someone say that the Yankees attacked and burned the city of Atlanta!

As you may expect from this exercise, *Taoist* and *Taoism* can also mean a lot of different things, depending on who's using the words. And just as with Yankees, you'll want to be careful not to mix up the various things that get called "Taoist" for one reason or another, which may not even be very good reasons. One person may be practicing Taoism by moving to the country, spending more time with nature, and making art out of stones and unfinished wood. Another person may be practicing Taoism by joining a monastery, wearing his hair tied up in a bun, and abstaining from sex. They're both Taoism all right, but they're not the same Taoism.

At this point, you've probably figured out that you'll be getting much less of a headache if you start resisting any temptation to try to find any "essence" of

Taoism, or to look for things that all Taoists have in common. In fact, there's probably not a whole lot that everything called *Taoist* has in common (just like New York baseball players don't have a lot in common with pot roast), and things they do have in common may just be coincidental rather than meaningful.

The words *Taoism* and *Taoist* may sometimes refer to very different things. There are, in fact, many different "Taoisms." Be careful not to assume that something true of one type of Taoism is true of every other type of Taoism. In fact, try not even to think of all these different Taoisms as variations of one Taoism. There really is no *one* Taoism.

Playing fast and loose with Taoism

Just because the word *Taoism* is ambiguous doesn't guarantee that people will use the term more carefully. When you're tuned in to how books and websites make generalizations about Taoism without specifying which way they're using the term or what kind (or kinds) of Taoism they're addressing, you'll start to notice that many of these claims just come off like little slogans or sound bites. Some of the following descriptions may sound familiar to you, and they may actually sound very appealing when you first hear them, but when you listen closely, you'll notice that they don't really say a whole lot:

- ✔ Taoism is a religion that teaches the natural way.
- ✔ Taoism is all about being spontaneous and going with the flow.
- ✔ Taoism imparts an experience that is beyond words.
- ✔ Taoism conveys a universal wisdom.
- ✔ Taoism emphasizes the balance of *yin* and *yang.*
- ✔ Taoists avoid religious dogma and organizations.
- ✔ Taoists are peaceful, calm, and in harmony with the universe.
- ✔ Taoists try to live simple, uncomplicated lives.

Every one of these jingles contains at least a grain of truth and reflects genuine familiarity with some Taoist texts, historical figures, or practices. But they also don't take into account all the ways they *distort* Taoism, the ways they may not apply at all to certain types of Taoism. Yes, one Taoist text cautions that we should avoid government and military affairs, but how does that explain Taoist-led rebellions or Taoist-run states? Yes, Chuang Tzu seems to turn up his nose at institutions of any kind, but then how do we square that with organized Taoist temples that have hierarchies of priests and structured daily rituals? Now that you know there are many different Taoisms, you can bring a much more critical eye to these types of clichés.

What do you mean there's no such thing as Taoism in China?

It may come as a surprise that the Chinese don't really have a single word that translates into English as "Taoism." In fact, they don't really have a word that translates as "religion" either; they only came up with the word *tsung-chiao* to create a Chinese equivalent of the English word *religion.* This doesn't mean that there isn't really any Taoism, or any religion, in China, but it does say a lot about how Chinese and Westerners think differently about the idea of religion and the various "religions."

Believe it or not, the word *Taoism* is actually a Western invention, coined only within the last couple hundred years. No matter how hard you look, you won't be able to find any English sources from before 1800 that mention Taoism, even though we knew about Chinese religion long before that. Even the word *Christianity* is a lot newer than you might have imagined. But don't worry — the same is true for *Hinduism, Buddhism, Shintoism, Sikhism, Jainism,* and a whole lot of other *-isms!* Stranger still, almost every one of the world's major religions originally got its name from "outsiders" — that is, from people who weren't members of that religion. And in almost every case, the name originally carried critical or negative connotations.

Maybe you're wondering if this is just a technicality? Sure, they must have had Taoism, but they just never had a name for it. Just as we all know that Christianity is 2,000 years old, no matter how old the name is. The point here is really not whether a religion existed before it acquired a name, but how naming something can influence the way we think about it. In the West, people only started naming religions during and after the period in Europe that we know as the Enlightenment, or the Age of Reason, which began in the mid-1600s. During this period, Enlightenment thinkers started to suppose that they could learn almost anything

through reason and scientific inquiry, and that they could organize all that knowledge into orderly and efficient encyclopedic categories. As a result of this approach to learning and knowing, people started to look *abstractly* at their own and other people's religious lives and started thinking of what they were doing as participating in *religious systems.* They began to think of religions as *things,* as coherent and systematic *-isms.* Before that, people recognized that Hindus and Buddhists and Jews all had different beliefs and engaged in different religious practices, but they had never imagined that they were following Hinduism and Buddhism and Judaism, respectively. When you hear people say things today like, "Islam tells you that you have to fast on Ramadan," or "Eating pork goes against Judaism," or "My religion says I can't do this," be aware that these all reflect a way of thinking that is primarily modern and Western. The way we think about religion today is a legacy of the Age of Reason.

So, why does this matter? It explains why our first inclination may be to seek out a religion's "essence," and why it's sometimes difficult to recognize or accept when religious traditions aren't stable, systematic, or internally consistent. Philosophers today often debate whether the "Enlightenment mentality" represents a net plus, but regardless, the key is simply to be careful not to bring "essentializing" habits to an encounter with Taoism. When you get out of the habit of asking, "What does Taoism say about such-and-such?" and instead start asking, "What does Lao Tzu say about such-and-such," or "What do medieval Taoist texts say about such-and-such," or "What does modern Complete Perfection Taoist practice imply about such-and-such," you'll be able to find answers you can trust.

Whenever you hear or read anything about Taoism, try to get in the habit of asking yourself, "Which Taoism?" That will help you recognize if something is oversimplified or presented out of context, and it will keep you from making overgeneralizations yourself.

Making Sense of the Chaos: Some Important Distinctions

It's time to start looking at some of the different Taoisms, and at some of the most important ways that people use the term *Taoism,* but this is actually a little more complicated than just listing different Taoist denominations. One big reason for that is that more than one Chinese term routinely translates into the English word *Taoism,* and those original Chinese terms came about for different reasons and had completely different frames of reference. To muddy things even further, the Chinese have sometimes mixed up these terms or used them interchangeably or applied them to people or situations where they really didn't belong. Add to that all the Western translators who made careless use of language or misinterpreted the Chinese background, and you've got a real mess.

In this section, I introduce you to the most important categories you'll need in order to sort out the different types of Taoism, explain where those categories came from, and offer tips for recognizing how to employ them wisely. Here, you'll get your first exposure to so-called Taoist philosophy and Taoist religion, learn about the distinction between Taoism and folk religion, and become familiar with one of the extended uses of the term *Taoist.*

From library classification to school of philosophy

When people talk about different kinds of Taoism, a term you'll hear often is *philosophical Taoism* or *Taoist philosophy.* What does it mean to say that there is a Taoist philosophy? You may be tempted to imagine that this term refers to the underlying philosophy behind Taoist practices, or to a systematic and coherent school of Taoist wisdom, or even just to a general way of thinking about life "Taoistically." And why shouldn't we think of Taoist philosophy this way? It certainly makes sense to picture that the great Taoist thinkers developed a consistent intellectual system, which gave rise to a set of religious practices and which any one of us can adopt in our own lives.

Unfortunately, the term *Taoist philosophy* is something of a misnomer, which lends itself to a bunch of misinterpretations. You could even say that it's a translator's invention. In this section, I explain the origin and meaning of the term, introduce you to some of the key figures from this type of Taoism, and give you a brief look at some of the important themes you'll run into when you look at Taoist philosophical texts.

The place of philosophical Taoism

The terms *Taoist philosophy* and *philosophical Taoism* are somewhat awkward approximations of the Chinese term *Tao-chia,* which actually has a narrow, fairly technical meaning. *Tao-chia* translates literally as "family of *Tao,*" but it means something more along the lines of "school of *Tao*" or "lineage of *Tao.*" When an astrologer and librarian hired by the emperor first used that expression a little more than 2,100 years ago, he was marking out one category for classifying earlier authors and texts in terms of how they approached the question of governing the country. These authors may never have considered that they were participating in a single "school of thought," and their texts often contradicted one another. But they sounded enough alike that people who made lists of such things began to think of them as all on the same philosophical page. And so, the Chinese had themselves a retroactive "school of *Tao.*"

What's more, for all the talk of a "school of *Tao,*" there doesn't seem to have ever been any self-conscious "school" that continued after this first round of writings. Yes, the Chinese studied and took inspiration from the main texts for centuries, but they never continued any sustained philosophical tradition in the same vein. When you look at the history of Chinese philosophy and religion across 2,000 years, you really won't find any "philosophical Taoists" or people creating "Taoist philosophy."

The invented Western terms *Taoist philosophy* and *philosophical Taoism* pretty much refer to a cluster of thinkers and texts from what we know as China's "Classical Period," the stretch from the late 6th century B.C.E. until the end of the 3rd century B.C.E. It's probably more accurate to think of the writings from this period simply as "Classical Taoism."

Important names in Classical Taoism

Classical Taoist thought has exerted a tremendous influence on Chinese culture and education, and it has so fascinated Western audiences that you may get the idea that it's the be all and end all of Taoism, but only a handful of thinkers actually seem to fall into this category. Here are the names that you'll hear most often, in roughly descending order of importance:

- **Lao Tzu:** The legendary founder of Taoism who was the supposed author of the *Tao Te Ching,* the best known and most widely translated Taoist text. Most classical Chinese texts are simply named after their author, so the *Tao Te Ching* is also known as the *Lao Tzu.*

- **Chuang Tzu:** The author of the most important chapters of the *Chuang Tzu,* a funny and often brilliant text that contains allegorical stories, poems, imagined dialogues, and essays about logic and language.

Chinese have often referred to Classical Taoism as "the Lao-Chuang Tradition," because of the importance of Lao Tzu and Chuang Tzu.

✔ **Lieh Tzu:** An author who may have written in a style similar to that of Chuang Tzu, but whose writings did not survive. There is an existing book called the *Lieh Tzu,* but it's most likely a much later forgery (though still a fun read).

✔ **Yang Chu:** A mysterious figure who is sometimes described as a "hedonist." He's the focus of one chapter of the *Lieh Tzu,* and a few chapters by his followers are tucked into the *Chuang Tzu.* The Confucians gave him a pretty bad reputation for his emphasis on physical pleasure.

✔ **Shen Tao, T'ien P'ien , and P'eng Meng:** Thinkers who get mentioned in other texts but whose writings are either lost or survive only in fragments that are quoted elsewhere. It's hard to tell how many others there were like them whose names were simply lost to history.

Classical Taoism, philosophical Taoism, Taoist philosophy, and the *Lao-Chuang tradition,* as well as a few other terms you might bump into every once in a while (for example, *Hundred Schools Period Taoism, Warring States Taoism,* and *Pre-Han Taoism*), all refer to more or less the same thing.

Important themes in Classical Taoism

Lao Tzu, Chuang Tzu, and the other Classical Taoists may not always put forth the same philosophy, but they do all address a number of recurring themes. Here are some of the topics you'll find most often:

✔ *Tao: Tao* translates literally as "the Way," the empty, timeless principle underlying all of existence. Classical Taoists talk about experiencing the Way, harmonizing with the Way, becoming one with the Way, and so forth.

✔ **Skepticism:** The Classical Taoists do a lot of questioning, and they can sometimes get pretty snarky about it. They question the value and purpose of language, they question learning and knowledge, and they question moral categories. They even question their own questioning. This can start to make your head hurt.

✔ **Returning:** Lao Tzu and Chuang Tzu are convinced that our conventional intellectual and moral habits have dragged us down to a state in which we're distant from and out of touch with the original Way. They chide us to return to that original state of perfection.

✔ **Unlearning:** If everything we've learned has distanced us from the original Way, the only method for getting back to it is to *unlearn* everything we already know. Classical Taoists talk about abandoning knowledge and intentionally striving to forget.

✔ **Spontaneity:** Once we've gotten back in touch with the Way, and letting our bad mental or moral habits dictate our lives, we can act in a way that harmonizes naturally and effortlessly with the flux and flow of the cosmos. Lao Tzu especially introduces the ideas of "doing nothing" or "actionless action," which he paradoxically understands as an effective way to rule a country.

✔ **Simplicity:** The spontaneous life brings us back to our original, simple natures, free of scheming, calculating, and conniving. Lao Tzu and Chuang Tzu usually portray this as living an unambitious and uncluttered life, not bothered by fame, rules, or social obligations. Sometimes, they suggest this might look like a kind of primitive utopia.

The fuzzy line between philosophy and religion

Another important term you hear a lot is *religious Taoism* or the *Taoist religion.* If the word *religion* brings to mind things like deities, priests, rituals, sacred scriptures, organized institutions, and places of worship, you wouldn't be too far off. Religious Taoism refers to actual religious stuff, not just ideas in old texts — the historical and living practices and communities that you can see, visit, and maybe even join. It only gets tricky when you assume certain things about it just because we call it "religion," or try to put together the relationship between Classical Taoism and religious Taoism. In this section, I'll talk about the term *religious Taoism,* how it relates to Classical Taoism and other types of Chinese religion, and some of its most significant types and characteristics.

The development of the Taoist religion

Just as *philosophical Taoism* is an imperfect translation of a Chinese phrase, so, too, *religious Taoism* and the *Taoist religion* are also approximations of specific Chinese terminology. The original expression *Tao-chiao* literally means "the teachings of the *Tao,*" which over time came to refer to a range of organizations and practice groups that traced their origins back to one specific social and religious movement that began almost 2,000 years ago. And to some extent, almost everything Taoist that occurs after the Classical Period now falls under the heading of "religious Taoism."

But don't be fooled into thinking the Chinese came up with this term to distinguish religious Taoism from philosophical Taoism. They were actually differentiating the teachings of the *Tao* from the teachings of the Buddha, the missionary Buddhism that had been coming into China during much the same period. Eventually, the Chinese would think of "three teachings" — the "teachings of the *Tao,*" "the teachings of the Buddha," and "the teachings of the Confucian scholars." You may recognize these as what people today sometimes call the "three religions" of China: Taoism, Buddhism, and Confucianism.

So, what's the relationship between Classical Taoism and religious Taoism? There isn't really a clear answer, though there are plenty of people fighting about it, and some Chinese have even used the terms *Tao-chia* (see "The place of philosophical Taoism," earlier in this chapter) and *Tao-chiao* more or less interchangeably! Sometimes, it seems that there are really obvious connections, like when you see images of Lao Tzu in Taoist temples, or Taoist monks studying the *Tao Te Ching*. But other times, it's much harder to put them together, like when Taoist practice focuses so much attention on healing, longevity exercises, and the search for immortality, which doesn't square with Chuang Tzu's argument that we should be indifferent to matters of life and death.

Try not to think of religious Taoism as the outward expression of Taoist philosophy, or of philosophical Taoism as the intellectual basis of the Taoist religion. They really aren't just two versions of the same thing. *Taoist philosophy* refers to classical texts from a specific period; *Taoist religion* refers to a complicated and diverse set of practices and organizations spanning a much longer period.

Important subdivisions of religious Taoism

So, *Taoist philosophy* is a misnomer, but is it okay to use the terms *Taoist religion* or *religious Taoism?* Mostly yes, but because this category covers such a huge range of Taoist religious practices, communities, and lineages, it's usually more helpful to think of these terms as just umbrella terms for the many different flavors of Taoism, which people sometimes sort out by historical period (for example, "Six Dynasties Taoism"), region ("Mao-shan Taoism"), and social structures ("monastic Taoism"). But even with all this diversity, you really only need to keep track of a manageable number of specific sects and denominations. Here's a sampling of the most important ones, listed in roughly chronological order of their formation:

- ✔ **The Way of the Celestial Masters:** The first organized movement that can really be called Taoist. It formed in about 142 C.E., and almost all subsequent Taoist organizations are in some way descended from it.

- ✔ **Highest Purity and Numinous Treasure:** Self-cultivation groups that began in the 4th and 5th centuries and produced a large number of revealed texts and practiced meditation or alchemy. They imported many ideas and practices from the Celestial Masters tradition.

- ✔ **Celestial heart, Spiritual Firmament, and Perfect Great Way Taoism:** Some of the short-lived sects that arose from the 11th through 13th centuries. They didn't last long, but they provided important links between the earlier sects and the two lineages that still exist today.

- ✔ **Orthodox Unity Taoism:** One of the two Taoist denominations that survive in China today. This branch is primarily *liturgical,* which means that its members conduct rituals and preside over various public and private ceremonies. It understands itself as the direct descendant of the original Way of the Celestial Masters.

✔ **Complete Perfection Taoism:** The other Taoist denomination that you can find in China today. This branch is primarily *monastic,* which means that its members receive their training or live in monasteries. Founded in the 12th century, this is the newest existing branch of Taoism.

Important characteristics of religious Taoism

In some ways, there's nothing at all mysterious about the different branches of Taoism; they look a lot like other religions you may already know, particularly some of the others from East Asia, like Buddhism or Shinto. Here are some of the characteristics that show up in most religious Taoist lineages:

✔ **Deities:** There are numerous Taoist gods and goddesses, but not every denomination venerates the exact same figures. Some of the most important include the "Three Pure Ones," one of which is a deified Lao Tzu, and various historical and legendary persons.

✔ **Scriptures:** There are well over a thousand sacred Taoist texts, though almost certainly no single person has ever read them all from cover to cover. They deal with subjects as diverse as ritual formulas, alchemy, morality, and physiology.

✔ **Priests:** Taoist organizations developed an intricate and elaborate hierarchy of different priestly ranks. Ordained priests wear special clothing, have access to secret interpretations of texts, and preside over ritual functions.

✔ **Sacred places:** Through most of its history, a big part of Taoism has been its "sacred geography," places that are considered to possess a special religious charge. Several important Taoist temples are built into the landscape of sacred mountains.

Not every hermit, magician, or exorcist is a Taoist

If you already feel challenged because the word *Taoist* is ambiguous and can refer to so many different types of Taoist philosophers or religious practitioners, you'll probably go a little bit crazy when I tell you that it can also refer to people and things that aren't even Taoists!

Because many Chinese haven't always understood a lot of the murky or even secretive aspects of Taoist practice — like the elaborate rituals and the highly technical texts — they didn't always know who really was and who really wasn't a Taoist. But they did recognize that plenty of people did the same kinds of things they associate with Taoists, like performing ceremonies for communication with or safe passage of the dead, exorcising unwelcome spirits, or producing potions thought to heal illnesses or help one to achieve immortality. And they got in the habit of referring to these other characters as "Taoists," without really caring whether they were actually ordained in a Taoist lineage.

It's a lot like seeing one of your neighbors decorating her home with crystals, worshipping goddesses, and celebrating old pagan holidays, and then coming to the conclusion that this person is a Wiccan, a practitioner of the old religion that was often pejoratively identified as witchcraft. And it may not matter to you that she actually has no relationship with any Wiccan coven, has never learned any of the Wiccan oral traditions, and has never been initiated into any Wiccan community. For all intents and purposes, she may seem like a Wiccan to you, but only because you're just not familiar with how the Wiccan "insiders" understand their own tradition.

What makes this such an edgy issue is that many of the Chinese who made this kind of mistake were conservative Confucian intellectuals, many of whom were already sensitized to Western ideas of "superstition." They simply dismissed all this stuff as irrational nonsense, and they had no interest in differentiating "ordinary" charlatans and sorcerers from charlatans and sorcerers who had supposedly received some kind of special training. They were the ones who got to write the textbooks and history books, and they were often the ones who gave Western travelers and scholars their first information about China. As a result, there's a longstanding habit of people assuming that when local and folk religious practices are obviously not Buddhist or Confucian, they must be Taoist. And some Chinese today may brand someone as a Taoist as another way of calling him a huckster! You can probably imagine how much havoc this has brought to studies of Chinese religion, and how much this may have bothered actual Taoists, who saw what they were doing as something very different from folk practices.

There is a difference between Taoists who have been trained and initiated into Taoist lineages and the various local priests and folk religious practitioners who are erroneously called "Taoist."

Chapter 3

Don't Believe Everything You Think

Sometimes, the biggest barrier to getting something right is what you already know about it, or what you *think* you know about it because you've heard it repeated in many places, so many different times, and on good authority. And that's especially true for Taoism. Because most people would be pretty hard-pressed to find Taoist neighbors, Taoist co-workers, or Taoist classmates to correct the record, textbooks, websites, and plain old word-of-mouth have all been pretty much free to define Taoism as they pleased, and no one was around to tell them they got it wrong. And I'm sure you know that once something goes viral, whether on the Internet or in ordinary chatter, it can be pretty hard to stuff the genie back in the bottle. How many times have you heard the baloney about the Great Wall of China being visible from space, or even the moon? Ironically, that one was going around decades before humans ever made it into space.

But it's not just preconceived notions about Taoism that can get in the way; it can also be preconceived notions about religion itself. For obvious reasons, people are likely to be most familiar with their own traditions, and they often assume that what's important in or true of their own traditions are important in and true of others. When this happens, it's usually a lot more subtle than just mixing up the doctrine, like Christians mistakenly thinking Jews accept the divinity of Christ. And it's those subtleties that often cause the biggest problems.

In this chapter, I address some of today's stubborn misconceptions about Taoism, as well as certain misconceptions about religion that have a habit of getting in the way of understanding Taoism. Here, you see how we can debunk the single most popular and enduring Western myth about Taoism, become familiar with some unexpected characteristics of Chinese religion in general, and get to try on for size a totally different way of thinking about religion.

Debunking the Main Myth about Taoism

So, what is this dominant myth about Taoism that has been feeding us all these misconceptions and mistaken impressions? It's one that deals with the origins of the tradition and the relationship between so-called "philosophical Taoism" and so-called "religious Taoism" (see Chapter 2), and it actually goes back at least a century. Most people who have believed and passed along the myth have almost always done so with sincere intentions and a genuine interest in the subject, unaware that this particular interpretation of Taoism employed a kind of loosey-goosey understanding of history and, unfortunately, passed along the religious biases of the people who first created the myth.

It's really quite astonishing how badly this myth has mucked up the story of Taoism. In this section, I fill you in on all the important parts of this myth, explain the odd combination of circumstances that produced it, and show you how profoundly this has affected almost everything that Western sources — at least those not written by egghead scholars — regularly say about Taoism.

A pure teaching corrupted by superstition and religious opportunists

The main myths about Taoism are that there is a "real" Taoism, that it's easy to point to what that real Taoism is, and that all other types of Taoism can be understood in relation to that real Taoism. So, what is this real Taoism? It can be broken down as follows:

- Lao Tzu founded Taoism in the 6th century B.C.E. when he wrote the *Tao Te Ching*.

- Lao Tzu had several disciples or followers, most notably Chuang Tzu, who continued and spread his teachings. The *Tao Te Ching* and the *Chuang Tzu* are the two most important books of Taoism.

- The Taoism of Lao Tzu and Chuang Tzu celebrates and encourages a mystical state of naturalness, which anyone can pursue without gods, rituals, scriptures, or any of the other trappings of organized religion.

✔ This religion of mysticism and naturalness is one of China's three religions, next to Confucianism and Buddhism. It's especially at odds with Confucianism.

An almost secondary byproduct of this thinking is an acknowledgment that there is some kind of institutional religion in China that calls itself Taoism, but that it isn't as important or as interesting as the pure Taoist philosophy of Lao Tzu and Chuang Tzu. Often, this myth incorporates an even more explicit dismissal of "institutional," "organized," or "church" Taoism, which it sees as a pale imitation of the "original" Taoism. You may hear any or all of the following statements about this kind of Taoism, though they basically spin variations on the same theme:

The Myth	*What It Supposedly Explains*
Religious Taoism represents a failed attempt to put original Taoism into practice.	That's how the tradition adopted conventional religious forms, including rituals, priesthoods, the worship of deities, and many other things Lao Tzu specifically taught against.
Religious Taoism represents the contamination of original Taoism by superstition and shamanistic practices.	That's how the tradition adopted practices like exorcism, astrology, and the concocting of immortality potions.
Religious Taoism reflects the infiltration into original Taoism by ambitious opportunists.	That's how the tradition became involved in military rebellions, political maneuvering, and internal power struggles.

All these myths share the assumption that religious Taoism is a later, imperfect, *version* of some original Taoism, whether a misinterpretation, a corruption, or a usurpation of Lao Tzu's pure, timeless, and wise philosophy. However cool you may find alchemy, shamans communicating with spirits, and rituals to guarantee safe passage of the dead, these are all additions to and distortions of the real deal.

The biggest problem with all this — *aside from the fact that none of it is accurate* — is that it has encouraged generations of Americans and Europeans to pay disproportionate attention to Lao Tzu, Chuang Tzu, and an imagined philosophical Taoism, while virtually ignoring (or even denigrating) 2,000 years of Taoist religious history.

Now don't get me wrong. I'm *not* saying that Lao Tzu and Chuang Tzu were not *immensely* important; the classical texts really did alter China's philosophical world in breathtaking ways. But I *am* saying that focusing on them exclusively would be like talking about Christianity without any mention of church history or the Vatican, of Augustine or Thomas Aquinas, of the medieval Christian mystics, of the Inquisition or the Crusades, of the Protestant Reformation, or of Mother Teresa and Martin Luther King, Jr. In short, there's a whole lot of other important Taoist stuff, too.

This myth is so pervasive that it's common for reputable world religion textbooks to omit religious Taoism altogether, which then perpetuates the misconception for yet another generation. That's why if you Google Lao Tzu, you'll find literally millions of results; but try Googling the Way of the Celestial Masters, which is the oldest established sect of religious Taoism, and you'll be lucky to find a hundredth as many results. Google the *Tao Te Ching,* and you're back up in the millions, but Google the *Kan-ying P'ian* or some other important text in the Taoist Canon, and you're back down in the thousands.

The pervasive idea that real Taoism is the original teaching of Lao Tzu and Chuang Tzu is simply not true. No other stubborn fallacy has done more to obstruct Western attempts to understand Taoism and Chinese religion.

A Victorian spin on Taoism and Chinese religion

So, where did this myth of a pure Taoist philosophy and a corrupt Taoist religion come from? Back in the late 1800s and early 1900s, Americans and Europeans didn't have too many ways to learn about China. Few resources were available for learning Chinese language or culture, overseas travel was difficult and prohibitively expensive, and China itself was so torn apart by rebellions and the collapse of its final dynasty that few Westerners (other than diplomats) had much incentive to travel there in order to learn about it. But there was, however, one group of people who felt driven to live among the Chinese and learn about their civilization: Christian missionaries. Most people today have no idea how thoroughly missionaries dominated and defined the first generations of Western scholarship about China. Most of what we first learned about Taoism, we learned from them.

Some people may imagine missionaries as arrogant colonialists who barge into foreign countries for the sole purpose of "converting the heathens." But more often than not, missionaries historically recognized the importance of learning the cultures of the countries they visited, respecting their native traditions, and establishing personal relationships with those whom they recognized as local religious and community leaders. One scholar-missionary who followed this pattern was James Legge, a Scottish member of the Congregationalist church. Legge contributed numerous translations of Chinese texts to what was then a groundbreaking achievement, a 50-volume series titled the *Sacred Books of the East,* which took more than 30 years to complete. As it turns out, through his many translations and other books he wrote about China, Legge probably did more to define the Western picture of Taoism than did any other single person.

The story of another missionary to China

Another interesting 19th-century missionary who followed Legge's model — living for years in China, establishing personal connections, and making clear his respect for Chinese religious traditions — was an independently wealthy German named Paul Kranz. In fact, Kranz respected Chinese religion so much that he directed much of what he wrote to help the Chinese better understand their own traditions. Kranz wrote many books and articles (in Chinese) about Christianity, but he also translated classical Confucian texts from literary Chinese into colloquial Chinese, because many modern Chinese could not read the ancient language well.

But what really made Kranz a controversial figure among many of his fellow missionaries was his theory about the relationship between Christianity and Confucianism. Kranz was so sensitive to how loyal the Chinese were to their traditions and cultural heroes that he took the position that Christianity could never *replace* Confucianism — it could only *complete* it. What's more, he wrote a book about how people should view Confucius and Christ as friends, not enemies. Some of the more hard-line missionaries didn't particularly like these compromises and wasted no time in trashing Kranz's opinions.

Though Kranz was writing mostly about Confucianism and Christianity, he actually contributed indirectly to some of Germany's first exposure to Taoism. One of his Chinese protégés, a Confucian loyalist named Chingdao Wang, went to Germany for four years to work at a major university, perhaps on Kranz's advice or with his support. While he was there, Wang met a young Martin Buber, who would one day become an important existentialist Jewish philosopher and write an influential book, *I and Thou*. Wang got Buber interested in Chinese religion and literature, and he acted as sort of a "ghostwriter" when Buber published two books, including the very first German translation of the *Chuang Tzu,* which became very popular. So, a large chunk of the Western audience got its first look at Taoism from a translation by a Jewish philosopher, who got his Taoism from the Confucian student of a Christian missionary!

Legge recognized Confucian intellectuals who worked in public service as important religious and cultural leaders, and he relied on them for much of his information. Unfortunately, these Confucian scholars, who wanted both to preserve traditional Chinese culture and accommodate challenges from the West, were invested in the idea that cream-of-the-crop Chinese religion was philosophically sophisticated and didn't include any silly "superstitions." They told Legge that Taoism as practiced was basically a hoax perpetrated on the illiterate and "unenlightened" masses and that it had degraded the original Taoism of Lao Tzu and Chuang Tzu.

But why did Legge buy this without a fight? Because this explanation made perfect sense to a Protestant missionary who was conservative, somber, and Victorian. Legge had already thought that Catholicism was a vulgar degradation of Protestant Christianity, and he had no trouble seeing Taoism, with its priests and over-the-top rituals, as just another funky degradation of an originally good idea. As far as Legge was concerned, just as people should identify "real" Christianity with Protestant theology and simply dismiss Catholic excesses, so, too, people should identify "real" Taoism with the early Taoist philosophy and simply dismiss Taoist "superstitions."

The myth of a pure Taoist philosophy and a corrupt Taoist religion originated with late 19th-century Protestant missionaries. Their anti-Catholic bias made them receptive to the anti-Taoist bias of the people who supplied them with most of their information.

A perfect fit for spiritual seekers

Even though many scholars know that the myth of a pure philosophical Taoism is not accurate, and they've been able to trace its origins to the missionary scholars of the 19th century, you may be wondering why the myth still persists. Yes, the Taoism specialists don't mind us having our fun with Lao Tzu and Chuang Tzu, but they do keep barking reminders that we should hurry up and get on with the rest of the story. So, why is it so hard to fix this? Why do people still hold on to the fascination with Taoist philosophy and pay lip service to Taoist religious practice?

In large part, it's for exactly the same reason that James Legge bought the myth in the first place. Not the anti-Catholic part, but the part about how much sense it made for him and how compelling he found the philosophy itself. No matter how you slice it, ever since the first translations of the *Tao Te Ching* made it into English and other Western languages, enthusiastic audiences have found Taoism intriguing, stimulating, and captivating. People just love this stuff, and with good reason! The legendary story of Lao Tzu's birth and composition of the *Tao Te Ching,* the mysterious principle of the *Tao,* the paradoxical wisdom that "the sage does nothing, and yet nothing is left undone" — these have all touched the Western spiritual imagination in some profound way. And even if you don't really know much of anything about Chinese culture, what spiritual seeker can resist the image of the Taoist sage, a Chinese version of Henry David Thoreau, who warns against social obligations, technology, and the rat race, and encourages us to seek our own spiritual paradise through simplicity and naturalism?

That may explain the continuing fascination with Taoist philosophy, but what about the last 2,000 years of Taoist religion? Why do so many people still treat that as Taoism's less interesting younger brother? The reasons for this can best be summarized as follows:

- **Accessibility:** Taoist religion can be incredibly difficult to understand, with all those secretive practices, shadowy deities, and hundreds of texts that have never been translated. Taoists can also be very protective of their rituals and teachings, so they're in no hurry to make it any easier.

- **Context:** Although people have easily found timeless and universal messages in the classical texts, the Taoist religion has from the beginning been utterly *Chinese* through and through. A lot of Westerners just don't relate as easily to practices that are tied so closely to Chinese geography, historical figures, and local community interests.

✔ **The "cool" factor:** Once you learn about the actual practice of Taoism, you may be disappointed to learn that it includes a lot of things — like ordination certificates, rigid rules of morality, and public confessions of sins — that make it seem less exotic. A real-life Taoist monk can sometimes seem less magical than an imaginary, idealized Taoist sage.

✔ **The ivory tower:** As much as I hate to admit it, experts in Chinese religion haven't always done a good job of explaining why Taoist religion is important or why we should find it interesting. Most of the time, they make the conversation so technical that only people with the same level of training can follow what they're talking about.

Getting Oriented to Chinese Religion

Although specific dominant myths about Taoism haunt the Internet, it's an offbeat-enough subject that you may never have actually encountered those myths and aren't approaching Taoism with any of those assumptions. It's actually a lot harder with assumptions about religion in general, however. Because almost everyone is familiar with at least something about religion — even the most hard-core atheists must bump into religious people every now and then — you may have certain expectations about what the major world religions are all about, what kinds of questions they all deal with, and what particular features they all share. But Chinese religion has a habit of throwing a monkey wrench into many of those expectations.

In this section, I orient you to some important, but probably unexpected, features of Chinese religion, which should make Taoism a whole lot less mysterious. I explain how an exercise with a peculiar logic problem can tell you boatloads about Chinese religion, what it means when people say that Chinese religion is "syncretic," what particular place Chinese religion gives to gods and various spirits, and how certain religious practices like divination function in day-to-day Chinese religious life.

Circles, triangles, and thinking concretely

You can gain some unexpected insight into some of the basic characteristics of Chinese religion by trying an unlikely exercise. Do you have an idea that things like math, logic, and geometry are pretty universal? If so (or even if not), take a stab at the following logic problem:

If all circles are large, and if all triangles are circles, then are all triangles large?

What did you answer? Did you say yes or no? Or were you afraid to take a crack at it because you figured I was trying to trick you?

My guess is that you did something like this: Okay, let's assume the first part, that circles are large. Now let's look at triangles, which are now somehow circles. Don't ask me how a triangle could be a circle — these kinds of problems always have silly stuff like that. In any case, those triangles, which are now circles, have to be large, because we already know that circles are large, right? So, yes, if all circles are large, and if all triangles are circles, then all triangles must indeed be large.

And if you did it more or less like that, you're right in line with the more than 80 percent of Americans who answered a similar question that way in a study done several years ago. But incredibly, when the researchers posed the question in Chinese to a sampling of educated people from Taiwan, the vast majority either answered no or complained that there were just too many things about the question that didn't make sense. How could a triangle be a circle? If it becomes a circle, is it not a triangle anymore? And so on. As a result, most of them just ignored such a "counter-factual" statement (the part about triangles being circles) and then trusted their own experience and judgment, which told them that no, not all triangles are large.

Why did this happen, and what's the point here? Most Americans in the test — and probably you, too — tended to approach the problem abstractly, to do it as a kind of mathematical puzzle. If all A is B, and all B is C, then all A is C, a type of sequence that experts in logic call a *syllogism*. But most of the Chinese — and maybe you, too — didn't do it that way, not because they lacked any ability to think abstractly, but because they naturally approached the problem concretely, thinking of it in terms of real-life situations and experiences. And in real life, no matter how you draw them, triangles aren't circles, and not all triangles are large.

For the most part, the Chinese have traditionally brought the same concrete orientation to their religious concerns as they did to that logic problem. If you ever find anything confusing about Taoism or Chinese religion, try to remind yourself about the circles and triangles.

What are some ways a concrete orientation can influence how religion develops? For starters, here are just a few:

- **What matters is the "here and now."** Chinese religion generally addresses the concerns of *this* world and of *this* lifetime. Even when it does get into stuff like heady metaphysics or speculation about what happens after death, the emphasis is almost always on what that means for us here and now, for the responsibilities you have and for the choices you can make in your own life.

- **The universe you see is the universe you get.** Chinese religion treats the universe as a self-sufficient *organism,* where all the parts relate to one another in complicated ways. Whenever it introduces any spirits or deities, these are always treated as vital parts of that universe. Judaism, Christianity, and Islam all think of an omnipotent god who stands some-how separate from existence and creates the universe out of nothing. You won't find that in Chinese religion.

✔ **It has to matter.** Chinese religion always has a practical component, even if it isn't always obvious to someone watching it from the outside. You probably can't expect the Chinese to participate in religious activities unless they expect them to have some practical effects for themselves, for their families or communities, or even for the whole universe.

Religious syncretism: One from Column A, two from Column B

One of the most interesting aspects of Chinese religion is the way the Chinese make use of what more than one individual tradition has to offer. In the West, even though interfaith families are becoming more and more common, most people identify themselves (if they identify at all) exclusively with one reli-gious affiliation. By and large, you'll find people who say they're Jewish or Christian or Muslim or Buddhist, for example. And even if they're inclined to "borrow" from other traditions — some Jews celebrate Christmas, some Christians practice Buddhist meditation, and some Buddhists read Muslim texts — most still maintain one primary religious identification and are fully aware when they're crossing into someone else's religious territory. And of course, many people who think of the religions as completely separate may find it irreverent or just feel uncomfortable when others try to mix and match.

Apart from religious "professionals" (like priests), Chinese seldom identify with only one religion. Many textbooks say that there are three religions in China — Taoism, Confucianism, and Buddhism — and that most Chinese practice all three, or some combination of the three. But this is still not quite on the money. Here's a better way to understand this: The Chinese have had some distinct, recognizable ways of being religious, and those very often involve using or participating in whatever available resources best serve their religious needs. If they visit a Taoist temple, they don't suddenly think of themselves as "being Taoists" or "practicing Taoism." Likewise, they don't think of themselves as "being Confucian" when they learn a traditional Confucian art like calligraphy, or "being Buddhist" when they read Buddhist morality texts to their children. They're simply being Chinese, and they don't "belong" to Confucianism, Taoism, or Buddhism. If anything, Confucianism, Taoism, and Buddhism belong to them!

The term for this way of using resources from multiple religious traditions is *religious syncretism*. You can describe someone taking this approach as *reli-giously syncretic*. Historically, the Chinese have almost always been religiously syncretic.

Three for the price of one?

If you enjoy detective work, it can be fun to watch specific instances of Chinese religion closely to see if you can pick out the various Taoist, Confucian, and Buddhist elements that have been syncretized into one location, celebration, practice, or text. For instance, there's an old temple in Singapore that's dedicated to a Taoist deity called the Jade Emperor, but it also hosts Buddhist deities, and it has a statue of Confucius to boot. A popular Taoist text warns that if you don't follow Confucian morality, you'll be subject to the Buddhist law of karma (where bad actions bring bad effects later in this life or in the next life), implemented by Taoist deities that inhabit your body. Sometimes it really does seem like one from Column A, two from Column B, and three from Column C.

Most of the time, these syncretic practices happen because that's just way the Chinese practice their religion. But there have been times when Chinese scholars worked intentionally to develop ideologies that they thought combined the best of all three religions. Starting around the 1500s, Confucian scholars and Taoist adepts (and sometimes Buddhist monks) began to repeat the slogan that "the three teachings harmonize as one," imagining that they all somehow shared the same goal and could be combined into a kind of "super-syncretism." The funny thing is that these religious "leaders" were probably just responding to cues from the "ordinary" people, who were *already* combining practices from multiple places, without seeing any internal contradiction.

This slogan about the fundamental harmony among the three religions got a lot of traction, and many Chinese routinely echo that point today. So, are they really all that harmonious? Do Taoism, Confucianism, and Buddhism all, at some level, teach the same Way? In one basic sense, sure they do, because they together somehow speak to Chinese religious needs. That is, it *works* for the Chinese to draw from them all. But the truth is that almost every religious tradition maintains some myth of unity, and followers often take great pains to insist on that unity even when there are obvious internal doctrinal contradictions, sectarian divisions, or ethnic factions. Jews, Christians, and Muslims even have specific rituals or holidays that celebrate the unity of their respective traditions. So, in one way, the idea of three harmonious teachings probably more reflects the way the Chinese prefer to see themselves than any reasoned conclusion about the unity of the three teachings themselves.

What does Chinese religious syncretism look like? As you can probably imagine, there isn't any single blueprint, but there are some patterns you'll find more than others. Here are a couple common syncretic practices:

✔ **Temple worship:** People may visit both Taoist and Buddhist temples to make offerings to their respective deities without feeling that they're "changing sides." They may even schedule these trips on the same day, which is especially easy to do when the temples are in close proximity to each other. Some local temples are not affiliated with either Taoism or Buddhism but house deities from both.

✔ **Holidays and public celebrations:** Much as they do with temple worship, Chinese generally don't give a second thought to celebrating holidays that originated with different traditions. Public holidays that are not exactly religious but might have some small religious component or overtones — Chinese New Year is the most obvious example — may have events where Buddhist and Taoist priests both preside.

Try to keep in mind that in terms of actual practice, almost everything you find out about Taoism contributes to a larger religious composite. The Chinese seldom feel that they have to accept any one tradition whole, and that may go especially for Taoism, which can sometimes suggest ways to live that would be hard to carry out. Just because Lao Tzu says to throw away weapons, tools, and technology, doesn't mean that there are actually any Chinese Taoist communities of homesteaders reading by candlelight.

Deities, spirits, and the concern for concrete effects

Chinese religion has always included many deities, spirits, ghosts, and other beings whose presence isn't obvious to the naked eye. If you want to know every deity the Chinese have ever honored, you'd probably need a scorecard or the kind of computer program that keeps track of complicated family trees. But for the most part, you can keep track of them by sorting them into the following categories:

✔ **A high god:** The Chinese name *T'ien* translates literally as "Heaven" or "the Heavens." This deity is more impersonal than anthropomorphic, which is to say that it doesn't really possess human features. Heaven is associated with things like fate, cosmic order, and the protection of a righteous ruling regime.

✔ **Sectarian gods and goddesses:** These are deities that originated from particular religious traditions, like the Buddha named Mi-lo (that's the round, smiling guy you may see on the counter in Chinese restaurants), a compassionate female Buddhist goddess named Kuan-yin, or Hsi Wang Mu, the Taoist Queen Mother of the West.

✔ **Functional and local deities:** These deities fulfill particular purposes (like healing, agriculture, or protecting travelers) or occupy and protect particular regions. Rural villages would often have their own earth gods, and individual families to this day may still have images of kitchen gods in their homes.

✔ **Deified historical or legendary figures:** Most deities are thought to have once been people, who for one reason or another earned "promotions" to god status over time. The best known of these is Ma Tzu, an ordinary fisherman's daughter from the 10th century, who is now honored as the goddess of the sea.

✔ **Spirits of ancestors:** Your parents and grandparents continue to deserve your respect, even after they die. The Chinese holiday called Ch'ing Ming is a time when people visit their family cemeteries, lighting firecrackers, burning incense, and making other offerings to their ancestors. Spirits of the dead who have no descendants or have been forgotten by their descendants turn into unhappy, restless ghosts.

So, which of these deities are the most important in Chinese practice? You may be imagining that the most powerful ones or the ones commanding the most territory get the most attention, but actually the exact opposite is true. Think of it this way: The most powerful person in the country is (depending on which country) the president, the prime minister, or maybe the chief justice of the highest court. So, naturally, whenever you need something from the government — like getting your dog released from the pound or acquiring a building permit — you get on the phone and call the president, right? Well, no. Instead, you call the local official — the animal control officer or the director of planning and zoning, whoever has the direct authority to take care of your particular problem. The Chinese think of their deities much the same way, as though they were organized like a government bureaucracy. People pay less attention to the higher and more remote figures and more attention to the ones that influence their immediate concerns. The Chinese worship deities based not on their overall importance, but on their *ling,* their "spiritual efficacy," the quality the deities possess to bring concrete effects into people's lives.

For the Chinese, the deities that matter most are the ones that *matter* — that is, the ancestors, local spirits, and other figures who have the spiritual efficacy to influence their day-to-day lives. If they don't think a spirit is efficacious, they won't worship it.

Because the Chinese measure deities by their efficacy, they may have some religious habits that strike non-Chinese as strange, until you remember that they tend to employ religious resources that have a practical, concrete value. For example, if they think that a deity isn't "doing its job," whoever is in the position of authority to make such decisions can simply replace that deity with a different spirit who's more up to the task. The relationship between humans and deities is mutual; each side has its obligations to fulfill, and even deities are held accountable if they don't fulfill theirs.

Divination and the practical side of religion

If you understood that all sorts of gods, spirits, and other non-obvious beings inhabit our world, and if you had the idea that those beings can influence our lives, you'd probably want to devote some time and attention to figuring out exactly what their intentions are and what they want from us. Christians and

Jews usually find those answers through the Bible, through prayer, or perhaps through conversations with clergy or other religious counselors. One important way the Chinese have traditionally sought to answer those questions is through various forms of divination.

In its most basic sense, *divination* refers to predicting the future or figuring out things we can't normally see, through some kind of specialized practice. Reading tea leaves, telling someone's fortune, palm reading, and even the Magic 8-Ball are simple forms of divination. You can even think of interpreting nice weather as a sign that God wants you to go the beach as a kind of divination. Here are several important types of Chinese divination, many of which the Chinese (and others) still practice today.

- ✔ **Oracle bones:** In ancient times, experts would write or carve questions on animal bones, heat them, and then interpret the cracks on the bones as answers to the questions. Archaeologists discovered these bones early in the 20th century and learned a lot about ancient China through them.

- ✔ *Feng-shui:* This term literally translates as "wind and water," and it refers to ways of reading the physical environment in order to decide the best location to place a dwelling, like a house, school, or cemetery. Chinese also employ *feng-shui* to determine changes they should make to an existing dwelling, like where to place furniture or hang a mirror.

- ✔ *The Book of Change (I Ching):* The *Book of Change* is a manual that contains a divination system, based on different combinations of *yin* and *yang*. Both Taoism and Confucianism regard it as a classic, and many people find a lot of philosophical and cosmological significance in the commentaries on it.

- ✔ **Spirit writing:** This refers to several different methods of suspending racks or trays so that a stick or wand, which is presumably occupied by a specific spirit, can trace Chinese characters in sand or on a flat surface. This is also sometimes called "automatic writing."

- ✔ **Oracle blocks:** This is a very common practice at temples and shrines, where someone asks a yes-or-no question (presumably of the appropriate deity) and tosses a pair of blocks that are round on one side and flat on the other. Landing one round block and one flat block up usually means yes, while the other combinations normally mean no (though there are other interpretations as well).

Most of these methods require some level of expertise, either to perform the divination or interpret the information, and that helps explain why there are professional diviners and hereditary priests in China. Critics tend to regard all forms of divination as unscientific or pseudo-science, in part because they don't really withstand scientific testing, but also because the "experts" guard their territory closely and don't normally explain how it works. In spite of this, many Chinese take these practices quite seriously. For instance, recent surveys indicate that a surprisingly large number of Chinese would consider using *feng-shui* before making certain important decisions. Some people have speculated that *feng-shui* persists among the Chinese because their basic worldview allows for the possibility that different things sometimes connect to one another in ways that are not immediately apparent. But it may be simpler than that. Many people get their first chance to employ *feng-shui* at some kind of crucial moment of transition in their lives, like when a newly married couple has to figure out where to build their first home or a grieving son has to decide where to bury his father. And often during those crucial moments, it can feel safer and more comforting to choose the traditional option. There's an old adage that people all over the world are inclined to "get religion" during three momentous events: births, marriages, and deaths — or, to put it more playfully, when you're hatched, matched, and dispatched.

Believe It or Not, It's Not about Belief

One last aspect of Chinese religion that can be so difficult for Western audiences to grasp is that *belief* in religious doctrine does not hold a particularly important place. This might strike you as pretty curious. After all, when you want to know about other people's religion, isn't one of the first questions you ask, "What do they believe?"

One reason that so many people are in the habit of thinking of religion that way is that Western traditions, particularly modern Christianity, emphasize things like getting the doctrine right or making clear that you *believe* in God's existence. This implies that the act of believing in some way determines your fate, or that it actually matters to God what you believe.

But the Chinese don't really think of their practices in terms of belief. If you ask a Chinese why he or she burns incense at an ancestor's grave, that person is not likely to say, "Because I believe that my ancestor's spirit is still alive, that it likes the smell of incense, and that I'm going to have bad luck if I don't do it." You're more likely to hear an answer like "To show respect," "To fulfill my family duties," or "To repay the kindness my grandfather showed me when I was younger." In other words, there's no special virtue in believing; there's only virtue in doing the right thing with sincere feelings. What's more, the spirit truly doesn't care if you believe it exists; it cares that you don't forget it and continue to tend its grave respectfully.

Try thinking of it this way: You're taking a college course in which your teacher requires that you attend class regularly, keep up on the assigned readings, and take four tests in order to pass. But she never requires that you believe she exists! How would you feel if I held up your exams as evidence that you "believed in" your professor? Most likely, you never even gave that matter a second thought, and that would be kind of a funny conclusion. So, try to remember that even when Chinese are discussing religious doctrine, it's not for the purpose of dictating what someone should believe; it's for the purpose of making clear how you should understand the world and what that means for how you should act in it.

Part II
Looking At the Development of Taoism

In this part . . .

Taoism has reinvented itself more times than Madonna. There are classical Taoist texts like the *Tao Te Ching,* but also Taoist-inspired governments, Taoist communal organizations, Taoist revelations, Taoist immortality practices, and two thriving sects of Taoism in China today. And don't forget: Taoism has also come west, and that's probably the most dramatic reinvention of all!

This part tells the story of Taoism, from its beginnings two and a half millennia ago, to its various faces and incarnations in the modern world. It's a complicated family tree, and in this part, you see that each branch produces different-colored leaves and sometimes bears some pretty unusual fruit!

Chapter 4

Classical Taoist Philosophy

. . . .

In This Chapter

▶ Getting oriented to the Hundred Schools

▶ Meeting the wise, old Lao Tzu

▶ Greeting the snarky, young Chuang Tzu

▶ Remembering some nearly forgotten thinkers

▶ Considering Taoism and government

. . . .

*T*aoism first began about 2,500 years ago, during an extraordinarily creative time in Chinese history known as the Classical Period. This doesn't
mean that there were Taoist communities, or Taoist temples, or even people
walking around identifying themselves as Taoists back then. But it *does* mean
that several authors during this period wrote or compiled texts on a range
of subjects — logic, language, government, ethics, physical cultivation —
that later record-keepers catalogued under the heading "School of *Tao*," the
term that you often see misleadingly translated as "philosophical Taoism" or
"Taoist philosophy." These authors and texts make up the core of Classical
Taoism.

No other aspect of Taoism gets more attention than these Classical authors
and their texts, which do contain some of the most profound, most intriguing,
and most perplexing philosophy you'll find anywhere. In this chapter, I bring
you up to speed on the development of Classical Taoism, and introduce you
to the most important Taoist figures from the period. You'll learn your way
around the historically foundational "Hundred Schools" of ancient China, get
to know Lao Tzu, Chuang Tzu, and other lesser-known Taoist thinkers, and
discover how Taoism may have briefly talked its way into one dynasty's official
ruling ideology.

Try not to think of Classical Taoism as an institutional religion or even an
organized school of philosophy. Instead, think of it as the name given to a
cluster of texts written during a particular period of Chinese history, which
share a general approach to the political and social problems of that time.
And try to think of Lao Tzu, Chuang Tzu, and the others as distinct authors,
each of whom made his own separate contribution to that conversation.

The Hundred Schools

When the Chinese first recognized a "School of *Tao*," they saw it as one of several intellectual "schools" that for a few centuries took part in a lively public debate about how to rule the country, how to instill moral values and conduct in the people, and how to achieve a sense of personal fulfillment living in the world. Even though the Chinese never specifically identified much more than a half-dozen or so different schools, they came to refer to this era as the "Hundred Schools Period" (roughly 550 B.C.E. to 200 B.C.E.) simply because so many original thinkers flourished at this time. Almost everyone who knows Chinese history well recognizes this period as the Golden Age of Chinese Thought.

Classical Taoism developed as part of the Hundred Schools Period of ancient China. It's important to try to understand the part that it played in that period.

In this section, I bring you right into that "Hundred Schools" conversation that produced so many influential figures. You find out what historical factors set the stage for this period, how all these scholars got involved in the discussion in the first place, what kinds of philosophical issues they were addressing, and which scholars had been pretty much setting the agenda that Lao Tzu and Chuang Tzu were trying to wrestle away from them.

Nostalgia for the good old days

The Hundred Schools Period didn't just drop out of the blue, like a geranium stuck suddenly in a flower pot; it grew from a specific constellation of social and political crises. These particular circumstances enabled and nurtured the intellectual climate of the Hundred Schools Period. The following sequence summarizes how China came to such a place.

Disruption of the dynasty

The Chinese Chou Dynasty, a loosely integrated feudal political structure that went back to around 1046 B.C.E., suffered a major crisis in 770 B.C.E., when it was attacked by a non-Chinese ethnic group from the north, who killed their king and took over much of their territory. This shattered any image of a stable, unified country that the dynasty's rulers had been trying to project.

Decline of moral authority

The survivors of the ruling family fled to a new capital, marking the beginning of the Eastern Chou Dynasty. The defeat at the hands of northern "barbarians" gave the family a major black eye, and many blamed the loss on the ethical drift of the dynasty, whose current leaders couldn't seem to hold a moral candle to the legendary wise kings of the past.

Decentralization

With the rulers losing both moral authority and political power, several states began to sever their ties (or maintain only minimal ones) to the dynastic family. Eventually, these states began military campaigns against one another for control of the country. Because of this, the Chinese call the time from 475 B.C.E. to 221 B.C.E. the Warring States Period, which roughly coincides with the most important part of the Hundred Schools Period.

The need for new ideas

As China was basically falling apart and lots of ambitious local leaders (or aspiring leaders) were competing with each other for power, many of them invited intellectuals (or self-styled intellectuals) to share their ideas about how to unite and rule the country. Some even sponsored academies to encourage the exchange and debate of ideas.

Unemployed intellectuals looking for a job

With Chinese officials looking earnestly for solutions to an increasingly unstable government and fragmented society, hundreds of men began to travel from state to state, trying to find an audience for their ideas. These eager, would-be political advisors would eventually develop into a self-conscious class of professional scholars. Many of the Hundred Schools thinkers addressed their texts specifically to local officials, and some of the texts chronicle conversations among the scholars and those officials. Some of the texts argued about morality, others gave advice on how to get subjects to follow the law, and others gave advice on military conquest. The scholars sometimes challenged or rebutted one another, and some saw themselves as the standard bearers for earlier scholars or imagined allies. These debates continued for generations.

Nearly a century after the end of the Hundred Schools Period, Chinese historians began to sort out all the scholars and devise categories for organizing their texts. They never really developed one system, which explains why one account could list only six schools, while another could list up to ten, some of which almost no one has heard of today. Here are the ones that seem to have been the most significant or at least the ones who had a lot of their texts survive. (I list them here with both the English translations you normally see and a more literal translation from the Chinese in parentheses.)

- ✔ **Taoism (the School of Tao):** This group included Lao Tzu and Chuang Tzu, but also lesser-known figures like Lieh Tzu, Yang Chu, Shen Tao, T'ien P'ien, and P'eng Meng.

- ✔ **Confucianism (the School of the Scholars):** This group included the self-appointed guardians of the conservative intellectual and cultural traditions that they saw as endangered by the collapse of the country and fragmentation of society. The most important representatives of this school were Confucius, Mencius, and Hsun Tzu.

✔ **Mohism (the School of Mo):** This group included Mo Tzu and his later followers. They taught an ethic of universal love and opposed the Confucians on many key points, including fate, spirits, ritual, and music.

✔ **Legalism (the School of Law):** This group included experts on law, the art of statecraft, and the maintenance of political power. The most important representatives were Han Fei Tzu, Shang Yang, and Shen Pu-hai.

The following schools did not leave behind a whole lot of material, and they may have been even less organized as real "schools" than the preceding four. Still, some seem to have exerted significant influence on the overall conversations, and the writings and fragments of theirs that do survive can get pretty interesting.

✔ **The Logicians or Dialecticians (the School of Names):** The Logicians often discussed the formation of categories and the relationship between language and reality. One of their most interesting entries was Kung-sun Lung-tzu's essay, "A White Horse Is Not a Horse."

✔ **The Naturalists (the School of Yin-Yang):** The Naturalists were interested in the ways in which the *yin* and *yang* forces of nature interacted, and how that could be used to understand history, physiology, and even morality.

✔ **The Agriculturalists (the School of Tillers):** The Agriculturalists wrote about the possibility of forming (or returning to) a peasant utopia based on farming and land cultivation.

✔ **The Diplomats (the School of Alliances):** The Diplomats addressed practical political matters like negotiating treaties, establishing coalitions, and planning military strategies.

✔ **The Militarists (the School of Soldiers):** The Militarists wrote about military affairs, with special attention to strategic components like how to deceive an enemy or employ spies. Sun Tzu's *Art of War* falls into this category.

✔ **The Eclectics (the School of Miscellany):** The Eclectics drew from many different schools, though it's not clear if they were really making a conscious attempt to synthesize them into one unified teaching.

Basic assumptions and terminology of the period

The Hundred Schools thinkers often proposed very different answers from one another, but at least their answers usually addressed many of the same basic questions. That is, they were really all participating in a network of intersecting and overlapping conversations. For the most part, these philosophers were all focused on very *humanistic* and *concrete* concerns, like how to reunify the empire, what moral values people should follow, what kind of teaching is necessary for a person to do good, what our obligations are to one another, and even how a person can live his or her life happily. Even when they talked about things that might seem kind of heady or abstract — like what conferred on a ruler the authority to keep power, or whether human nature was good or evil — it was almost always for the purpose of figuring out what that meant for human practices or responsibilities.

Not every Chinese philosopher had precisely the same concerns or used exactly the same terminology, but they did share some similar starting places and began to develop a common language. Here are some of the important assumptions and terms common to the Hundred Schools:

- ✔ **Heaven:** The philosophers generally understood that the high deity, Heaven, fated certain circumstances (like giving a dynasty the responsibility for ruling) and somehow decreed that humans should follow a particular "way." They didn't always see eye to eye on what Heaven was actually mandating or how that translated into which particular human responsibilities. The Chinese term we normally translate as Heaven (or sometimes "the Heavens") is *T'ien*.

- ✔ **Family values:** Chinese culture was very family-centered, and almost all the thinkers pretty much took family ties and loyalties as a given. They would never argue, for example, on whether to respect your father — but they might disagree on how you should learn that respect or what the exact signs of that respect should be. The term *hsiao* translates as "filial piety" or "familial loyalty."

- ✔ **The emperor as the son of Heaven:** Kind of combining the importance of Heaven with the prevalence of family values, the Chinese accepted the idea that the emperor had both the Heavenly mandate to rule and the responsibility to be worthy of that mandate. This concept serves as a reminder that Chinese religion was, at least until the modern era, never really separable from Chinese government.

- ✔ **Spirits and ghosts:** Few authors from the time of the Hundred Schools challenged the assumption that the world is populated by various helpful and destructive spiritual forces, including ancestors, local deities, and spirits associated with particular places or functions. They often understood that it was no less necessary to negotiate relationships with these spirits than to do so with members of your family or community. The good, well-tended spirits were called *shen* ("good spirits"); the forgotten or unhappy spirits were called *kuei* ("ghosts").

- ✔ **The human heart-mind:** The Classical Chinese philosophers recognized that humans possessed a unique faculty that allowed them both to feel and to think, and so they conceived of the heart and the mind as essentially one organ. They believed that humans had the responsibility to educate and exercise their heart-minds appropriately. The Chinese term we translate as heart-mind is *hsin*. Try not to confuse this with *hsing*, which translates as "human nature."

The Tzu brothers? Not really

You may be starting to wonder why so many important Hundred Schools philosophers — Lao Tzu, Chuang Tzu, Lieh Tzu, Mo Tzu, Hsun Tzu — have the last name Tzu. Could it be that there was one big extended clan, with siblings, cousins, and generations of grandchildren all pursuing the same family business?

As fetching an idea as that might be, none of the different Tzus came from the same family, or at least very few of them did. The name *Tzu* was actually an *honorific* (an honorary title that means something like "sir" or "master," not in the sense of a master over a slave, but as one who has mastered a subject or skill and possesses the relevant expertise). So, Chuang Tzu is simply the Chinese way of saying "Master Chuang," Mo Tzu is the Chinese way of saying "Master Mo," and so forth. History pretty much decides who's a Tzu and who isn't.

And speaking of history deciding people's names, you may also be wondering why some of the ancient scholars *not* named Tzu seem to have pretty un-Chinese sounding names, specifically Confucius and Mencius. In fact, we know them by these names because the original Christian missionaries who first introduced Chinese thought to the West recognized the important historical place that some key figures occupied, and they thought it would be respectful to give them Latin versions of their names. The Chinese normally referred to Confucius as K'ung Tzu (Master K'ung), but they sometimes called him K'ung Fu-tzu, which translates as something like "Venerable Master K'ung" or "Sagely Master K'ung." The missionaries simply turned K'ung Fu-tzu into Confucius, and Meng Tzu into Mencius.

What if the missionaries had gotten their information from Chinese people who thought that Taoism was the most important of China's religions? Then today we'd probably be calling Lao Tzu and Chuang Tzu Laocius and Chuancius, respectively!

The moralists: Confucians and Mohists

A great deal of Classical Taoist thought was directed to challenging or providing some kind of alternative to the Confucians and the Mohists, who dominated much of the Hundred Schools conversation. Although they were themselves often at each other's throats, the two groups did have something in common: They spent most of their time talking about ethics and moral conduct. Both of them were intent on explaining what it takes for an emperor to rule morally, what kinds of virtues humans should learn and aspire to inculcate in their children, and what practices bring about good people and an ethical society.

But as they say, the devil's in the details, and on those actual details, Confucians and Mohists were usually pretty far apart from each other. Here are some of the main points where they disagreed:

   ✔ **What is moral teaching?** The Confucians taught that morality involved the cultivation of your character, that you should be virtuous for the sake of being virtuous, and that morality is something completely different from matters of personal benefit or profit. By contrast, the Mohists taught that morality involved nothing other than bringing the greatest benefit to the greatest number, that benefit was the only yardstick for measuring moral accomplishment, and that defining virtue otherwise would necessarily result in selfishness. Some philosophers think of Confucians as *virtue ethicists* (emphasizing virtue and overall character) and Mohists as *utilitarians* (emphasizing utility and tangible benefit).

✔ **What are the primary virtues?** The Confucians taught that most virtues were extensions of family values, that proper conduct was contingent on your place in different social relationships. For example, the respect you have for your father is different from the proprietary love you have for your child, and so your duties as a son should be different from your duties as a father. The Mohists taught that Confucian ethics were guilty of *partiality,* of teaching that you only are obliged to certain family and social relationships, which would restrict how much benefit you would bring to the community and the world. They advocated instead an ethic of "universal love."

✔ **What are moral actions and expressions?** The Confucians taught that you should follow prescribed rituals, so that you relate to others and express your feelings in accord with established patterns of decorum and modesty. The Mohists opposed any rituals, ceremonies, or artistic expression that wasted resources and didn't bring benefit. They taught instead that you should simply observe the socially beneficial moral habits of your superiors and make every effort to put them into practice.

✔ **How do you become a moral person?** The Confucians taught that becoming good involved a lifelong process of learning, becoming educated in everything from specifically moral lessons to cultural and literary arts. The Mohists had little patience for such process-oriented brainiacs, and instead taught that you should simply weigh carefully how much benefit an action will bring and make the direct and conscious decision whether to do it.

✔ **How should you treat spirits and ghosts?** The Confucians recognized the importance of extending family and social rituals to relationships with other types of beings, but they generally seemed more invested in keeping them at a polite distance than trying to predict their actions or manipulate their power. The Mohists had a more literal understanding of ghosts and spirits as very real beings capable of bestowing reward and punishment, whom you ignore only at your own peril.

Whenever you hear certain buzzwords — like virtue *(te)*, humaneness *(jen)*, sincerity *(ch'eng)*, ritual propriety *(li)*, and filial loyalty *(hsiao)* — that should tip you off that the source is Confucian, though the exact language may vary a bit from translator to translator. When you hear talk of benefit and universal love *(chien-ai)*, that's almost certainly Mohist. Both groups frequently talk about rightness or righteousness *(i)*, so you have to pay attention to see whether it's being tied in to character (Confucian) or utility (Mohist).

A hot spot in human history

Once you start digging into the history of religion and philosophy, it can be quite the shock to discover that a number of really important figures around the world all lived at the same time, and that different parts of the world were going through their own versions of the Hundred Schools Period. Check out the dates — at least the traditionally recognized dates, which are always subject to scholarly tinkering — of the following important movers and shakers:

- **Lao Tzu (604 B.C.E.–531 B.C.E.):** The reputed founder of Taoism and author of the *Tao Te Ching*.

- **Confucius (551 B.C.E.–479 B.C.E.):** The first important scholar in the Chinese tradition known in the West as Confucianism.

- **Siddhartha Gautama (563 B.C.E.–483 B.C.E.):** The Indian man who assumed the title "the Buddha" after having an enlightenment experience, which gave rise to the Buddhist tradition.

- **Mahavira (599 B.C.E.–527 B.C.E.):** The founder of the Indian tradition called Jainism, which is best known for radical teachings of non-violence.

- **Zarathustra (628 B.C.E.–551 B.C.E.):** Also known as Zoroaster, the founder of the ancient Persian tradition known as Zoroastrianism.

- **Thales (624 B.C.E.–546 B.C.E.):** Probably the first of the ancient Greek philosophers, who set in motion what would become the Socratic era.

Astonishingly, the architects of Taoism, Confucianism, Buddhism, Jainism, Zoroastrianism, and Greek thought all lived during roughly the same period, around the 6th century B.C.E., a time that is now often called the Axial Age. What's more, a pair of religious traditions that don't really have "founders" had important texts come into their finished forms right around this time, even though the materials the texts contain are much older:

- **The Torah:** The first five books of the Hebrew Bible, which Christians call the Old Testament.

- **The Upanishads:** A collection of important Hindu texts that contain, among other things, memorable discussions about the nature of a human's true self.

So, why did this Axial Age even take place? Is this just the greatest coincidence in 2,500 years, or did something happen in human history that caused such incredible developments in China, India, Greece, Persia, and the Middle East at about the same time? Folks have been trying to figure this one out for a long time, and some of the theories they've come up have been real doozies, like a global epidemic of psychedelic drug poisoning or the possibility that a spaceship landed and seeded people all over the world.

The most convincing answer is that this is when human beings developed the ability to engage in *second-order thinking*. What is this second-order thinking? Well, if first-order thinking is just ordinary thinking, like noticing that the sky looks nice or wondering what's for lunch, second-order thinking is *thinking about thinking*. In other words, asking yourself what is worth thinking about and how you should do that thinking, a kind of thinking with a different sense of self-awareness and critical perspective. Questions about ultimate meaning, ethics, life and death, and so forth are all examples of second-order thinking. According to this theory, it was during the Axial Age that China, India, Greece, and the Middle East each collectively worked out which questions they decided were important — and then spent the next several hundred years entertaining different possible answers to those questions.

Lao Tzu: The Traditional Founder of Taoism

When most people think of Taoism, they think of Lao Tzu, and with good reason. Lao Tzu's name and image are splashed across almost anything you can think of that calls itself Taoist. Multiple translations of the main book that bears his name sell like hotcakes from the major bookstore chains, statues of him sit in pretty much every Taoist temple, and websites invariably identify him as the founder of the tradition. To put it plainly, if it ain't got no Lao Tzu, it ain't no Taoism.

Although Lao Tzu occupies an immensely important place in Taoism, he is still subject to considerable confusion and misunderstanding. In this section, I separate the fact from the fantasy and give you a more realistic and believable picture of this legendary sage. You discover just who Lao Tzu really was (or wasn't), pick up a new perspective on the many tales about his life, and take a first look at the *Tao Te Ching,* that mysterious book that gets quoted by poets, philosophers, musicians, and even modern politicians. You also find out what this text has to say about the concept of the *Tao,* how it criticizes the Confucian virtues that were prevalent at that time, and how it crafts an odd and paradoxical understanding of what makes a person wise and how a sage should act (or not act) in society.

The old sage who probably never was

As the traditional story goes, the man we call Lao Tzu lived a pretty extraordinary life. At some point around the early 6th century B.C.E. (or just before that), he was born with white hair and a long beard, after having hung out in his mother's womb for more than six decades. He was an elder contemporary of Confucius, who served as a historian, astrologer, or administrator of the imperial archives, depending on which version of the story you hear. He attracted many students, including Confucius, who once consulted with him about ritual. Eventually, perhaps at the age of 160, he got fed up with the moral decline all around him and bolted for parts unknown, heading somewhere off to the unspecified "west" to live out his remaining years as a recluse. But as he was about to leave the city, a gatekeeper recognized him and demanded that he write down his wisdom before disappearing for good. The document he composed was the *Tao Te Ching,* the text that started Taoism.

The problem is, to put it plainly, that all the Lao Tzu stories just don't wash. After you put all the pieces together, you find that his biography consists of a conglomeration of snippets about several different people, and even these people were only pretty unconvincingly identified as the historical Lao Tzu. For example, one story described a man named Li Er, another Lao Lai-tzu, and still another Lao Tan. It would be convenient to say that these are all just different names for the same person, but it's more likely they were different people who were *conflated* (that is, confused and then combined) into one by historians who were desperate to assemble some kind of coherent biography of the reputed author of the *Tao Te Ching.* And to ice the cake, almost everything in the Lao Tzu biography is really legendary or idealized folk tales, what historians call *hagiography.*

Okay, so what if we just accept that we don't have any reliable information about Lao Tzu, can't we just think of him as the author of the *Tao Te Ching,* whoever he might really have been? Well, sort of, but maybe not. Though not everyone agrees on this point, it looks like the text never actually had one author, and that it may have taken a long time — perhaps even centuries — to come into the form that we now know. In the 1970s, a team of archaeologists unearthed two silk manuscripts of the *Tao Te Ching* from the 2nd century B.C.E., and they looked considerably different from each other and from the "official" version. Twenty years later, more archaeologists found a bamboo strip version that was at least a hundred years older than those two, and it too indicated that the text was still changing. The best guess now is that a lot of orally transmitted material took quite some time to "settle" into one relatively stable text. And that material may have poked around for a while before anyone ever attached the name Lao Tzu to it. So, even thinking of Lao Tzu as the author of the *Tao Te Ching* could be a little misleading, unless you remind yourself that doing so is just adopting a handy label for what were probably many different authors.

And by the way, what does the name "Lao Tzu" even mean? If you don't speak or read Chinese, it's actually a little more complicated than it first appears. Here are some possible translations of Lao Tzu, and some of the possible problems with them:

✔ **Master Lao:** This is the explanation that you would come to expect, because that's how it works with all the other classical authors, like the way Chuang Tzu is Master Chuang, Mo Tzu is Master Mo, and so forth. But Lao was not a standard family name in China, so it's pretty certain that it meant "old," not someone's actual name.

✔ **The Old Master:** This is the most common translation, the one that is most faithful to the figure appearing in the dubious biographies, the wise old sage who authored the *Tao Te Ching* and started the Taoist tradition. This translation would probably make the most sense . . . if there actually were one Lao Tzu!

✔ **The Old Masters:** Chinese nouns don't indicate whether they're singular or plural — you have to figure that out by context — so when people first attached the name Lao Tzu to the *Tao Te Ching,* they may have already understood that the text was a collection of sayings that had come down from various wise men of the past. This is probably the most helpful translation when it comes to thinking about how the text actually came together, but it's not the way the Chinese have thought about Lao Tzu for at least 2,000 years.

> ✔ **The Old Child:** Because the Chinese character *Tzu* can also mean "child," it's possible that the name Lao Tzu was kind of a play on words, describing someone who was both young and old at the same time. That would fit nicely with the story about his being born as an old man, but it probably happened the other way around, that the story developed in response to the ambiguity of Lao Tzu's name.

The person we know as Lao Tzu probably didn't exist, but that shouldn't stop us from using "his" name to refer to the philosophical voice(s) that come through in the *Tao Te Ching*.

The Tao Te Ching: A classic in 5,000 characters

The text that Lao Tzu supposedly authored, the *Tao Te Ching*, can stimulate your imagination, get you scratching your head for hours, or just leave you bewildered and impatient. Its authors composed it in a peculiar style that lends itself to many different interpretations, which partially explains why hundreds of Western translators over the last century have all taken a crack at it.

The legendary conversations of Lao Tzu and Confucius

In about 100 B.C.E., the Han Dynasty's Grand Historian chronicled a meeting between the two grand old men of Chinese thought, Lao Tzu and Confucius, which had supposedly occurred some 400 years earlier. Although this spectacular account was almost certainly pieced together from a mix of folk legends and whimsy, it captured such a dramatic meeting of opposites that it still periodically shows up in popular Chinese art, theater, and storytelling.

In the official story, Confucius paid a visit to the more senior Lao Tzu (naturally), superficially to request instruction about ritual. Lao Tzu pretty much lowered the boom on Confucius, chiding him for arrogance, self-centeredness, and putting on airs, and rubbing his nose in the fact that the bones of the people he wanted to honor with rituals had all turned to dust anyway. After this scolding, Confucius retreated with his tail between his legs and acknowledged to his disciples that Lao Tzu was like a dragon, well beyond his own limited knowledge. Lao Tzu followed with a few words of his own, bashing Confucius for pursuing the virtues that would eventually lead to his undoing.

The Grand Historian relayed this narrative in an attempt to get the story right, but Chuang Tzu — or at least the author of several passages spread across different chapters of the *Chuang Tzu* — fabricated a series of encounters between Confucius and Lao Tzu, for the purpose of making Confucius look like a sincere but malleable recipient of Lao Tzu's wisdom. In most of the stories, Lao Tzu talks down to Confucius, who ends up acknowledging that he's finally beginning to see the light. The Taoist light, of course.

That said, there are still a few things about the *Tao Te Ching* that are a lot easier to sort out. Here are some features of the text in its current form.

- ✔ The text contains approximately 5,000 Chinese characters. The number varies slightly depending on which version you're reading.

- ✔ The text contains 81 chapters, though these chapter divisions may have come quite some time after the text first started circulating.

- ✔ The 81 chapters are divided into two sections. The first part contains chapters 1 through 37; the second part contains chapters 38 through 81. In at least two versions unearthed by archaeologists, the order was reversed.

- ✔ The first Chinese character of the first section is *Tao,* so the Chinese traditionally call that the "*Tao* section." The first important character of the second section is *Te* ("virtue," "power," or integrity"), and so the Chinese call that the "*Te* section."

- ✔ The two sections of the text together explain the title, the *Tao Te Ching.* It means the "Way-Virtue Classic," or "The Classic of the Way and Its Virtue," or something similar.

After this basic stuff, the *Tao Te Ching* gets a lot dicier. It lacks most of the details that other texts of the period have, like names of people or places, references to historical events, or even some clear indication of what specific audience it has in mind. Most of the chapters contain clipped, often poetic-sounding adages, and they don't develop any sense of narrative or continuity from chapter to chapter. Sometimes, it reads like the disconnected musings of a contemplative spiritual seeker, at others like a secret trove of military strategies. It has plenty of enigmatic images too, like the "valley spirit," the "uncarved block," and the "mysterious female."

Still, out of all this obscurity, the text does develop several recurring themes. In the rest of this section, I talk about how Lao Tzu put an unexpected spin on the concept of *Tao,* how he distinguished between the "true" *Tao* and mundane Confucian virtues, and what this all meant for his understanding of the sage or wise person.

The Tao that cannot be Tao-ed

In a nutshell, the Hundred Schools philosophers, including Lao Tzu, were arguing about the *Tao,* about the Way that Heaven decreed and what humans have to do in order to follow that Way or help realize it on Earth. So far, the Confucians and the Mohists, who dominated much of the debate, mostly fought about *which* way was the *right* way to fulfill our human obligations. Should you relate to people differently depending on their relationships to you, or should you love all people equally? Should you practice rituals in order to build character and refine relationships, or should you avoid waste and seek what brings benefit to the greatest number? Should you adopt a deferential, somewhat distant posture with ghosts and spirits, or should you treat them as omnipresent players that you're responsible for satisfying? In short, the Confucians and the Mohists argued about how to follow the way and which path makes up the right way, but they never really questioned the human capacity to know the way, or asked themselves what it even means to talk about a "way." Enter Lao Tzu, who brought discussions of the Way back to the drawing board.

In the first line of the *Tao Te Ching* — at least in the traditional version that's still the most common one in circulation — Lao Tzu assaulted all the elemental assumptions that his audience may have had about the *Tao*. With one six-character phrase — *tao k'o tao fei ch'ang tao* — Lao Tzu turned conventional thinking on its ear. He also baffled both translators and modern Chinese readers, who still struggle with how many different ways there are to read this single line. For starters, the passage says something about the *Tao,* and whether you can *Tao* it, which is already confusing! What does *Tao* mean when you use it as a verb like that? What does it mean to *Tao* a *Tao* or say that a *Tao* can't be *Tao*-ed?

Lao Tzu also said something in that opening line about a "constant *Tao,*" or an "eternal *Tao,*" or an "absolute *Tao.*" Does that mean there's a difference between a "changing *Tao*" and a "constant *Tao,*" or between a "provisional *Tao*" and an "absolute *Tao?*" What would a provisional *Tao* even look like? How long do we have to watch a *Tao* to figure out whether it's "eternal" or only "temporary"? If this is starting to make you a little crazy, you might want to brace yourself, because this is still only the first line of the text.

Check out the following plausible readings of this ambiguous set of six characters. You may also want to notice when a translation uses capital letters for "the Way" (even though Chinese characters have no uppercase or lowercase), and see if it changes the mood and tone of the passage:

- The way that can be named is not the absolute way.

- A way can be named, but not the constant way.

- As for the Way, it can be spoken, but not the eternal Way.

- The way that can be walked is not the permanent Way.

- As for ways that can be walked, they are not the constant Way.

- Way-making that can be put into words is not really way-making.

- To guide what can be guided is not constant guiding.

Confused? Well, no matter how we read it, Lao Tzu did seem to be warning us about (at least) two things. First, there is some limit to what we can know through language; and second, knowing the *Tao* is going to get a lot more complicated than we may have initially thought. Suddenly, what had been framed by the Confucians and Mohists as a straightforward *moral* question starts to take on elements of *mystery*. Here are some more elusive descriptions of the *Tao* in the *Tao Te Ching:*

- ✔ The great Way appears dark.
- ✔ The smooth Way appears uneven.
- ✔ The Way is constantly nameless.
- ✔ The Way is shadowy and nebulous.
- ✔ The Way floats and drifts, flowing left and right.
- ✔ The Way of Heaven is like the flexing of a bow.
- ✔ The Way is the wellspring of the 10,000 things.
- ✔ The ancients who knew the Way were subtly profound and mysteriously perceptive.

Passages like these may make you wonder if Lao Tzu invented the first fortune cookie. But for all these paradoxes and Chinese puzzle boxes, he does give the strong impression that *knowing* or *experiencing* the Way requires extraordinary insight and sensitivity, and that it probably doesn't follow from conventional book learning. This could also explain a huge part of this text's appeal. When you read the *Tao Te Ching,* you may feel like you've entered a journey to solve a high-stakes cosmic mystery!

The *Tao Te Ching* never really defines the *Tao.* Try to think of the text as a series of indirect *pointers* that together evoke a quality that can't be expressed easily through standard language.

The critique of Confucian virtue

Even if Lao Tzu had no inclination to tell us what the *Tao* is, he certainly had no problem telling us what is *isn't.* The biggest mistake you can make would be to *confuse* the *Tao* for all the traditional virtues that the Confucians and Mohists had been trying to peddle. What's more, the only reason those virtues even exist is because they represent mistaken, confused, and failed attempts to understand the *Tao.* This is a huge knock on moral philosophers, in particular the Confucians. To drive home this point, Lao Tzu portrayed a sort of collective "fall" of humankind, where we gradually fell from some pure state when we could really know the *Tao,* descending lower and lower through all the so-called "virtues," and eventually landing in a spot that is superficial rather than substantial, chaotic rather than well ordered. Here's Lao Tzu's narration of this decline:

1. In losing the Way, afterward follows virtue *(te).*

2. In losing virtue, afterward follows humaneness *(jen).*

3. In losing humanness, afterward follows rightness *(i).*

4. In losing rightness, afterward follows ritual propriety *(li)*.

5. Ritual propriety is the thinnest husk of loyalty and sincerity, and the beginning of disorder.

Because Lao Tzu sees all these so-called virtues as things that emerge when people fail to understand and follow the *Tao,* it can require some effort to remember that he's identifying these qualities as *negative* characteristics. You might normally expect that humaneness and rightness are *good* things, but he's referring to them in an almost tongue-in-cheek manner. When Lao Tzu says something like "the highest virtue is not virtuous," he means that whatever it takes to be *really* virtuous, to get to the place where he *really* wants you to be, that's very different from (but easily confused with) the so-called "virtue" of the Confucians and other moralists. Similarly, when Lao Tzu says that loyalty and compassion arise when human relations are not in harmony, you may initially think he's saying that people will step up to the challenge and practice loyalty and compassion to fix the messed up relations. In fact, he's saying much the opposite, that the so-called virtues of loyalty and compassion are actually *symptoms* of disharmony. Just like the *genuine* Way differs from the *contrived* virtue of humaneness and rightness, *genuine* human harmony differs from the *contrived* virtues of loyalty and compassion.

Lao Tzu rejects traditional moral virtues as signs of having lost the Way. Most of the time, when the *Tao Te Ching* mentions humaneness, rightness, or ritual propriety, it's employing the terms pejoratively.

Backward sagehood: I alone am muddled and confused

Because Lao Tzu sees ordinary virtues as a *decline* from an original state of knowing the Way, he feels that the only way we can get back to that perfect starting place is through a process of *returning* or *reversal.* That is, we somehow have to work our way backward and undo all the junk that got us here in the first place. That's why Lao Tzu admonishes us to "abolish humaneness" and "abandon rightness"; it's the only way we can rediscover genuine loyalty and compassion.

However, this process of reversal involves more than just tossing away useless virtues. If you think about it, how would you ignore your own humaneness or rightness? Certainly, these character qualities won't just disappear if you click your heels and try to wish or will them away. That's why Lao Tzu demands that we actually *unlearn* the things we've already absorbed, that we somehow abandon the so-called knowledge and wisdom that's keeping us from getting things right. If we can eliminate learning, he tells us, we'll have no unnecessary worries; if we eliminate knowledge, it will bring great benefit to the people. So this, like just about everything else in Classical Taoism, comes out on a paradox that flies in the face of ordinary intuition. Learning takes you forward and moves you to "increase" each day, but hearing the Way takes you backward and moves you to "decrease" each day. The goal is a *regressive* one.

What does someone look like who has returned, who has unlearned, and dropped away all his or her artificial trappings? You may imagine that some-one without knowledge looks like kind of a doofus who just tends to his or her own survival, and Lao Tzu doesn't always try to dissuade us from that image. He says the sage is for the "belly," not the "eye," because all the stuff you see, hear, and think about — colors, valuable goods, difficult tasks — just confuse and distract you. The sage rejects excess and extravagance; he won't brag or show off. Lao Tzu even describes himself as "muddled," "confused," "stupid," "lacking," and "uncivilized." He really does take this returning and unlearning thing pretty seriously.

You may be asking what it is that makes such a clumsy clod worthy of the label "sage," and it's certainly a fair question. Lao Tzu answers this with one of his most perplexing ideas: *wu-wei,* which can be translated as "inaction," "doing nothing," "non-doing," or "actionless action." Somehow, this newly obtained simplicity is *efficacious;* the "act" of acting without action *accom-plishes* things, but it does so without having a specific goal or selfish intent. More than once, Lao Tzu puts forth some variation of his claim that the sage "does nothing, and yet nothing is left undone."

According to the *Tao Te Ching,* the best way to follow the *Tao* is through *wu-wei,* through non-doing, an effortless and actionless kind of "action" that mysteriously leaves no tasks unfulfilled.

Chuang Tzu: Skeptic, Storyteller, Comedian

Next to Lao Tzu, no other Classical Taoist commands more attention than Chuang Tzu, and many people would argue that he's the one who really deserves the top spot on the Taoist hit parade. As with Lao Tzu, there's almost no reliable biographical information about the man identified as Chuang Chou; the one existing narrative of his life places him in the 4th century B.C.E., and a good chunk of the *Chuang Tzu* text does indeed seem to date from that era. But regardless of who the author really was, *someone* produced some incredibly sophisticated philosophy, some genuinely funny and memorable vignettes, and some snippets of literary genius. Even if no one had ever bothered to think of the *Chuang Tzu* as a religious text or a work of philosophy, millions of people would still be reading it today simply as great literature.

It's easy to see why the historians identified the *Tao Te Ching* and the *Chuang Tzu* as belonging to the same school; both texts develop similar understand-ings of the *Tao,* criticize the moral standards of the day, and go way against expectations when they depict the ideal sage. But Chuang Tzu had his own interests and his own quirks, and he took the conversation to some truly strange places.

In this section, I help you get to know this dazzling oddball. You see how he develops a unique skepticism about the nature of the world, and questions whether we can even trust our own senses and judgments. You also see how he holds up bizarre characters as role models and draws vivid pictures of what it means to follow the Way.

Deconstructing consensus reality

When you read the *Chuang Tzu,* you get the feeling that you're overhearing the thoughts of someone who for the first time realized that when people view things from different angles, they may actually see those things differently and come to different conclusions about them. This must have been an astonishing and — at least initially — disorienting insight. Suddenly, our *perceptions* seem to depend on our *perspectives,* and that calls into question exactly which of those perceptions we can trust and should act upon. How certain can we be of our notion of taste, when foods that seem like delicacies to us sicken other people? How certain can we be of our concept of beauty, when women renowned for their beauty repel fish, birds, and animals? If we think we're certain about anything, and feel that certainty reinforced by our families and communities, Chuang Tzu is always there to point out exactly what perspective we have that produced that certainty, and to show us another perspective that makes it all look different. There may be a *consensus* among people about what is true and what is good, but that consensus can always be *deconstructed,* can always be taken apart.

These little turnarounds are entertaining, but Chuang Tzu wasn't just fooling around like college students sitting in their dormitory hallways at three in the morning, wondering if our entire existence is really a tiny speck on some scientist's microscope slide in another galaxy. Chuang Tzu wasn't speculating abstractly but struggling with how humans can make wise and responsible choices when we can so easily deconstruct our own assumptions and opinions. In particular, he wondered how to make moral choices when the Confucians denied what the Mohists affirmed and affirmed what the Mohists denied, especially when each side seemed to come to its position so honestly. How can a wise person arbitrate such matters? How can you negotiate it when different perspectives produce different moral standards? Normally, you may think you can choose from one of a few different approaches:

- ✔ **One of them must be correct.** Your task is to choose the best position, defend it, and live your life by it. This would be an *absolutist* approach. Chuang Tzu would reject this because he would find it intellectually dishonest to embrace a position that can be easily deconstructed. Competing types of absolutism are what got him scratching his head in the first place.

- ✔ **All of them are correct.** You can adopt an attitude of tolerance, accepting that each position works in its own way. This would be a *relativist* approach. Chuang Tzu would reject this because it doesn't get you any closer to figuring out what you should actually do when you encounter different possibilities. If one side says an action is right, and another side says it's wrong, you can't really both do it and not do it.

✔ **None of them is correct.** You can just accept the reality that no one has it right, throw up your hands in frustration (or amusement), and somehow muddle through the best you can. This would be a *nihilist* approach. Chuang Tzu would reject this, in part because it would produce a chaotic and hostile world, but mainly because he was convinced from his own experience that there *must* be some right way.

As you might expect, Chuang Tzu didn't think you could follow the Way by choosing from, combining, or even ignoring different alternatives. Like Lao Tzu, Chuang Tzu understood the *Tao* as something distinct from (but easily confused with) the various moral paths that occupied most of the other philosophers. And like Lao Tzu, he relied on lots of figurative language and parables to evoke what he meant by the Way.

Dreaming he was a butterfly

In one of the *Chuang Tzu*'s best known — and best loved — stories, Chuang Tzu dreamed he was a butterfly, fluttering and flying so happily that he never for a moment thought about having ever been Chuang Tzu. When he woke up, he was startled to find that he was Chuang Tzu, physically and intellectually. At that point, he wondered if he was really Chuang Tzu, who had just dreamed that he was a butterfly, or if he was in fact a butterfly now dreaming that he was Chuang Tzu. In the final line of the story, Chuang Tzu recognized the obvious distinction between himself and a butterfly, and identified this movement from one to the other as an example of the "transformations of things."

Was Chuang Tzu saying that he really thought he turned into a butterfly and then back into a man? I doubt it. Be he *was* saying that *our own* perspectives may shift and produce different perceptions, and also that the world itself is in a kind of constant state of transformation. Though he didn't mention anything about the interactions of *yin* and *yang* in this story, he certainly shared the general Hundred Schools assumption that the universe functioned as a single, dynamic organism, in a constant state of flux and flow. For Chuang Tzu, the challenge was to adapt our perceptions and attitudes to that flux and flow.

Because of this, Chuang Tzu differentiated between an attitude that comes from your own perspective and situation (one that is stuck in your own starting place) and one that shifts effortlessly with the sometimes subtle alterations of the circumstances at hand and the entire cosmos. According to Chuang Tzu, the first attitude is the one most people have, though they're not usually aware of its *situatedness,* of the way that it's tied into their particular context. The second attitude is the enlightened one, a *liberated* one, which operates flexibly and fluidly. Chuang Tzu called the first one something like "artificial affirming" or "affirming based on one's own constructing" and the second one something like "adaptive affirming" or "affirming based on the circumstances." By necessity, following the Way would entail a total restructuring of the way you perceive, interpret, and act in the world.

Chuang Tzu encourages you to develop a habit of "adaptive affirming," rather than "artificial affirming," determining what is so and how to proceed from the *shifting circumstances of existence,* not from your frozen presuppositions, opinions, or intellectual constructions. This is one place where it makes a lot of sense to say that Chuang Tzu values the "natural."

Trashing scholars and glorifying misfits

Because Chuang Tzu thought most of the Hundred School philosophers were missing the mark when it came to figuring out the Way, he often portrayed traditional scholars as either a little bit slow or genuinely buffoonish, acting as dramatic foils for the unlikely heroes of his stories. For role models, Chuang Tzu had a fondness for trotting out grotesques, cripples, mutilated criminals, and various social outcasts. And what a perfect strategy! If he wanted to shock his audience into recognizing that their initial perceptions and interpretations were misguided, what better way than to introduce us to repulsive or scorned outsiders, only to flip things around and show us how they're the real sages?

Indeed, what a motley crew of misfits Chuang Tzu conjured up! Most of the time, he inserted them into dialogues with established figures, so they could get the better of the exchanges. Here are just a few of Chuang Tzu's memorable wise men who truly know the Way:

- ✔ **Shu-shan Choptoes:** This one-time criminal visits Confucius, gets an earful from him, turns around and lectures him on qualities that go beyond the crippled body, and eventually earns his praise. By the end of the vignette, Choptoes and Lao Tzu together lament how far poor dim Confucius still has to go.

- ✔ **Uglyface T'o:** Despite his appearance, men gravitate to him, and women all want to be his mistress. This time Confucius gets it, and describes Uglyface as someone whose virtue simply hasn't taken physical form but who dispassionately recognizes all the alternations of destiny.

- ✔ **Limpleg Hunchback Lipless:** The contrast between the fullness of his virtue and the defectiveness of his physical appearance caused those who saw him to view apparently healthy (but spiritually deficient) people as having outrageously long legs. His counterpart Pitcherneck caused others to see healthy people as having outrageously long necks.

- ✔ **Crippled Shu:** He had numerous deformities — his chin was stuck in his navel and his five internal organs were on top of his head — but he was able to support himself and fulfill the destiny that Heaven mandated for him.

Biblical scholarship and the *Chuang Tzu*

It may not seem obvious that Biblical scholarship has anything to do with the *Chuang Tzu,* but the same methods that scholars employed more than a century ago to do groundbreaking work on the Bible have also paved the way for some tremendously important revelations about the *Chuang Tzu.* Beginning at the end of the 19th century, and using something now called "historical-critical method," scholars analyzed the language, literary styles, historical references, and religious priorities of the authors of the first five books of the Hebrew Bible (the Torah, or the Old Testament), and they hypothesized that these books actually consist of four distinct sources that were written at different times and eventually became intricately folded into one continuous narrative. If you ever take a college-level course in Biblical studies (which is different from a church-based Bible study), you'll never again hear four English letters — *J, E, P,* and *D* — without thinking of the Bible. Those are the initials of the four textual strands: the Yahwist, the Elohist, the Priestly, and Deuteronomist.

For centuries, scholars recognized that many different hands contributed to the 33 chapters of the *Chuang Tzu,* though they were usually content just to try to separate the "authentic" chapters (those written by the original author in the 4th century B.C.E.) from the later additions. But over the last few decades, a handful of highly motivated individuals took on the demanding task of applying historical-critical method to the *Chuang Tzu,* to sort out who the different authors were, when they were writing, and what intellectual positions they represented. Probably the most important of these scholars was a British professor named Angus Charles Graham, who basically took the entire text apart and put it back together. Today, most scholars pretty much take for granted Graham's division of the *Chuang Tzu* into five different strands:

- ✔ **Chuang Tzu (CT):** The "authentic" portions include the first seven chapters and various related essays or fragments scattered throughout the book. Whether or not there was a historical Chuang Tzu, this material

seems to have had one author and dates to around the 4th century B.C.E.

- ✔ **School of Chuang Tzu (SCT):** Six chapters from the middle of the book are philosophically and stylistically similar to the authentic chapters, though they were probably written during the subsequent generations by followers trying to emulate his work. Despite the "school of" label that Graham chose, there's no evidence that these followers ever organized into a self-conscious school.

- ✔ **The Primitivist (P):** Close to four chapters were written sometime around 200 B.C.E. by an irritable gadfly who has absolutely no patience for scholars, morals, or anything he remotely considers excessive or unnatural. This author seems to reject society and longs for the days of a primitive utopia.

- ✔ **The Yangists (Y):** Four or so chapters, also written around 200 B.C.E., seem to come from various anonymous followers of Yang Chu, who taught that humankind's basic nature was *physical* and that our most important task is to gratify the sensory needs of the body.

- ✔ **The Syncretists (S):** The handful of chapters that make up the latest portions of the text (around the 2nd century B.C.E.) were written by authors trying consciously to blend Taoist thought with legal philosophy and other influences. In all likelihood, the Syncretists were also responsible for compiling the text (though others would monkey with it for the next several hundred years).

So, just as we know some of the different voices in the Bible, we now know the different voices in the *Chuang Tzu.* And just like it doesn't really make sense to ask the "biblical view" of something — because there's almost always more than one such "view" — it doesn't really make sense to ask what the *Chuang Tzu* says about something, unless you make clear which of the five sources you mean.

The stranger the character, the more likely that Chuang Tzu is presenting him as one who knows the Way. This provides a huge contrast with traditional Confucian or Mohist sages.

Getting into the Tao zone

When Chuang Tzu wants to illustrate concretely how someone adapts to the flux and flow of the Way, his main strategy is to present people who do very simple tasks, but do them with extraordinary, even superhuman ability. This is what you might want to think of as Chuang Tzu's "*Tao* Zone," where you're so *in touch* that you can effortlessly glide along with the natural ripples of the universe. One of his most memorable and lovable figures is Cook Ting, who has an uncanny dexterity for, of all things, carving oxen! He slides his blade so carefully through the tendons and ligaments that even though he's been doing his job for 19 years, he's never had to change or even sharpen his blade.

If you think about it, this makes perfect sense. If you're going against the flow, or against the grain of anything, it will take a toll and wear you (or your tools) down. But if you're really going with the grain, it's like you're coasting down a stream, or letting a breeze blow you where you need to go. Think of the old Grateful Deadheads in their tie-dyed shirts, who used to say, "The band doesn't play the music, the music plays the band!"

Many other colorful characters in the *Chuang Tzu* operate in the *Tao* Zone, performing the most inconsequential chores as if they were playing notes in a cosmic symphony. Here's a small sampler of these delightful eccentrics:

- A ghostly swimmer who breezes along the edge of treacherous waterfall, without ever losing control
- A hunchback who catches cicadas with a sticky rod, never missing a single one
- An engraver who fashions a bell stand with such ease that it seems to carve itself
- A wheelwright who employs his hammer and chisel with ideal tension and speed
- A metal forger who crafts perfect buckles, even when he is well into his 80s
- An archer who never misses a target, no matter how small

Did Chuang Tzu mean these stories literally? Was he exhorting us all to go out and carve oxen or swim on the crest of a waterfall? Probably not. More likely, Chuang Tzu intended these as *allegories*, vivid illustrations of how unusual and how profound it is to function in the *Tao* Zone. He probably had the same thing in mind when he described characters with *truly* superhuman abilities:

- ✔ A man living on a distant mountain, who rides on cloud vapor or flying dragons, and subsists on wind and dew.

- ✔ The unnamed "true men" of the remote past, who could somehow jump in water without getting wet, or walk into fire without being burned.

- ✔ Three men who aspire to climb up to the heavens, roam in the ether, and mingle with the infinite.

A Pair of (Almost) Forgotten Early Taoists

Enthusiasts of the Hundred Schools Period tend to identify Classical Taoism with Lao Tzu and Chuang Tzu, but several other Taoistically inclined thinkers did contribute much to the public debates. Unfortunately, very little authentic material apart from the so-called Lao-Chuang tradition has survived over the years, and so there are certain limitations to how much we can say about them.

Two figures in particular are worth examining, in part because others from the period mentioned them, but also because we do have a critical mass of textual material associated with them, even as there are legitimate doubts about their authenticity. In this section, I introduce you to Yang Chu, the man frequently reviled as an "egoist," and Lieh Tzu, a man who might have been as well known as Chuang Tzu had his writings survived.

Lieh Tzu: The man who was almost Chuang Tzu

Like Lao Tzu, the supposed author Lieh Tzu may or may not have ever lived. His questionable biography places him in the late 5th and early 4th centuries B.C.E., a couple of generations before Chuang Tzu. He does show up a few times as a character in the *Chuang Tzu,* but other authors from that period don't seem to have given him any thought. Still, the same historians who eventually sorted out the Hundred Schools authors and texts specified the existence of the *Lieh Tzu,* an eight-chapter text of Taoist philosophy. There is a text by that name that survives today, but unfortunately it's a forgery from about 300 C.E. But as forgeries go, it's a pretty useful one, because it gives us different versions of some stories that occur in the *Chuang Tzu,* and it also contains passages that may even have come from lost chapters of the *Chuang Tzu.*

It's a pity that we don't know much about Lieh Tzu, because he sounds like he could have been quite a character, and early historians speculated that Chuang Tzu may have actually gotten some of his best stories from him. In one place, Chuang Tzu says that Lieh Tzu could journey for 15 days with the wind as his chariot, though he still made a point to upbraid him for not riding a "true chariot" between Heaven and Earth. In another place, Lieh Tzu becomes fascinated with a shaman who can predict the future, but then decides that his learning has not yet begun and retreats for years to a life of simplicity, feeding pigs as though he were serving honored guests. But if it had been his text that survived and Chuang Tzu's whose was lost, we might be talking today about the Lao-Lieh tradition.

Yang Chu: Embracing bright colors and beautiful women

If indeed there was a Yang Chu, he probably lived around the same time as the equally uncertain Lieh Tzu, about 400 B.C.E. One chapter of the *Lieh Tzu* focuses on him, and his followers (or simply others writing in a similar vein) contributed several later chapters to the *Chuang Tzu* and other miscellaneous works of the period. So, we do have some sense of what a "Yangist" strand of thought might have been, even if we're not too sure about the actual person or know much about whoever wrote those essays.

Apparently, Yang Chu was one of the first Chinese philosophers to tackle the question of human nature, and his understanding of it led him to a set of clear, specific conclusions:

- **Humans are by nature *physical* beings.** Our primary endowment is not our intellect or a capacity to reason, but our actual physical bodies.

- **We can understand the body in terms of certain sensory and cognitive functions: eyes, ears, nostrils, mouth, body, and will.**

- **The physical functions desire specific gratification.** The ears desire music, the eyes desire female beauty (he doesn't talk about what female eyes desire), the nostrils desire flowers and aromas, the mouth desires to talk truthfully, the body desires comfort and good food, and the will desires freedom and leisure.

- **Humans should satisfy the desires of those particular functions.** To tend to our lives in that way is to fulfill our basic human natures. To neglect to do so, or to be distracted by morality or education or concern for the dead, is to fall short of fulfilling our own humanity.

Because of his concerns for the gratification of the physical body, Western scholars sometimes identify him as a "hedonist." Chinese critics were more upset by what they characterized as "egoism" — acting on behalf of oneself — which they saw as hostile to the fundamentally *social* character of their culture. In one notorious passage, Yang Chu says something about not being willing to sacrifice a single hair from his body, even if it would bring benefit to the entire empire. Either way, no one has been particularly quick to hold up Yang Chu as some philosophical genius.

At this point, you might want to ask yourself, what is it that even makes Yang Chu a Taoist? Yes, he did teach a kind of *natural* approach to living, and he did reject all the same moral preoccupations that Lao Tzu and Chuang Tzu did, and his writings did end up sitting smack dab in the middle of Taoist texts. But Yang Chu did not share any of the "mysterious" interpretations of the *Tao*, or have any similar misgivings about language, or envision anything special about a sage beyond an ability to cook a good meal. And of course to some extent, the question is really kind of a red herring, because there probably were no self-conscious Taoists during that period, and so it only makes so much sense to ask if he was one of them.

Yang Chu taught certain Taoist-flavored ideas, like an emphasis on being natural and a rejection of Confucian and Mohist moralizing, but he also lacked many of the qualities we normally associate with other Classical Taoists.

A Moment in the Sun for Taoist Government

If "Taoist government" sounds to you like an oxymoron, you'll be surprised to find that Taoism — or at least some form of it — nearly became China's official ruling ideology a few generations after the end of the Hundred Schools Period. A new dynasty finally unified China in 221 B.C.E., and its emperor adopted Han Fei Tzu's Legalist philosophy and harsh social controls as the means to maintain power. The regime did implement many important political and bureaucratic measures, but it quickly alienated the masses and gave rise to a successful peasant-led rebellion.

The new Han Dynasty, which took power in 206 B.C.E., quickly found itself in need of methods to govern — they apparently spent far more time thinking about how to take over the country than how to run it — and they looked again to the competing ideologies of the Hundred Schools. Eventually, they would settle on Confucianism as the official state ideology, but that couldn't happen right away. The new peasant emperor thought that Confucians were all arrogant eggheads; he even reportedly once took a whiz in a Confucian scholar's cap!

In this section, I introduce you briefly to a kind of Taoism that fleetingly had the emperor's ear in the early part of the Han Dynasty and may have functioned as a kind of unofficial state ideology. You find out about this short-lived tradition called Huang-Lao Taoism, and see how scholars creatively combined Taoist thought with that of other schools.

Huang-Lao and the School of Tao

In the early 100s B.C.E., when scholars first began to sort authors and texts into a "School of *Tao*" *(Tao-chia)*, they also began to mention the teachings of Huang-Lao, a reference to Lao Tzu and Huang Ti, the mostly mythic Yellow Emperor who was associated with everything from agricultural inventions to waging military battles. Historians have sometimes employed the terms *Tao-chia* and *Huang-Lao* more or less interchangeably, but the latter has come to refer to a loosely affiliated coterie of Han intellectuals who made up a new Taoist movement. Until recently, scholars knew very little about this type of Taoism, but they've begun to reconstruct the history and identify different sources that seem to be propagating Huang-Lao philosophy, though this is still at a very early stage. The following texts or pieces of texts are all good places to find some aspects of Huang-Lao:

- ✔ **Four or so chapters of the *Chuang Tzu*, usually identified as the *Syncretist* writings:** The authors of these chapters may also have been responsible for compiling the entire text.

- ✔ **Two chapters from the Legalist text *Hanfeizi*, though probably not written by Han Fei Tzu himself:** "Commentaries on Lao Tzu and "Illustrations of Lao Tzu" may be the oldest known systematic discussions of the *Tao Te Ching*.

- ✔ **The *Huang Ti Nei-ching*, the *Inner Scripture of the Yellow Emperor:*** This text discusses the basic elements of traditional Chinese medicine.

- ✔ **The *Huai Nan Tzu:*** This important document was sponsored by Prince Liu An, who commissioned several scholars to write it. He presented the text to the emperor, his nephew, who ultimately rejected it in favor of Confucianism.

- ✔ **The Ma-wang-tui manuscripts:** The archaeological excavation in 1973 that discovered two ancient silk versions of the *Tao Te Ching* also came upon four previously unknown texts. Some scholars tentatively identified these as the lost *Four Classics of the Yellow Emperor,* but others dispute this claim.

A synthesis of Taoism and other philosophies

Although Huang-Lao thought never enjoyed any official status and apparently lasted for no more than a couple of generations, it did present an innovative fusion of Taoist philosophy with other strands of Chinese thought. The Huang-Lao thinkers smartly integrated the following elements in this new Taoism:

- ✔ **Legalism:** Most of the texts were addressed to the emperor and dealt specifically with the questions of how to maintain power and govern effectively.

- ✔ **Daoism:** The emperor should rule by non-doing *(wu-wei),* so that human laws and social structures correspond to cosmic laws and structures.

- ✔ **Naturalism (the Yin-Yang School):** Huang-Lao thinkers often explained law, social relationships, physiology, and historical events through the interactions of *yin* and *yang,* and related systems of correspondence.

- ✔ **Confucianism:** Although the school seemed Taoist in many ways, the morality it taught pretty much reinforced traditional Confucian social relationships and responsibilities.

The Huang-Lao tradition may also have involved techniques for cultivating the body, or techniques that didn't differentiate between physical and spiritual cultivation. Many of the theories behind these techniques, if not always the techniques themselves, would play important roles in later Taoist practice.

Chapter 5

The Development of Institutional Taoism

In This Chapter

▶ Meeting the "real" founders of Taoism

▶ Tracing ongoing Taoist revelations

▶ Getting a sense of Taoist identity

Classical Taoist texts like the *Tao Te Ching* and the *Chuang Tzu* have left a lasting impact on Chinese literature and *intellectual* history, but if you want to get a handle on the role of Taoism in Chinese culture and *social* history, you need to take seriously the many organized, institutional types of Taoism that have ebbed and flowed for nearly 2,000 years. Many Westerners find the whole idea of institutional Taoism kind of an oxymoron; after all, didn't Lao and Tzu and Chuang Tzu protest against the kinds of dogma, rules, structures, and ceremonies that people often associate with organized religion? For sure, figuring out how these organized forms of Taoism connect to the classical philosophy can be difficult, but they're *not quite* different enough from each other to say that they're totally unrelated.

In this section, I cover the origins and development of various movements that eventually came together to form what we now know as the Chinese Taoist religion. You get up close and personal with the first "real" Taoist organization in China, discover how later religious ideas and practices merged with aspects of that original organization, and see how a distinct Taoist identity eventually emerged over a period of a few hundred years.

Try to understand Taoist institutions "on their own terms." If you keep trying to see how they're following Lao Tzu and Chuang Tzu's philosophies, you'll probably get frustrated and confused pretty quickly.

The Way of the Celestial Masters

The story of religious Taoism begins with a society called the Way of the Celestial Masters *(T'ien-shih Tao),* that took shape in the middle and late parts of the second century. This movement combined a number of religious themes — including divine revelation and a belief in a new age, spiritual healing — and set in motion a process that would eventually lead to the forms of Taoism that are still active in China today.

In this section, I talk about the early history of this remarkable movement, as well as some of its key leaders and religious innovations. You get a look at how the Chinese transformed Lao Tzu from a quasi-historical author into a divine being, meet up with the man who founded the Celestial Masters, and hear all about the community that he founded. You'll also find out about other similar groups, and how later communities initiated military rebellions with the goal of setting up a Taoist religious state.

The deification of Lao Tzu

Toward the end of the Han Dynasty, by the middle of the 1st century, all the folk stories circulating about Lao Tzu began to take on increasingly fantastic and mythic characteristics. This was partially because the Chinese were playing a protracted game of "telephone" with him — telling and retelling the stories with more and more drama and supernatural episodes — but also because various political and religious factions "adopted" the Lao Tzu figure and transformed both his story and his symbolism to suit their own purposes. They started to know him not as Lao Tzu, but as Lord Lao (Lao-chün), Yellow Old Lord (Huang-lao-chün), and eventually Most Elevated Lord Lao (T'ai-shang Lao-chün). He remains a central figure of worship and veneration in Taoism today.

The "new and improved" Lao Tzu (a.k.a., Lord Lao) was no longer simply an archivist, historian, and adversary of Confucius who wrote the *Tao Te Ching.* Rather, he morphed into a unique deity with extraordinary powers and a ranking position in any imagined hierarchy of Heavenly beings. The following are a few characteristics of the newly deified Lord Lao:

  ✔ **Personification of the *Tao:*** Even if the *Tao Te Ching* never portrayed the *Tao* as a deity, that didn't stop later followers from thinking of Lord Lao either as *identical* to the *Tao* or as some type of *manifestation* of the *Tao* and cosmic order. Because the *Tao* is a creative principle, Lord Lao becomes thought of as creator of the universe.

    ✔ **Role in earthly history:** Lord Lao is a *primordial* deity (that is, one who existed before time and space), but he also would manifest on Earth and play significant roles in human history. This is how he could still be identified with the *Tao Te Ching,* but also be conceived as imparting wisdom to different historical Chinese dynasties, or providing magic and charms to help the Han peasant rebels defeat the corrupt Ch'in Dynasty.

    ✔ **Source of revelations:** Lord Lao dwells in Heaven but periodically descends to reveal sacred scriptures to humans for various reasons. Many of the texts of the Taoist Canon are attributed to him.

Lord Lao is the defied Lao Tzu. He is associated with the *Tao,* creation, cosmic order, events in human history, and the revelation of sacred texts.

Chang Tao-ling: The "real" founder of "real" Taoism?

If anyone can lay claim to being the "real" founder of "real Taoism," it would be Chang Tao-ling, a figure whom you quite possibly never encountered before reading this book.

When you hear a statement identifying Chang as the "real deal," be careful not to think I'm claiming that Chang Tao-ling was a "better" Taoist than Lao Tzu, or that Chang somehow knew the "real" Taoist beliefs and practices, or that I have the authority to decide who's in and who's out of the "Taoist founders club." I'm really not making any judgment about who's more important, or who was more of a sage, or who better understood the Tao. What I'm saying is that when we start taking a historical perspective, when we start thinking not only about texts or conceptions of the Tao, but about actual historical practitioners and communities, we can see that none of this really happened until Chang Tao-ling came on the scene. Yes, the classical philosophers were writing texts centuries before Chang Tao-ling, and yes, there may even have been groups of like-minded people engaging in similar practices. But in terms of an observable and self-aware critical mass of people involved in a shared and sustained religious enterprise, Chang Tao-ling's community is really the first appearance of Taoism.

The claim that Chang Tao-ling is the real founder of Taoism is not a judgment about him in relation to Lao Tzu. It's a historical observation about him in relation to other religious events and developments in China. Did he know the *Tao* any better or any worse than Lao Tzu? Who knows. Whatever the answer, though, it has no effect on the simple fact that Chang was the first to found a community that would eventually be known as Taoist.

So, who was Chang Tao-ling, and what did he do? As you might expect, the available biographies often give unlikely and inconsistent information, and it's possible that stories about different historical figures have blended together over time. Still, the overall narrative depicts a broadly experienced child prodigy named Chang Ling (the "Tao" part of his name was added later) who was born near China's coast in the late 1st century C.E. or early 2nd century C.E., during a time when the Han Dynasty was growing increasingly unstable. As the story goes, Chang traveled inland to Szechwan (or Sichuan) Province, not in search of spicy cuisine, but to live as a hermit and seek religious secrets, though it's not really clear what those secrets might have been (or how much of that part of the story was added much later on).

Chang's pivotal moment occurred in 142 C.E. while he was living in an uncertain location called either Crane Call Mountain or Swan Call Mountain, when he received a revelation from a "Heavenly being" in a pretty dramatic fashion. Later lore identified this spirit as the Most Elevated Lord Lao, who descended from the sky riding thousands of carriages and golden chariots, accompanied by countless dragons and tigers. Clearly, this is not simply the Old Master who composed the *Tao Te Ching* and meandered off to parts unknown. Lord Lao's revelation contained some pretty astonishing news:

- **The vision of a new age:** Lord Lao informed Chang that the world was coming to an end in some type of unspecified apocalypse, presumably because of rampant moral decline. He told Chang to prepare for a "new age" by gathering together individuals who would repent their transgressions, become morally pure, and constitute the "seed people" of the new era, which would have a pantheon of previously unknown deities who were manifestations of the pure *Tao*. The term for belief in a new age is *millenarianism,* the belief that one millennium is about to end and another is to begin.

- **Healing powers:** In order for Chang to justify his claim that he was acting on Lord Lao's authority, he was given powers to heal the sick and exorcise evil spirits, which was important because of the rampant epidemics in China at that time. Whether Chang really did claim at the time to be acting on divine revelation, there's really no doubt that he established himself as a charismatic leader and healer. These were not incidental miracles, like those associated with Jesus's much broader ministry; the community really did rally around Chang and his healing powers.

- **The establishment of a covenant:** Lord Lao supposedly gave Chang a collection of scriptures that would serve as the blueprint for how his new society should live. These structures made up the Awe-Inspiring Covenant of Orthodox Unity. Lord Lao designated Chang as his earthly counterpart, and gave him the title of *T'ien-shih* (Celestial Master), a term that had appeared once in the *Chuang Tzu,* to refer to a boy who somewhat offhandedly equated governing an empire to herding horses.

The first community that we can legitimately identify as Taoist grew out of Chang Tao-ling and his revelations from Lord Lao. Believing that he was pursuing a millenarian mission, and armed with healing powers, Chang established a new community organized around the Orthodox Unity covenant, with himself serving as the first Celestial Master.

The covenant of Orthodox Unity

When Chang Tao-ling undertook his mission as a healer and exorcist, he was by no means the first Chinese to exhibit these skills. What made Chang's work so unusual was the way he *organized* his followers and required that each person joining the group would pay a tax of five bushels (sometimes called "pecks") of rice or the monetary equivalent in other goods. Although the rice tax doesn't seem to have much religious significance, it provided something that was hugely important but all too easy to overlook: a reliable source of income, something that every institutional religion needs to negotiate eventually. It also created a store of goods that the people could share communally. Because of this odd way of doing business, many people nicknamed them (usually pejoratively) the "Five Pecks of Rice Sect."

The "Way of the Celestial Masters," "Way of Orthodox Unity," "Five Pecks of Rice Sect," and sometimes simply (and misleadingly) "liturgical Taoism" are all names that people called Chang Tao-ling's organization at different times. It's easier to keep track of the different types of Taoism when you remember that these are all different names for basically the same thing.

Over the course of a couple generations, Chang, his son Chang Heng, and his grandson Chang Lu (who inherited the Celestial Master title) organized the loose association of people they healed into a full-blown religious community, possibly joining forces with other similar healing groups in the region. The Orthodox Unity covenant stipulated many beliefs, practices, bureaucratic structures, and so forth. Here are some of the important features of this growing community:

- ✔ **Administrative districts:** The Changs organized the community into 24 distinct districts, supposedly corresponding to the sacred geography spelled out in an earlier text, which identified several sacred mountains and the deities dwelling in them. Each unit had lodges to accommodate travelers and provide communal activities like public feasts.

- ✔ **Hierarchy of ordained priests:** Members of the community were divided into several levels, differentiated by how accomplished they were at various rituals. The highest were the *chi-chiu* (libationers) — as in someone who prepares and pours libations — who reported directly to the Celestial Master, led the 24 administrative districts, had access to secret texts, presided over rituals, performed healing, and worked as a kind of moral police force for their territory. A group called *demon soldiers* occupied a lower rank; they were responsible for the moral conduct of extended families. Other ranks included *register disciples* and *Tao officials.* Technically, all these offices could be held by men or women, and several women did become prestigious libationers.

✓ **Registers and talismans:** Depending on their rank, followers had access to texts called "registers," which listed not only basic census records, but also the names of spirits or other celestial beings that the person possessing them could in some way control. Marriage rituals included the symbolic joining of two people's registers, which may even have involved some sexual implications. Libationers also used texts called *talismans,* diagrams that offered protection against evil spirits. Members of the community attached appropriate registers and talismans to their clothing.

✓ **Moral precepts:** The revelations from Lord Lao made clear that physical illnesses requiring healing grew out of moral transgressions. Some of the moral precepts echoed classical Taoist ideas, like not pursuing fame and merit, practicing clarity and stillness, and practicing subtlety and receptivity. Others came off as more generic "family values," like being honest, performing good deeds, not killing other people, not speaking in self-aggrandizing ways, and being devout during religious ceremonies. But some reflected the specific interests of the new community, like not eating tasty food or animals that contained blood, not sacrificing to spirits of the dead, not wasting or harming your body's *ch'i,* and not teaching the *Tao* to outsiders. The last point guaranteed that only those in the community had privileged access to its ritual secrets.

✓ **Confession of sins:** Individual members of the community, especially those in need of healing, would retreat to quiet chambers to meditate on and confess their moral transgressions. Priests or senior officials would purge the sins through various rituals, many of which involved writing down the sins as a kind of divine record, and then petitioning deities by burning or burying the record or throwing it into a river. The priests might also direct the confessor to engage in physical or meditative practices, or drink water that had been mixed with the ashes of protective talismans.

✓ **Recitation of the *Tao Te Ching:*** Although it may be hard to see the connection, the Celestial Masters movement understood their morality as drawn, at least in part, from the *Tao Te Ching.* An important commentary on the text, possibly written (or commissioned) by Chang Tao-ling's grandson Chang Lu, translated Lao Tzu's ambiguous poetry into specific rules for living that would allow the community to dwell in harmony with the *Tao* in a state of "Great Peace." They believed that public recitation of the text could help cure illnesses, give you special vision to see spirits, and extend your lifespan. This represents a major change; they viewed the text as not only communicating a particular philosophy, but itself functioning as a source of power.

At this point, you can probably see why it makes sense to think of this as the start of the Taoist religion. So many of the features you normally associate with religious traditions — deities, institutional organization, clergy, sacred texts, rituals and ceremonies, moral precepts — show up here in a way they didn't in the classical texts. And it was Chang Tao-ling and his family, not Lao Tzu, who founded this community, though you could certainly make the claim that Lao Tzu's teachings may have inspired it.

The way of great peace

While Chang Tao-ling organized the Five Pecks of Rice community in the southwestern part of China, other similar communities developed in different parts of the country, though we don't always know whether they had much interaction with one another. The best known and most important of these other movements was the Way of Great Peace (T'ai-p'ing Tao), which took root in northeastern China under the leadership of a man named either Chang Chieh or Chang Chiao, who was probably not related to Chang Tao-ling. This movement may have employed a text called the *Scripture of Great Peace (T'ai-p'ing Tao),* though the book by that name that exists today is probably a mishmash of pieces from a number of different sources.

Chang Chieh's movement had much in common with the Celestial Masters organization, including administrative structures, healing practices, dietary restrictions, rituals to control evil spirits, public confession of sins, and drinking talisman water. The Way of Great Peace was also a millenarian movement, whose members believed that the Chinese government and much of Chinese society had inherited the moral corruption of previous generations and was beyond redemption. Using the kind of *yin-yang* theory that was common in the short-lived Huang-Lao Taoism, Chang determined that the Blue Heaven Period of the Han Dynasty was depleted, and that the new age, the Yellow Heaven Period, would soon take its place. To symbolize the new era, followers wore yellow headscarves and outsiders began to call them simply the Yellow Turbans. Just as Chang Tao-ling's movement was known by many different names, Chang Chieh's movement could be known as both the Way of Great Peace and the Yellow Turbans.

Unlike Chang Tao-ling, Chang Chieh actively broadened his organization, recruiting followers from several different provinces, and promising that the new era would begin in 184 C.E. At one time, he may have had close to a half-million adherents, a huge following for a 2nd-century organization. As far as the government was concerned, the Way of Great Peace was a serious force to reckon with and was anything but peaceful.

Rebellion and Taoist theocracy

Because both the Way of the Celestial Masters and the Way of Great Peace were not only millenarian movements, but also movements that thought the new age was imminent (not just coming at some indeterminate time in the distant future), both groups saw themselves as self-sufficient communities intending to break away from, or even overthrow, the Han Dynasty. In 184 C.E., the year Chang Chieh computed as the beginning of the new millennium, he led more than 300,000 soldiers in the Yellow Turbans Rebellion, an uprising against the Chinese government that took about 30 years to be subdued. After they were defeated, many of the remaining followers eventually hooked up with the Celestial Masters and probably blended some of their ideologies as well, which makes some of this early history quite difficult to untangle.

Though you could argue that the Yellow Turbans Rebellion wasn't technically Taoist — the Way of Great Peace probably didn't trace their revelations to Lord Lao, utilize the *Tao Te Ching,* or have any real connections to Chang Tao-ling's original movement — people often identify it as a Taoist rebellion. Whether Taoist or not, it left a huge mark on Chinese history. The famous 14th-century historical novel *The Romance of the Three Kingdoms* actually begins with the Yellow Turbans Rebellion.

The Celestial Masters, under the leadership of Chang Lu, also organized a military arm but ultimately struck a deal with the Han government, which gave Chang an official title and allowed the organization to function more or less autonomously, mainly because it occupied a more remote part of the country and posed less of an overt threat than did the Yellow Turbans. As a result, Chang controlled what amounted to a state within a state, the first Taoist *theocracy,* a quasi-autonomous political unit that understood itself as sanctioned by divine authority and operating on religious principles. As the architect of this Taoist sub-state, some argue that Chang Lu, not Chang Tao-ling, should be seen as the *real* founder of Taoism, but if you're still having trouble letting go of Lao Tzu as the founder, this step may be just a little too much to take!

The Han Dynasty collapsed in the early 3rd century, and for the next 400 years, China went through a long period of disunion, with many short-lived regimes controlling different parts of the country at the same time. Chang Lu surrendered just before the end of the Han, effectively ending the theocracy, but dispersing his followers — several hundred thousand of them — to different regions, taking their beliefs and practices with them. As a result, other brief Taoist rebellions and theocracies — as well as emerging Taoist strongholds — cropped up in other places. Here are a few important, or at least interesting, historical developments:

✔ **Sun En's rebellion:** In the late 4th century, Sun En, whose family had supposedly followed the Celestial Masters for generations, joined his uncle in a rebellion on the east coast of China. The rebellion may not really have been particularly Taoist, but he did recruit followers by enticing them with the health and longevity practices associated with the Celestial Masters and other local movements.

✔ **K'ou Ch'ien-chih's theocracy:** During the early 5th century, in the Northern Wei Dynasty (which was run by a non-Chinese tribe), K'ou Ch'ien-chih, another descendant of the Celestial Masters movement, received revelations from Lord Lao, instructing him to assume Chang's old title of Celestial Master, revive and reform the movement, and institute a new series of longevity practices. The Wei functioned as a Taoist theocracy until 450, two years after K'ou's death.

✔ **The Platform of Lou-kuan:** This was a state-sponsored Taoist learning center, a place where various unaffiliated Taoist students and practitioners, many of whom were followers of K'ou Ch'ien-chih before the Northern Wei dissolved the theocracy, could gather, study, receive revelations, and so forth. In a sense, this set the stage for the first Taoist monastery or abbey, and the term *kuan* is still frequently used for Taoist temples in China.

Hope and Chang?

So, have you noticed that a lot of figures from the early history of institutional Taoism have the family name Chang? You've got Chang Tao-ling, his son Chang Heng, his grandson Chang Lu (who may have defeated a leader from a rival movement named Chang Hsiu), and the Yellow Turbans leader Chang Chieh. What's more, Chang Tao-ling claimed to be descended from Chang Liang, whose revelation from Lord Lao 300 years earlier led to the founding of the Han Dynasty. In other words, the name Chang packs a heckuva wallop in Taoist history.

After the organized Taoist religion really got up and running, and the Chang "brand" became associated with Taoist authority, leadership, and ritual mastery, many people with that name recognized quite the incentive to discover (or claim) their descent from the Taoist Chang family. When the existing Cheng-i lineage traces their history of Celestial Masters, all of them are named Chang, because they supposedly descended from Chang Tao-ling. And when there have been disputes over who rightly held the title of Celestial Master, you can bet that all the claimants were named Chang.

Descent from Chang Tao-ling is important not only for establishing the right to claim the title of Celestial Master, but also for claiming Taoist authority more generally. For instance, a colorful modern *t'ai-chi* and *ch'i-kung* teacher, Grandmaster Yuanming Zhang (which would be spelled Yuan-ming Chang in the system this book uses), makes a point on his website and promotional literature to identify himself as heir to 17 generations of teachers, all descended from Chang San-feng (the legendary founder of *t'ai-chi*), Chang Tao-ling, Chang Liang, and even Lao Tzu. For transmissions of Taoism, the Chinese have always put great stock in the line of teachers and ancestral descent, and the Chang family tree counts for a lot.

The Next Wave of Taoist Revelations

Taoism as an organized movement began with Chang Tao-ling and the Way of the Celestial Masters, but the tradition evolved in anything but a straight line after that. After the dissolution of the Five Pecks community, remnants of the movement scattered to different parts of China, continuing some of their beliefs and practices, discarding others, and merging with the various local traditions they encountered. Some of those other religious strands had their own independent literature and traditions, sometimes with legitimate connections to earlier Taoism, and the ways they all combined, fragmented, took on still new influences, combined and fragmented again, makes for some pretty complicated history. If you're hoping to get a good Taoism timeline, you may have to settle for something more resembling a family tree, or a combining of multiple family trees, where pieces branch out, twine together, die out, reemerge generations later, and then continue the process over and over again.

During this still-formative period of religious Taoism, from about the 3rd through 7th centuries when China was largely in disarray, several new groups formed around new batches of revealed scriptures that originated from a number of different sources. But unlike the Way of the Celestial Masters, these groups didn't particularly emphasize new age beliefs and communal living as much as methods of individual cultivation. Many of the materials and practices from these groups ultimately combined with the Celestial Masters sources to give Taoism a whole new identity and flavor. In this section, I cover three of the most important of these mostly aristocratic self-cultivation groups — the Great Purity, Highest Purity, and Numinous Treasure lineages. Here, you see how their contributions fit in to the developing picture of organized Taoism.

While K'ou Ch'ien-chih's Taoist theocracy and the Lou-kuan center were flourishing in the northern part of China, the cultivation groups described here developed in the south. They represent different strands of the Taoist "family tree."

The Great Purity

The term *Great Purity* or *Great Clarity* (T'ai-ch'ing), which had occurred earlier in the classical Taoist texts to refer to the sage's pure knowledge, began in the 3rd or 4th century to refer to a Heavenly realm that granted a series of revelations, a realm even higher than the one occupied by Lord Lao. The texts that these revelations produced, some of which no longer survive or survive only in fragments, dealt with something that didn't seem to have been a concern of the Celestial Masters or Yellow Turbans, but which would eventually become a permanent feature (though in many different forms and incarnations) of the Taoist tradition: the practice of *alchemy* (the laboratory production of special elixirs made from various metals, minerals, and herbs).

Practitioners believed that by producing these elixirs under the appropriate ritual conditions, making offerings of the substance to the appropriate deities, and then swallowing the potions, they could achieve magical powers, keep dangerous (and illness-causing) spirits at bay, summon the protection of helpful spirits, and, perhaps most important, extend their lives or even live on after death as a special kind of spirit in the Great Purity Heaven. This idea of "postmortem" immortality — the Chinese term for such an immortal spirit is *hsien* — had been knocking around China for a while, not in exclusively Taoist circles, but it quickly became part of the basic Taoist vocabulary. The Celestial Masters may have already had a sense that a ritually advanced practitioner could become such an immortal, and they certainly performed rituals for the safe passage of the dead. Later folklore would describe how when Chang Tao-ling died, he transformed into an immortal in broad daylight.

If you think about it, you can probably see how these practices and goals might dovetail with the Celestial Masters and their Orthodox Unity covenant. True, they didn't have much to do with millenarianism, utopian communities, or even ethical precepts, but like the Celestial Masters, they were concerned with physical and spiritual healing of the body, identifying texts or materials that could confer divine protection or powers, and unlocking the secrets of deities and their Heavenly dwellings. The T'ai-ch'ing revelations and alchemical practices came from a different intellectual and religious lineage, but they could potentially fit together nicely with the displaced followers of the Celestial Masters community.

The Highest Purity

The Highest Purity or Highest Clarity (Shang-ch'ing) revelations, as well as the organized community of practitioners that grew out of them, made enormously important contributions to Taoism, in terms of their texts, doctrines, practices, and understandings of deities. Scholars have written whole books about specific Shang-ch'ing texts or historical periods, and a lot of it is unusually technical and not particularly accessible. But the following bite-size chunks may provide some order to all the complexities:

✔ The Shang-ch'ing revelations began in the 4th century when a pair of brothers from a wealthy family hired a spirit-medium to make contact with the deceased wife of one of the brothers. They got more than they bargained for, however, when the channeled spirit started telling them how the various Heavens were organized, and, over a seven-year period, brought on a whole bunch of other spirits — "perfected beings" — who dictated dozens of texts' worth of material. One of the significant channeled spirits was Wei Hua-ts'un, a female libationer in the lineage of the later Celestial Masters, so already they had some connections to that branch of the tree.

✔ The textual records of the revelations floated around in different circles and in different forms for quite some time, until the late 5th century, when an alchemist named T'ao Hung-ching came across one Shang-ch'ing manuscript and then spent the next several years collecting and reassembling the sources. He pretty much singlehandedly established Shang-ch'ing as a formal Taoist lineage, stationed at Mao-shan (Mt. Mao). Because of this, Shang-ch'ing Taoism is sometimes also called Mao-shan Taoism.

✔ The revelations included elaborate descriptions of multiple Heavenly realms (with the Heaven of Highest Purity at the top), populated by different hierarchical classes of divine beings, ranging from gods who were emanations of the *Tao* (like the Celestial King of the Primordial Beginning), to various immortals and ancestors. The spirits also in some sense lived in the individual human body, which itself comprised complicated "mountains" and "palaces" that mirrored the structures of the cosmos.

✔ Shang-ch'ing students and adepts engaged in a range of practices meant to transform themselves into divine "perfected beings," like those who transmitted the revealed texts and the deities inhabiting their bodies. These mostly involved meditations and visualizations of deities and colors, that allowed you to accomplish such things as sending your soul on an excursion through the cosmos, absorbing the light emanating from the stars, or otherwise developing intimate connections to various divine agencies, which was tantamount to becoming that kind of divine being yourself.

✔ Advanced adepts could practice alchemy. This was only for the advanced followers because swallowing many of the concoctions — which scientists today would simply identify as "poison" — resulted in death, or at least what appeared to be death. If you drank the elixir without all the appropriate intellectual and meditative training or ritual precautions, you would simply die, without transforming into a postmortem immortal. Supposedly, experienced teachers could tell who was prepared for what would look to the outsider like a ritual suicide, but you couldn't tell just by looking at the body who "made it" and who didn't.

✔ Accompanying these concerns about becoming a postmortem immortal, the Shang-ch'ing texts developed elaborate theories about different realms for spirits of the dead, the deities that occupy those realms, and the otherworldly processes for movement from one realm to another. As a result, they understood the attempt to do an end run around "ordinary" death — through meditation, visualization, or alchemy — as something akin to technical or scientific manipulation of cosmic processes.

The Numinous Treasure

In the late 4th century, another aristocratic self-cultivation group, the Numinous Treasure or Spiritually Efficacious Treasure (Ling-pao), accepted the authority of the Shang-ch'ing revelations, but added to the revelations a few dozen texts of its own, supposedly revealed by deities from an even higher Heaven than the Highest Purity. It also incorporated other earlier strains of thought, like astrology and *yin-yang* cosmology.

Led initially by a man named Ko Ch'ao-fu, Ling-pao Taoism built on the Highest Purity model of imagining multiple levels of Heaven and elaborate hierarchies of corresponding deities, while throwing in some divine characters of its own, like the Heavenly Worthy of the Primordial Beginning (a slight variation of the Highest Purity deity) and the Lord of the *Tao,* a compassionate being who revealed many of the Numinous Treasure scriptures. Here are a few more changes instituted by this particular group:

- ✔ **Movement away from physical cultivation:** Numinous Treasure texts discouraged physical practices like alchemy, gymnastics, and meditation.

- ✔ **Moral emphasis:** Practitioners were obligated to follow moral precepts, like not stealing or engaging in sexual misconduct, with the understanding that they or their family members would be punished after death.

- ✔ **Use of talismans:** Revealed Numinous Treasure scriptures included five sacred talismans, identified as tied in to the creation of the universe, which not only provided protection from spirits, but also could guarantee the safety of an entire family or community. Only a ritual specialist who knew specific sounds and gestures could employ these talismans properly.

- ✔ **Communal rituals:** Perhaps integrating some of the ritual form from the Celestial Masters, Numinous Treasure practitioners organized large public rituals of purification for the community and care for the dead. Some of these would provide the basis for important rituals that Taoists still perform today.

The Emergence of a Taoist Identity

Out of this not always consistent or organized conglomeration of communal organizations, rebellions and theocracies, revealed scriptures, and self-cultivation groups — about three or four centuries' worth — practitioners eventually began to understand themselves as loosely related to one another as Taoists. They never quite established a universally recognized central authority, and they never made substantial efforts to discourage Taoists in different regions and teaching lineages from continuing their own separate practices. Still, Taoism had sufficiently "arrived" that, by the early 7th century, T'ang Dynasty rulers imagined themselves as descendants of Lao Tzu and legitimated their rule by claiming to be instituting the "Great Peace" that the Celestial Masters and other healing groups had prophesied.

When you remember that these groups had begun as breakaway or even violent military factions, there's something quite ironic about the Taoists developing such cozy ties with the government. It's kind of like when counterculture rock bands suddenly find themselves embraced by mainstream culture, like when the famous San Francisco hippy band the Grateful Dead sang the national anthem before a baseball game or posed for pictures with Vice President Al Gore.

If you have any associations of Taoism as being anti-government, that just doesn't wash with the close relations Taoist institutions often enjoyed with the ruling dynasties. Eventually, these relationships would grow strained, but more because of changing political circumstances than any rebellious aspect of Taoist ideology.

In this section, I talk about some of the features of this emergent Taoist identity. You'll see what it meant for the Chinese to talk about a "Taoist religion," find out how the up-and-coming presence of Buddhism in China forced some lasting changes in the tradition, and take a quick look at some later Taoist sects that had brief moments in the sun.

The teachings of the Tao

By the 5th century or so, as Taoists (and other Chinese) began to conceive of the diverse groups and practices as pieces snuggling under the same broad Taoist umbrella, perhaps even with fantasies that they somehow fit together into a unified whole, they started referring to this fragile unity as *Tao-chiao,* the "teachings of the Tao." This is a slightly different term from the one historians and librarians had earlier used to describe classical Taoist texts — *Tao-chia,* the "School of *Tao*" — and it developed for very different reasons. Although *Tao-chia* differentiated classical Taoist philosophers and texts from other "schools" of the Hundred Schools Period (like Confucianism and Mohism), the term *Tiao-chiao* differentiated the coalescing Taoist religion in two important ways:

> ✔ **It provided a contrast — not with Confucianism, or with some other philosophy, or even with *Tao-chia* — but with Buddhism, a missionary religion that by that time had been making inroads into China for at least a few hundred years.** The Buddhism that came to China

was also tremendously diverse; it included a range of highly technical philosophies, elaborate meditation practices, and worship of numerous divine and semi-divine beings. But they all came with an unambiguous Buddhist identity, and Taoists suddenly felt the need both to distinguish themselves from Buddhists and to demonstrate that they had the same sense of participating in one overarching tradition that the Buddhists did.

✔ **The concept of a _Tao-chiao_ served to differentiate Taoism from the various local traditions that dealt with much the same territory, with things like hereditary priests and exorcism of spirits.** This was actually very similar to the way major religious traditions today try to differentiate themselves from "cults." The Taoists portrayed themselves as having access to authentic and sophisticated religious teachings, and cast the local cults as primitive, crude, and misguided.

There are a few specific ways that the Taoists understood themselves as superior to the local cults:

- **Deities:** Taoist deities were manifestations of the _Tao_. The deities existed at the beginning of time or occupied the highest Heavens. Local, popular deities were simply the "vulgar" or "ordinary" spirits of the people, competent for dealing with small local matters but ultimately limited in their scope and powers.

- **Revelation:** Taoists recognized their own texts as revealed scriptures, which came from Lord Lao or other authentic deities. Local texts, if there even were any, could boast no such divine origin.

- **Priesthood:** Taoist priests, by virtue of their initiation into the tradition, had privileged access to the pure deities and the powers that could be tapped through appropriate practices. Local diviners and hereditary experts had the same limitations that their spirits and texts did.

- **Rituals:** The Taoists touted their own rituals, which only their priests had access to, and which drew from revealed texts and were directed toward pure deities. They especially rejected the "blood sacrifices" still carried out in many local (and even state) cults.

The new term _Tao-chiao_ contrasted the Taoist religion not with Confucianism or with the earlier Taoist philosophy, but with both the Buddhist religion and the ordinary local cults.

The influence of Buddhism

Even though the Taoists made every effort to set their traditions apart from Buddhism, they must have developed at least a twinge of "Buddha envy," because they picked up or adapted many Buddhist beliefs and actually copied a number of Buddhist forms. Part of it was simply that they appreciated a lot of what Buddhism had to offer, but it was also that Buddhism was already nearly a thousand years old and — to put it plainly — the Buddhists already knew how to do organized religion right!

The following are a number of the ways that Chinese Buddhism influenced Taoism. These range from specific changes in doctrine to institutional structures:

- ✔ **Deities:** The main Numinous Treasure Taoist deities, Heavenly Worthy of the Primordial Beginning and Lord of the Dao, sometimes sounded a lot like the Buddha, compassionate beings trying to save the world during times of moral decline.

- ✔ **Morality:** Numinous Treasure adopted many Buddhist ideas of morality, especially the idea that you could feel the effects of your evil deeds later in this life or in the next one. This seemed to echo the Buddhist idea of karma.

- ✔ **Scriptures:** Taoists began to collect their many scriptures and revealed texts and organize them into a canon, copying the three-part structure of the Buddhist Canon.

- ✔ **Monasticism:** Taoist monasteries didn't really exist before practitioners observed how important they were in spreading Buddhist teaching and providing centers for their communities. A monastery created a place where serious seekers could train under established teachers, and laypeople could have the opportunity to venerate deities and address issues in their day-to-day lives.

- ✔ **The *Tao*-nature:** Some Taoists began to combine Chuang Tzu's idea that the *Tao* is found is all things with the Buddhist idea of *Buddha-nature,* the thought that all pieces of reality, no matter how microscopic or temporary, embody the quality of "Buddha-hood."

Later Taoist lineages

As is the case with almost every major religious tradition, after the Taoist religion established itself in China, it eventually began to fragment into various sects and sub-sects, many of which survived for only a brief period of time. This kind of development is really inevitable, because as political and cultural circumstances change, traditions adapt (or not) to the times, where history sorts out the "winners" and "losers" through a kind of survival-of-the-fittest endurance test. Some branches speak to the needs of the people and appeal to their religious imagination, while others wither.

Taoists and Buddhists, oil and water

Because Taoism and Buddhism developed similar forms and approaches, they actually began to "compete" with each other for the same clientele — not only the ruling families who could favor one tradition over the other, but also the religiously syncretic and unaffiliated masses who could basically take their "religious business" wherever they wanted. Sometimes, the Taoists and Buddhists came up with pretty ingenious ways to demonstrate their superiority to each other:

✔ **Competing histories:** Frustrated by the inroads Buddhism began to make, a Celestial Masters libationer concocted a story of how Lao Tzu had gone to India to "convert the barbarians" and in effect "became" the Buddha. The Buddhists countered by devising stories that depicted Lao Tzu as a disciple or later incarnation of the Buddha.

✔ **Mutual accusations:** Sometimes, each tradition rewrote histories showing how chaotic things were when the other had

the upper hand. The Taoists claimed that the Buddhist worship of demons brought about natural disaster and political rebellions, while the Buddhists anachronistically linked ancient Chinese tyrants to Taoist rule. When 13th-century Buddhists accused some Taoists of exploiting their power by taking over Buddhist temples and mistreating their followers, they actually had a legitimate claim.

✔ **Public debates:** At different times, the Chinese government sponsored public debates or contests between Taoist and Buddhist intellectuals, demanding that each defend their respective teachings and explain why they should be viewed as superior to the other. They pretty much fought to a draw in the 6th and 7th centuries, though the Taoists took a beating in the 13th century in the eyes of Mongol rulers who, at least initially, were suspicious of the indigenous Taoist tradition and favored the "foreign" Buddhists.

Here's a brief summary of several schools that (mostly) lived for a short time, may have made some interesting contributions to the overall Taoist picture, but ultimately faded into obscurity:

✔ **The Teaching of the Great Unity (T'ai-i chiao):** This was a 12th-century sect that left behind no writings, so we can only speculate what they actually taught. It looks like one of their main concerns was to liberate the Taoist priesthood from the hereditary lines that controlled it and open the teaching more to the lay population.

✔ **The Perfect Great Way (Chen ta-dao):** This sect began in the 12th century and lasted until about the early 14th century but also left behind no writings. They seem to have performed the kinds of healing associated with the Celestial Masters but also encouraged their followers to practice austerities such as not eating meat, drinking wine, or taking medicine.

- **The Way of Pure Brightness (Ch'ing-ming tao):** With connections to a set of local traditions that dated back almost as far as the Celestial Masters, the Way of Pure Brightness was a 12th-century self-cultivation group similar to Ling-pao Taoism. They lasted for several hundred years, before being absorbed by Ch'üan-chen, a contemporary lineage.

- **The Correct Method of the Celestial Heart (T'ian-hsin):** Utilizing some material from the 10th century, this 12th-century tradition of exorcism and healing involved a ritual where the priest "transformed" himself into a deity from a complex Heavenly bureaucracy, in order to command troops of "spirit soldiers." Though the sect didn't last much more than a century or so, some forms of the tradition still exist in parts of Southeast Asia.

- **The Great Rites of Youthful Emergence (T'ung-ch'u Ta-fa):** This 12th-century sect pitched itself as a revival of Highest Purity (Shang-ch'ing) Taoism, but also took cues from the healing rituals of the Celestial Masters.

- **The Spiritual Firmament (Shen-hsiao):** This 12th- and 13th-century sect practiced exorcism and healing rituals, before they were absorbed by the Celestial Masters, though some local traditions may have their roots with this sect.

- **The Pure Tenuousness (Ch'ing-wei):** This 13th- and 14th-century movement was less a distinct sect than system for performing rituals, especially a set of mysterious "thunderclap" rituals that may have integrated forms of Tantric Buddhism.

Chapter 6

Types of Taoism in China Today

hinese Taoism continued to grow for the nearly 2,000 years since the founding of the original Celestial Masters community. Various sects and lineages came and went, newly revealed texts made their way into the Taoist Canon, and regional tastes and sensibilities continued to add many different flavors and shapes to the tradition. In other words, Taoism behaved a lot like many of the other world's religions: growing, changing, fragmenting, synthesizing. By the middle of the 20th century, even after decades of criticism from Confucian intellectuals and Chinese Christian converts, thousands of Taoist temples dotted the Chinese landscapes, and tens of thousands of priests practiced their crafts all over the country.

But the political climate of the late 20th century inflicted some major body blows to Taoism, and it's fair to say that the tradition has never fully recovered. In fact, over a period of about 30 years, Taoism nearly went extinct in China. Here are the main political causes:

✓ **The Communist Revolution:** When the People's Republic of China was founded in 1949, official documents guaranteed the freedom of religious belief. However, because the Chinese had close relations at that time with the Soviet government, they took on much of the Soviet suspicion of religious institutions as corrupt, superstitious, and power hungry. The government confiscated temples, censured religious leaders, and otherwise turned public opinion against Taoism. Some Taoists fled China for Taiwan or Hong Kong, but many just rejoined lay life as ordinary laborers.

✓ **The Anti-Rightist Movement:** In 1957, the Chinese government initiated this policy, trying to purge the political party of officials and teachings they saw as disloyal to the continuing Communist Revolution. One such person was the first leader of a newly established national Taoist association, who committed suicide as a result of the public sanction. The thousands of Taoist temples dwindled to the hundreds, and the tens of thousands of priests shrank to fewer than 5,000. By this point, Taoism was seriously on the ropes.

✔ **The Cultural Revolution:** For more than a decade beginning in 1966, Mao Tse-tung, the chairman of the Communist Party, instituted what he called the Great Proletariat Cultural Revolution, a movement officially intended to cleanse the country of forces hostile to communism, such as capitalism and traditional Chinese values. In practice, this amounted to an extended (and brutal) persecution of any constituencies the government deemed dangerous, including teachers, intellectuals, landlords, and, unfortunately for Taoism, religious institutions. During this period, the Chinese government either caused or authorized the wholesale destruction of Taoist temples, burning of Taoist books, and abuse of Taoist leaders. When Mao died in 1976, he had virtually wiped Taoism off the face of China, and some people were wondering if it was essentially gone for good.

Shortly after Mao's death, new leaders began to undo the earlier restrictions on Taoism (and other traditions), and sometimes worked aggressively to restore Taoist temples. Since then, the government has stayed closely involved in all religious activities, by regulating temples, monitoring the ordinations of priests, and holding Taoist academies accountable for their curricula. Even though many modern Chinese, especially those who lived through the Cultural Revolution and its aftermath, don't know a whole lot about Taoism now, it's in the midst of something of a comeback. And the "new" Taoism has its own characteristics.

In this chapter, I talk about the state of Taoism in China today. You find out about the specific lineages of Taoism that survived the test of time and repressions of the recent past, as well as the administrative and bureaucratic structures that provide a bridge between the lineages and the Chinese government.

The Taoism in China today is largely a *revival* of traditions that had been fairly dormant, having been under assault for nearly 30 years. Parts of contemporary Taoism are consistent with the way the tradition had been practiced before the persecutions, but other parts are new developments and still changing every day.

The One (and the Many) Gave Birth to the Two

Although Taoism historically mushroomed into a number of lineages and sub-sects, most of the Taoism in China today falls into roughly two categories: a liturgical branch and a monastic branch. If you find an ordained Taoist priest, or someone who trained with a Taoist teacher, he almost certainly is affiliated with one of two specific lineages or can trace his (sometimes loose) connection to one of those lineages.

I say "loose" connections, because sometimes "private" teachers don't really think of themselves as one or the other, but they almost always cite some teaching pedigree to justify their authority — often through a specific family, and often with a name that carries some cachet — and these lineages tend to have at least some resemblance to the two common branches today.

Of course, sometimes people just make up or exaggerate these connections, just like people in other traditions (or other areas not related to religion) sometimes make up or exaggerate entries on their résumés, but that's just an occupational hazard of the "religious territory." There have always been (and always will be) religious figures who are unscrupulous and manipulative, just as there have always been (and always will be) religious figures who are sincere and inspiring.

Most Westerners, even those who attend Taoist practice centers to learn *t'ai-chi* or *ch'i-kung,* or purchase books and DVDs on Taoist healing and sexual techniques, haven't heard of the two lineages by name. This is probably the best indicator of how poorly understood Taoism is among the Western rank and file. It would be kind of like a Buddhist or a Sikh knowing something about Christianity, perhaps even being familiar with some of the important texts and admiring the teaching, without ever having heard of Catholicism or Protestantism.

In this section, I try to fix that oversight and talk about the two existing branches of Chinese Taoism. You see where they fit in to Taoist history, what their day-to-day practices look like, and how each is distinguished from the other.

The liturgical branch: Cheng-i Tao

The Cheng-i Tao, the Way of Orthodox Unity, is the more ritualistic and liturgical branch of Taoism. You can find this Taoist lineage all over China, though it flourishes mainly in the southern parts of the country and in Taiwan. Its spiritual center, the Palace of Highest Purity, is located on Dragon Tiger Mountain (Lung-hu Shan) in the southeastern province of Kiangsi (Jiangxi), which has the added bonus of being traditionally recognized as Chang Tao-ling's ancestral home. A pair of important, older Western experts in Taoism, American scholar Michael Saso and Dutch scholar Kristofer Schipper, received initiation and ordination in this lineage well before many other scholars had ever heard of it, though Saso, who was originally ordained as a Jesuit priest, later sought (successfully) to have his Roman Catholic ordination reinstated.

In this section, I fill in the details on the Way of Orthodox Unity. I explain the connection between this lineage and the original Celestial Masters movement, the current controversies around the lineage's leadership, the respective places of priests and laypeople, the normal responsibilities that priests fulfill, and the differences between Orthodox Unity clerics and other non-Taoist hereditary priests.

The Celestial Masters legacy

You may recognize that the name Orthodox Unity comes from the covenant that Chang Tao-ling received in the revelation from Lord Lao and established in the original Celestial Masters community. And there's a good reason for that, because this lineage understands itself as directly descended from Chang Tao-ling and that movement. What's more, they trace an uninterrupted line of Celestial Masters, all in the Chang family, with the title normally passed down to sons and nephews.

In actuality, the history is probably a little more complicated, for a number of reasons:

- In the early history of the Celestial Masters, particularly during the few hundred years after the original organization dispersed, many people not named Chang claimed (or were recognized by the government as having claim to) the Celestial Master title. One important example was K'ou Ch'ien-chih, the 5th-century architect of a short-lived Taoist theocracy.

- Many scholars now suspect that the hereditary Chang family actually died out some time around the 7th century, at a time when the lineage was losing some of its imperial clout and the Celestial Master title was sometimes scooped up or applied kind of indiscriminately.

- In the 11th century, a Chang family assumed leadership of a newly regrouped Way of Orthodox Unity (which probably absorbed several other fledgling lineages), claiming descent from the original Changs and piggybacking on the Celestial Masters legacy. Although scholars aren't so sure the Changs haven't confused their family trees, the newly resurgent Way of Orthodox Unity filled in the early history based (presumably) on their own family's traditions, cataloguing two dozen generations of Celestial Master Changs.

Although the actual historical line connecting Chang Tao-ling and the original Five Pecks of Rice community to the current Orthodox Unity lineage has a lot of zigzags, breaks, and swirls, the modern sect regards itself as a 2,000-year-old tradition and has no motivation to question its own authenticity.

The current office of Celestial Master

The myth of historical unity is actually kind of ironic, because although they did have a clearly articulated lineage of 64 Celestial Masters — beginning with Chang Tao-ling, up through Chang Yuan-hsien, who died in 2008 — the lines of succession are still in dispute even today, and sometimes it gets kind of wildly and almost comically tangled.

Here's the current state of affairs, but keep in mind that even this can change if new claimants show up on the scene, the government makes new determinations, or different factions of the tradition (which is very loosely organized, if at all) struggle over power:

- All hands are pretty much in agreement that the 63rd Celestial Master, Chang En-p'u, who held court at Dragon Tiger Mountain, left China for Taiwan in 1949, the year of the Communist Revolution. Once he found his place there, he remained a public figure, establishing local Taoist associations, training priests, and extending Taoism to Malaysia and elsewhere. He died in 1969.

- Chang En-p'u's only son had already died in the 1950s, but his nephew (some sources say his grandson) Chang Yuan-hsien, a former soldier, inherited the title as the 64th Celestial Master and continued living in Taiwan, though he never assumed quite the activist public profile of his predecessor. Chang Yuan-hsien died in 2008, and this is when things got confusing, because many in the Chinese mainland never particularly recognized his right to the title in the first place.

- Shortly after Chang Yuan-hsien's death, Chang Chin-t'ao, with the approval of the Chinese government, assumed the title as the 65th Celestial Master at Dragon Tiger Mountain. At least one American, Dr. Jerry Alan Johnson, who directs the Temple of the Celestial Cloud in Monterey, California, reports that he was ordained by Chang Chin-t'ao in the Orthodox Unity lineage.

- In 2009, the leadership backtracked on Chang Chin-t'ao's assumption of the position, possibly because of disagreements between factions in China and Taiwan. They turned back the Celestial Master clock and decided that Chang Yuan-hsien, who had been the 64th Celestial Master for nearly 40 years, as Chang En-p'u's nephew was never really a true heir to the position. They declared Chang Tao-ch'en the retroactive 64th Celestial Master, and (at least according to reports in Chinese newspapers) Chang Chin-t'ao willingly abdicated and accepted a position as "Taoist Diplomat." One source claimed that Chang Tao-ch'en was a biological son of Chang En-p'u but was too young to serve when his father died, and that Chang Yuan-hsien only became 64th Celestial Master *pro tem* (for the time being). Another source indicated that a letter from Chang En-p'u to Chang Tao-ch'en's father indicated the correct line of succession.

- No sooner than everything got "settled" with Chang Tao-ch'en taking over as the retroactive 64th Celestial Master, a Taiwanese man named Chang I-chiang produced a will and Japanese documents indicating that he is the grandson of one of Chang En-p'u's brothers. He does not accept the nullification of Chang Yuan-hsien's status as 64th Celestial Master and claims that he is the rightful heir as 65th Celestial Master. Reportedly, at least one upper-level Taoist administrator has supported his claim, though Chang Tao-ch'en and his inner circle have declared the whole thing a phony.

✔ Another Taiwanese man, a schoolteacher in his 50s named Chang Mei-liang, also claims to be a son of 63rd Celestial Master Chang En-p'u. Those who reject the claim say that he was "only" an adopted son or that he fabricated his story.

✔ Finally, reports that chronicle these disputes sometimes mention that as many as four others — though not identified by name — from China have stepped forward and claimed rights to the title.

To some extent, it's not entirely clear what all the fuss and feathers are about. Although Chinese newspapers (and Western scholars from a century ago) labeled the Celestial Master the "Taoist pope," the role today is largely ceremonial, because there's really no central authority with far-reaching power in Orthodox Unity Taoism anyway. Celestial Masters do have the sanction to confer ordination, and claiming that kind of direct transmission may create added prestige for individual priests, but as the preceding list reveals, there's never any guarantee who will interpret what claims as authoritative or significant. What's more, the day-to-day practice of Orthodox Unity Taoism continues, and will continue, regardless of who holds the title of Celestial Master or perhaps whether there even is one.

Who should legitimately hold the title of Celestial Master is currently contested, just as it had been sometimes contested during different periods of Orthodox Unity history.

Orthodox Unity priests and ordinary Chinese people

One of the hardest things for Westerners to understand about modern Taoism is how it has so many "regular" features of religion — priests, deities, rituals, scriptures, moral precepts — and yet it seems to be missing one important thing: *followers*. What I mean is that the only people who are actually Orthodox Unity Taoists are the priests themselves (and their students and assistants), not the community or the people they serve. This may seem a little strange, because ministers serve Christian congregations and rabbis serve Jewish synagogues, so shouldn't you expect that Taoist priests serve Taoist communities?

Because of the Chinese habit of syncretism, the laypeople make use of the services of Taoist priests and other religious professionals, generally without self-identifying as Taoist, Buddhist, or otherwise. In fact, many of them make use of Taoist resources without even self-identifying as religious, understanding their own practices simply as Chinese or local cultural traditions. Regardless, families, individuals, or entire communities hire Taoist priests for their expertise, the skills that you can obtain only by training in the lineage, probably with your father or a respected local priest as your teacher.

Aspiring Orthodox Unity priests usually "climb the ladder" of the religious hierarchy, starting their training by taking on mundane tasks and assisting with ceremonies, and gradually gaining access to more technical aspects of the practice. The formal ordination ceremony, which may involve a literal "climbing the ladder," generally involves textual recitation and dramatic symbolism. Ordination basically initiates a person into a set of ritual and scriptural secrets and authorizes him to call on (or exorcise) specific deities, depending on his clerical rank. Because the tradition pays so much attention to hereditary lines — of both the priests and Celestial Masters themselves — you probably won't be surprised to discover that people who are ordained in this tradition generally do not abstain from sex or live in a monastery or temple; they marry, raise children, and live in the community. They may not even be affiliated with any single temple, but they may conduct specific ceremonies in them.

In the modern era, Orthodox Unity Taoism has virtually become a religion of priests. Although they may serve the broader Chinese community, and many laypeople may engage in Taoist practices or celebrate Taoist festivals, it's generally only the religious professionals who identify themselves as Taoists.

The duties and prerogatives of a Taoist priest

Because Orthodox Unity Taoism is the liturgical branch, it makes sense to look not so much at their doctrines as at their types of ritual practices. Here are the types of events where you can find Orthodox Unity priests playing an important role:

- ✔ **Rites of passage:** As is the case with most other traditions, Taoist priests can preside over events related to different stages in the life cycle, like births, weddings, and death. But because so much of earlier Taoism dealt with the search for postmortem immortality, the Orthodox Unity priests seem to have developed a special patent on funerals, which can last several days and are conducted both to ensure the safe passage of the dead and to free the living from any negative repercussions related to the deceased person's spirit.

- ✔ **Annual festivals:** These can include specifically Taoist festivals, like the Jade Emperor's birthday (which occurs during the extended New Year celebrations or the respective feast days of the "three offices" of Heaven, Earth, and Water. They can also include more generically Chinese community festivals, like the Dragon Boat Festival, where Taoist and Buddhist priests can both play a ceremonial role.

- ✔ **Healing and exorcism:** With access to secret ritual formulas and protective talismans, Orthodox Unity priests may perform healing ceremonies comparable to those that first united the original Celestial Masters movement. These may be performed on behalf of individuals with specific needs or the general health of the community.

> ✔ **Rituals of purification and offerings:** These are the major public rituals associated with Orthodox Unity priests. Performed at periodic intervals and sometimes lasting several days, these dramatic and colorful events can alternately address the care for ancestors, the welfare of the nation, or even the "renewal" of the entire cosmos (setting the cosmos back in harmony with the *Tao*).

Blackheads and redheads

Another way the Orthodox Unity sect continues its Celestial Masters legacy lies in how they understand themselves as having a secret, privileged access to the special deities in their pantheon and the stylized rituals they perform. As far as this tradition is concerned, you can't just buy a set of robes, imitate the rituals you've watched, and call yourself an Orthodox Unity Taoist. The priesthood functions, at least theoretically, as a closed and guarded order, and only those who have obtained "insider" status have the authority to make use of its sacraments.

You become an Orthodox Unity Taoist not by believing a set of doctrines or praying to a group of gods, but by being initiated and ordained in the lineage by an authorized teacher.

Because of this, Orthodox Unity Taoism carries on the Celestial Masters idea that they cover more select (and more important) territory than do the various unaffiliated local cults. An important sign of this is the distinction between "blackhead priests" and "redhead priests," or simply between "blackheads" and "redheads." To put it plainly, those who have been ordained specifically in the Taoist lineage wear distinctive head-coverings that look something like creatively creased black chefs' hats. On the other hand, local priests who have specific religious expertise, which may have been passed down in the family, wear softer hats that look like red bonnets with scarfs hanging down the back. The blackheads are the Taoists, the redheads (who are most common in Taiwan and southern China) are the local priests.

In terms of function, the blackhead Taoists can generally do anything the redheads do — mainly healing, exorcism of unhappy spirits, and various specific rituals for health and prosperity — and more. By virtue of their official Orthodox Unity authorization, they can also perform funeral services and other rituals on behalf of the dead, as well as the trademark Taoist rituals of purification and cosmic renewal. In some ways, it's almost like the difference between a clinical psychologist and a medical psychiatrist. They often do similar things, like conducting therapy sessions and evaluating people's competence for making financial decisions or standing trial, but they have different training, and the psychiatrist has some privileges that the psychologist doesn't, particularly with regard to prescribing medication.

Because of the overlap in functions between the blackheads and redheads, many people (especially those who don't take either of them particularly seriously) refer to them as "blackhead Taoists" and "redhead Taoists," which perpetuates the confusion between religious Taoism and Chinese folk religion. But the so-called redhead Taoists aren't really Taoists at all, and Taoism is certainly not just another name for any Chinese religious practices that don't look particularly Buddhist.

The monastic branch: Chüan-chen Tao

The Ch'üan-chen Tao, the Way of Complete Perfection (sometimes translated as the Way of Complete Reality), is the monastic branch of Taoism. It's also something of a relatively modern reform movement in Taoism, because it only goes back to the 12th century, when it was founded by a man named Wang Ch'ung-yang (also known as Wang Che). The Complete Perfection sect comes closer than the Orthodox Unity branch to being the official Taoism of China, because the government has been more directly involved in its revival and maintenance, though this hasn't necessarily translated into making it more popular or better known. Complete Perfection Taoism flourishes more in the northern parts of the country, and it has its center at the White Cloud Monastery, a popular tourist destination in Beijing.

Complete Perfection Taoism and Taoist history

Unlike the Way of Orthodox Unity, the Way of Complete Perfection does not try to piggyback on the legacy and history of the Celestial Masters. Although it acknowledges the historical and religious importance of Chang Tao-ling (many Complete Perfection temples have images of him), it doesn't pay much attention to the historical line of Celestial Masters (or the current Celestial Master) and doesn't have a similar line of recognized leaders in its own tradition. The closest it comes to that would be the inclusion of historical or quasi-historical figures in its extensive roster of deities, including the "Eight Immortals," the "Seven Perfected," and the "Five Patriarchs." Likewise, it downplays the Orthodox Unity focus on ritual and liturgical formulas.

So, you may be asking how it connects with Taoist history, if it doesn't follow the Celestial Masters and has added its own favorite deities? Good question. Mostly through the medieval self-cultivation groups like Shang-ch'ing and Ling-pao. Much of the work of Complete Perfection monastics concerns their own meditative training and personal cultivation.

More than anything, the development of the Complete Perfection lineage epitomizes the "Buddha-fication" of China and Taoism. Buddhism started scoring many successes in China about 1,500 years ago, and the Taoists were eager to pick up a lot of Buddhist tricks, like the way it organized its scriptures or articulated the relationship between moral conduct and your fate in the next life. But the development of monasteries and temples in Taoism may represent the biggest accommodation to Buddhism. Once the government (which by the late 13th century was run by the conquering Mongols) decided that the Buddhist way was the "right" way to do religion, many Taoist leaders — perhaps just for their own survival — started copying that model, with residential temples marking a clear break between monastics and laypeople, a celibate (and vegetarian) priesthood, and an emphasis on self-cultivation along the lines of Buddhist meditation. As a result, Taoist temples started looking a lot like Buddhist temples, and to this day many Chinese can't really tell them apart, because their layouts and day-to-day functions can be so similar.

Taoism as a monastic tradition developed only in response to monastic currents in Buddhism. The Complete Perfection lineage continues today as a monastic tradition along Buddhist lines.

Moral education in monastic training

When people get their first exposure to Complete Perfection monastic life, they're often confused by what seems to be an incongruous combination of mundane activities and advanced cultivation practices. On the one hand, Taoist monks engage in extensive manual labor — another tidbit picked up from Buddhism — which can include preparation of food, working in gardens, or maintaining the grounds. But on the other hand, they also engage in textual study, chanting scriptures, practicing musical instruments, and, of course, long hours of contemplative training.

Although Taoism at different times competed with both Buddhism and Confucianism for imperial attention and followers among the masses, the Complete Perfection moral principles reflect a deliberate attempt to blend Taoism with Confucian and Buddhist morality. That's because Complete Perfection Taoism was one of the first religious institutions in China to claim to be putting forth a synthesis of the "three teachings" of Taoism, Confucianism, and Buddhism. And so, part of the training may even include reading classical Confucian texts. What's more, the "ten precepts" that any Complete Perfection monk follows (or at least should follow) cut right across the three traditions. For instance, one precept might sound like a Buddhist directive but have a Taoist explanation attached to it. Each one includes a Chinese version of "thou shalt not," as well as encouragement for what "thou shall."

By way of summary, here are some of the ethical values that show up in these precepts:

   ✔ **Confucian ethics:** The precepts affirm Confucian virtues like sincerity, family loyalty, and allegiance to your social superior. They also have a vaguely Confucian flavor when they remind you to praise others for their good qualities, caution you not to exploit others for personal gain, and encourage you to support families so they can live with one another in harmony.

✔ **Buddhist ethics:** The precepts combine generic Buddhist admonitions against injuring or killing other living beings (including worms), with more specifically monastic Buddhist ideals like living as a vegetarian and abstaining from sex, alcohol, and other defilements. The Buddhist concerns for compassion and universal salvation translate here into general nods toward helping "the host of living beings."

✔ **Taoist ethics:** The precepts include some traditional Taoist concerns like warnings against boasting of your skills or parading your good qualities, usually linked to general ideas like "purity" and "emptiness." They also justify some of the precepts as ways to avoid harming your *ch'i.*

✔ **General Chinese ethics:** The precepts also include some general moral directives that don't seem specifically Taoist, Buddhist, or Confucian, as much as they just seem "Chinese," like warnings not to steal (or even to be greedy), or encouraging humbleness, moderation, and sympathy to people less well off.

✔ **Insider ethics:** The precepts also include reminders that Complete Perfection Taoism is a closed, or at least privileged, group, encouraging you to devote serious attention to matters of the *Tao,* to keep your virtue hidden, and to maintain a distance from those who are unwise, unclean, or defiled.

Complete Perfection Taoism is ethically syncretic (see Chapter 3). It studies Confucian classical texts, and their precepts combine Taoist ideas with Confucian and Buddhist ethics.

Complete Perfection and self-cultivation

Probably the most important (and most complicated) feature that distinguishes Complete Perfection Taoism is the emphasis on self-cultivation. Just as Buddhist monks and nuns living in temples engage in meditation as a crucial part of their daily regimen, Complete Perfection monastics participate in practices that to the casual observer look a lot like Buddhist meditation. But in addition to meditation and visualization, Complete Perfection Taoists receive training in a unique method self-cultivation, known as *internal (or inner) alchemy (nei-tan).*

The whole idea of internal alchemy is pretty fascinating, and it's basically a lot like it sounds. Internal alchemy does what traditional alchemy (which we now call "external" or "outer" alchemy) used to do, but it both internalizes and spiritualizes it. If the point of external alchemy was to produce special elixirs in the laboratory that could allow you to control spirits and become a postmortem immortal after your death, internal alchemy has the same goal but applies the process *metaphorically*.

What could it possibly mean, to do metaphorical alchemy? Here are a few basic elements of it:

✔ When alchemical instructions talk about how to prepare the laboratory, internal alchemy recasts them as metaphorical instructions for how to prepare your own body ritualistically and spiritually. Internal alchemy takes place in *yourself,* not in any actual lab.

✔ When alchemical instructions talk about the elements that are to be prepared in a crucible, internal alchemy recasts them as the physical and spiritual organs or energies of your own body. Just as internal alchemists don't actually make use of a lab, they don't really handle dangerous substances like mercury sulfide.

✔ When alchemical instructions talk about smelting metals in a stove or furnace, internal alchemy recasts that as the physical and meditative techniques that cultivate, circulate, or transform your body's energies.

In practice, internal alchemy may combine various methods of breathing, gymnastics, meditation, and even sexual hygiene. Some Taoist or quasi-Taoist practices that have gained popularity in the West — like *ch'i-kung* — may have grown from strands of internal alchemy. Depending on whom you talk to, Complete Perfection Taoists may explain the goal of these practices as becoming an immortal or more generally uniting your spirit with the *Tao*. And just as most Buddhist monks value the spiritual benefits of meditation even if it doesn't bring them to enlightenment during this lifetime, most Complete Perfection monks and nuns appreciate the physical and spiritual benefits of cultivation practices even if they're not so sure they've succeeded in earning "deliverance from the corpse" after death.

Internal alchemy is an advanced, specialized form a self-cultivation training that interprets alchemical traditions metaphorically and internalizes the theory and practices. Once the Taoists embraced internal alchemy, the practice of external alchemy began to die out.

When laypeople visit the temple

Like Orthodox Unity Taoism, Complete Perfection Taoism is more or less a tradition of religious professionals, but that doesn't mean that laypeople don't make use of the temple resources. If you visit a typical Complete Perfection temple, unless it's inactive or in some out-of-the-way place, you'll almost certainly see more ordinary men and women milling around than monks and nuns, but they're not usually there to practice inner alchemy, read Taoist texts, or partake in any rituals. Instead, they come to make offerings to Taoist deities — for very specific things like safety, health, a successful career, a happy marriage, or the general well-being of family — to participate in festival celebrations, or maybe just to watch the monks and nuns do their business.

In some ways, the Taoist temple is laid out like a rectangular Buddhist temple complex (with the obvious exception of the characteristic Buddhist pagoda), which makes it pretty lay-friendly (unless it's up on a mountaintop or something like that). The main attractions include several adjacent shrine halls, usually connected by paths or walkways, a lot like classroom buildings on a small college campus. Each hall is usually dedicated to a particular deity or cluster of related deities, with paintings or statues of those deities, sometimes on an altar. Many altars have a small container with burning incense sticks and a small prayer mat in front, where visitors kneel and make offerings to the deity. Often, the laypeople don't really know the basics, like how many times to bow, how to hold their hands, or even to which deity they should direct certain requests, but they can usually find other laypeople and sometimes monks to instruct them. And by the way, when you make a prayer, you also might want to drop some money into the collection box nearby, because that's part of the offering too. On the one hand, the act of generosity is for the deity, but concretely it's also for the support and upkeep of the temple and the monks who live in it.

Apart from the shrine halls themselves, larger temples usually have huge, ornate, metal incense cauldrons in front of the buildings or in the courtyards between them, and these are a sight to see. They can be 15 feet high or wide, sometimes with elaborate canopies over them, or with bells, dragons, or Chinese characters making up part of the design. These cauldrons don't contain just a few random incense sticks either. People often throw in whole bundles of lit sticks, perhaps 20 or more, which you can always buy from a temple shop or the numerous vendors that line the road to the front temple gate. Most of the cauldrons are burning constantly, so a smoky, aromatic scent permeates the entire complex, which certainly contributes to the exotic atmosphere.

When Complete Perfection temples started reopening after the brutal persecutions of the Cultural Revolution, most of the laypeople making offerings were elderly women. This actually makes a lot of sense when you consider that younger people had absorbed years of indoctrination dismissing religion as superstition or bourgeois indulgence, and men often couldn't spare the hours in the middle of a daytime workday. But the elders would bring their grandchildren, and the new generations started poking around to see what it was all about. Today, the lay visitors are growing increasingly younger, and it wouldn't be all that unusual to see teenagers or young men and women who go the temple to take informal lessons from the monks and nuns, or to practice things like *ch'i-kung* in the inspiring (and comparatively quiet) surroundings of a temple courtyard.

Visiting China? Why not do some temple hopping?

When you travel to China on tour, you can bet that your guides will take you to a bunch of well-established (and well-loved) tourist destinations, like the Great Wall, the Forbidden City, the Temple of Heaven, the excavations of the terra-cotta warriors, the Shaolin Temple, a few select Buddhist pagodas, and maybe even the remnants of the Silk Road. But if you ask, you may be able to score a special trip to one of the hundreds of Complete Perfection temples that have revived over the last three decades, and you may get lucky enough to observe some interesting activities, whether it's monks chanting prayers and making offerings, pilgrims gathering for a local festival, or even just lay-people praying to specific deities in the various shrine halls. Some temples have already turned into popular tourist sites, but others are off the beaten path, and it may take a while before you find the guide or cab driver who knows exactly where to go — so be persistent and don't get discouraged!

Here are a few of the places you may want to visit, depending on where your Chinese adventures take you:

- **Beijing: The White Cloud Monastery (Pai-yun Kuan):** You probably won't have to ask to go there, because it's already one of the main stops on any Beijing tourist jaunt. Because it's the central Complete Perfection temple and the home of the Chinese Taoist Association, you're sure to see some activity.

- **Xi'an: The Temple of the Eight Immortals (Pa-hsien An):** Yes, you absolutely *have* to see the terra-cotta warriors while you're in Xi'an, but make sure to put this famous temple on your itinerary, too. A former nunnery, it has beautiful frescoes, colorful shrine halls, and really cool incense cauldrons.

- **Shanghai: The White Cloud Monastery (Pai-yun Kuan):** Complete Perfection Taoism is not as big here as it is in other parts of China, and this smaller temple (which has the same name as the major one in Beijing) may accommodate both Complete Perfection monks and Orthodox Unity priests, sometimes in a bit of an uneasy truce. It's a much newer building than the "classic" temples in Xi'an and Beijing, and it houses the Shanghai Taoist Association.

- **Shenyang: The Great Purity Palace (T'ai-ch'ing Kung):** Once you get past the main tour of Beijing, Xi'an, and Shanghai, there are still a bunch of major industrial cities with lots to see, including Shenyang in the northeast. The name Great Purity derives from the 3rd-century cultivation group and was also the name of at least two other now-defunct temples dating back to at least the 8th century.

- **Fuzhou: The Temple of the Nine Emperors (Chiu-huang Kuan):** Okay, Fuzhou isn't exactly on everyone's list of main tourist destinations, but more Chinese Americans probably come from Fujian (where Fuzhou is the capital) than any other Chinese province. The Temple of the Nine Emperors is a tiny cluster of a few shrine buildings, but it's a great example of the "local" Taoist experience, and you'll get up-close access to the art and statues that you wouldn't get at a bigger, more official temple.

- **Chengdu: The Black Goat Palace (Ch'ing-yang Kung):** Chengdu is the capital of Sichuan (Szechuan), where Chang Tao-ling's movement got its start, so this temple carries with it a special (and spicy) sense of history. Make sure to check out the beautiful metal statue of the smiling black goat!

The White Cloud Monastery

The White Cloud Monastery (or the White Cloud Temple or Abbey of the White Clouds) in Beijing is the central temple of Complete Perfection Taoism, the best-known Taoist temple in the country and a perennial tourist stop. It actually predated the founding of Complete Perfection Taoism, when the government established the Celestial Perpetuity Temple as a Taoist institution, and it fell under Orthodox Unity control a few hundred years ago, but it has been the Complete Perfection institutional center for most of the last thousand years. It's the place to go if you want to see Complete Perfection Taoism in China.

The temple functions as a major training center for Taoist monks, conducts ordination ceremonies, owns an important collection of documents and paintings, and hosts various celebrations, including the birthday of Ch'iu Ch'u-chi, one of the "Seven Perfected" who first brought the temple under Complete Perfection control. The temple is constructed on a north–south axis, where you can find the four most important of the shrine halls in the temple complex (other small shrines are located along the east–west axis) once you walk through the dramatic front gate. These four shrine halls are as follows:

✔ **The Jade Emperor Pavilion (or the Pavilion of the Jade Sovereign):** The Jade Emperor is sometimes regarded as the highest deity of the general folk religion of China, but he also has a high ranking in the Taoist celestial bureaucracy.

✔ **The Hall of the Regulations of the Elders:** This shrine is dedicated to the early patriarchs of Complete Perfection Taoism. It's also the main community meeting hall and place for ordination.

✔ **The Patriarch Ch'iu Pavilion:** This shrine is dedicated to Ch'iu Ch'u-chi, the Complete Perfection temple founder.

✔ **The Three Pure Ones Pavilion (or the Pavilion of the Three Clarities):** The Three Pure Ones are sort of a Taoist "trinity," three related deities at the top of the pantheon that emerged from the Ling-pao revelations. They're the Heavenly (or Celestial) Worthy of Numinous Treasure, the Heavenly Worthy of the Primordial Beginning, and the Heavenly Worthy of the Way and Its Virtue.

Comparing the two modern branches of Taoism

Now that you've picked up a little bit about the Orthodox Unity and Complete Perfection sects of modern Taoism, it may help you keep them straight if I compare them directly with each other. Keep in mind that each lineage has a lot of variation *within* it, so generalizations about either one are just that: *generalizations,* not hard-and-fast rules. That said, here are some basic differences between them:

- Orthodox Unity Taoism is more common in Taiwan and southern parts of China. Complete Perfection Taoism is more common in the northern parts of China. Orthodox Unity's institutional center is the Palace of Great Purity in Kiangsi, while Complete Perfection's institutional center is the White Cloud Monastery in Beijing.

- Orthodox Unity Taoism traces its history directly to Chang Tao-ling and sees itself as continuing the generations of Celestial Masters, with the 64th currently presiding in China (though that's a controversial point). Complete Perfection Taoism developed much later in the 12th century and is not interested in the line of Celestial Masters, though it does acknowledge its connection to the Chang Tao-ling and his original revelations and honors its own historical patriarchs.

- Orthodox Unity Taoism is the more liturgical lineage. Orthodox Unity priests regularly preside over funerals, festivals, and rituals of offering and purification. Complete Perfection Taoism is the more monastic lineage, which makes it look more like Buddhism. Complete Perfection priests, monks, and nuns tend to train or live in monasteries, where they engage in personal self-cultivation.

- Orthodox Unity Priests are not usually affiliated with a specific temple; they perform their services for hire (sometimes at a local temple) by families or communities. Complete Perfection monks, nuns, and priests are usually teaching or training in a specific monastery, though they may leave and continue their work elsewhere at other temples or return to lay life (sometimes spreading their teachings to other lay students).

- Orthodox Unity priests usually marry and have children; they live very much as "ordinary" members of society. Complete Perfection monks, nuns, and priests generally practice celibacy; they usually live as cloistered monastics.

- Orthodox Unity priests generally do not follow the austerities you might associate with monastics. They may eat meat, drink alcohol, and cut their hair like a layperson. Complete Perfection monks, nuns, and priests practice traditional monastic austerities. They generally grow their hair long and tie it up in a bun under their hats. They're supposed to refrain from meat and alcohol.

The Chinese Taoist Association

If you do an online search for "modern Chinese Taoism" or something like that, you may eventually come across something called the Chinese Taoist

Association (CTA), though you may not easily find good descriptions of what this group actually does. Think of it as kind of a cross between a national YMCA and a regional chamber of commerce: a bureaucratic organization with no real *religious* authority, but that works to educate the public about Taoist history and practice, spearhead various Taoist initiatives, and act as a liaison between the Taoist lineages and the national government. The CTA only traces back to the late 1950s, when Taoists (once again) copied the organizational model that Chinese Buddhists (and this time, Chinese Muslims as well) had established a few years earlier. The timing probably couldn't have been much worse, because this happened just before Mao initiated the "Anti-Rightist Movement," which would eventually inflict considerable damage to Taoism. After the dust of the Cultural Revolution cleared 20 years later, the CTA opened up shop again.

Because the CTA falls under the supervision of the Chinese government (which keeps a close eye on all religious businesses and activities), it does have access to a lot of Taoist happenings all over the country, but you may want to remember that it'll usually give you the "official" line on Taoism and its history. In other words, the Chinese authorities have their own agenda, and the government-eye-view of the tradition may tailor what they present to suit that agenda. This is actually hard-wired into the CTA mission — its original movers and shakers founded the organization based on the stated principles of uniting Taoists and temples from different lineages, encouraging loyalty to the country (and to Taoism), and contributing productively to Chinese socialism. So, even when the CTA acknowledges that the government hasn't always been hospitable to Taoism, it usually makes sure to mention the country's official guarantee of religious freedom and downplay the darker sides of history. For example in a recent English-language textbook on Taoism written by a CTA official, the author refers to the CTA founder by name but neglects to mention that an Anti-Rightist purge had driven him to suicide. As a source of Taoist information, the CTA is usually accurate, if not always complete.

But even though the CTA sometimes has a tendency to sanitize Taoism, it has still been an important player in many Taoist projects and events. Here's a sampling of some of the many places where the CTA has left its mark or even been the main driving force:

- **Establishment of an ecumenical Taoist identity:** Despite its affiliation with the Complete Perfection White Cloud Monastery in Beijing, the CTA traditionally appoints board members from both the Complete Perfection and Orthodox Unity lineages, with the hope of fostering greater communication and cooperation between the two. It has also established (or coordinated) provincial and city chapters all over the country, as well as reached out to Taoist groups in places like Hong Kong, Taiwan, and Macao, to the point that large contingents from each place have participated together in major public rituals.

✔ **Preservation of Taoist resources:** The CTA has worked to repair or restore damaged temples, catalogue existing Taoist texts, and publish scholarly studies of Taoism. It founded the China Taoist College at the White Cloud Monastery.

✔ **Sponsorship of Taoist symposiums:** One of CTA's academic branches has organized symposiums on Taoism that have attracted scholars from all over the country and overseas. One of them, held at Mount Mao (the home of Shang-ch'ing Taoism), was titled "Prospects for Taoism in the 21st Century."

✔ **High-profile philanthropic activities:** The CTA is eager to influence Taoism's reputation in China as a fundamentally benevolent religious entity. When a flood of the Yangtze River in 1998 killed thousands of people, left millions homeless, and caused billions of dollars of damage to property, the CTA donated nearly three-quarters of a million dollars for disaster relief.

✔ **Restoring Taoist ordination ceremonies:** Beginning in 1989, the CTA sponsored periodic group ordination ceremonies for both Taoist lineages, conferring hundreds of Orthodox Unity registers and Complete Perfection ordination certificates.

✔ **Environmental conservation:** Apart from specific ecological activities like planting trees and "beautifying the natural environment," the CTA has issued public statements that the Taoist teachings of non-action and naturalness lead to respect for the harmonious relationships among all forms of life and discourage the exploitation of nature.

The Chinese Taoist Association doesn't really have religious authority — it doesn't "speak" for Chinese Taoism — but it *is* an active player in modern Taoist affairs and a helpful (though sometimes limited) resource for learning about Taoist history, philosophy, and practice.

Chapter 7

Go West, Old Tao, Go West

In This Chapter

▶ Searching for North American Taoism

▶ Exploring the appeal of Taoism in the West

▶ Reading Chinese texts in Western languages

▶ Finding American Taoist temples and practice groups

▶ Addressing contemporary social and political issues

*T*aoism got its start in China, but it eventually spread to many other Asian countries — Korea, Japan, Malaysia, Singapore, Vietnam, and the Philippines — and it's beginning to poke its way into the Western world as well. But for many reasons, the Taoism that's taking root in North America doesn't look much like the Taoism that originated and flourished in China, which has led some critics to say that it isn't even really Taoism.

Is that a problem? Not really. One of the most important things to keep in mind about religions is that they grow and change, and sometimes the later interpretations and developments are even more interesting than what came before. It's only a problem when we confuse American Taoism with Chinese Taoism, or look at American Taoism and assume that the rest of Taoism must somehow be that way (and vice versa).

American Taoism takes some funny and unexpected turns, and in this chapter I unpack a bunch of the more interesting twists and twirls. You see exactly why it's so hard to find Taoism in America, the reasons why Taoism continues to appeal to the Western religious imagination, the fascinating story of how Taoist texts have been translated into Western languages, who the colorful characters were who founded American Taoist temples and practice groups, and how Taoism has gradually entered modern social and political debates.

American Taoism differs considerably from Chinese Taoism, but try not to worry about whether it's "real" Taoism, any more than you should worry about whether it's really "American"! American Taoism adds to and transforms the global story of Taoism, just as it adds to and transforms the increasingly diverse story of American religion.

Taoism and the Western Imagination

You probably can't even find American Taoism without a great deal of detective work. When's the last time you saw a listing for "Temples, Taoist" in a phone book or online directory, saw a neighbor decorate his house for a Taoist holiday, or heard a classmate say she had to attend Taoist Sunday school? Believe it or not, most American Taoism is actually a product of our own imaginations!

In this section, I explain why American Taoism is such a mystery. You see how and why American Taoism is different from American Buddhism and why it hasn't taken root here the way other Asian religions have.

Deviating from the Buddhist model

Of all the Asian religions that have spread to America, Buddhism has been here the longest and is probably the easiest to find. Unlike with Taoism, you really *can* find Buddhist temples and retreat centers just by looking through the Yellow Pages, even outside cities where there are large Asian populations.

You may expect Taoism to follow a kind of "Buddhist model." After all, at first glance, Taoism and Buddhism have some similar philosophies, both developed in Asia at about the same time, and Americans visiting China can't easily tell the difference between Taoist and Buddhist temples. But for a variety of reasons, it just doesn't work that way with Taoism.

American Buddhism is tremendously diverse. There are at least a dozen different denominations, and many American Buddhists borrow resources from several or don't identify with any, but almost all American Buddhist practitioners and communities pretty much fall into two main categories:

- **Immigrant Buddhism:** The people in this category follow denominations that flourish in immigrant communities, mostly centered around neighborhood temples. These ethnic clusters — Chinese, Japanese, Tibetan, Thai, Burmese, Sri Lankan, Vietnamese — usually follow their original traditions when they first arrive and gradually become increasingly Americanized. Technically, not all people who practice immigrant Buddhism are immigrants; they may have been born in America and follow the religion of their parents or grandparents.

- **Convert Buddhism:** The people in this category aren't really "converts" in the ordinary use of the term. Instead, they're the whole cement mixer of people born and raised in America whose religious roots are Christian, Jewish, Muslim, humanist, secular, or whatever — and who, for one reason or another, seek out Buddhist philosophy and practice, often drawing freely from more than one denomination. They attend Buddhist meditation and retreat centers, join small "sitting" groups, and practice privately.

American Taoism just doesn't work like American Buddhism. Few Chinese immigrants maintain much of a "Taoist identity," and even fewer Americans have "converted" to Taoism.

Looking for Taoism in all the wrong places

So, why is Taoism such a mystery in America? How come it hasn't taken root the way Buddhism and some other Asian religions have? Here are a few of the many reasons:

- **Taoism never developed much of a missionary movement.** Taoist organizations in China simply lacked motivation to spend resources and manpower ministering to overseas Chinese or "selling" their traditions to non-Chinese. And because they sometimes had to deal with periods of overt hostility from the government, Chinese Taoists usually had their hands full with more immediate concerns.

- **The first waves of Chinese immigrants brought with them the religious customs that were most relevant for their practical needs, and these did not include a whole lot of Taoism.** The first Chinese temple in the United States was not specifically Taoist or Buddhist. Instead, it was dedicated to Ma Tzu, the goddess of the sea and protector of seafarers, which makes a lot of sense given that the first immigrants tended to come from coastal parts of China and settle in coastal parts of the United States.

- **In China, Taoism provided one wellspring of religious resources for people who would habitually weave together numerous religious options.** It would've been unusual for a layperson to identify specifically as a Taoist. So, there was never any critical mass of Chinese Taoists in America to form a self-conscious community.

- **China was virtually closed to the West during much of the middle and late parts of the 20th century.** Americans and Europeans who went off to Asia in search of "Eastern wisdom" (which was quite common in the 1960s and 1970s) found plenty of Western-educated Buddhist and Hindu teachers in other countries eager to enlighten earnest religious seekers, but most of these pilgrims couldn't even get into China, except under very controlled circumstances.

- **Much of the available information about Taoism glorified the classical texts and ignored or even bad-mouthed contemporary Taoist practices and institutions, portraying them as "degradations" of an imagined Taoist ideal.** Most Westerners who wanted to pursue Taoism assumed that they wouldn't find anything useful in China anyway.

But this doesn't mean that there is no American Taoism! It just explains why, when we do find Taoist influences in America or American things that call themselves Taoist, the connections to the Chinese roots are usually pretty tenuous.

Taoism as a Spiritual Path

Westerners almost always gravitate to Taoism because it appeals to them spiritually, because it addresses some intellectual ideas or emotional needs that they don't find satisfied in their own religious backgrounds. This characteristic is something that's completely new about American Taoism, not only because Taoism never really served that role in China, but because even the notions of "spirituality" and following a "spiritual path" are themselves relatively recent and Western ways of thinking about religion and philosophy.

The Chinese have seldom thought of Taoism as a "spiritual" tradition. But that doesn't mean that you can't think of it that way.

In this section, I talk generally about what it means to think of Taoism as a spiritual path. You discover something about the language of spirituality, how people have commonly "spiritualized" Eastern religions, and how the concept of the *Tao* transforms into a universal principle.

Deciphering the confusing language of spirituality

Spirituality. You hear this word all the time — it slides off people's tongues like ice cream off a cone on a hot day — but few people pay much attention to how it's defined or what exactly makes something "spiritual." If you listen in on enough "spiritual" conversations, you get the idea that the participants are talking about matters that are deeply private, about special feelings and experiences, and about ultimate concerns in life or the whole universe. This probably isn't very surprising. What *is* surprising, however, is that these types of concerns — which seem so fundamental and so basic — really aren't as universal or as timeless as you may assume. The emphases on individuality, privacy, and internal experience are some of the hallmarks of modern Western thinking and civilization. But they've never occupied the same place in China or many other parts of the world.

But hey, don't we all know spirituality when we see it? Don't we understand what a friend is talking about when he tells us he's "spiritual, but not religious"? Yes, but what we're really doing is separating what seems personal and authentic from what seems lifeless and programmed (formal religion). The distinction between religion and spirituality is actually a value judgment, not a formal classification.

And though, after this exercise, you may never think of religion and spirituality the same way again, just reflect for a minute on how the imagined relationship between the two is a lot like the relationship between male and female sex organs. That's right, you heard correctly! When you hear talk about religion and spirituality, try to make the connection with penises and vaginas:

- **Religion is external; spirituality is internal.** Religion is about actions, practices, ordered participation in prayer and ritual, and adherence to prescribed forms and structures. Spirituality, on the other hand, is about faith, feelings, and experience.

- **Religion is overt; spirituality is concealed.** Religion is out there for everyone to see; we can observe how it works and what it does. Spirituality, on the other hand, is camouflaged, never fully revealed through outward appearance, but sometimes we can catch a glimpse of it.

- **Religion is hard; spirituality is soft.** Religion deals with doctrine, moral directives, institutional organizations, hierarchical structures, and public demonstrations of faith. Spirituality deals with intuition, impressions, emotions, imagination, and indefinite ideas about transcendence.

- **Religions are measured by their size; spirituality is measured by its depth.** Religions institutions always want to grow bigger. Spiritually motivated people always want to deepen their faith and awareness.

- **Religions can commit acts of violence, while spirituality can be victimized by that violence.** The world has frequently been blighted by "wars of religion." But has anyone ever heard of a "war of spirituality"?

- **Ideally, religions and spirituality can join together harmoniously.** Even those who are "spiritual but not religious" often have the idea that it's not really possible to separate spirituality and religion. Religion needs a spiritual foundation, while spirituality needs concrete ways of expression. They can ultimately fit together as seamlessly as the *yin* and *yang* symbol.

When you find out about different types of Taoism in America, watch for how they come across as a set of "spiritual" teachings, how they address intuitive insights and an internal sense of wholeness and peace but don't have much to say about rules, regulations, religious institutions, and so on.

Spiritualizing Eastern religion

When you say that a Taoist text, idea, or practice speaks to you spiritually, the other side of the coin is that you're probably *spiritualizing* Taoism in some way. What does this mean? To spiritualize a religious tradition is to read or experience it in a way that pays less attention to the contexts in which it originated (language, history, cultural norms, social relationships, and so on) and instead abstracts from it what you perceive as eternal, universal lessons that can apply to your own life.

If this sounds disrespectful and makes you a little nervous, just be aware that this is an inevitable development in the life of religious traditions. For example, many Christian stories from the New Testament spiritualize Jewish stories from the Hebrew Bible (Old Testament), and modern Christian holidays spiritualize earlier Jewish holidays. Did you know that Easter spiritualizes the Jewish holiday of Passover, by generalizing the Jewish idea of God liberating the people of Israel from the bondage of slavery in Egypt, and changing it to the Christian idea of God liberating all people from the bondage of sin?

The spiritualizing of religious resources is very common when religious traditions grow and change, especially when they travel to new places and are translated into new languages.

How has Taoism been spiritualized? How can you imagine spiritualizing Taoist texts and practices for yourself? Here are a few common ways Taoism is spiritualized in the West:

- ✔ **The concept of "non-doing" in the *Tao Te Ching* refers mainly to ruling a state and conducting military affairs, with certain assumptions about social and political relationships.** But many Americans read it as advice on how to act more spontaneously or interact with nature.

- ✔ **The practice of *tai-chi ch'uan* was originally a martial art, with specific historical enemies in mind.** Today many Americans participate in it for exercise, fun, and relaxation; because it's similar to dance; or just because it gives them a general sense of "spiritual" well-being.

- ✔ **Taoist priests conduct rituals for the safe passage of the dead and guide laypeople in making offerings to deities in a large *pantheon* (an officially recognized group of gods and goddesses).** Many Americans simply don't connect with these local, culturally specific aspects of the tradition and choose to ignore them, usually focusing on the rarefied philosophy instead.

The Taoist force is with us

You may have noticed that some of the common (if somewhat vague and romantic) descriptions of the *Tao* — as cosmic principle, as boundless source of power, as metaphysical essence upon which the universe depends — begin to sound a lot like the descriptions of the "Force" in the *Star Wars* movies. When the sagely Obi-Wan Kenobi says, "It surrounds us and penetrates us. It binds the galaxy together," you wonder if he has been sneaking peeks into the *Tao Te Ching* between adventures.

And speaking of the *Tao Te Ching,* the title of that book gives reason to think that the name of one of the *Star Wars* saga's most compelling characters, Yoda, sounds suspiciously Taoist! The Chinese character *Te,* which is pronounced just like the second syllable of Yoda's name, can actually be translated as "force," and it means something like "the undifferentiated power of the Way." In Chinese, a person who is

You-Te (which is pronounced almost identically to "Yoda") is one who possesses that power or force! No wonder Yoda famously says that "you must feel the Force around you."

Ironically, *Star Wars* creator George Lucas doesn't seem to have pulled this directly from Taoism — he drew much more directly from the mythic themes of Joseph Campbell's *The Hero with a Thousand Faces.* But Campbell frequently discussed Taoism in his book, and the language there often sounded Yoda-esque: "*Tao* underlies the cosmos. *Tao* inhabits every created thing." Incidentally, Campbell was one of the 20th century's most creative (or most notorious, depending on who you ask) "spiritualizers" — he frequently drew themes from multiple religious traditions, bleached out their original contexts, and made them all sound pretty much the same.

Universalizing the Tao

No Taoist concept has been spiritualized more often, or more colorfully, than the basic principle of the *Tao.* The technical jargon of Chinese philosophy can be so complicated, and the subtleties of the original language so difficult to pick up, that it's just easier to portray the *Tao* through vague (but incredibly important-sounding) phrases like *metaphysical ground of being* or *cosmic source.* Plus, because of the universalizing tendency of American spirituality, many people think of the *Tao* as virtually interchangeable with other "cosmic" terms from other religions, like Nirguna Brahman, Buddha-nature, the Godhead, and so forth. Now, when you get deeply into all the original traditions, you do learn that these "cosmic" terms don't really all refer to the same thing, but the distinctions usually just don't matter to spiritual enthusiasts.

The most conspicuous sign of the spiritualization of the *Tao* is the way it has come into common English usage, mainly through the explosion of "*Tao* of" books, blogs, CDs, and workshops. In one of the first of these, *The Tao of Physics,* the Austrian-born Fritjof Capra never really explained what it meant for physics to have a *Tao,* but everyone pretty much understood that the book would borrow from Asian religions to communicate the "essence" of physics in a way that made it all seem to fit together into some mystical unity. And now, thanks to this "one *Tao* fits all" attitude, you can hop online or into your nearest bookstore and learn the universal, metaphysical basis of dating, peppermint tea, healing, Twitter, travel, photography, motherhood, healthy eating, coaching, sobriety, personal leadership, network security monitoring, watercolors, old-time banjo, and even Warren Buffet or Willie Nelson! Chuang Tzu said that the *Tao* was everywhere, and he wasn't kidding!

Translations of the Classical Texts

In kind of an odd twist, Taoism came to America initially through its primary texts, mainly the *Tao the Ching* and the *Chuang Tzu* — and through the enthusiastic reception that they received. If this sounds like Taoist texts took hold well before Taoism itself did, it also means that Americans without exposure to Chinese culture pretty much had to guess what Taoism looked like through those texts.

This may not seem like such a big deal, until you stop to realize that this is totally the reverse of how religious traditions usually spread from one place to another. Normally, the movement of religion coincides with the movement of actual *people* and institutions, not just the translation of books. Here are the main ways this typically occurs:

- ✔ **Immigration:** When people migrate to other places en masse, they usually bring their religions with them, like when the Puritans brought Christianity to the Americas, or when Muslims today are bringing Islam to Europe.

- ✔ **Missions:** Religious organizations often send missionaries to other countries. Sometimes this occurs when the home authority sends an intentional mission to members that have *already* immigrated, like when the Pure Land Buddhist leadership sent priests and teachers to minister to a growing Japanese population in America. But it also occurs when an established institution tries to introduce their tradition to someplace new, like when Jesuit priests brought Catholicism to Japan.

- ✔ **Religious quest:** This is sort of a reverse mission, where people interested in a particular religion that they can't find locally go out in search of it, and then bring it back with them. This is what happened for many of the first-generation American convert Buddhists, who sought teachers in Asia and then returned to America and opened meditation and retreat centers.

But Americans were reading Taoist texts and drawing spiritual inspiration from them for generations before any real American Taoist identity emerged, and many readers even fancied themselves philosophical Taoists without ever having met an actual Chinese Taoist or learned anything about actual Taoist practices. As a result, they were completely dependent on the translators, a diverse group that included not only scholars, but also monks, priests, and other religious figures who were themselves inspired by Taoist thought.

In this section, I talk about how specific translations of the *Tao Te Ching* and the *Chuang Tzu* shaped (and continue to shape) the American spiritualization of Taoism. You become acquainted with the philosophical and religious background of several of the early translators, discover how one modern fantasy and science fiction author has intentionally embedded Taoist thought into her books, and see how one adroit American writer managed to put Taoism and *Winnie the Pooh* on the same coffee table. You also hear what the China specialists have to say about all those translations out there by people who don't actually speak or read Chinese.

Inspiring Theosophists and Trappist monks

Unofficial tallies report that the *Tao Te Ching* has been translated into English and other Western languages more than any other book except the Bible. What's funny is how an astonishingly large number of the translators acted more as missionaries than scholars; they published their work not primarily to educate the West about Taoism, but to spread Taoist wisdom to the West. Funnier still, these Taoist quasi-evangelists were seldom either Chinese or Taoist, but were usually Westerners who for one reason or another took proprietary interests in Taoism and expended considerable effort to make the texts available. Funniest of all, many of these "translators" didn't speak or read Chinese, or had only limited exposure to the language. But when you really love something, who's going to let a little detail like that stop you?

Apart from the scholars, a roster of Taoist translators reads like a who's who of 20th-century religious and philosophical figures. Here are a few of the clergy, theologians, mystics, and dilettantes who took a crack at the *Tao Te Ching,* in each case bringing his own religious preferences with him and projecting those preferences onto his translation:

✔ **C. Spurgeon Medhurst:** Apart from having a great name, Medhurst was a British Baptist missionary to China, who eventually came under the sway of the Theosophical Society, an intellectual and spiritual movement that theorized a universal mystical wisdom lying at the heart of all the world's religions. His 1905 translation made the text sound like a Theosophical handbook.

- ✔ **Paul Carus:** A German immigrant to the United States, Carus was a philosopher who attended the 1893 Parliament of World Religions, and paradoxically described himself as both a theologian and an atheist. An early advocate of interfaith dialogue, especially with Buddhism, Carus saw his 1913 translation as contributing to a universal religious brotherhood of humankind.

- ✔ **Aleister Crowley:** A controversial dabbler in magic, the occult, and bizarre sexual escapades, Crowley is normally classified as an important voice in Western Esotericism, an umbrella term given to a broad range of eccentric philosophies and practices. Crowley had been to China but was no scholar. His 1918 translation treated the text as a bridge to Kabalistic mysticism.

- ✔ **Witter Bynner:** An American poet, Bynner did not know classical Chinese and took intellectual cues from American icons like Henry David Thoreau and Ralph Waldo Emerson. His 1943 poetic rendering of the text made it hard to tell the difference between a Taoist sage and a New England Transcendentalist.

- ✔ **Timothy Leary:** Yes, *that* Timothy Leary. A psychologist and former Harvard professor, Leary supervised experiments with LSD and other hallucinogenic drugs, and eventually exhorted his students to "turn on, tune in, and drop out." He didn't read Chinese either, but his 1996 *Psychedelic Prayers* included portions of the text as a companion for psychedelic journeys. Kids, don't try this at home!

- ✔ **Stephen Mitchell:** An American poet who also doesn't read Chinese, Mitchell felt that his training in Zen Buddhism and overall poetic attunement put him in a place where he could intuit Lao Tzu's mystical truths. His 1988 translation is probably the one that shows up most often in popular bookstores, a fact that drives scholarly translators of the text totally crazy.

Some memorable religious notables also played with the *Chuang Tzu,* though that text never inspired the cottage industry of self-appointed propagators as did the *Tao Te Ching.* For example, Thomas Merton, a prolific Trappist monk, in 1965 published loose versions of several of the stories not because he saw *doctrinal* similarities between Christianity and Taoism — he specifically said he wouldn't try to pull Christian rabbits out of Taoist hats — but because he simply felt a kind of monastic and contemplative kinship between them.

Regardless of what motivated all these different translators, most American readers simply haven't had the expertise to differentiate between scholarly and poetic translations, between versions done by people who know the language and versions by those who don't. As a result, Taoist texts in English could alternatively sound Theosophist, Kabbalistic, Transcendentalist, Buddhist, or druggie, which together merged into a doctrinally vague, universalist stew.

Many translators of the *Tao Te Ching* and *Chuang Tzu* projected their own religious or intellectual tastes in their translations, which most American readers had no way to know.

Always coming home to the Tao

Of all the non-specialists to work with Taoist texts, no one has done so with more ingenuity, creativity, and integrity than Ursula K. Le Guin, a widely acclaimed author of fantasy and science-fiction novels, as well as children's stories, poetry, and social and political commentary. Le Guin's engagement with Taoism began during her childhood, when her father, Alfred Kroeber, an important cultural anthropologist, read frequently from the Paul Carus translation of the *Tao Te Ching,* and requested that portions of it be read at his funeral. From then on, Le Guin studied Lao Tzu and Chuang Tzu herself and frequently embedded Taoist philosophical themes in her fiction.

The following Le Guin novels especially draw considerably from Taoism:

- ✔ *The Lathe of Heaven:* This novel, which quotes Lao Tzu and Chuang Tzu throughout, follows a battle of wills between an introverted loner who has the power to change reality retroactively through his dreams and a doctor who tries to harness that power to make the world a better place. The dreamer's unwillingness either to intervene in existence or to use his own mind to rewrite history illustrates Taoist ideas of naturism and non-doing.

- ✔ *The Dispossessed:* In this complicated novel (events are not really presented chronologically), Le Guin constructs one vision of a Taoist utopia. Instead of just touting the philosophy of non-doing, Le Guin speculates here about what kinds of social ethics may follow from that approach to life. Her later novel *The Telling,* a sequel of sorts to *The Dispossessed,* continues many of the same themes.

- ✔ *The Left Hand of Darkness:* This much esteemed novel takes place in a genderless society, or at least in a society where people have no gender except when they're reproducing. Here, Le Guin explores the problems of exploitation, dominance, and alienation from the natural, as well as the challenge of recognizing the mutual dependence of all life and the need to achieve balance and integration.

- ✔ *Always Coming Home:* Sometimes described as an "archaeology of the future," this story envisions a race of people who live in harmony without striving for knowledge or seeking progress. Like many of Lao Tzu's imagined sages or communities, these people have a basic technology but seldom use it, have relations with the people beyond their borders but have little motivation to wander beyond their own horizons.

In addition to these and many other writings that show Taoist influence, Le Guin also published her own version — she insisted it wasn't a "translation" — of the *Tao Te Ching.* To do so, she adopted a genuinely careful and painstaking method, where she compared multiple translations against the original Chinese text character by character, and she provided explanations whenever she made intentional changes for personal, spiritual, or aesthetic reasons. Le Guin's Lao Tzu comes off as kind of vaguely mystical but unambiguously egalitarian, in clear opposition to hierarchy, unchecked authority, and narrow-mindedness. She understands the idea of non-doing as something that can radically transform the way people think.

For a stimulating look at thoughtful American transformations of Taoism, read Ursula Le Guin's novels.

Pooh-poohing Taoism

Just mention to anyone that you've really enjoyed reading Taoist texts, and sooner or later you'll be finding *The Tao of Pooh* and *The Te of Piglet* wrapped up in red and green paper under your Christmas tree. Through a clever pairing of Taoist philosophy with the characters from A. A. Milne's *Winnie the Pooh* stories, Benjamin Hoff has convinced three decades of Western readers that you, too, can be a Taoist sage if you'll just mimic a bear of very little brains. Hoff's books are playful, lighthearted, and easy to read; they nibble at some basic Taoist concepts, and brush aside anyone who would tell you that the secret Taoist wisdom is anything more complicated than simply learning to *be.*

In other words, Hoff really has written the quintessential American Taoist texts. If you pick up either *The Tao of Pooh* or *The Te of Piglet,* you'll see just how thoroughly — and how cheerfully — these books typify the American spiritualization and universalization of Taoism, how they include and exclude exactly the right things for an American audience.

Consider the following characteristics of the two books:

- They acknowledge different types of Taoism, but they're most interested in the classical texts, mainly the *Tao Te Ching* and *Chuang Tzu,* occasionally including some material from the *Lieh Tzu* and the *Huai Nan Tzu.*

- They create a mood that suggests familiarity with Chinese folklore and values — Hoff did study various Asian arts and practice both *t'ai-chi ch'üan* and *ch'i-kung* — but they never really tie Taoism in to Chinese history or culture. This gives them a flavor of authenticity, but keeps them from getting bogged down in details the reader can't easily relate to.

- ✔ They don't so much present a systematic philosophy as much as they use familiar characters to illustrate a handful of basic themes from the primary texts, such as the concept of Tao, *wu-wei,* spontaneity, the mirror symbol, and the uncarved block. In fact, the Chinese character we normally translate as simplicity or the uncarved block is *p'u,* which is (of course) pronounced the same as Pooh!

- ✔ They recognize Taoist wisdom in the teachings of many Western intellectual and artistic heroes, including Henry David Thoreau, the poets William Blake and Ezra Pound, and even Thomas Edison and Claude Debussy. What would be the point in talking about Chinese wisdom if it's only for the Chinese?

- ✔ They are utterly *merciless* to scholars, whether it's the Confucians whom the classical Taoists always show up or the modern scholars who always seem to miss the essence of Taoist teaching. According to Hoff and his characters, those who don't have Taoist wisdom have no business talking about the Taoist way.

Defending the Taoist Territory

Texts like *The Tao of Pooh* may get good mileage poking fun at the stiff academics who supposedly are missing the essential Taoist point, but many scholars of Chinese religion and philosophy turn utterly apoplectic at the popularity of non-scholarly translations of the *Tao Te Ching* and the many pseudo-Taoist paperbacks about everything from cooking to country music. Some of them even tar the translators as "frauds" or "narcissistic" and write off their readers as intellectually lazy.

Maybe you can understand at least some of this on a personal level. An ambitious academic trains for years in the classical Chinese language, develops expertise in all the philosophical intricacies of the Hundred Schools texts, and publishes a scholarly translation of the *Tao Te Ching,* only to find that glossy (but inaccurate) versions by entrepreneurial poets outsell it ten to one. A Chinese religion professor once joked, with more than a tinge of outrage in his voice, that while bookstores can barely keep up with the demand for the fun Taoist stuff, the rigorous course he offered at a top-tier university on liturgical Taoism attracted only *two* students (both of whom loved it, by the way). It's clear what the American audience wants.

So, are the academics all worked up just because of professional jealousy? Well, there's actually a little more to it than that. Some of them have honest concerns that "imaginative" retellings of Lao Tzu and Chuang Tzu may not only *distort* China and the Taoist tradition — which makes their jobs as teachers a lot harder — but also somehow constitute a *violation* of Chinese Taoists. Their argument goes something like this:

- Many American readers enjoy non-scholarly versions of Taoism because those accessible texts appeal to them spiritually or aesthetically.

- Many of these readers don't know that these texts *misrepresent* the historical Taoist tradition or, worse, believe that these versions have captured some "spiritual essence" of Taoism that doesn't really require knowledge of the language or cultural context. Either way, they end up misunderstanding Taoism in some important ways.

- When readers presume that they actually know Taoism and feel free to make use of it to suit their own spiritual or aesthetic needs, they are doing to Taoism what far too many people have done historically to Native American traditions. By taking pieces of those traditions out of context for their own use, they're, in fact, showing profound disrespect for the people to whom those traditions have belonged for centuries, effectively engaging in acts of "cultural imperialism."

In short, some of these scholars see themselves as defending Taoism from misinterpretation and misuse. Of course, these problems all go away if everyone will just agree that Western transformations of Taoism are just that: Western *transformations* of Taoism. You can keep reading Hoff and Le Guin as you please, and scholars will get off your case, right? Of course, this can be a touchy subject. People don't always like to be told that their spiritualized readings aren't historically accurate, and who can blame them? But it's part of scholars' jobs to tell them, so this tension may never really go away.

Think twice before you tell your new Chinese religion teacher that you're a Taoist because you absolutely loved *The Tao of Pooh!*

American Taoist Temples and Practice Groups

Although the most significant transmission of Taoism in America has been through translations of texts, recent years have seen the emergence of American Taoist temples, practice groups, and study centers. Because most of these were founded by Chinese immigrants, you'd probably expect that they were established in Chinese neighborhoods to serve immigrant communities with traditional practices and worship. But that's not where the demand was, and so individual Chinese teachers, many of whom had left China during political turmoil, intentionally catered to American audiences and in effect established new American Taoist lineages.

The novelist and the nerds

With so many China scholars ready to pounce on Westerners who misunderstand the Taoist tradition or read it out of context, you'd think that would-be *Tao Te Ching* translators who don't know Chinese would set foot at academic conferences only at their own peril. So it's hard to imagine what must have been running through Ursula K. Le Guin's mind when she received an invitation to attend the Taoism and Ecology Conference at Harvard in 1998, and give her response to a professorial discussion of her Taoistic novels and "non-translation" version of the *Tao Te Ching*. Was this the academy's chance to get back at the popular authors who have been outselling them like crazy? Would the polite, 70-ish writer have to sit and endure accusations of "cultural strip mining" or "gimcrack integument"?

Happily, the meeting between the novelist and the nerds went delightfully well. Le Guin actually pre-empted most of the likely criticisms by acknowledging that her work with the *Tao Te Ching* took a lot of chutzpah, but also by discussing at length how aware she was of the challenges of being both "passionately sympathetic" to Taoism and "exceedingly conscious of possible transgression." In short, she admitted thinking deeply about how to take, without taking away.

Perhaps because of the persuasiveness of Le Guin's response, perhaps because of her sincerity and personal magnetism, the scholars treated her as a colleague, not as an interloper. And some of them even treated her as a celebrity, carrying in their well-worn copies of *The Left Hand of Darkness* and *The Dispossessed*, and bashfully asking her to sign them!

Most of these American lineages do trace back in some way to Chinese Taoist sources, but they often combine the quirks of their particular Chinese background with an astute sense of what works for American audiences. They tend to emphasize practices like *t'ai-chi, ch'i-kung,* meditation, and various gymnastic or health techniques (which may or may not be technically Taoist), with occasional doses of classical philosophy thrown in for good measure.

In this section, I introduce you to four important Chinese immigrants and the American lineages they founded. You discover something about their personal stories, important followers, particular teachings, and the legacies of their lineages. You also see how, in every case, the Chinese characteristics of the traditions have gradually pulled back and been replaced with goals and methods that appeal more to American sensibilities.

Most American Taoist organizations were established with a specifically American audience in mind.

Share Lew, Khigh Dhiegh, and the Taoist Sanctuary

Share K. Lew can boast the distinction of having co-founded the first publically recognized, tax-exempt Taoist institution in the United States, the Taoist Sanctuary, which was established in 1970 just outside Los Angeles, but has since relocated to San Diego. Lew's biography plays like a kind of modern Chinese mythology. He was orphaned in southeastern China, taken in by a Taoist monk, put to work at the Yellow Dragon Monastery, and eventually taught variations of internal alchemy. He fled China before the Communist Revolution and settled in San Francisco, where he learned *ch'i-kung* to complement his earlier Taoist training.

Lew founded the Taoist Sanctuary in collaboration with, of all people, an American actor named Kenneth Dickerson, who went by the name Khigh Alx Dhiegh and (thanks to his mixed North African ancestry and shaved head) managed to have a successful career portraying Chinese villains in movies and television. Lew died in July 2012 at the age of 94, just a couple months before he was scheduled to teach meditation classes at the Esalen Institute in Big Sur, California.

Although it's clear what institutions Lew founded, the legacy of his teaching can be a little harder to sort out, mainly because he didn't remain affiliated with those institutions. See if you can follow these twists and turns:

✔ The original Taoist Sanctuary in North Hollywood has since become the Taoist Institute, run by an American clinical psychologist who was trained in Reiki, *ch'i-kung,* and martial arts. The Institute offers classes in *t'ai-chi, ch'i-kung,* what it describes as "internal martial arts," and a trademarked version of Kung Fu, as well as workshops on Taoist and Buddhist philosophy.

✔ The "second" Taoist Sanctuary in San Diego is currently run by an American Taoist named Bill Helm, who studied under Dhiegh but received ordination though a lineage different from Share Lew's. The Sanctuary now emphasizes traditional Chinese healing and martial arts, offering classes in *ch'i-kung,* meditation, and herbal medicine. Its website includes information about a form of Chinese medical massage that Lew had introduced with the founding of the Sanctuary.

✔ Kenneth Dickerson eventually moved to Arizona and established a spinoff temple outside Phoenix, which over time evolved into the Sanctuary of Tao, which now sponsors "*Tao* talks," a "*Tao* blog", retreats, and courses.

✔ A few years before his death, Share K. Lew publically announced that he had never ordained any priests and that most (but not all) teachers claiming a connection to him did so without permission and were exaggerating the extent of their relationship. His widow has encouraged those interested in studying Lew's internal alchemy-based meditation (which she also taught) to contact her directly for a list of approved teachers.

The first American Taoist?

If we think of American Taoists not as people who read Taoist texts and tried to integrate the philosophy into their own lives (like Ursula K. Le Guin's father, Alfred Kroeber), but as people who actually trained in specific Taoist practices from Chinese Taoist teachers, it may be a fitting bit of irony that the very first American Taoist may have been Kenneth Dickerson (also known as Khigh Dhiegh), the man who founded the Taoist Sanctuary in 1970 with Share K. Lew.

Dickerson made a career out of pretending to be Chinese, and he almost always played the heavy. With his slanted eyebrows and wiry mustache, Dickerson affected a shady (if not exactly sinister) grin and a squeaky, menacing laugh, conjuring up the very worst (albeit pretty funny in retrospect) American stereotypes of Chinese villains. He portrayed the head "brainwasher" in the political thriller *The Manchurian Candidate,* as well as the recurring nemesis Wo Fat on the TV crime drama *Hawaii Five-0.* In the greatest coincidence of all, Dickerson guest-starred in an episode of the cult classic *Kung Fu,* taking on the ambiguous role of a magician and martial arts adept who rescues young Caine from bandits, teaches him techniques of breath control, and then unexpectedly steals a priceless scroll that Caine had been sent to deliver to a remote temple. And what were the contents of that scroll that made it so priceless? The story about Chuang Tzu dreaming he was a butterfly! The man who "stole" Chinese identity for his acting career got to portray a character who stole a Taoist text!

You may be wondering if Dickerson "stole" Taoist identity as well, when he trained with Share Lew and co-founded the Taoist Sanctuary. It's not a bad question — he may have actually made up the seasonal Taoist rituals he performed there. But if Taoist was just one of Dickerson's many faux-Chinese roles, he never broke character during most of his life. He reportedly studied Taoist texts as early as the 1930s, published commentaries on Taoist philosophy, was active in an offshoot of the Taoist Sanctuary in Arizona (where he held weekly services and sponsored tea ceremonies), and talked about his commitment to Taoism in one of his last interviews.

Given that Lao Tzu probably didn't really exist, and that Chuang Tzu could find cosmic irony in almost anything, you can't help but wonder if both of them would be genuinely amused by Dickerson's story and his role and transmitting Taoist thought to the West.

Master Moy, the Taoist Tai Chi Society, and Fung Loy Kok

Moy Shin-lin founded what has probably done more to facilitate the spread of *t'ai-chi ch'üan* than has any other institution. Like Share K. Lew, he was born in southeastern China. Before the Communists came to power, he fled to Hong Kong, where he studied at an institute affiliated with a branch of Ch'üan-chen Taoism, though it's not clear whether he was ever ordained (biographical information does frequently describe him as a monk). Eventually, he settled in Canada and began what would eventually become the International Taoist Tai Chi Society, which currently has branches in nearly 30 countries, as far afield as Costa Rica, New Zealand, Norway, and the

Slovak Republic. The Taoist Tai Chi Society of the USA has its national center in Tallahassee, Florida, and sponsors centers in close to 30 states.

Long before you could sign up for *t'ai-chi* classes at the YMCA or in synagogue basements, Master Moy was turning a once obscure martial art form into an accessible, largely unreligious physical and spiritual practice. He originally taught more faithfully to what he had learned in Hong Kong, but he soon hit upon the right formula for American audiences, downplaying the martial component of the practices and emphasizing the physical and mental health benefits. For example, he taught that practicing *t'ai-chi* would lead to spiritual equanimity and a generally cultivated and calm inner life.

In tandem with the Taoist Tai Chi Society, Moy and his followers also opened a string of temples, first in Canada and then in the United States, called the Fung Loy Kok, which is the Cantonese pronunciation of P'eng-lai Ko, or P'eng-lai Pavilion (P'eng-lai was an imaginary island paradise in Taoist folklore, thought to hold secrets of immortality). Although the temples would normally house Taoist shrines and host traditional ceremonies, these pretty much appealed to Chinese-American immigrants exclusively and seldom blended with the more broadly popular *t'ai-chi* lessons. The temples now function largely as a subsidiary of the Society, which is very much in line with the American spiritualization of Taoism. The historical and liturgical features have faded into the background, while *t'ai-chi* has morphed into a universally beneficial practice.

Master Moy died in 1998, and the Society has arguably grown more American and less traditionally Taoist over time, which has caught some criticism but kept it visible and accessible. One of Moy's senior students, Eva Wong, a prolific author and translator, founded the Denver arm of Fung Loy Kok, but she broke from the tradition after Moy's death. She now teaches *ch'i-kung* in the Denver area, and her official biography specifies her training in a fairly obscure inner alchemy lineage but makes no mention of Moy Shin-lin, Fung Loy Kok, or the Taoist Tai Chi Society.

Ni Hua-ching's integral way

Ni Hua-ching rates as a truly American Taoist success story, climbing from working as a local doctor and teacher to overseeing a dynasty that produced numerous publications, shrines, institutes, medical facilities, teaching centers, online resources, and a pair of sons who have continued the "family business." Though his biographies sometimes contradict one another, you can get still get a general sense of his story. He was born in China, fled to Taiwan, and claimed to have been trained by Taoist hermits for more than three decades. In the mid-1970s, an American student living in Taiwan who had been affiliated with the Taoist Sanctuary in Los Angeles, "discovered" Ni and brought him back to America, where other students had been clamoring to learn from authentic Chinese Taoist masters.

Ni has never really provided many specifics about his teachers or lineage, but he's often characterized the teaching as a form of internal alchemy that is "nonreligious" and "nonmonastic." OmNi (as he is known to his followers) calls his teaching the "Integral Way," which recasts Taoist philosophy as something of an American self-help movement, instructing you in how to repair and restore your own damaged spiritual energies.

When he settled in California, he began teaching private groups and opened a small Taoist shrine in his home. Since then, he and his sons have expanded into a number of different Taoist enterprises, some of which have since broken off in their own directions:

- **Schools and institutes:** Ni founded the College of Tao (now called the College of Tao & Integral Health) in Santa Monica, which produced various specialized branches, including Yo San University of Traditional Chinese Medicine in Los Angeles (named for Ni's father), and the Chi Health Institute and the InfiniChi International Institute, both housed in the original college. They offer courses in *t'ai-chi,* medical *ch'i-kung,* and traditional Chinese medicine.

- **Affiliated societies:** In 1983, Ni founded the Universal Society of the Integral Way, a nonprofit organization that established local centers for the spreading of Ni's teaching. This has since evolved into the Friends of the Integral Way, an umbrella term for various organizations and online affiliates, including the Sisters of the Integral Way, an informal network of female followers, and the Integral Way online resource, which provides blogs, shopping, information about classes, and instructions for maintaining physical, mental, spiritual, moral, and financial health.

- **Wellness centers:** Ni established a basic medical practice, which has since expanded into the Tao of Wellness, two comprehensive health centers in Santa Monica and Newport Beach. The centers are now run by his sons Daoshing Ni and Mao Shing Ni, both trained in acupuncture and Chinese herbal medicine, though they also have several other specialists on staff. The centers not only treat patients, but also publish newsletters, offer online advice for diet and exercise, sponsor public events, and sell a variety of products related to Taoism and physical health.

- **Publishing:** Ni has translated and authored multiple Taoist texts, some that he claims to be secret teachings passed down through his family, though the sources are not always clear. His two sons have also written books on longevity and fertility techniques, and they periodically go on book tours.

Mantak Chia's healing Tao

Like Ni Hua-ching, Mantak Chia mainly emphasizes Taoism as a healing and overall wellness resource. Chia is ethnically Chinese, but he was born in Thailand and initially learned Buddhist mediation as a small child. He eventually studied *t'ai-chi* from one teacher, and a variety of practices from a teacher in Hong Kong affiliated with a branch of Ch'üan-chen Taoism. In 1974, he opened the Universal Healing Tao school in Thailand. He moved to New York in 1979 to open the Taoist Esoteric Yoga Center, which has since been renamed the Universal Healing Tao Center.

The New York Center sponsors retreats, offers online courses, gives free advice on things like Taoist astrology, includes the Tao Garden Health Spa & Resort, advertises Chia's touring and speaking engagements, and, of course, sells various products online. In other words, the Universal Healing Tao Center has evolved into just that, a massive one-stop shop for any and all your Taoist medical and spiritual needs. Chia insists that the practices are not religious, which means that anyone from any religious background can do them. The development of your *ch'i* is utterly nondenominational!

One of Chia's disciples who assisted in the editing of many of his books, Michael Winn, runs Healing Tao USA, located in Asheville, North Carolina. Most of the Healing Tao resources concern variants of *ch'i-kung* and wellness practices, again marketing in the inimitably American style. One advertisement, for example, promises to teach you the secrets of Taoist masters in "simple, easy steps." All the products eventually tie in to giving you some variant of spiritual joy, physical health, and realization of your destiny.

The following are just some of the topics covered in DVD and audio resources:

- ✔ **Fusion of Five Elements,** a comprehensive method including such things as "emotional alchemy" and "fusion meditation"

- ✔ **Healing Love & the Tao of Sex,** including "Taoist bedroom love secrets" and "medical sexology"

- ✔ **Inner Sexual Alchemy,** which discusses the concepts of "spiritual orgasm" and "inner male-female copulation"

- ✔ **Sun-Moon Alchemy,** which includes lessons on how to "dissolve evil *ch'i*" and "birth your immortal child"

- ✔ **Taoist Dream Practice,** which involves "lucid dreaming," "dream commands," and "power napping"

Taoism as a Social and Political Resource

You probably haven't seen much American Taoism at the forefront of public debate on social and political issues, but that hasn't stopped a number of Americans from drawing on Taoist sources in order to justify, inspire, or advance certain social and political actions. Ironically, while American

Taoists may be less politically visible than American Christians, Jews, and Muslims, many American *non-Taoists* frequently find that Taoism lends itself easily to various social and political causes.

In this section, I talk about some of the ways Americans have pressed Taoism into the service of a few of those causes. You hear about Taoism's unlikely place in presidential politics, its influence on modern feminist thought, and its increasing presence in conversations about environmental issues.

Taoism in U.S. presidential politics

When you think about religion in American presidential politics, Taoism probably isn't the first subject that pops into your mind. Perhaps you'd think of John F. Kennedy giving a major speech where he promised he wouldn't take orders from the Vatican. Or of Barack Obama distancing himself from a minister at his church who made inflammatory statements about America. Or of Mitt Romney, the first Mormon from either major American political party nominated for national office. Or perhaps you'd recall how certain hot-button religious issues — like abortion, or the reference to God in the Pledge of Allegiance, or the question of vouchers for parochial schools — have a way of showing up in plenty of presidential campaigns. But Taoism? Come on. What Taoist has ever run for any office in the United States? What presidential candidate ever spoke about issues related to a Taoist community? What presidential candidate quoted Taoist sages in his or her speeches?

Okay, you're right, Taoism hasn't really penetrated all that much into American presidential politics, but believe it or not, on separate occasions in the late 20th century, leading figures from *both* political parties have, indeed, quoted the *Tao Te Ching,* one while running for president and the other while actually *serving* as president! This is especially interesting because these dudes represented utterly opposite sides of the political spectrum, but both quoted the text because they thought it captured their ideologies so well, no matter that one was a liberal lion and the other a pillar of conservatism.

So, who were they? Well, let's take the one who didn't win first. In 1984, Alan Cranston, the senior senator from California, vied for the Democratic presidential nomination. Cranston ran as an unashamed liberal, supporting a nuclear freeze and campaigning against American military expansion. In his stump speeches, Cranston periodically quoted one passage from the *Tao Te Ching* that he always carried with him in his wallet, the chapter where Lao Tzu states that the best kind of leader is one that the people barely know exists, which is even better than a leader the people all love. When such a leader's work is done, the people are of the mind that they accomplished all the good work themselves, because they felt free to follow their natural hopes and dreams without intrusion from the government. For Cranston, this expressed his sentiment that government should function altruistically but not interfere with people's private lives or burden them with fears of military confrontations. Cranston took this sentiment so seriously that the Lao Tzu passage appeared on the cover of the program at his memorial service.

Cranston never came close to getting the nomination, never got the chance to run against the incumbent Republican president Ronald Reagan, so perhaps America wasn't ready for Taoism in 1984. Or was it? Because the Republican who quoted Lao Tzu was Reagan himself, and he quoted him at the 1988 State of the Union address! Toward the beginning of his last major address to the joint session of Congress, Reagan cited Lao Tzu by name and said "Govern a great nation as you would cook a small fish; do not overdo it," a line the legislators greeted with laughter. Reagan related this to his desire to "get government off the backs of the people," to lower taxes, remove regulations from businesses, and refrain from intervening in people's lives with social welfare programs. He had earlier invoked the doctrine of *wu-wei* to explain his admittedly "hands-off" leadership style, how his preference was to appoint people to do their jobs and then recede into the background while the system he set up would run itself.

How could this be? How could two such different candidates claim that their philosophies were justified by the same Taoist text? I suppose you could just blame it on the vagueness of the text itself; with a "*Tao* that can't be spoken," couldn't you support just about any position through a text like that? But then again, Jews and Christians of all political persuasions routinely justify their political and social positions through Biblical quotations and theological arguments. And Muslims with different ideologies do the same with the Qur'an.

If you're in a particularly cynical mood, you could probably say that politically savvy people could justify almost *any* political position if they would interpret the scriptures creatively enough. Either way, it would've been fun to see Cranston and Reagan argue about whose interpretation was the *right* one! When was the last time you saw two politicians fighting about how best to read a Taoist text?

The Yin strikes back: Taoism and feminism

Because the *Tao Te Ching* makes such frequent use of feminine images — "mysterious female," "female of all under Heaven," "mother of Heaven and Earth" — and because most people have a vague sense that Taoism is interested in the balance of *yin* and *yang,* you may expect that Taoism and feminism would fit together like two peas in the proverbial pod. But while there have been always been women Taoists in China, they've struggled with their institutions much as their sisters in other traditions have around the world. For example, women may play significant roles at Ch'üan-chen temples, but the Cheng-i lineage has never permitted them full ordination. In short, Taoism enjoys no special status as being particularly open to (or particularly hostile to, for that matter) feminist concerns.

Still, none of this has stopped Americans (who get most of their Taoism from the classical texts, practices like *t'ai-chi,* and Chinese traditional medicine) from finding the tradition simpatico with feminism, and they frequently draw out those connections in personal blogs, newspaper articles, academic papers, and so forth. Here are a handful of themes that they seem to mention most often, even as some of them reflect broad overgeneralizations about Taoism or a lack of familiarity with Taoist history in China:

✔ **The harmony of masculine and feminine:** Taoism does not think of *yin* and *yang* as competitive, hierarchical, or contradictory. Instead, it imagines a harmonizing of two complementary but fundamentally good and equal principles.

✔ **The emphasis on freedom and authenticity:** With ideas like naturalness, spontaneity, and the uncarved block, Taoism values people who are genuine, not those who construct, perpetuate, or give in to oppressive social structures.

✔ **Respect for female power:** Taoism has historically recognized female immortals, supported the worship of female deities like the Queen Mother of the West, and portrayed women warriors (like in *Crouching Tiger, Hidden Dragon*). It also values feminine sexual power and has practices specifically designed for the cultivation of it.

Taoism and ecology

In 1993, the Chinese Taoist Association sponsored a national ecological conference, which led to a declaration of intent to spread the ecological teachings of Taoism, continue a tradition of planting trees and building forests, and publicize Taoist mountains as modes of environmental engineering. But if you Google "Taoism and ecology," you'll find that most of the American conversation about this subject doesn't really say much about the Chinese initiatives. In fact, you'll find that most of those involved in the American conversation about Taoism and ecology aren't even American Taoists.

So, who's having these conversations? Oddly enough, a sometimes uneasy combination of environmental advocates, environmental studies scholars, and religious activists from *other* religious traditions have been responsible for most of this material. Why? Because they all share the assumption that the world's major religious traditions — some more than others — contain the blueprints for coming up with authoritative, ethical, and transformative responses to the full range of contemporary ecological crises.

To put it in a somewhat simple nutshell, because the world is faced with such serious environmental challenges, and because religion is such a big part of people's lives, maybe it would be a good idea to use religion to teach people environmentally responsible ways of thinking about the world.

If this sounds like a somewhat indirect way of achieving a political end, just keep in mind the roles that churches and visible religious leaders have historically played in things like the abolition of slavery, the Civil Rights movement, and anti-war campaigns. Religion carries a great deal of authority for many people, so there is a concerted effort to apply that authority to environmental issues.

The following are all non-Taoist organizations and initiatives that have been trying to put Taoist philosophy to work:

- ✔ **Alliance of Religions and Conservation (ARC;** www.arcworld.org**):** Conceived in 1986 and eventually launched in 1995, ARC is actually a British nonreligious body that works to build alliances between religious communities and environmental organizations. In 2006, ARC facilitated a partnership between the Chinese Taoist Association and the Ecological Management Foundation, which together built an "ecological Taoist temple" in central China.

- ✔ **Religions of the World and Ecology conference series** (www.hds. harvard.edu/cswr/about/history/ecology.html)**:** Between 1996 and 1998, the Center for the Study of World Religions at Harvard University sponsored a dozen individual conferences, each focusing on the environmental contributions and possibilities of a different major tradition, and culminating with an inter-religious conference at the United Nations and the American Museum of Natural History. The Daoism and Ecology conference included contributions on Taoist attitudes toward nature and wilderness, the relationship between *feng-shui* and environmental planning, practical implications of *wu-wei,* and many other subjects.

- ✔ **The Forum on Religion and Ecology** (http://fore.research.yale. edu)**:** Building on the momentum provided by the Religions of the World and Ecology conference series, the conference organizers subsequently established this project at Yale University. Through various print and online media, the Forum tries to build bridges between religious traditions and other institutions and academic disciplines in order to find solutions to both local and global environmental challenges. Its website includes a discussion that characterizes the Taoist worldview as one of "cosmic ecology."

Part III
Examining Important Taoist Concepts

The 5th Wave By Rich Tennant

"Taoism is based on keeping the qi in balance using the complementary opposites of yin and yang. Like right now, I'm a little short on yin, so it would be really yang of you to pay for lunch."

In this part . . .

*I*t's time to start answering some of the most important questions about Taoism. What is the *Tao?* How can you follow the *Tao* by doing nothing? What are *yin* and *yang,* and how do you balance them? How is Taoism a new age movement? Are there really more than a thousand sacred Taoist texts?

This part goes into depth on some of these big Taoist ideas. So, turn off your cellphone, take a break from social media, and get ready to hit your head against Taoism at its most compelling.

Chapter 8

What Is the Tao, and What Does It Mean to Follow It?

In This Chapter

▶ Putting the *Tao* into words

▶ Thinking of the *Tao* as the source of existence

▶ Getting inside the empty *Tao*

▶ Experiencing the *Tao*

*I*n some ways, the Chinese concept of the *Tao* is incredibly easy. It simply means "the way," (or "ways," since all Chinese nouns could be singular or plural, depending on context), and there's nothing particularly mysterious about it. Much like the word *way* in English, the modern Chinese *Tao* can connote a path (a way to get someplace), a direction (which way to go), a method (which way to do something), or a principle (a way to act). Modern Chinese people probably use the term dozens of times a day, without thinking that it carries any particular mystique. The most common contemporary Chinese word for "know" is *chih-tao* ("to know the way"), and the word for "street" is *tao-lu* ("roadway").

But in religious or philosophical circles, the term turns a bit more nuanced. It still means "the Way," but it can refer to matters of ultimate truth (the way of the universe) and matters of human moral responsibility (the way you ought to act). And very often, the natural and the ethical aspects of the Way tie in closely to each other: The way the cosmos is structured and functions (the "way of Heaven") determines the way that human beings are supposed to behave. But it should come as no surprise that not everyone in China has agreed on exactly what the "Way" is or how you should follow it. In the Classical Period, the Confucian Way differed considerably from the Mohist Way, which in turn differed from the Legalist Way. And in later centuries, when the Chinese begin to speak of the "three teachings," Confucians, Taoists, and Buddhists argue among themselves about the "Way," just as

Jews, Christians, and Muslims argue with one another over doctrine. They all use the term *Tao,* and they all agree that it somehow provides the blueprint for human obligations, but in terms of what it actually means, well, for that the devil really is in the details.

But doesn't Taoism have some unique meaning for *Tao,* or some special place for it? It is, after all, the only Chinese tradition that's actually named after it, right? To tell you the truth, even that's not quite true. The Chinese sometimes refer to Confucianism as the "Way of Confucius and Mencius," and *Neo-Confucianism* is just an invented Western term for an 11th-century movement the Chinese originally called the "Learning of the Way." Still, you're right to notice that the *Tao* is especially loaded in Taoism, but attempts by scholars (and others) to pin down what it really is often produce descriptions that may sound a lot like philosophical doubletalk, even if they're technically accurate. Consider the following characterizations of the Taoist *Tao* that you can easily find online:

✔ The Metaphysical Ground of Being

✔ The Underlying Principle of Universe

✔ The Unconditioned Principle of Reality

✔ The Matrix of Spiritual Transformation

Easy as pie, right? If this somehow makes sense to you, if it helps you to think of the *Tao* as an "unconditioned principle" or related to the "ground of being," that's great, but I'm not really sure that it does much more than give you the kinds of slogans that play nicely into the more spiritualized interpretations of Taoism, which make the *Tao* more or less synonymous with some vague, generalized notion of "transcendence" or "the transcendent."

It's probably better to hold off on actually defining the *Tao,* and instead try to get some clarity on the qualities that Taoist texts regularly ascribe to the *Tao* and on the advice they give on how one actually follows it. And because the Chinese have traditionally been more interested in concrete significance and practice than abstract philosophy, this approach is probably more faithful to the overall Taoist mindset.

In this chapter, I unpack the single term that seems to lie at the heart of this complicated and diverse tradition. You get a feel for the Taoist attitudes toward language, the creative (and procreative) aspect of the *Tao,* the importance of the *Tao* as "empty," and what Taoists mean when they talk about following or harmonizing with the Way.

Understanding the Paradoxical Language of the Tao

You can probably understand why people have come up with all sorts of bizarre definitions of *Tao.* Just look at the first chapter of the *Tao Te Ching:*

As for the *Tao,* the *Tao* that can be expressed is not the constant *Tao.*

As for names, the name that can be named is not the constant name.

As for the nameless, it is the beginning of the 10,000 things.

As for the named, it is the mother of the 10,000 things.

Therefore, be constantly without desire, and by this perceive its subtlety.

Be constantly with desire, and by this perceive its manifestations.

The two emerge together.

They have different names, but are called the same.

A mystery of mysteries.

The gateway of all subtleties.

Probably the first thing that jumps out at you in the opening lines is the idea that you can't *really* talk about whatever it is they're talking about. Both Lao Tzu and Chuang Tzu mention a "wordless teaching," which is, of course, paradoxical. After all, why would they spend so much time — Lao Tzu's 5,000 characters and Chuang Tzu's 33 chapters — talking about what can't be spoken?

On the one hand, this shouldn't come as a surprise. Almost a century ago, a German scholar noticed that whenever someone says something can't be described, that person pretty much always has a "copious eloquence" in spite of his or her supposed linguistic shortcomings. On the other hand, this also carries an implicit warning that the reader should take the texts cautiously, perhaps reading them as containing allegories and figures of speech, as evocative and suggestive of moods and feelings rather than only descriptions of ideas.

In this section, I talk about some of the paradoxical language in the Classical Taoist texts and try to give some pointers for how you can best navigate it. You'll see how the authors treat the supposed limitations of language, how they nevertheless have to use language in saying something about their subject, and where that leaves you in terms of understanding the *Tao.*

Those who know do not speak, those who speak do not know

You don't have to turn too many pages of Taoist texts to find that the authors regard language as inadequate. But inadequate for what? Somehow they keep telling us not just that words miss the point or garble the real meaning, but also that people who use words must not really get it. It's certainly possible that they're putting forth a sophisticated theory of language or a general skepticism about the relationship between words and actualities, but whether or not that's the case, they mainly just come off as pretty suspicious of language. Just look at some of the words Lao Tzu uses to describe words:

- Beautiful words can be bought and sold.
- Sincere words are not beautiful, beautiful words are not sincere.
- Correct words say the opposite.
- To speak seldom is naturally so.

So, what exactly is wrong with words and language? Why does speaking about the *Tao* fall short of describing the "constant *Tao*"? Why does applying a name fall short of the "constant name"? Probably for the same reason that classical Taoists say Confucian or Mohist morality falls short of capturing the true way. Both specific language and defined morality narrow and restrict something that, in the case of the *Tao,* doesn't lend itself easily to such restrictions. By its very nature, language creates discriminations between ideas and conceptual borders between phenomena — and that's a good thing, because these discriminations and borders allow us to function concretely, to sort out the world in useful ways, to know the difference between a bicycle and a persimmon. But if the *Tao* is something that is somehow "beyond" discriminations or borders, then applying any language to the *Tao* — at least the way we normally apply language — will necessarily distort its meaning. Or, to put it more simply, if language is finite and the *Tao* is infinite, then the one can't possibly do justice to the other. That isn't actually too far from a basic principle of Kabbalistic mysticism. The early Jewish scholars described God as *ein sof* (literally, "without limit"), but they always added that even saying that God is without limit is already saying too much about God!

This guarded attitude toward language also relates to Chuang Tzu's observation that any localized, specific perspective on reality — any concrete "situatedness" — inherently creates limited perceptions, attitudes, and ways of understanding. Any use of language — the specific vocabulary, the grammatical structures, the symbolic associations, even the linguistic habits that reinforce the unquestioned distinction between "self" and "other" — localizes you in your own linguistic universe and, therefore, determines (at least partially) the intellectual structures you use to construct and even experience reality.

Lao Tzu and Chuang Tzu tell us that if we use our customary linguistic and cognitive mechanisms to try to know the *Tao*, doing so may accomplish *something,* but it won't work for knowing the "constant *Tao.*"

Classical Taoists express suspicion of language not only because the *Tao* is somehow beyond words, but because language itself is one human resource that habitually binds us to particular perspectives and narrows our range of possible experience.

Effing the ineffable

Scholars sometimes use the word *ineffable* to describe something that language can't describe satisfactorily. To some extent, lots of things and experiences are actually hard to describe. If you think about it, how would you describe the taste of coffee, or the feeling of love, or even the sensation of a sneeze? You don't really have to sit at the feet of a sage to understand some of the limitations of language.

But the implication throughout the classical Taoist texts is that there's much more at stake if you don't understand the *Tao* than if you can't find just the right language to describe a sneeze. When people don't know the Way, they have to deal with confusion, disorder, disharmony, or coming to an early demise.

Both Lao Tzu and Chuang Tzu seem to be writing, in part, to rescue a world that's being misled by the fraudulent (or incomplete) "ways" of the Confucians and Mohists. This sets up quite the catch-22. It's absolutely crucial that we know the *Tao,* but utterly impossible to describe it. Quite the no-win situation, to say the least.

Fortunately, for every time Lao Tzu or Chuang Tzu says something like "those who speak do not know," they also remind us that "those who know do not speak." This may not inspire any great confidence in the power of language, but at least it acknowledges that there really are, somewhere, "those who know," and there really is something to know. And as frustrating as it is to keep running into red flags about language, it's equally intriguing to chase down clues about the "constant *Tao,*" the "nameless," or the "mystery of mysteries," and to get some sense of what it means to enter the "gateway of all subtleties." Regardless of whether the *Tao* falls into the philosophical category of "ground of being" or "principle of reality," Lao Tzu and Chuang Tzu seem intent on reminding their readers at every turn that it holds the key to some mysterious and extraordinary type of knowledge or experience. And you could even say the classical Taoist texts represent the authors' best attempts to "eff" that mysterious and extraordinary ineffable.

The gateway of all subtleties

At times, Lao Tzu almost sounds like he's having a ball dangling the *Tao* right in front of us, dropping little hints without actually giving away the answer, the way a mystery writer builds suspense while narrating a whodunit. But Lao Tzu's whodunit is really more of a "whatisit" (or a "howdoyougetit") where he gradually reveals tantalizing details about the *Tao*. In one passage, he describes it as something "undefined and yet complete" that was "born before Heaven and Earth," something "silent and shapeless" that "stands alone and doesn't change." But even Lao Tzu acknowledges that it's somehow beyond even him, that he doesn't know its name and simply makes use of linguistic convention to identify it as "*Tao*." And when push comes to shove, if he has to call it something, the best he can dredge up is to regard it simply as "great."

Lao Tzu reinforces the sense of mystery by suggesting that it's more than just our language that's in the way — it seems that none of our other regular cognitive or sensory processes is sufficient for grasping this "silent and shapeless" *Tao* either. If you look for it, he says, you can't find it. If you listen for it, you can't hear it; if you reach out to touch it, you can't hold onto it.

Chuang Tzu also gets in on the fun, in one place characterizing the *Tao* through a series of baffling paradoxes:

✔ *Tao* has actuality and reliability but no action or form.

✔ *Tao* can be transmitted but can't be received.

✔ *Tao* can be gotten but can't be seen.

✔ *Tao* is above the Great Ultimate, but you can't call it high.

✔ *Tao* is beneath the six extremes, but you can't call it deep.

✔ *Tao* was born before Heaven and Earth, but you can't call it longstanding.

✔ *Tao* is elder to antiquity, but you can't call it old.

What's more, Lao Tzu says that the *Tao* is the good person's "treasure." And the person who knows this treasure is "subtle," "profound," "mysterious," and "wise." And what's the payoff for this knowledge? Well, if kings and their ministers could somehow maintain it, Heaven and Earth would "unite to disburse sweet dew." How's that for a beautiful image of a cosmos working generously and beneficently?

Understanding the Tao as the Source of Existence

It's a good idea to stay away from jargonistic descriptions like "ground of being" or "ontological reality," but it probably doesn't push too many esoteric buttons to say that Taoist texts frequently describe the *Tao* as a creative principle. This doesn't necessarily mean that the *Tao* created the universe the way God does in the Bible or the Qur'an, or that the *Tao* has any specific will or interest in creating things, but it does point out how the classical Taoist authors often associate the *Tao* with creation and with the idea of creativity itself. The *Tao* is not only the way of existence; it's somehow also the source of that existence. Without the *Tao,* there would be no cosmos.

In this section, I talk about some of the textual references to the *Tao* as the source of existence and explain some of the implications of that idea. You'll see how Lao Tzu often compares the *Tao* to a "mother" (and various other feminine images), what it says about a cosmos that somehow springs from the *Tao,* and whether it's appropriate to imagine the *Tao* as something of a creator god.

Here's someone who calls it more than "great"

In a 1974 episode of the classic *Kung Fu* television series titled "The Cenotaph" (a cenotaph is an empty tomb), David Carradine's character, the half-Chinese Shaolin monk Kwai Chang Caine, quotes almost an entire verse of the *Tao Te Ching,* that passage that describes the mysterious *Tao* as "silent and shapeless." Mistaken for a "Sasquatch priest" by a guilt-ridden Scotsman with an enigmatic past (and an unusually phony-sounding accent), Caine presides over the mock funeral of the man's imaginary wife, Anna White Eagle. Except that after he recites the line "for lack of a better word, I call it great," he tacks on the coda, "for lack of a better name, we call her Anna," which brings a tear to the Scotsman's eye.

It was a pretty amazing piece of dramatic entertainment (and really ahead of its time) for a TV character to be quoting the *Tao Te Ching*

in 1974. This was back when China was still a pretty bewildering entity for most Americans. The press (and politicians) still called it "Red China," and Richard Nixon had made his presidential visit there only two years earlier. In fact, the taciturn hero quotes from the *Tao Te Ching* in several episodes, usually in that pinched, fortune-cookie dialogue that became his trademark. In one scene, he sums up his entire character with a *Tao Te Ching* sound bite: "I was taught a good soldier is not violent. A fighter is not angry. A victor is not vengeful."

But in retrospect, it's even more amazing that while the action on *Kung Fu* was supposed to be taking place sometime in the 1870s, Caine quotes a translation that is obviously adapted from the 1972 version by Gia-fu Feng (a Chinese-born crony of many of the Beat writers) and his wife Jane English. Now, *that's* ahead of its time!

The mother of the 10,000 things

Lao Tzu frequently describes the *Tao* as "mother" or uses more generic feminine imagery, but he also states right off the bat that these are metaphorical, not literal, images. We can regard the "nameless" *Tao*, the ineffable *Tao*, as simply the beginning of the 10,000 things. It's only when we start talking about the named (which is not the "constant name"), that we can think of the *Tao* as the "mother of the 10,000 things." So, the *Tao* may be a *creative* principle, but it's certainly not anthropomorphic and it's technically not really a *procreative* principle, at least not in the way we conceptualize ordinary human procreation.

The classical Taoist reference to the *Tao* as "mother" is almost certainly a metaphorical way of conveying the idea of the *Tao* as a source of existence, as a principle that somehow enables the process of creation.

Despite his suggestion not to go too far overboard with the mother metaphor, Lao Tzu puts it to ample use throughout his text. Here are some of the ways he spins that particular image:

- **Symbolizing originality and antiquity:** Perhaps one-upping Chuang Tzu's paradoxical references to the *Tao* as "born before Heaven and Earth" (though "not long-lasting") and "elder to antiquity" (though "not old"), Lao Tzu alternately refers to the *Tao* as the "mother of Heaven and Earth," "mother of the world" (literally the mother of "that which is under Heaven"), and "mother of the kingdom." The *Tao* is in some way *prior* to everything, including Heaven and Earth, and in some way lying at the basis of their creation.

- **Functioning as a nurturing source:** Although the mother imagery naturally suggests a progenitor, don't overlook the role of the *Tao* as *nurturer* (something that you can tap into for nourishment or sustenance). Lao Tzu periodically talks about the positive things that occur if you "attain," "hold onto," or "possess" the mother, often in terms of avoiding harm or living an extended period.

- **Feminizing the *Tao:*** Whether or not Lao Tzu is talking specifically about the maternal images of creativity and nurture, he also employs more generically feminine metaphors when he describes the *Tao*, ascribing to it the qualities of receptivity and tranquility. In one instance, he relates the "valley spirit" to the "mysterious female," equating them both with the "roots of Heaven and Earth." In another, he casts the "female of the world" as the "meeting point of the world," which can overcome the male with stillness.

The *Tao Te Ching* may seem to put forth what was then a fairly radical view of the "feminine," but that doesn't quite justify seeing it as explicitly supporting any kind of feminist revolution. In fact, there's no evidence that the authors of the text didn't share most of the basic Hundred Schools Period assumptions about a stratified social order, a male king, and the role of sons in carrying on the family name and legacy. Some modern feminists do embrace the *Tao Te Ching* for its feminine images, but it would require a pretty free-wheeling imagination to view it as challenging traditional Confucian gender roles.

Spontaneous self-generation and self-perpetuation

The role of the *Tao* as creative principle is very different from the role of a creator God in the monotheistic traditions. By identifying the *Tao* as the source of existence, this doesn't really serve the purpose of explaining why things are as they are, or establishing humankind's place in a divine plan, or even instilling any sense of gratitude in the created beings — all of which are common associations in Jewish, Christian, and Muslim thought. The metaphor of the *Tao* as the "mother of the 10,000 things" doesn't mean that we should accept as an article of faith that the universe was created that way, or that we were forged in the *Tao*'s image, or that we should give thanks to the *Tao* for creating us. As Lao Tzu says, "The 10,000 things rely upon it, yet it does not act as their ruler."

So, what, then, does it mean to characterize the *Tao* as a creative principle? What are the implications of imagining the *Tao* as the mother of the 10,000 things? The main point seems to be that the entire cosmos, the ongoing transformations of the universe, somehow participate in a single order, by virtue of their flowing from a single source. What's more, the *Tao* — which has no action or form, can't be seen or received, and can't be called old, high, deep, or long-standing — doesn't seem to *do* anything to or impose itself on these transformations. Yes, the *Tao* lies somehow at the root of all existence, but because of that, the universe takes care of itself perfectly well, on its own accord. In that sense, it is the way of the universe for it to be in spontaneous self-generation and self-perpetuation. That is to say, the cosmos *is,* the cosmos *transforms,* and the cosmos *endures.* The *Tao* is the source of that existence, transformation, and endurance — to know the *Tao* is to be able to understand that self-generating and self-perpetuating process, and to take your place in it.

That's why Lao Tzu says that the *Tao* "accomplishes tasks and completes affairs," that it's by virtue of the *Tao* that Heaven is clear and Earth is stable. Chuang Tzu has his own language for characterizing the hundredfold transformations: "As for things alive or dead, square or round, none knows its source, yet from antiquity the 10,000 things have remained firmly in existence."

Chuang Tzu adds, "There's nothing under Heaven that doesn't float or sink, remaining unchanged throughout its lifetime," and though the *Tao* doesn't seem readily apparent, it is indeed the source of this ebb and flow.

The idea of the *Tao* as a single source of a perpetually transforming universe sets up a really interesting tension between the unity of the *Tao* and the obvious diversity of phenomena in that universe. On the one hand, everything springs from and participates in the single source. On the other, nothing remains the same from moment to moment. The Chinese see this not as any kind of contradiction, as much as a creative ambiguity. One *Tao,* but 10,000 things.

The temptation to think of the Tao as a deity

If your primary exposure to religion is one or more of the monotheistic religions of the West, you may have initially read the *Tao Te Ching* and the *Chuang Tzu* and come to the conclusion that they must mean that the *Tao* is some kind of a god or spirit. On the surface, this doesn't seem like a particularly bad interpretation of the texts. After all, the *Tao* is older than Heaven and Earth and the mother of the 10,000 things, it's the mystery of all mysteries that goes beyond language or conventional boundaries, and it's the formless "something" that stands alone and doesn't change. That describes a deity, doesn't it? Well, if you thought so, you'd have plenty of company. Some Christian theologians have asserted that *Tao* (as well as plenty of other charged terms from various traditions) is just another name for the monotheistic God, and some early translators even rendered *Tao* simply as "God."

But of course, there's almost no way that either Lao Tzu or Chuang Tzu intended the term theistically. For one, most of the Hundred Schools Period thinkers — Mohists, Confucians, Legalists, and Dialecticians — regularly employed the term (as did plenty of others engaged in non-philosophical and non-religious conversations), and none of them seemed to have a deity in mind. What's more, the various commentaries on the text never talk about the *Tao* as a deity, and there's no evidence of anyone from that period ever worshipping the *Tao* itself.

I bring up this point not to rub anyone's nose in this (or any other) misinterpretation of the texts, but to point out how the early Taoists didn't seem to share the common (though not unanimous) Western impulse to ascribe certain processes, like creation and cosmic order, to a deity. Today's advocates of "intelligent design" often justify their position by noting that certain aspects of existence are so microscopically complex, so delicate in their construction and subtle in their functioning, that they *must* have some kind of intentional, willful, and personal engineer behind them. But one of the most fascinating aspects of classical Taoist philosophy is the idea that the source of existence is utterly without intent, will, or personality, which is why the process of transformation is equally "soulless."

The Tao works in mysterious ways

Mistaking the *Tao* for the Biblical God is not just a peculiar misreading that some spiritual dabblers produce the first time they read the *Tao Te Ching* — it's a habit that actually enjoyed a long history in European theological circles. Perhaps the earliest scholar to try to identify the *Tao* with God was the early 18th-century Parisian Jean-Pierre Abel-Rémusat, who noticed that the initials of three Chinese characters used to describe the *Tao* in one chapter of the *Tao Te Ching* — *yi* (level), *hsi* (rare), and *wei* (subtle) — bore a superficial resemblance to the *Tetragrammaton* (the four Hebrew letters in the Old Testament, YHWH, that represented a liturgical name for God). Somewhat later, a German translator of the *Tao Te Ching*, Victor von Strauss, backed off a bit on the relation between the Chinese terms and YHWH, but he still basically viewed the *Tao* as a metaphor for God.

In one of the first English language translations of the *Huai Nan Tzu*, the Welsh scholar Evan Morgan translated *Tao* as "cosmic spirit." And in addressing Lao Tzu's identification of the *Tao* as "great," Morgan wrote, "This word *great* may be compared with *Lord*. In a way, it may be synonymous with Jehovah." His comparisons are quite telling. Traditional Bibles still substitute the word *Lord* for YHWH, which is actually the source of the name Jehovah.

Still, if you initially gave the *Tao* a theistic spin, you can take some solace that the concept of the *Tao*, though not exactly becoming a deity in and of itself, eventually takes on a close association with the later Taoist pantheon. Barely a century after the unofficial conclusion of the Hundred Schools Period, many saw Lord Lao — the deified Lao Tzu — as somehow synonymous with (or at least an incarnation of) the *Tao*. And when the Way of the Celestial Masters established its own roster of gods, it understood those as manifestations of the *Tao*, in contrast to the ordinary popular spirits worshipped by local cults. So, while you can't really say that the Taoist philosophical discussions of the *Tao* are describing it as a deity, you really do have to acknowledge that the modern worship and channeling of Taoist deities is really the worship and channeling of the manifest *Tao*.

Seeing Emptiness as the Wellspring of Power

One important implication of identifying the *Tao* with creativity is the idea that it's effective, that the *Tao* is the creative impetus that informs the universe and its flow. In that sense, you can also understand the *Tao* as a source of power, not necessarily political or social or even hydroelectric power, but the source of real, concrete, and effective transformations of the 10,000 things. That's why it's such a big deal to know or experience the *Tao* — to have access to the *Tao* is to be able to tap into cosmic power par excellence.

But one of the overarching paradoxes of classical Taoism — and this is not just an odd theoretical point, but something that genuinely matters for Taoist practice — is that the texts repeatedly describe the *Tao* as "empty," as a "void," or as a field of "non-being." This doesn't seem to be just another strategic way of expressing ineffability and mistrust of language. Instead, Lao Tzu and Chuang Tzu are emphatic that the quality of emptiness is itself the *Tao*'s source of creative power. Of all the Taoist paradoxes, all of the "elder to antiquity but not old" formulations, this one may seem the most boggling and counterintuitive. How could a creative principle actually be empty, and how could emptiness actually be effective? And why does any of that matter?

In this section, I answer those questions, and try to give you a sense for the Taoist idea of an empty source of creativity and power. You get acquainted with the metaphors Lao Tzu employs to demonstrate the relationship between emptiness and effectiveness, and also start to appreciate what this means for human moral conduct and for the world in which we live.

Thirty spokes unite in one hub

If you don't quite get how something empty can be a creative source, you may want to think again about the metaphor of the *Tao* as mother of the 10,000 things. In human procreation, the womb, an empty space, is quite literally the cradle of life. And if a womb weren't empty, it wouldn't be able to accomplish what it does. Just as a womb engenders, nurtures, and transforms a single life, the *Tao* engenders, nurtures, and transforms all of existence.

Lao Tzu drives this point further home by using the image of a wheel. The most visible parts of a wheel — at least of wheels from 2,500 years ago — are the spokes, the physical material that makes up the wheel itself. But what makes those materials function, what makes them actually a wheel rather than just a pile of metal or stone, is the empty center around which the spokes converge. The spokes all stem from, revolve around, and return to that center. Even in simple geometry, you can see the curved line that makes up the outside of a circle, but it's the fact that every point on that line is the same distance from the empty center that makes it a circle. And just as it's the empty hub that gives a wheel its potential to turn, and the empty center that gives a circle its definition, it's the empty *Tao* that gives the universe its potential to transform.

Lao Tzu employs several similar images throughout the *Tao Te Ching*, each one illustrating how an empty space actually provides the value or usefulness of something. Here are a few examples:

> ✔ **Clay pots and other vessels:** As with the wheel, we notice the physical materials used to make a pot or other vessel, but it's the emptiness of the pot that allows it to hold things. Think about it — people may compliment the materials in your coffee mug or the design on it, but when's

the last time you heard someone compliment the empty space that holds the coffee?

✔ **A room inside a building:** For all the decorations and furniture you move around a room (through *feng-shui*, perhaps?), it's only the empty space itself that actually makes it useful as a room. And of course, it's an absolute necessity to carve out spaces for windows and doors, all of which are, when you think about, empty spaces themselves.

✔ **A pair of bellows:** There's nothing inside of a bellows — well technically, there's air, but we don't have to go there — but the bellows always has the capability to blow wind, to stoke a fire, or perhaps to move an object. What's more, it's because the bellows is empty that it can never be depleted; using it never actually drains it in any way. That's why Lao Tzu says that although the *Tao* is empty, you can use it without ever having to fill it, and that someone who preserves the *Tao* doesn't need to be renewed.

Because emptiness represents the effective aspect of the *Tao,* Lao Tzu admonishes the reader to "attain emptiness to its utmost limit" and "maintain stillness to the utmost." Chuang Tzu has his own spin on this, pointing out that few people have the capacity to understand the "use of the useless." As always, part of Chuang Tzu's point is that we should question how we make determinations of "value" and "utility," but he's also mirroring Lao Tzu's idea that the source of effectiveness is actually something empty and "useless."

The idea of the *Tao* as the source of creativity and effectiveness is closely tied to the idea of the *Tao* as empty.

Heaven and Earth are not humane

Okay, you've probably got it down by now that the *Tao* is nameless, formless, and shapeless; that it has no discriminations or borders; and that its very emptiness is essential to its creative functions. Even when Lao Tzu and Chuang Tzu make suggestions that the *Tao* ultimately enables the health of the universe or is somehow on the side of the sagely person, they're still quick to remind you that it's dull, bland, and even insipid. What could they have possibly been thinking by arguing that the most important principle in their entire philosophy is insipid? You've got to wonder if the classical Taoist public relations experts were taking an extended lunch break.

They seem to push this to an almost comical extreme when Lao Tzu volunteers things like "Heaven and Earth are not humane." It's one thing to say that human beings "miss" the *Tao* when they pursue conventional virtues like humaneness or ritual propriety — that's just part of the whole critique of Confucian and Mohist ethics — but it's quite another to say that the ongoing transformations of Heaven and Earth (which is basically the movement of the *Tao*) are them-selves not humane. What could this possibly mean? Does this say that the universe treats us callously, without feeling, indifferent to our happiness or prosperity? Actually, some translators of the *Tao Te Ching* seem to go out of their way to give us that idea, rendering the key phrase as "Heaven and Earth are inhumane," "Heaven and Earth are ruthless," or "Heaven and Earth are heartless." So, not only is the *Tao* empty, but it doesn't give a hoot either?

Of course, Lao Tzu really does have a method to his apparent madness, and his point is not that the *Tao* is evil or cruel or any such thing, but that any expectation we may have that the *Tao* is a moral principle or that the flux and flow of the cosmos is in any way invested in the lot of humankind comes only from our own human-centeredness. It's actually an act of vanity, of human narcissism, of trying to construct a *Tao* in our own moral image — to imagine that the human virtues we recognize somehow apply to the *Tao*. But the *Tao* really is empty; it really is bland and insipid. And it engenders the 10,000 things and their continuous transformations, without will, without intention, without any sense that the created universe fulfills any moral plan or carries any moral obligations, at least not "moral" in the sense that humans ordinarily use the term. The *Tao,* Lao Tzu tells us, is impartial; it truly plays no favorites, and simply treats the 10,000 things as "straw dogs," as ceremonial objects that wear lavish adornments during the ritual but afterward get discarded with other trash out in the back alley. The straw dogs are not "sacred" during the ceremony, not "profane" in the aftermath; they're just neutral (and temporary) participants in the process at hand. Likewise, the 10,000 things enjoy no special status under Heaven; they're just impersonal participants in the transformations of existence.

Theologians and scholars sometimes talk about what they call *teleology* or a *teleological* view of the world. This is the perspective that there is a *telos* (an end purpose) of existence. If theology examines questions like who the gods are, how they created the universe, and what they expect of created beings, then teleology asks why the universe exists, what divine plan the deities had in mind when they created it. For the most part, the classical Taoist texts seem to be non-teleological — they portray the *Tao* as a natural principle, a principle that lies at the source of existence and that forms the basis of the spontaneous creation and perpetuation of the universe, but has, so to speak, no horse in the cosmic race. The *Tao* is impartial, soulless, and uninvolved.

When you hear quick summaries identifying the *Tao* as a "natural" principle or the principle of "nature," it's tempting then to ask if this nature is good or bad, if the universe that has the *Tao* as its source is ultimately a good or bad one. The classic Taoist answer is neither — the question is itself badly framed and misleading. "Good" and "bad" are moral categories, and those rubrics simply don't apply to the *Tao* or to nature. If you need to characterize nature, just think of it simply as, well, natural. Nothing more, nothing less. This is one more explanation for why harmonizing with the *Tao* requires something other than moral conduct; if the *Tao* is natural and amoral, it stands to reason that humans should be as well.

The sun and moon can only go their courses

When you watch television news coverage these days — whether about truly important matters like presidential elections or global warming, or trivial tabloid fare like the man who ate an entire lawnmower or the woman who raised hyenas as family members and taught them all Pig Latin — sooner or later one of the reporters is bound to ask the question on every viewer's mind: "How did you feel about this?" Along those lines, how do you feel — or rather, how *should* you feel — about the Taoist ideas of the *Tao* and a non-teleological universe? Or, to put it more broadly, where does it leave us, knowing that the Way of Heaven and Earth doesn't particularly care too much about us? Should we be jumping for joy at this revelation, or crying in our beer?

If you come from a religious tradition that has a decidedly teleological bent — traditional Judaism, Christianity, Islam, Hinduism, and many others fall into this category — this may seem like a pretty harsh, cold, or lonely understanding of humankind's place in the cosmos. Instead of a just, wise, compassionate, loving, salvific, and good creator god, you've got an empty source of existence and a cosmos that treats you like a straw dog. Who wouldn't feel a little unnerved by that? If our world had once seemed to us like a bountiful, nurturing greenhouse where we were secure and protected, now it seems like a borderless vacuum, void of any underlying meaning or purpose. Indeed, I wouldn't be surprised if some readers find this a pretty terrifying thought.

And yet, the classical Taoist texts convey an overall flavor — an overall *mood* — that there's no reason in the world why anyone should have the slightest problem with any supposed teleological shortcoming. The universe may not, technically, be good or meaningful or purposive, but it does still reflect, for lack of a better way to put it, a fundamental "okey-dokey-ness"! Yes, I know *okey-dokey* isn't exactly a technical term, but it does capture the Taoist idea that there's something basically healthy, intact, and otherwise just fine about a universe that operates this way — insipid *Tao*, impartial universe, amoral cosmos, and all. This is, of course, another typical Taoist paradox; absolutely everyone, every single one of the 10,000 things is an equally straw dog, an equally comfortable and appropriate co-participant in this fine mess we know as existence. In other words, the universe really is okey-dokey, but we have the challenge of following its rhythms and adapting to its movements.

Chuang Tzu especially finds this whole deal not a cause for despair, but an endless succession of opportunities to celebrate the transformations with a kind of intoxicated glee. Why else would he be having so much obvious fun reveling in every offbeat butterfly dream and chattering songbird, while impishly upsetting as many philosophical apple carts as he can? He even has the *cojones* to insist that the *Tao* is to be found in urine and excrement. "Heaven cannot but be high, Earth cannot but be broad, the sun and moon cannot but go their courses, the 10,000 things cannot but prosper. Is this not *Tao?*" When you put it this way, the universe sounds like a pretty cool place after all.

Following, Experiencing, and Harmonizing with the Way

Keeping with the traditional Chinese emphasis on concrete realities, the classical Taoist texts discuss the *Tao* not in order to indulge the authors' abstract philosophical yearnings, but to offer instructive lessons to their audience. All the speculation about the nature of the Way and how it works — this only matters to the extent that living human beings can apply what they learn to their own lives in the here and now.

For Confucian and Mohist authors, learning and following the Way was pretty much synonymous with inculcating discrete virtues and cultivating your character, but the kind of application to your own life that the classical Taoist authors have in mind — what exactly you're supposed to do with the *Tao* — isn't always totally clear. Yes, the texts talk about "following" the Way or "knowing" the Way, but they also conjugate a boatload of other interesting verbs. You can "practice" the Way, "devote yourself" to it, "hear it," "possess" it, "preserve" it, "submit" to it, "care about" it, "draw close" to it, or "use it to govern." And as you've probably come to expect by now, Lao Tzu and Chuang Tzu employ some characteristic metaphors to illustrate the uniquely Taoist understanding of what it means to *experience* the Way.

In this section, I flesh out the most significant classical Taoist metaphors about "getting" the *Tao* and explain how they fit with Taoist philosophy more generally. You get to take a closer look at the recurring theme of "returning" or "reversal," as well as the image of the sage as one who emulates the qualities of the *Tao* in his or her own life. You also have a chance to start thinking about what some people mean when they describe Taoism as a "mystical" tradition and consider some of the pluses and minuses of thinking of it that way.

The theme of returning

Once you're comfortable with the idea of the *Tao* as the source or principle of creation, it's probably not such a huge leap to consider the value of getting back to that original source. But this isn't just the intellectual process of doing an end run around all the "false *Taos*," all the mistaken ways you've been taught. This really involves somehow tapping directly into that primary source, experiencing the *Tao* in its fullest, most foundational power. And why shouldn't you want to do that? The *Tao* is the creative principle at the root of all existence, the cosmic impetus informing the transformations of things, the wellspring of power par excellence. To return to that source is in some way to harness that creative power.

It's really important to keep in mind that the image of returning to the Tao isn't just an accidental or strategic one, or just another enigmatic turn of phrase; Lao Tzu really does reiterate that the movement toward the Tao is a type of backward movement toward the source. In fact, Lao Tzu even says that "the movement of the Tao" is itself "reversal," and he illustrates vividly the multifold transformations as a process of returning:

> The 10,000 things arise side by side,
>
> And by this, I observe their return.
>
> Heaven's things proliferate,
>
> Yet each returns to its root.
>
> Returning to the root is called stillness.
>
> And this is called returning to destiny.
>
> Returning to destiny is called "the constant."
>
> To know the constant, that's simply "illumination."

Lao Tzu concludes this verse by adding that "knowing the constant" — an ambiguous phrase that seems to be identified generally with maintaining equanimity in the face of "destiny," of acceding to the transformations of the 10,000 things — triggers a provocative chain reaction of reversal:

> To know the constant — is to be fully embracing.
>
> To be fully embracing leads to impartiality.
>
> Impartiality leads to kingliness.
>
> Kingliness leads to Heaven.
>
> Heaven leads to the *Tao*.
>
> And the *Tao* leads to the enduring.

The classical Taoist version of "knowing the Way" does not involve the acquisition of moral knowledge or the development of character, as much as it involves the direct, experiential return to the *Tao,* to a more pristine state than humans ordinarily occupy.

The emulation of the Tao

To a great extent, the real significance of every quality of the *Tao* — its mystery, its ineffability, its role in creation, its emptiness, its amoral impartiality, its power — points to the implication that it could (or should) be the goal of your life to emulate the *Tao,* that you should seek in some way to embody the *Tao* by returning to it, and in that way have access to its creative potential. That's why when Lao Tzu and Chuang Tzu ascribe qualities to the Way, they often follow up those descriptions by ascribing similar qualities to the sagely person. So, just as Heaven and Earth treat the 10,000 things as straw dogs, the sage also treats the "common people" as straw dogs. Just as Heaven and Earth live and endure without concern for themselves (which would actually sound kind of strange), the sage thrives by eliminating his or her own private interest. Just as the *Tao* is empty and without purpose, the sage chooses not to strive or contend with other people or things.

One particular passage from the *Tao Te Ching* sets this idea of emulating the *Tao* in a deceptively simple series of relationships, starting with humankind and metaphorically working "up the ladder":

> Humanity takes on the pattern of (or models itself on) Earth.
>
> Earth takes on the pattern of Heaven.
>
> Heaven takes on the pattern of *Tao.*
>
> And *Tao* takes on the pattern of that which is so of its own accord.

 Try to think of this as kind of a progressive telescoping of the pattern from microcosm to macrocosm, which is actually a reversal of the creative process of the *Tao.* Whoa! Getting a little too jargonistic here? Let me try it again without quite so much metaphysical gobbledygook. If you start with the *Tao* as the source, as a sort of cosmic blueprint of or template for existence, it somehow imparts its own pattern — which is, of course, utterly empty and insipid, the simple quality of being "so of its own accord" — onto all aspects of the cosmos, beginning with Heaven. And then Heaven, as a kind of conduit of the Way, transmits that same pattern to Earth. And finally, Earth, which functions as the (metaphorically) tangible "theater" where the transformations of existence occur (and where the 10,000 things cannot but prosper), likewise transmits that pattern to humankind. So, to put it simply, in this ongoing metaphysical drama, the pattern of the original blueprint flows from the macrocosm (the *Tao*), through Heaven and Earth, all the way to the microcosm (each individual person).

When you turn this process around, it more or less summarizes the human potential for returning to the *Tao* and at least one way such a return can occur. Maybe you wouldn't have the slightest idea how to emulate the ineffable *Tao,* But humans can discern, adapt to, and ultimately take on the patterns of Earth because we're all participants in its multifold transformations. And the patterns of Earth are nothing other than the imprinted patterns of Heaven, which are nothing other than the imprinted patterns of the *Tao,* which are ultimately nothing other than the patterns of empty, spontaneous creativity. The ability to return to the Way is inherent in all of us — it's like a metaphysical birthright — because the Way lies at the root of our very existence, and the existence of all other beings as well.

The question of mysticism

All this talk of emulating the *Tao,* progressive telescoping, and metaphysical birthrights must make it obvious why many people, both scholars and dabblers in the *Tao,* are quick to portray Taoism as a "mystical tradition" or espousing a "mystical philosophy" or "mystical practice." And to tell you the truth, it's probably more accurate than not to portray at least some aspects of Taoism as mystical. But it's also unfortunate, because most sources that use the terms *mystic, mystical,* or *mysticism* don't really have a clear, critical sense of how to define the terms, a working knowledge of how mystical traditions have operated historically, or an understanding of the relationships between particular mystics and their broader traditions. They also tend not to recognize ways that the category of mysticism can actually be problematic and misleading, especially when it's applied indiscriminately to any tradition or historical figure whose ideas seem paradoxical, not entirely rational, or boasting "transcendent" insights. Unfortunately, you'll far too often hear people talking about "mysticism" as a substitute for analyzing something critically and carefully.

Because mysticism is so important a concept for understanding Taoism, but is also such a widely misunderstood concept itself, I take some time in this section to walk the conversation back to a more realistic and helpful starting place. You'll come away with a working definition of mysticism and a bit of a road map for exploring whether it's helpful to think of Taoism as a mystical tradition.

Defining mystical experience

Just hop online, and you can find literally millions of websites that talk in one way or another about mysticism. You'll also find no shortage of definitions of *mystical,* possibly without ever stumbling across any suggestions that it's actually a contested category — that is to say, there really isn't widespread agreement as to what people even mean by *mysticism,* what texts or traditions fall into that category, or even whether the description is itself accurate or historically justified. English-language authors have been writing about it for more than a century, though the vast majority of theories and general claims have been discredited over time and are now woefully out of date. Perhaps even more than with Taoism, outmoded scholarship (and nervy armchair philosophizing) on mysticism created and still perpetuates misconceptions that just won't die.

So, keeping in mind that scholars are genuinely fighting with one another about mysticism, here's a pretty broad definition that shouldn't outrage too many of the combatants. Think of mysticism simply as the pursuit of an experience (or a succession of experiences) that the experiencer believes reflects contact with a higher reality or with the true character of reality. There are two especially important aspects of this definition that are worth looking at in detail:

✔ **Experience:** First and foremost, mysticism refers to experiences that you undergo, as opposed to doctrines that you believe or prayers and rituals that you practice, which brings it closer to perception than to conception. For this reason, the phrase *mystical philosophy* is really a misnomer. It doesn't matter if an intellectual argument contains complex theosophical speculation or metaphysical maps of the universe — we should only think of a particular philosophy or text as mystical if it describes, chronicles, evokes, or facilitates a particular type of experience.

✔ **Something higher:** Whether it's a "higher reality" or the "true character of reality," the key is that the experience is (felt to be) qualitatively different from "ordinary" experience and carries with it a profound sense of authority. This can take many different forms, including apprehension of a deity or a heightened state of knowledge. Either way, no one would ever call an experience mystical if he or she didn't think it was a very big deal, like meeting God face to face, or feeling yourself dissolve into a greater unity.

The advantage of thinking of mysticism this way is that it narrows the topic in a very specific way, but it also accommodates a range of experiences from many different traditions. It doesn't foist certain stereotypically mystical ideas — like oneness, union, transcendence, or even God — into the definition, or pass judgment about which experiences are "real" or which experiences are somehow more revelatory than others.

Mysticism: Expanding universe or black hole?

Normally, reading about subjects of scholarly debate can be about as interesting as watching grass grow or paint dry. But the discussion about mysticism can be especially enlightening, as there are few other subjects where educated, experienced professionals see the same thing so differently and disagree on it so vehemently. You may be blissfully unaware that such ivory-tower battles have been raging, but right now they actually matter a lot to issues related to curricula, disciplinary divisions, and even funding.

One of the biggest issues on the table is what actually makes up "experience," and what the relationship is between experience and interpretation. Although many different theories about mysticism are currently circulating, the scholarly approaches can pretty much be divided into two distinct academic factions: the contextualists

and the contemplatives. Here are some of the basic positions of the contextualists:

✔ **No "pure" experience:** The contextualists argue that all experience — even mystical experience — is at least partially constructed by the person's previous ideas, training, expectations, language, and so on. This is a departure from the idea that experience is simply something that "happens to you," and it implies that much of what you might mistake as interpretation is actually part of the experience itself.

✔ **The primacy of context:** Because contextualists link experience with prior notions the person brings to it, they argue that you can only really understand mystical experience by analyzing the relationship between the experience and the person's context. They suggest that mystical experiences are so different from one another because the contexts that produce them are so different from one another as well.

✔ **Detached analysis:** Contextualists are basically "agnostic" about mystical experience — that is, they have no opinion as to whether all such experiences refer back to a single "ultimate reality" or whether one experience is more "true" than another. Basically, they treat mysticism just as they treat any other aspect of religious traditions, trying to analyze and understand without passing judgment.

On the other hand, the contemplatives stake out a different set of positions:

✔ **Mysticism as pure experience:** The contemplatives are interested in mysticism less as data points that illustrate aspects of particular religious traditions than for the higher truths that mystical experiences reveal. They contend that such experiences are not products of your own construction, but genuine breakthroughs to the "absolute" or "ultimate."

✔ **Transcendence of context:** Because they don't believe that mystical experiences are constructed by one's previous positions, they feel that the "essence" of the experiences lies outside of context. In fact, they argue that many mystics (including Chuang Tzu) teach methods for undoing your own context.

✔ **Contemplative education:** With the understanding that mystical experiences are both revelatory and independent of context, contemplatives are eager to teach various practices — meditation, t'ai-chi, yoga, visualization — in nonsectarian environments, in order to help cultivate students' "interior" lives. They've established programs in "contemplative education" or "contemplative studies" at several American universities.

You can probably anticipate where some of these disagreements go. Contemplatives pejoratively called the contextualists "constructivists," as if to suggest that they think people just "make up" their own experiences. On the other hand, contextualists call contemplatives "perennialists," suggesting that they're trying to see all mysticism as variations of a core experience. To the contemplatives, contextualists look like clinical, soulless social scientists; to the contextualists, contemplatives look like closet theologians. Contemplatives think contextualists are ducking the big questions; contextualists go ballistic about contemplative education programs. In some ways, following the *study* of mysticism can be more exciting than studying mysticism itself!

Try to keep in mind that there is no one "mysticism" — instead, there are many different types of mystical experiences. And try to think of mysticism as one aspect of the religious life, rather than as something separate from (or superior to) "ordinary" religion.

Relating mysticism to Taoism

A number of people who represent Taoism as a mystical tradition usually tell you that the goal of Taoism is "union with the *Tao*," "becoming One with the *Tao*," or "merging with the *Tao*." And although these descriptions may not be entirely inaccurate, they can potentially create more confusion than clarity. For one, different mystical traditions may have radically different understandings of *oneness* and what they mean by things like *union* or *merging*.

Authors who aren't familiar with these types of subtleties may use an expression like "union with *Tao*" without making explicit what it means for a human being to "unite" with an ineffable principle, or explaining how it differs (if at all) from a Christian understanding of "union with God" or a New England Transcendentalist's understanding of "communion with nature." In any event, this is especially problematic for discussions about Taoism, mainly because the Taoist texts most often regarded as mystical don't particularly use that kind of language. Yes, Lao Tzu and Chuang Tzu do use expressions like "become one with spirit," "come into accord with the great thoroughfare," and "deem the 10,000 things as one," but these aren't necessarily even saying the same thing as one another, let alone just describing "union with the *Tao*" in different ways. It's important to resist the temptation to spiritualize such passages into a single homogenized "oneness."

So, what types of mysticism can we find in Taoism? Unfortunately, there isn't just one answer. With more than a thousand texts in the Taoist Canon (many of which have very little to do with mysticism) and at least a half-dozen different authors of the *Chuang Tzu* alone, there's really no reason to expect that all of them are describing the same kinds of experiences. And even when there's widespread consensus that something mystical is going on (like with the *Chuang Tzu*), no one can really seem to agree on anything. One important scholar describes Chuang Tzu as an *intraworldly mystic* — that is, someone who doesn't seek any kind of unity, but rather, in line with the idea of the *Tao* as transformative process, develops a new way of being present in the changing world. Such a mystic is fully involved with, fully attached to, each moment as it comes, and then fully detached from that moment as it passes, turning life into an endless slide show of new beginnings. However, another scholar argues that Chuang Tzu is a *bimodal mystic,* who eases back and forth between, on the one hand, an introverted loss of self and individuality and, on the other hand, a concrete apprehension of the oneness of the *Tao* in all things. And regardless of what type of mysticism Chuang Tzu actually practiced (if he did at all), at least one linage of Orthodox Unity Taoists today regard the first seven chapters of his book as a coded meditation manual, leading to a kind of "union" based on exorcising both *heterodox deities* (deities not part of the official Taoist pantheon) and one's own selfish desires.

The *Tao* is not necessarily a "mystical" concept in Taoism, but there certainly are Taoist authors, texts, and practices that point toward experiences of the *Tao* that are, indeed, mystical, in the sense that those who have those experiences understand them as revelatory of a higher reality or the true character of reality. Because not many scholars have sufficient expertise on both Taoism and mysticism, we don't really know the whole story yet about what types of mysticism Taoism represents, though more of this kind of analysis could be coming our way over the next decade or two.

Chapter 9

Doing Everything by Doing Nothing

In This Chapter

▶ Introducing actionless action

▶ Ruling by doing nothing

▶ Seeing non-doing in everyday life

▶ Longing for a primitive utopia

All that talk in Chapter 8 of the "creative and empty source of existence," or the "spontaneous self-perpetuation and self-generation of the cosmos," or the "emulation of the *Tao*" may be all well and good, but where does this leave human beings in terms of their day-to-day lives? After Lao Tzu and Chuang Tzu reject all the conventional human virtues, what does the Taoism of the classical texts have to say about ethical conduct, or interpersonal relations, or social organization? Doesn't religion usually include at least a couple paragraphs about what people are supposed to *do?* Or is mulling over how to return to the *Tao* doing enough?

The classical Taoist answer sounds astonishingly similar to one you might expect to hear from certain politicians, enthusiasts for mind-numbing video games, and couch potatoes of all persuasions: *There's no problem anywhere — ethical, social, governmental, or whatever — that's so big that it can't be solved by doing absolutely nothing!* That's right, you heard correctly. Although other Hundred Schools thinkers debate which actions will best transform society and solve the world's ills (and later texts from the Taoist Canon offer no shortage of ethical precepts), Lao Tzu and Chuang Tzu seem to be advocating not just taking no action, but actively pursuing the task of taking no action. And no, they're not just messing with your head either.

In this chapter, I do everything I can to make some sense of this peculiar Taoist idea of "doing nothing." You see exactly what the classical texts mean by *wu-wei,* as well as how this idea relates to government and military affairs. You also see examples of how this is supposed to work when you're dealing with ordinary matters, and how some strands of Taoist thought translate this into a kind of primitivist revolt against technology and progress.

Considering the Counterintuitive Concept of Wu-wei

The Chinese term that appears nearly a dozen times in the *Tao Te Ching* (and frequently in both the *Chuang Tzu* and *Huai-nan Tzu* as well) is the ordinary two-character couplet *wu-wei,* where the first character translates easily as "not" or "without," and the second means either "do" or "make." (The latter can also mean something like "on behalf of," but the grammatical structure indicates that's not what they have in mind here.) So, in its most basic sense, *wu-wei* really does mean "not doing," "not making," "not acting," or something very similar. It seems like a pretty straightforward concept, even if a slightly dull one.

But naturally, the Taoist texts wrap up this concept in their usual predilection for paradox and counterintuitive formulations. For one, Lao Tzu talks a couple times about *wei wu-wei,* about "doing the non-doing," or "acting without acting," which suggests that the non-doing actually entails some kind of doing, and possibly even that there's something *intentional* or *willful* about this puzzling type of "deed." Hmmm. So, what kind of doing can non-doing possibly be? Looking at the Chinese characters again, maybe you can think of it as *wei*-ing in a *wu* way — that is, acting, but in a "without" kind of way! A "without" *what* kind of way, you may ask? Without intention, without affect, without calculation, in short, without any specific cognitive motivation that brings you out of synchronicity with the *Tao*. This may be why some translators have chosen to render *wu-wei* as "actionless action" or "non-ado," to differentiate it from a kind of mindless passivity.

Try not to take the Taoist idea of "non-doing" or "doing nothing" too literally. It seems to be describing not an abstention from action as much as an utterly different kind of action, one that's so dissimilar to action that follows from ordinary human motivations and passions that it barely makes sense even to think of it as "action" at all.

In this section, I flesh out some of the implications of non-doing, as it's developed in the classical Taoist texts. I explain the idea of *wu-wei* as an effective principle, the way it relates to ideas of the *Tao* as empty and natural, and some of the most memorable images that Lao Tzu uses to illustrate this idea.

Nothing left undone

Probably the most important and compelling characteristic of Taoist *wu-wei* is the idea that somehow the proper performance (using the term *performance* very loosely) of this non-doing is effective, that it actually accomplishes particular ends more efficiently and more thoroughly than ordinary action does. The texts explain this point best in a few different places, where they say that the *Tao* (or Heaven and Earth) *wu-wei er wu pu-wei* ("does nothing and yet nothing remains undone"). And by extension, the sagely person, who aspires to emulate the Tao, likewise strives to do the non-doing and likewise accomplishes the same end of leaving nothing undone.

So, how does non-doing work? What's the mechanism by which nothing remains undone? It sounds like the classical Taoists are promising the philosophical equivalent of lowering taxes and increasing human services, claiming that you can accomplish more by actually doing less. Of course, they never quite explain this in so many words, but the entire calculus is implicit in the basic understanding of the *Tao*. Because the *Tao* is empty, impartial, insipid, and soulless, because it gives rise to and sustains the 10,000 things, the ongoing transformations of existence, without conscious will, moral investment, or anything remotely resembling *effort,* the process of purging yourself of willful intent, of the accumulated human cognitive "stuff," is tantamount to "plugging yourself into" the *Tao* and, therefore, plugging yourself into its all-encompassing efficaciousness.

Just as the *Tao* accomplishes infinitely by virtue of non-doing, so, too, can the sagely person successfully leave nothing undone in the same manner. This may not exactly explain the messy details of how tasks get fulfilled when no one's making a conscious effort to do them, but it does explain the philosophical basis that informs the overall idea.

The spontaneous and the natural

You may be getting the message from this discussion of non-doing that our ordinary doing is somehow unnatural, that action following from our own cognitive habits and values — especially Confucian morality, political guile, and clever calculating — are artificial, manufactured, contrived actions, as opposed to actions in step with the *Tao.* The implication throughout is that "*Tao*-ful" action, the action accomplished through non-doing, is genuine, authentic, and, of course, utterly natural, in that it harmonizes with the wholly natural flow and rhythm of the cosmos. In this way, you can think of returning to the *Tao* as a return to your authentic self. And there's probably no Taoist expression that captures this idea better than *tzu-jan,* yet another confusing term that's boggled generations of well-intentioned translators.

You can best understand the term *tzu-jan* not through its usual translations — like "spontaneity," "naturalness," or "the course of nature" — but through a more direct look at the Chinese characters themselves. The first one, *tzu,* means "self," but not in the sense of, say, "understanding your true self." It's really more like "I accidentally poked myself in the eye," what your grammatically correct friends would call a *reflexive pronoun.* The second character, *jan,* means "such" or "so," like the way Captain Jean-Luc Picard of the USS *Enterprise* gives an order to "make it so," or Kurt Vonnegut muses that "so it goes," where "so"

simply refers to the quality of being as it is. Together, *tzu-jan* translates into something like "of itself, so" or "so, of its own accord" or more descriptively (if more ponderously) "that which follows by virtue of its own nature." On balance, "naturalness" isn't such a bad translation after all, as long as you keep in mind that this describes harmonizing with the creative and shifting flow of existence, not simply eating granola, doing wilderness exploration, or hanging out at "naturist" (a.k.a., nudist) camps.

The hard part, of course, lies is differentiating what is genuinely natural from what "feels natural," in not confusing true spontaneity from knee-jerk reaction or mere impulsiveness. You may then want to think of Taoist non-doing, the following of what is "so, of its own accord," as something of an *enlightened* spontaneity, a heightened (yet direct and intuitive) apprehension of how to "act" that (quite ironically) doesn't come easily, thanks to all the dysfunctional habits we've acquired all our lives. In short, the path of simplicity isn't always easy.

Kicking butt the natural way

The term *tzu-jan* has a distinct place in Taoist philosophy, but it also carries a bit of cachet in some non-Taoist (or marginally Taoist) circles as well. In particular, a recently developed form of martial arts, one with some connections to the *ch'i-kung* movement, calls itself *tzu-jan men,* the "gate of what is of itself so," though it's usually translated simply as Natural Boxing or Natural-Style Boxing. Tracing its roots to a 19th-century figure referred to as Dwarf Hsu, Natural Boxing integrates martial arts with both breathing techniques and vaguely Taoist ideas.

Though it hasn't emerged as one of the biggest draws on the belts-and-mats circuit, the Natural Boxing lineage has slowly but surely begun to spread all over the world, and I mean all over. Here are some places where you can find it:

✔ **The Zi Ran Men Kung Fu Academy, in Sydney, Australia** (www.ziranmen.com): The founder Liu De Ming, who claims to be a fifth-generation master in the *tzu-jan* lineage (the academy's name uses the *pinyin* system of Romanization), teaches a version called Six Harmony Natural Boxing, which stresses conditioning, physical training, and combat techniques.

✔ **The Liu He Zi Ran Men/Wushu Training Center, in New York City** (www.sifuchenying.net): This center is run by three Chinese-born teachers with an extensive background in competitive martial arts. They also offer the Six Harmony version of the school, which they present as a method that pares away unnecessary steps and produces unpredictable movements.

✔ **The Tzu Jan Martial Art Institute, in Athol, Idaho** (http://tzujanmartialart.weebly.com): The American instructors here have backgrounds in a wide range of Asian arts — Chinese, Japanese, Filipino — and they understand *tzu-jan men* as a "reality-based" teaching that doesn't mandate specific styles, as much as translating basic principles and adapting them to the needs of the individual student.

✔ **Triangle Kung Fu Arnis Academy, in Raleigh, North Carolina** (www.kungfuarnis.com): Although this academy mainly teaches *t'ai-chi* and *kung-fu,* one of its instructors, a local police officer named Rick Ward, is a "tenth-degree grandmaster" and founder of a lineage called Tai Yang Tzu Jan Men, which he translates as the Sunburst Natural Fist System.

The metaphor of the uncarved block

One of the recurring metaphors for the *Tao* in the *Tao Te Ching* is *p'u* (the probable inspiration for *The Tao of Pooh*), which translates as something like "unhewn log," "uncut wood," or, most often, "uncarved block." You can probably imagine why this metaphor has historically been so compelling, how a raw, unfinished piece of wood poetically captures much of what is so difficult to express about the concept of Tao: its basic simplicity and naturalness, its utter lack of specific features or characteristics, and its potential for creative manifestation. But most important, this image serves as an important reminder that when you start differentiating the *Tao,* when you start carving it up into particular virtues, goals, or purposes, you've somehow lost that pure, original, whole. It is, in fact, the uncarved quality of the block that makes it so special.

If the uncarved block acts as a metaphor for the *Tao,* then emulating the uncarved block acts as a metaphor for returning to the *Tao,* for settling into a state of pure non-doing. Lao Tzu mentions this image half a dozen times, in each case subtly reinforcing this principle:

- **Describing the ancient sages who were adept at the Way:** Lao Tzu says these shadowy figures were subtle, profound, and wise, but also so profound that you could barely recognize them. Still, if you look closely, you notice that they're tentative, cautious, solemn, broad, and genuine. And also elementally plain, like an uncarved block.

- **Abandoning virtues and calculations:** Lao Tzu repeatedly tells the reader to cast off Confucian virtues like humaneness and rightness, to eliminate selfish desires for profit or material gain. So, what's left? Embracing the simplicity of the uncarved block.

- **Maintaining the original integrity:** Lao Tzu notes that you can certainly start carving the block, but doing so will produce "vessels," which may indeed be conditionally useful but which will no longer be the original block. Great carving, Lao Tzu tells us, doesn't involve any actual cutting apart.

- **Enabling spontaneous transformation:** Lao Tzu describes the uncarved block as small and insignificant, but if rulers could somehow harness it, the 10,000 things would all fall in line of their own accord.

- **Setting right the universe:** Building on the previous reference, Lao Tzu notes that once the 10,000 things transform, their desires may yet become active. The solution? Subdue them with the uncarved block, and then Heaven and Earth will spontaneously be rectified.

- **Transforming the people:** When the sage engages in non-doing, holds fast to tranquility, detaches from ordinary affairs, and desires not to desire, the people transform, repair, and enrich themselves, ultimately taking on the quality themselves of the simple uncarved block.

An uncarved Flux of Pink anarchy

The image of the uncarved block may never have gotten much attention in later Taoist circles — the 1,600-plus-page *Encyclopedia of Taoism* doesn't have even a brief entry on it — but that hasn't stopped it from piquing the Western imagination. Whether you read the most sterile scholarship or flights of fancy like *The Tao of Pooh,* you're bound to find some analysis or clever repartee devoted to this single metaphor from the *Tao Te Ching.*

So, what's the strangest place you can find reference to the uncarved block? Well, there's plenty of competition, but I'd have to give the prize to the third album by Flux of Pink Indians titled, simply enough, *Uncarved Block.* So, who were Flux of Pink Indians, and what's their connection to Taoism? Well, if you have to ask, you must not be up on your 1980s "anarcho-punk" music, the name given to a short-lived British musical genre (using the term *music* loosely)

that espoused a crude amalgam of anarchist or quasi-anarchist ideologies, embracing a range of activities from civil disobedience to Dumpster diving.

Obviously struck by classical Taoism's apparent rejection of intrusive government, restrictive laws, and artificial structures, Flux of Pink Indians lighted on the uncarved block as a perfect symbol of the anarcho-punk ethos. More than half the album's song titles echo Taoist language, and surprisingly, some of it is Taoist language from sources other than the classical texts: "Nothing is Not Done," "Value of Nothing," "Backward," "Just Is," and "Youthful Immortal." If you're used to the *Tao Te Ching* presented with sublime calligraphy, pastoral landscapes, and earthy musical tableaux, the Flux's discordant synthesizers and bizarre sound effects are sure to jolt your picture of Taoism.

The role of feminine imagery

Taoism has never been shy about pressing feminine imagery into service, whether in the form of the procreative "mother of the 10,000 things," as half of the *yin-yang* dyad, or as sexual energy in esoteric alchemical practices. But when the *Tao Te Ching* encourages you to "know the male, yet hold onto the female," this is one piece of a sustained strategy to illustrate how something as counterintuitive as *wu-wei* actually works.

The Chinese of this time identified the female as quiet, receptive, and submissive, and yet just as non-doing accomplishes more than emotionally invested doing, the female overcomes the male *through* (not in spite of) its stillness. Along these same lines, Lao Tzu presents several narrative sequences where something less powerful or possessing less overt physical potency unexpectedly proves to be more effective than its more powerful, more potent counterpart. Taken together, these vignettes reinforce the image of effective non-action.

Here are some of the parings that Lao Tzu has in mind, where the "victorious" side is analogous to the female:

- ✔ **Low vs. high:** Whether a low-lying river, or a state lying low before doing battle, it's always the lower one that ultimately commands and controls the other. This recurring emphasis on staying low is one theme some interpreters pick up on to justify claims that the text is encoding secret messages about military strategy.

- ✔ **Soft vs. hard:** Softness, suppleness, weakness, and flexibility are all characteristics of life, while hardness, firmness, and rigidity are characteristics of death. That's why, Lao Tzu tells us, the softest things under Heaven can often run roughshod over the hardest and stiffest things. It's hard (so to speak) not to relate this particular pair directly to female and male.

- ✔ **Weak vs. strong:** Just as reversal is the movement of the *Tao,* so, too, weakness is its application. That's why Lao Tzu claims one whose muscles are weak and pliant nevertheless has a firm and tight grip on the *Tao.* The weak-strong couplet shows up frequently in the text.

- ✔ **Water vs. solidity:** Toward the beginning of the text, Lao Tzu compares the highest good to water, as it passively and effortlessly brings benefit to the 10,000 things. What's more, while nothing is softer and weaker than water, its relentlessness will allow it eventually to overcome any other substance, no matter how dense. The British-born, San Francisco philosopher Alan Watts labeled Taoism the "watercourse way," the same title used for an album by the New Age music band Shadowfax in the 1970s.

Ruling by Not Doing

When you first hear about the doctrine of non-doing, you could easily come to the conclusion that classical Taoism supports a kind of radical anarchism or individualism, and that the intended audience must be a whole slew of hermits, anti-government libertarians, and social dropouts. But the Taoist idea of *wu-wei* seems less to be advocating your right to be left alone, your right to be free from political intervention or social coercion, than demonstrating how much you can accomplish by leaving others alone, by engaging the world in a non-coercive, non-interventionist manner. After all, Lao Tzu and Chuang Tzu were writing during Axial Age China, not 21st-century America or Europe, and they never really questioned the basic political and social givens, like a dynastic ruling family or hierarchical family-centered relationships.

When you look at it this way, it starts to make sense that the *Tao Te Ching* introduces non-doing not primarily as an individual ideal, but as a model for ruling society (or the world), as the guiding principle that can produce a stable (but not static) social harmony. Why else would Lao Tzu say that it's through quietude and stillness that you can become the one who rectifies the world? And just in case you don't get the point, consider the following sequence from the *Tao Te Ching*:

1. The Way is great.

2. Heaven is great

3. Earth is great.

4. And the king, also, is great.

5. This realm possesses four greats, and the king occupies one place among them.

When the *Tao Te Ching* mentions the king and how to rule, these aren't incidental, passing references just to placate some bureaucratic eavesdropper, or metaphorical allusions to being the master of your own fate or anything like that. The text really does assume that ruling is a primary concern, and the adoption of *wu-wei* is the primary means of doing it well.

In this section, I examine some of the political and governmental aspects of non-doing. I discuss the classical Taoist attitude toward rules and regulations, how Lao Tzu understands the proper role of a king, and the not always consistent comments on the place for military conflict.

The trouble with laws and government

So, why do governments institute laws? Why does every school, church, and social organization have policies, guidelines, or by-laws? Why do games and competitive sports have rules? Why do you have to produce an electronic signature certifying that you've read and understand the "terms of use" every time you do something on a commercial website? I'm sure a lot of readers will think these questions are too obvious (or too stupid) to take seriously. If you don't have these kinds of rules, they're probably thinking, you have no way to make sure that (other) people do what they're "supposed to do" or prevent them from doing what they're "not supposed to do." In other words, laws, rules, and regulations all represent attempts to control how people act or don't act, which seems like a pretty important thing if people have to live together, share resources, and so forth.

But the classic Taoist logic dictates that anything you attempt with self-willed, goal-oriented motivations will ultimately backfire. Consciously adopting a particular virtue will miss the mark, seeking valuable goods produces no satisfaction, and even something as basic as looking to gratify your senses only dulls and confuses them. That's why Lao Tzu points out that laws and other methods of control invariably bring about the opposite effect:

- ✔ The more taboos and prohibitions in the world, the more the people will be poor.

- ✔ The more sharp weapons the people possess, the more the states will be confused.

- ✔ The more skill and artistry the people have, the more peculiar things emerge.

- ✔ The more legal decrees become pronounced, the more robbers and thieves come to be.

In other words, the wrongdoers only exist because, well, we've just concocted so many wrongdoings! But this isn't just a dash of armchair psychological speculation that people don't like to be told what to do and will violate rules as an act of rebellion or self-assertion. Instead, it's keeping in tune with the idea that deliberate action doesn't work because it deviates from the Way; attempts to control people through laws represent the imposition of an artificial order onto society, a situation that's always doomed to fail. If Confucian virtues like humaneness and ritual propriety fail to live up to the Way, then laws fail even to live up to Confucian virtues.

The sage-king as the empty center

So, if Classical Taoism has a profound distaste for rules and regulations, what exactly is a sagely king supposed to do? You may have guessed that the answer is to engage in non-doing. And yes, Lao Tzu says that ruling a state is like cooking a small fish, that indifference to affairs will both reinforce the ruler's power and benefit the people, and that not pursuing greatness is the paradoxical means by which to accomplish greatness. But more important, by positioning himself as the human embodiment of the *Tao,* as the empty center that lies at the source of all creative transformation, the sage-king extends the "nothing left undone" dynamic beyond his immediate sphere, expediting (through non-doing) the spontaneous accomplishment of everything in the kingdom or perhaps the world. In short, non-doing is generally efficacious, but non-doing in the hands of the ruler effectuates the wide-ranging common good.

So, the kingly person should be impartial, like the *Tao,* exercising remote and seemingly insubstantial leadership, which causes the people to be genuine and honest. There's also a recurring whiff in the *Tao Te Ching* that this figure should adopt a paternalistic posture in relation to the masses, "emptying their minds" and "filling their bellies," so they respond like children who attentively "fix their eyes and ears on him," but without recognizing that he's the actual source of their strength. Lao Tzu's ideal world seems to flow as smoothly as the mutually attuned members of an improvisational jazz band, where the solos melt into one another effortlessly, coordinated only by a subliminal nod from the bandleader who lurks quietly in the shadows. Maybe that's why Lao Tzu "ranks" various types of rulers in the following way:

1. With the best kind of ruler, those below know only that he exists.

2. With the next kind, they feel intimately connected and offer praise.

3. With the next kind, they fear him.

4. With the last kind, they insult him.

The ideal ruler portrayed in the *Tao Te Ching* is one who's out of sight and out of mind. His emptiness and *wu-wei* facilitate the well-being of the people, who barely notice him and experience all accomplishments simply as their own.

Mixed messages on military affairs

When you think of a non-interventionist doctrine like *wu-wei,* it would seem to be a no-brainer that classical Taoism should have a pacifistic bent. After all, what could be more intrusive and coercive than a military campaign? But the *Tao Te Ching* especially comes off as decidedly schizophrenic on warfare and military matters. On the one hand, it contains numerous passages that put forth the Gandhi-esque non-aggression and non-violence you may expect:

✔ Those who assist their rulers in the Way do not employ the force of weapons in the world.

✔ All the fine weapons are ill-omened instruments.

✔ Those who are strong and violent do not come to a natural death.

✔ Those who act upon the world under Heaven are defeated by it.

And yet, Lao Tzu often seems utterly resigned to the necessity of military battle, counseling that we should respond to the killings of masses of people with sobs of grief and sorrow, and treat victories in battle with the gravity of a funeral ritual. What's more, he even seems to be offering subtle suggestions that *wu-wei* is the best strategy for accomplishing those lamentable ends, advocating the use of surprise tactics when employing troops, indifference to affairs in order to gain control of the world, and the concealment of weapons from the people once you're actually in power. In short, Lao Tzu presents non-doing as something that can accomplish a lot, and that holds true for political and military undertakings as well.

When you look at *wu-wei* in this light, it starts to make sense why many legalist philosophers and rulers took such a keen interest in the *Tao Te Ching,* how

Huang-Lao philosophy integrated Taoist thought so easily into a political ideology, and what various interpreters were thinking when they started seeing the text as a blueprint for guerilla warfare. The main themes of guerilla tactics — flexibly employing fewer combatants, harassing and withdrawing quickly, concealing obvious targets, advancing only after the enemy has exhausted itself — show up throughout the text, though not necessarily in so many words. Using typical paradoxical language, Lao Tzu suggests that armies go into battle without armor or shields, that you should retreat a foot rather than advance an inch, that a good warrior doesn't appear militaristic, that you can defeat an enemy without actually engaging him. In some ways, it reads like one long reflection on a rope-a-dope strategy, where a reader who sees mysticism rather than militarism may actually be the one getting roped!

So, what's the point of following the *Tao* anyway?

You may have noticed that the doctrine of *wu-wei* seems to come equipped with more potential for self-contradiction than any of the other Taoist paradoxes, especially with regard to political or military affairs. For example, the country should only be run by someone who doesn't want to run the country, right? If you *want* to run it, the logic goes, you can only accomplish this end if you *don't want* to run it. But doesn't choosing not to want to run the country for the sole purpose of getting to run the country kind of defeat the whole idea of *wu-wei?* If you do non-doing for a particular purpose, then is it even really non-doing?

One scholar, whose name you don't hear much these days but who was quite influential a half-century ago, tried to find some rhyme or reason in this apparent contradiction. His name was Herrlee Creel, and he spent nearly 40 years as one of the big China cheeses at the University of Chicago. Creel noticed that you can find side-by-side in the classical texts — not just the *Tao Te Ching* — one voice that seems to be pushing *wu-wei* simply because it harmonizes you (and/or society) with the Way, and another that seems to be encouraging *wu-wei* as an effective strategic means to an end. Creel thought that the former expressions came out of something he called "contemplative Taoism," and

he imagined that followers of this approach sought to ponder and experience the *Tao* for the sheer contemplative delight of it. On the other hand, he thought the latter represented a "purposive Taoism," populated by calculating strategists and entrepreneurs who sought to ply the Taoist philosophy toward specific ends. He speculated that contemplative Taoism was chronologically and intellectually primary, that purposive Taoism represented a later, degenerate attempt to "cash in" on the philosophy, and that both were still superior to the missing-the-point "immortality Taoism" that would later become the dominant historical and cultural face of the tradition.

Creel was almost certainly incorrect to imagine distinct contemplative and purposive lineages, and wrong-headed to assume uncritically that "immortality Taoism" lacked the depth of the "original" philosophy, but he did correctly identify that the formative texts of Taoism didn't speak with one voice, contained internal contradictions, and anticipated the diversity that would characterize the tradition in subsequent generations. But it's probably best not to try to figure out which strain of Taoism represents its "essence," and instead to let go of the idea that Taoism (or any other tradition, for that matter) has to possess such an essence.

Adapting to the Existential Circumstances

Although Chuang Tzu doesn't employ the term *wu-wei* as often of Lao Tzu does, he does capture the spirit of non-doing in a number of places throughout his text. But rather than offering provocative ruminations on the efficacy of *wu-wei* or its application to political and military affairs, Chuang Tzu is more concerned with modeling how you should adapt to the puzzling circumstances that real life seems to present at every turn, including the contending ethical positions of the Confucians and Moists, the mysteries of life and death, and even the challenges of ordinary, mundane tasks. For Chuang Tzu, the question in each instance is how to follow not your own (or someone else's) private motivations, but the natural and non-affected movement of the Way.

In this section, I talk about the literary devices Chuang Tzu employs to illustrate the appropriate means of adapting to existential circumstances. You become familiar with some of his most memorable images, including the hinge of the Way, the whetstone of Heaven, and the mind as a mirror. You also see some colorful examples of Chuang Tzu's literary heroes putting these principles into practice.

The hinge of the Way

If Lao Tzu was troubled that our acquired intellectual habits produce actions that don't easily fall into line with the Way, Chuang Tzu was equally troubled that every single human perspective on reality seemed to be somehow "stuck" in a localized, situated viewpoint. These lenses for interpreting and orienting to the world may superficially make life easier to negotiate — they offer a kind of conditional validity and comfort — but none of them puts you in a position to follow the natural intricacies of the Way. As Chuang Tzu saw it, our biggest impediment to engaging in genuine, spontaneous action was what brainiac philosophers would identify as *epistemological* — the root of the problem lies in how we perceive, learn, process, and integrate information. The only way to engage in *Tao*-ful, non-purposive action is somehow to arrive at a place that isn't locked into a fixed, inflexible perspective, but that liberates you to participate in that "free and easy wandering" that harmonizes naturally with the Way.

So, where is this perspective-less place, and how do we get there? In one passage, Chuang Tzu describes it as the "hinge of the Way" (or "axis of the Way"), a state that doesn't demand the selection of a cognitive affirmation of either something or its opposite, but instead lets you hold the world up to the light — actually, the light of Heaven — and proceed with lucid clarity. The image of a hinge or axis is such an effective metaphor because it illustrates an ability to *pivot* effortlessly with the changing circumstances, that quality of malleability and adaptability that both Lao Tzu and Chuang Tzu value. When you position yourself on the hinge of the Way, you can always discern the answer to that timeless bumper-sticker question — what would the *Tao* do? — and spontaneously act in a manner guided by that, rather than your own (or someone else's) personal motivations.

Chuang Tzu employs similar language later in the same chapter, when he encourages you to deal with contending voices by "harmonizing them on Heaven's whetstone." With just a slight variation, he also says that the sage harmonizes the different alternatives and "comes to rest on Heaven's potter's wheel." Collectively, these three images — hinges, whetstones, potter's wheels — suggest that constructive action should be based on intuitive and aesthetic out-of-the-box insights, rather than conventional and deliberate decision making. Of course, none of these vignettes actually tells you how to get to such a place, and it's hard to imagine that Chuang Tzu just thinks he can grab you and shake you into a new perspective, but certainly intellectual honesty about your own limitations is a good starting point.

The potter's wheel of Heaven revisited

The Chinese terms that translate as the hinge of the Way, Heaven's whetstone, and Heaven's potter's wheel are actually quite obscure and have given translators fits for at least a century. If you compare translations side-by-side, you'll find that one version translates Heaven's whetstone as "Heavenly equality," while another renders it as "framework of nature," both of which improve on an older version that tried "invisible operation of Heaven." For the reader who doesn't know Chinese, it can be kind of a crapshoot.

But the particular term *t'ien-chün*, the potter's wheel of Heaven, which appears on two occasions in the *Chuang Tzu*, has gained some modicum of Taoist immortality in modern American popular literature, thanks to a wonderfully memorable mistranslation. The 19th-century missionary-scholar James Legge, who translated both the *Tao Te Ching* and the *Chuang Tzu*, committed what today would be an elementary faux pas of translation, when he translated the same phrase two completely different ways. In

the first instance, he rendered *t'ien-chün* as the "equal fashioning of Heaven," which was relatively consistent with the way he was translating similar terminology. But in the second case, perhaps because it appeared in one of the later mishmash chapters and was threatening what would happen if you couldn't get things harmonized, Legge came up with a pretty menacing-sounding sentence: "Those who cannot do this will be destroyed on the lathe of Heaven."

Does this sound familiar? That's the translation that inspired the title of Ursula K. Le Guin's short novel, *The Lathe of Heaven*, and Legge's phrase actually gets quoted early on in the story. The irony here, which Le Guin has since acknowledged and rolled with in characteristically Taoistic fashion, is that Chuang Tzu really couldn't have possibly intended the term *chün* to mean "lathe," because the lathe hadn't been invented yet during that period in ancient China! But to tell you the truth, I'm not sure "Heaven the Equalizer" or "Potter's Wheel of Heaven" would have made as compelling a title.

A Buddhist reflection on the mirror-mind

If you've dabbled in more than one Eastern religion, you may already know that the image of the mind as a mirror gets considerable mileage in Buddhist, as well as Taoist, traditions. This holds especially true for Zen, the lineage of Buddhism that originated in China (under the name Ch'an) and came to be pretty much synonymous with rigorous meditation practices. Scholars used to think that Ch'an-Zen developed in China as a result of the crosspollination of Buddhism with Taoist philosophy, though that's probably an oversimplification. Still, there's no question that a lot of terminology and some key practices bounced back and forth between the two traditions.

The mirror-mind plays a crucial role in one of the most important early Ch'an-Zen Buddhist texts, *The Platform Sutra of the Sixth Patriarch*, which chronicles a (probably fabricated) leadership struggle in the Buddhist monastic community. As the story goes, the patriarch of the lineage announced an "open call" for poetic submissions, soliciting poems from monks on the "Buddha-nature" that he would judge in order to designate a successor. The heir-apparent wrote a lovely tetrad where he compared the mind to a clear mirror, which each person must constantly polish so no dust (that is, mental defilements) accumulates to obscure the original pure nature, a perfectly reasonable take on the process and goal of Buddhist meditation. But in response, an illiterate, ethnically mixed novice composed his own poem, stating that the original mirror was so clear and pure that there wasn't even any room for dust to gather, effectively "out-Buddha-ing" the earlier entry. Taoism is Taoism, and Buddhism is Buddhism, but it's hard not to notice how they both relate the mirror metaphor to the realization of one's pure, original nature.

The mind as a mirror

Another useful metaphor that Chuang Tzu employs briefly, but significantly, is the image of a mirror. Later Taoism would come up with various ritual and symbolic functions for mirrors, but Chuang Tzu brings it up for much the same reason that he introduces the hinge of the Way — that is, to describe a condition where you respond to the world not by constructing your own ideas and preferences, but by *reflecting* whatever presents itself to you. In the key passage, Chuang Tzu reminds you to let go of desire for fame, of purpose-driven calculations, of investment in ordinary affairs, and of the accumulation of knowledge, directing you instead to use your mind like a mirror, neither being effected by impressions as they come or holding onto them as they go. And echoing the language of *wu-wei*, doing this accomplishes every end without taking any toll on yourself. The passage on the mirror-mind is certainly one of the places where it makes great sense to think of Chuang Tzu as putting forth some type of mysticism, though not in the sense of either merging with things or dissolving one's self. If anything, it describes a quality of presence, and the accompanying ability to adapt reflexively and spontaneously to the passing present moments.

You may be able to get a better grip on the mirror-mind metaphor if you contrast it with some other ways that people have understood the functioning of the human mind. One image is of the mind as a lamp — something that sheds light on objects of its awareness, that helps to differentiate one object from another, and selects which objects are more deserving of attention. Another image, which is popular in some philosophical circles, is of the mind as a transformer — something that processes outside stimuli and converts them into symbols, perceptions, sensations, and so on. Both of these images, to a lesser or greater extent, depict the mind as an active agent, which brings a constructive element to its engagement with (and subsequent action in) the world. By contrast, the mirror-mind is receptive and attuned, not passively being blown over by the world, but fluidly reflecting and responding to it.

The connection between wu-wei and nurturing life

Many of Chuang Tzu's best-loved vignettes fall under the heading of "skill" or "knack" stories, where characters like the ox-carving Cook Ting and the cicada-catching hunchback accomplish their mundane tasks to perfection. Whether it's the elderly fisherman who reluctantly takes the reins of government or the picture-painter who's so oblivious to the demands of the moment that he nonchalantly doffs his clothes, all these figures have a few important things in common:

- **Zero expenditure:** Neither the heroes of the stories nor the tools they employ ever seem to expend any energy or exhibit any signs of being worn down. This may not really be possible — at least not according to modern laws of thermodynamics — but it makes for a striking image that Cook Ting can go nearly 20 years without ever sharpening his blade.

- **Ambiguous personal agency:** In most of the stories, the main characters deny that they possess any special skills, instead suggesting that they're merely following the Way or yielding to the "spirit-like" qualities that possess them. Whatever personal will or agency they have, it doesn't stand over and against the function of the Way.

- **Superhuman success:** None of these fables would be worth telling if they didn't end magically, with perfect executions of what the *Chuang Tzu* calls "nurturing life." The individual feats mirror the accomplishments of Heaven — which consequently casts the individual artisans as companions of Heaven in the cosmic processes.

The mysterious literary career of non-doing

One way to measure the impact of Taoist philosophy on the Western imagination is the sheer number of places where Taoist terminology shows up under a completely new guise in pockets of popular culture. For example, the Taoist term *p'u* lives on in both Benjamin Hoff's *Tao of Pooh* and the Flux of Pink Indians album *Uncarved Block,* and *tzu-jan* is kicking around in the practice of Natural-Style Boxing (it was also the name of a vegetarian restaurant in San Jose). But what about *wu-wei?* Isn't that the big enchilada of Taoist thought? How has that shown up in Western popular culture?

Actually, more places than you can probably imagine. But the most intriguing is the case of the shadowy literary figure who adopted the pseudonym Wei Wu Wei, a three-character phrase that would translate into English as "doing the non-doing." Beginning in 1958, for a period of about 15 years, a man calling himself Wei Wu Wei published a series of books meant as companions for the spiritual seeker. Many of them ostensibly dealt with Buddhism, but Wei didn't particularly distinguish one Eastern philosophy from another, because he imagined them all to be spiraling in on the same universal wisdom. His book titles alone — *Open Secret, Unworldly Wise: As the Owl Remarked to the Rabbit, Fingers Pointing Toward the Moon: Reflections of a Pilgrim on the Way,* and *The Tenth Man: The Great Joke (Which Made Lazarus Laugh),* among others — cover plenty of obscure territory, but it's the individual chapter titles that go well up into the philosophical stratosphere: "Description of No-Space," "Reality is Necessarily Intemporal," "To-o-Wha-a-t," and "Is the Man-in-the-Moon in the Puddle?" represent just a sniff of Wei's cosmic cork.

To make things a little more interesting, Wei's books tried to create a mystique about the author's true identity — the preface to one of them even included a riff on the overly cozy connection between name and ego, and (of course) a reference to how "one of the greatest books in the world" opens with a passage about how the *Tao* can't be named. Even now, many of his latter-day followers still try to perpetuate Wei's anonymity, but some good detective work ultimately identified Wei Wu Wei as Terence James Stannus Gray, an Irish intellectual from a wealthy family who had a brief career as an Egyptologist and then, while in his 60s, reinvented himself as an enigmatic and sagely quasi-Taoist. Photographs of Gray/ Wei reveal a stately, pipe-smoking, white-bearded man with a cane, looking more like an Oxford intellectual than a mountain recluse. And although he may have heeded Lao Tzu's advice on not seeking fame or profit, he was independently wealthy when he died in 1986, owning a private home in Monaco.

Incidentally, is Wei Wu Wei such an impossible name for a Chinese person to have? Actually, no, and there's an internationally known Chinese musician named Wu Wei (though it's not clear whether that's a pseudonym), who plays the *sheng,* a traditional instrument you often hear in the Chinese opera. And speaking of music, "Wu Wei" is also the title song from an album by the Algerian-Parisian guitarist extraordinaire, Pierre Bensusan, whose swirling arpeggios and graceful harmonics seem tailor-made for bringing non-doing to life through melodic imagery. Indeed, for something that does nothing, *wu-wei* sure gets around.

In short, these three qualities together embody the *wu-wei* principle, the effortless, egoless, and effective performance of basic human functions. Those who perform the tasks experience them as though they're doing nothing, like the way Artisan Ch'ui could replicate both the straight lines of a T-square and the curves of a compass, with his fingers simply following the natural transformations and his mind tucked safely out of the way. And at the same time, the actors never show any surprise that their performances leave no task undone, no chore unaccomplished.

Although the characters in Chuang Tzu's "knack" stories partake in various discrete actions, they illustrate perfectly the principle of non-doing. Perhaps they provide a glimpse of what society might look like if everyone were to follow classical Taoist notions.

Looking at Images of a Primitive Utopia

More than one person has looked at classical Taoism and come to the conclusion that the authors are, at least sometimes, depicting a utopian world, a perfect society where all participants left to follow the Way through their own natural devices will spontaneously and effortlessly accomplish their ordinary tasks, without ever interfering with one another or the basic order of existence. But not every idealist imagines the same utopia, and the strand of utopianism in the classical texts has its own particular flavor, one that readers have alternately identified as primitivist, pre-social, or *autarkic* (which is a fancy word for economically self-sufficient). That is to say, a number of passages hint at a return not only to the *Tao* itself, but to a time before the development of technology, commerce, law, and just about every other earmark of so-called civilization. According to this view of things, simplicity really does mean simplicity.

In this section, I unpack some of the classical Taoist portrayals of a primitive utopia. In particular, I take a close look at one particular passage from the *Tao Te Ching* and the chapters written by the cranky "Primitivist" contributor to the *Chuang Tzu*.

Carriages no one rides, weapons no one wields

Many passages in the *Tao Te Ching* suggest that we'd all be better off if we just chucked the trappings of "modern" life. The penultimate chapter of the text in particular reads like a whimsical daydream about the kind of world Lao Tzu really longs for. It makes no philosophical pretenses, offers no paradoxical images of empty circles or uncarved blocks, and completely ignores moral terminology, instead simply articulating the characteristics of his paradise:

- An insignificant state with a small population.
- People who appreciate their food, clothing, customs, and homes.

✔ The existence of weapons, but without anyone using or even displaying them.

✔ The existence of boats and carriages, but without anyone riding them.

✔ The use of simple tools for matters like keeping records.

✔ Close proximity to neighboring states, though without interaction between them.

Or as Lao Tzu puts it, even though people may be able to catch sight of the neighboring state, even though they may be close enough to hear the noises of their neighbor's animals, they're content to remain where they are, utterly indifferent to the source of the nearby sights and sounds. Ultimate happiness, Lao Tzu says, lies in a small community turning its collective back on progress and the tangled complications it produces.

So, is this *wu-wei?* Certainly, there are some people who interpret non-doing not as a sophisticated philosophical principle about intent, will, and aligning with the Way, but as a pragmatic observation that "less is more," that simple living can be gratifying, and that "civilized living" can get messy. And hey, if you've ever spent a couple weeks at an undeveloped island or wilderness, listening intently to the rhythms of the tides or sunsets, does it really seem like that crazy an interpretation?

Struggling to preserve one's nature

Nearly four chapters of the *Chuang Tzu* were written at the very end of the Hundred Schools Period by a single author whom scholars usually call the "Primitivist," a testy and irritable (and stylistically dull) maladroit who tosses verbal grenades at whatever moralist, logician, profiteer, adventurer, or ambitious politico gets in his way. Instead of musing poetically about any aspired-for utopia, he uses most of his ink beating up on everything that has turned his utopia into such a near impossibility.

The Primitivist author's primary concern is an idea that doesn't appear at all in the *Tao Te Ching* or the authentic "Inner Chapters" of the *Chuang Tzu:* that of human nature (though you could make a case that it appears implicitly throughout both texts). Employing metaphors like webbed toes and sixth fingers, the Primitivist argues that moral preaching, the quest for fame, and even stylized tasks like music and carpentry are all *accretions* foisted onto the original human nature, extraneous accumulations that prevent our real humanity to prosper. Somewhat more cynically, and perhaps justifiably so, he also sometimes casts the usual suspects as "robbers," who with their ambitious prattling and intrusive structures, have stolen an innate endowment from the people. Horses, the Primitivist says, do just fine when you leave them to graze and drink, to rub necks together when they're happy or issue warning kicks when they're agitated. But after you rein them in with poles and yokes and crossbars and shafts, they chew at all the apparatus and cause all sorts of trouble. People will invariably act the same way.

Sometimes in the classical texts, the idea of *wu-wei* translates into less a doctrine of transformational non-doing than a general rejection of all social and moral structures, based on the simple presupposition that such structures are unnatural and, therefore, harmful to people.

Chapter 10

For Every Yin, There Is an Equal and Opposite Yang

*I*f you've read classical Taoist texts, taken classes in *t'ai-chi* or *ch'i-kung,* or heard bits and pieces about Taoist physical cultivation practices, you've probably gotten the impression that the concepts of *yin* and *yang* figure pretty prominently in Taoist thought and practice. You may also have an unspecific sense of what those terms mean: *Yin* is the "feminine principle," associated with things like night, coolness, and receptivity, while *yang* is the "masculine principle," associated with things like day, heat, and activity. And you may even have a fuzzy understanding that the goal of Taoism is somehow to keep (or put) these two principles in some kind of balance. If this is what you're thinking, you're actually not too far off, but there is, of course, a whole lot more to it.

For starters, try to think of *yin* and *yang* — which originally meant nothing more complicated than, respectively, the shady and sunny sides of a hill — not so much as aspects of uniquely Taoist doctrine, but as ingredients within a general Chinese worldview that helped to shape not only Taoism, but also the Buddhist and Confucian traditions, as well as other disciplines like medicine, psychology, and even political history.

 The theory of *yin* and *yang* is a quintessentially Chinese innovation. It's not exclusively Taoist, though there's really no doubt that Taoism takes the *yin-yang* ball and runs with it much farther and to more interesting (and often obscure) places than just about anyone else does.

In this chapter, I talk about the basics of *yin-yang* theory, catch you up on its historical roots, and start unpacking its significance in Taoist thought and practice. You'll get clear about how *yin-yang* thought relates to both the concept of *ch'i* and to the Taoist understanding of creation. You'll also see how what began as a fairly mundane pair of categories eventually became the subject of philosophical speculation as an integral part of an elaborate cosmological system.

The Concept of Ch'i: The Psychophysical Stuff of Existence

Whenever you read a Taoist reference to *yin* and *yang,* unless it's using the older and more conventional meanings of dark and light (or night and day), chances are that it's referring at least implicitly not just to general ideas of femininity and masculinity, but specifically to *yin ch'i* and *yang ch'i.* This concept of *ch'i,* which goes back at least as far as the earliest Taoist texts, has one trait in common with other Asian religious terms like *Tao, karma,* and *nirvana:* It has pretty much made its way into the English language and even shows up from time to time in crossword puzzles and Scrabble tournaments. But it's a tough term to define exactly, and even Chinese people sometimes stop to ponder its many meanings and applications.

In this section, I fill in some of the background on this "stuff" the Chinese call *ch'i,* stuff that can somehow be either more *yin* or more *yang.* I talk about what it is and what it isn't (which can be just as important as what it is), but also explain why you should resist the temptation to think of *ch'i* as the Chinese version of atomic theory.

What is ch'i?

In one way, this is an incredibly easy question to answer. In modern Chinese, the word simply means "air" or "breath." The Chinese term for *balloon* is a "*ch'i*-ball," and your trachea is your "*ch'i*-pipe." When Chinese Americans first encounter lectures or essays on this mystical Chinese theory of *ch'i,* they're often amused (and baffled) that anyone's making such a fuss over it. I've heard more than one student or friend declare, "It's just air!"

But in religious and philosophical texts, and as a technical term in a number of fields, *ch'i* is, indeed, virtually untranslatable, not because there's anything magical about it, but because there just isn't one single English word that captures all its nuances. For the last hundred years, translators have driven themselves crazy trying to find the best equivalent of this term, and they've generally settled on language that wasn't exactly wrong, but just didn't quite tell the whole story. Here are some of the most common choices, any one of which is plausible in its own way:

Breath	Energy	Ether
Life force	Matter	Passion-nature
Pneuma	Substance	Vital energies

If we adopt sort of an all-of-the-above approach, maybe you can see that *ch'i* refers to some kind of "stuff" but also seems to cut across the conventional Western boundaries separating matter from energy, or physical substance from spirit. So, yes, all types of what you think of as *matter* — solids, liquids, gases — are *ch'i* (or, more accurately, composed of *ch'i*), but so are more tenuous "substances" like energy, thought, or will. In short, *ch'i* really is the "stuff" of existence, the raw materials (though not necessarily "material" materials, if that makes any sense) from which everything in the universe is put together.

One really helpful translation of *ch'i* is "psychophysical stuff," because it captures the idea of "substance" that is simultaneously psychological and physical. If the Western term *psychosomatic* indicates an interest in how the mind and body relate to each other, the term *ch'i* indicates how the Chinese never really separated mind and body in the first place.

Although *ch'i* is an all-encompassing category, not every Taoist concept or practice that has the sound *ch'i* (or something similar) in it is actually using that term. For example, the *ch'i* of *ch'i-kung* is indeed the psychophysical stuff, but the *chi* of *t'ai-chi* is not (it means something more like "ridgepole").

What isn't ch'i?

If *ch'i* runs the gamut of everything from matter and physical substance to energy and thought, it doesn't leave a whole lot of room for anything that isn't *ch'i,* does it? Well, no, it doesn't. The Chinese have never conceived of anything (or any "thing") that doesn't consist of *ch'i,* and they haven't wasted a whole lot of time trying to speculate abstractly about what kind of *ch'i*-less materials might exist somewhere in the universe. Not all *ch'i* is as hard as concrete, but the Chinese generally think pretty concretely about it.

But on the other hand, for about the last thousand years anyway, Chinese thinkers did find it helpful to conceptualize the principle (or principles) that govern *ch'i* and make it function coherently as somehow "above form," while *ch'i* itself was "below form." And so, you might occasionally hear someone say that Tao is not composed of *ch'i,* but that it somehow is inherent in the *ch'i* or is somehow manifest in it.

Or, you can try thinking of it this way: You'll never find any existing thing, any configuration of *ch'i,* that doesn't embody some underlying or organizing principle (or replicate the *Tao,* as some Taoists may be more inclined to say). On the other hand, such an underlying principle doesn't ever really exist abstractly or independently of reality; there must be some real *existence* that this principle actually underlies.

Contrasting ch'i and atomic theory

Once you hear that "everything is made up of *ch'i,*" you may be inclined to suspect that what they're really talking about are molecules, atoms, quarks, subatomic particles, and so on, but that they're doing so in a kind of romantic and impressionistic way. In other words, it may sound like the theory of *ch'i* isn't much more than a pseudo-scientific version of atomic theory. That's actually a pretty natural conclusion to draw, but it misrepresents the Chinese worldview in some subtle ways.

The main differences really concern what people mean when they say "everything is made up of" something else, and how they understand the significance of that information. At some risk of overgeneralization, Western atomic theory is concerned with the *composition* of matter, of definitively identifying exactly what the smallest building blocks are that combine to form more complex substances or organisms. It also investigates the *properties* of these building blocks, explaining how and why they function, combine (or not), and so forth. It's really like taking something apart to find out what it's made of and why it works.

On the other hand, the theory of *ch'i* is concerned much less with figuring out the *structure* of existence than with recognizing patterns of how different aspects of existence relate to one another, much less with isolating what the stuff *is* than with gaining insight into the *processes* of change and interaction. The Chinese generally think of existence as a fluctuating field of various configurations of *ch'i,* not as an accumulation of completely separate entities; so, *ch'i* refers more to shifting states than to static elements. At any moment, *ch'i* can have a preponderance of *yin,* a preponderance of *yang,* or an equal balance between the two, but this can ebb and flow over time. It can be refined or crude, clear or dense, active or sluggish, but those describe *conditions,* not essential realities.

Oh, and what's more, your *ch'i* and my *ch'i* are in some way the very same stuff. For that matter, your *ch'i* and my *ch'i* and a rock's *ch'i* and the Earth's atmosphere are all the same stuff. They're all parts of the same living organism and participate in the same cosmic processes.

In Taoism, *yin* and *yang* are not abstract principles of femininity and masculinity; they're ways of characterizing specific configurations of *ch'i.*

The *Tao* of Western Yin-Yang Philosophy

Despite the very specific definitions of *yin* and *yang* in Chinese history, that hasn't stopped Westerners from spiritualizing the two terms into a metaphor for any kind of dualism, polarity, or dichotomy, whether describing personalities, social roles, or political parties. One fun result of this *yin-yang*-ification of English is the endless sequence of American books with *yin* and *yang* in their titles, though probably not as many as the notorious "*Tao* of" books. Most of these don't dig terribly deeply into Chinese philosophy, if they do so at all.

Here's a brief smorgasbord of what you'll find out there:

- *The Yin and Yang of Creativity,* by Mary Heather: This self-help book explains how the balance of *yin-yang* can be applied to such things as business, social relations, and getting yourself to stand out in a crowd.

- *The Yin-Yang Life of a Baby Boomer,* by Marilyn Cugel (Rocket Science Productions): This autobiographical narrative uses *yin-yang* more or less synonymously with "highs and lows." The author relates acquiring *yin-yang* balance to the precariousness of Jewish life in *Fiddler on the Roof.*

- *Testosterone-Free Marketing: The Yin and Yang of Marketing for Women,* by Denise Michaels (Personal Transformation Press): This advice book talks about how women can discover a *yin-yang* balance that allows them to succeed in business without abandoning their feminine identities.

- *The Yin and Yang of Marriage,* by Stephanie Ager Kirz and Howard L. Kirz, M.D. (White Dog Press): A former public relations executive and a former emergency room doctor give advice on how to deal with several topics, including personal space, in-laws, and sex.

- *The Yin and Yang of American Culture,* by Eun Y. Kim (Nicholas Brealey Publishing): In kind of an interesting turnaround, the Asian-American author uses the theory to praise what he understands as American "*yang* virtues" (like individuality and romanticism) and critique "*yin* vices" (like wastefulness and lack of attention to character education).

Yin and *yang* seem to have acquired some other meanings in English vernacular as well. The popular newspaper comic strip *Baby Blues* once showed the parents walking by a shop called "Ringtones up the Yin Yang," which was right next to a shop called "Cheese Logs 'n Nose Studs!"

The Role of Yin-Yang in the Taoist Creation Stories

Although several religious traditions — Judaism, Christianity, and Islam are the most obvious — understand God's intentional and self-sufficient creation of the universe as a kind of paradigmatic moment outside of ordinary time, Taoists think of *cosmogony* (that is, creation of the cosmos) in very different terms, and they don't attach anywhere near the same significance to a single creation story.

First off, they usually understand creation as *ongoing process* rather than a distinct *event*. For all intents and purposes, creation has *always* been occurring, is continuing now as you read these words, and will continue to occur long after you've put down this book.

Second, they usually view the whole process as self-generating and self-perpetuating; even when they do ascribe it to a deity like Lord Lao or the Heavenly Worthy of the Primordial Beginning (they're not always consistent about which one), they don't really think of a personal *will* informing the process.

And third, although they think of creation as bringing *order* to the universe, they don't really think of it as fulfilling any divine *purpose*. Asking theological questions like why the universe exists or whether it has an ultimate plan hasn't really made up a substantial part of Taoist thought.

The Taoists may not have a single creation myth that makes up part of a regular liturgy or shows up in pastoral sermons, but they do have some interesting, brief narratives that take up the cosmogonic theme, and many of them integrate (or at least imply) some aspects of *yin-yang* theory. In this section, I examine a pair of "creation stories" from the classical texts, and illustrate how an understanding of *yin* and *yang* may call to your attention aspects of those stories you may not have noticed otherwise.

Order from chaos

One especially provocative passage from the *Tao Te Ching* narrates what sounds like a numerically coded series of events, culminating in some kind of reflection on *ch'i, yin, yang,* and how they combine. Although Taoists (and others) haven't always agreed on exactly what some of the terms represent, or whether some phrases sneaked in that probably shouldn't have, they're pretty much all on the same page that this depicts a Taoist shorthand of the process of creation, the gradual movement from chaos to order, and to the quality of harmony inherent in that order.

Here's one translation of this sequence, with line-by-line interpretations to fill in some of the blanks:

1. **The *Tao* gives (or gave) birth to the one.** This sequence begins with the *Tao,* which functions as a kind of creative impetus for the whole process. Some people have interpreted the "one" as *t'ai-chi,* the Great Ultimate (yes, that's the *t'ai-chi* of *t'ai-chi ch'üan*), the boundless cosmic pole that allows the universe to cohere. The "one" can also represent the entire repository of "original" or "primordial" *ch'i,* an undifferentiated chaos that contains a field of unlimited possibilities.

2. **The one gives birth to the two.** Somehow, out of this field of chaos, of undifferentiated *ch'i,* the first signs of order begin to take shape with the complementary emergence of the "two," the *yin* and *yang.* This is still somehow before the materialization of actual *things,* but it's nevertheless a huge step in the transition from disorder to definition. And by thinking of yin and yang as perfectly complementary qualities, the state is still fundamentally balanced and harmonious.

3. **The two give birth to the three.** This is actually where things get a little dicey, because interpretations of the "three" can vary pretty widely. One standard reading is Heaven, Earth, and humankind; another, which shows up in some later Taoist texts, is *ch'i,* form, and substance. Either way, the implication here is that the interaction of *yin* and *yang* gives rise to increasingly more differentiated configurations of *ch'i,* to increasingly more distinct constituents of existence.

4. **The three gives birth to the 10,000 things.** And here Lao Tzu opens the floodgates of creation, with the "three" giving rise to the "10,000" (sometimes translated as the "myriad") things, a standard shorthand in Chinese texts for the multiplicity of creatures and things that inhabit our existence.

5. **The 10,000 things carry *yin* on their backs and embrace *yang* in their arms.** Have you ever noticed how in the *yin-yang* symbol (the one on the cover of this book), there's always a little dot of *yin* inside the thickest part of *yang,* and vice versa? That's just to remind you that you'll never find *yin ch'i* or *yang ch'i* in total isolation, even in women and men. All of the 10,000 things, at least to some extent, embody both *yin* and *yang.*

6. **They blend *ch'i* and, through this, harmonize.** And what's more, the 10,000 things are naturally in a state of harmony, through a blending of *yin* and *yang ch'i.* Is this a simple statement of how the universe functions? A cryptic blueprint for how human beings can exist harmoniously in that universe? An invitation somehow to join and share in this ongoing process of creation and harmonization? No matter what, it's certainly one early clue that there's a lot of stake in understanding the flux and flow of *ch'i* — including your own!

The Taoists understand creation as an ongoing movement from chaos to order, with an important implication that humans can somehow participate in or harmonize with that process.

The chaotic wanton

A very different narrative in the *Chuang Tzu* puts an interesting spin on the idea of creation as the transition from chaos to order and orientation. This short allegorical vignette refers to chaos by name — Hun-tun — and depicts "him" as the hospitable emperor of a nebulously defined "central" region, periodically welcoming the respective emperors of the northern and southern regions.

Wishing to thank Hun-tun for his kindness, which they've apparently never reciprocated, the two emperors observe that he has no "holes," none of the seven openings that all other beings have in order to see, listen, eat, and breathe (they don't seem to be interested in apertures that allow for other non-sensory bodily functions). In response to this outward "flaw," they begin to bore holes in Hun-tun, one each day. And as you might expect, Hun-tun dies on the seventh day, having been (literally) bored to death. The story ends there, with no explanation, no moral. For readers who have no idea what Hun-tun represents, they may wonder if Chuang Tzu had been dipping into the brandy peaches without the peaches.

In here, as well as other Taoist (and some non-Taoist) stories, Hun-tun is a shapeless, featureless blob, an infinite and nondescript jumble with no clear qualities or borders, exactly what you may imagine before the first stirrings of *yin* and *yang*. In fact, you've almost certainly encountered Hun-tun before, or at least some version of him, not in religious texts or mythic narratives, but in Chinese restaurants!

Have you figured it out yet? He's that amorphous mass you find floating in a popular — if kind of *boring* — soup: the ever-present wonton! Yep, the Cantonese word *wonton* is pronounced *hun-tun* in Mandarin, and the word for chaos and the word for the thing in your soup are etymologically and linguistically related. So, from now on, maybe you should think of the dinner appetizer as "chaos soup," and the pre-creation chaos as nothing but a big, plump, primal "wonton."

Back to the story, chaos (a.k.a. Hun-tun) endures until two complementary forces — never specifically equated with *yin* and *yang,* but the parallels do jump out at you — act on that chaos and do away with it, implicitly replacing it with more defined components of existence. The narrative doesn't quite match up exactly with Lao Tzu's step-by-step recitation — chaos giving birth to the *yin* and *yang* differs noticeably from *yin* and *yang* boring holes in chaos — but they both illustrate the general principle that *yin* and *yang* appear early in the cosmogonic process and are the most elemental forms of order.

The theme of order from chaos shows up in later Taoist texts as well, and many of them incorporate descriptions of Hun-tun, sometimes much like Chuang Tzu's inchoate blob, sometimes as kind of a cosmic egg. The term *Hun-tun* is also related to a phrase in the *Tao Te Ching* that translates as "something confused, and yet complete." Who'd have thought you could have so many different ways of imagining the state of pre-creation chaos?

There's more than one way to create a cosmos, and more things to create than just the cosmos

When you get a handle on Lao Tzu's narrative from the One to the 10,000 things, Chuang Tzu's image of boring holes in a chaotic wonton, and allusions to a cosmic egg, you may start to notice that religious traditions tell many different types of creation stories, that they incorporate various cosmogonic myths. In fact, most Jews and Christians probably aren't aware that the book of Genesis from the Hebrew Bible (Old Testament) begins with not one, but *two,* accounts of creation. The first account describes how an impersonal God created the world in six days, culminating in the creation of humankind (both male and female) in his "image" on the sixth day, and concluding with the day of rest and sanctification of the Sabbath. The second account describes how a much more personal deity (who actually talks with his created beings) formed a man from dust (or clay), breathed life into him, placed him in the Garden of Eden, and created a companion for him from his own rib, a sequence that leads to a dramatic encounter with a serpent and the eventual expulsion from paradise. If you move outside the Western traditions, you find considerably more variation. One ancient Indian myth, for example, portrays the divine sacrifice of a thousand-headed primal man, whose body parts give rise to different aspects of existence, including not only the heavens and Earth, but the four Hindu castes. Evidently, there really is more than one way to create a cosmos.

And to boot, not every creation story talks about creating the universe. What on Earth (or what else on Earth), you may be asking, could be created in a creation story? Some stories describe the creation not of the cosmos, but of the gods. To keep these types of stories straight, scholars classify god-creation stories as *theogonies* — just as a *cosmogony* is a creation of the cosmos, a *theogony* is a creation of a deity or deities. This may be a little surprising, since Western creation stories all *start* with God, without any explanation of where this deity came from, and move on to describe how God does the creating. But as you can see from both Lao Tzu's and Chuang Tzu's cosmogonic accounts, not every creation has a divine agent running the show, so it's interesting to find cases where the divine agents actually get created *during* the show. And who creates the gods in theogonies? Well, sometimes no one, through some variation of the chaos-to-order theme. And sometimes, the gods create the gods — perhaps even by sacrificing to the gods. For the time being, let's not ask where *those* gods came from!

The Yin-Yang School

Although the ideas of *yin* and *yang* did get swallowed up by Taoism, and other Chinese traditions as well, they really did much more than just float around as a pair of vague ways of classifying specific entities or configurations of *ch'i*. They also figured prominently as the foundational terminology of an elaborate philosophy. In fact, the same historians of the Hundred Schools Period who first classified Lao Tzu, Chuang Tzu, and others into a "School of *Tao*" also created a category called the "School of *Yin-Yang*," which is sometimes translated as the "Naturalists." When you hear that Taoism incorporates *yin-yang* thought, or something like that, it really means that it incorporates the original teachings (and later interpretations) from this School of *Yin-Yang*.

In this section, I introduce you to these first rumblings of a systematic philosophy of *yin* and *yang*. You get to know a little something about the supposed (and rather mysterious) founder of this "school," see how scholars have picked up the breadcrumbs to piece together some of his original ideas, and get a first look at how the *yin-yang* theory expands to something increasingly complex and integrative.

Tsou Yen: The architect of a lost school

Chinese scholars traditionally attributed the School of *Yin-Yang* to a man named Tsou Yen, who probably lived in the early part of the 3rd century B.C.E. Biographies written a few hundred years after his death describe him as educated in a number of different fields, including math, astrology, politics, and geography, which helps explain why he'd be interested in developing some kind of comprehensive theory of how things interact with one another. The historical accounts also credit him with writing many long essays about the "production and dissipation of *yin* and *yang*," although none of these — absolutely none — survives.

So, how do we know anything about Tsou Yen's early *yin-yang* theory if we don't actually have any of his writings? The only choice we have — though it may not be entirely reliable — is to gather up every place where he was *quoted* in texts from his time or not too much later, lay the passages end to end, and see if you can find any consistency or coherence in them. This is actually a fairly common strategy in reconstructing "lost" authors and schools, especially with some of the more elusive figures from the Hundred Schools Period. It may amount to little more than a game of "telephone," but at least it gives us something to work with.

According to these various fragments (which you may want to take with a grain of salt), Tsou Yen had his fingers in many pieces of intellectual pie, all of which he would try to relate to the fluctuations of *yin* and *yang*. Here's a sampler of some of the many things that caught his attention:

- ✔ **History:** Tsou had an interest in coordinating time, dynastic cycles, and the stories of great sages from the past, imagining all the way back to a time of mythic pre-history.

- ✔ **Natural sciences:** Biographies report that he wanted to classify animals and vegetation, as well as geological and topographic occurrences, with the intention of extrapolating things like what one would find beyond the oceans.

- ✔ **Morality:** Though it apparently made up a small piece of his theory, he did address the typical family and relation-based ethical concerns that were common to his day. Later *yin-yang* theory often, but not always, incorporates some kind of implicit component.

✔ **Divination:** This is probably the piece that held all these other interests together. Tsou was especially concerned with reading and interpreting signs and omens, trying to determine the connections among things that weren't immediately obvious. In one sense, Tsou was always trying to understand the past; but more important, he was trying to figure out how to act in the present and take a peek into whatever was coming in the future.

The five elements theory

Although there's considerable doubt about the extent of Tsou Yen's actual contributions, traditional histories credit him with one especially important innovation in the naturalistic system: the pairing of *yin-yang* theory with another theory that may have had its own historical roots, that of the "five elements." Where the basic dualistic *yin-yang* theory understood existence as the alternation of two rising and falling complementary configurations of *ch'i*, the five elements approach allowed for a much more complex and potentially expansive network of interactive cycles.

In actuality, the Chinese term *wu-hsing* should be more accurately translated as "five phases" or "five agents" rather than "five elements," a suggestion that may make a little more sense once you remember that the Chinese idea of *ch'i* concerns processes and patterns of relationships, not atoms or molecules. Try thinking of them as *phases* of transformation, or *agents* of mutual influence, rather than static *elements*. So, what are these five phases? They're usually listed in this order:

✔ **Wood:** This phase refers to much more than two-by-fours, including a whole range of vegetation, minerals, and even substances like wax or carbon.

✔ **Fire:** This includes various things associated with heat and light, like the sun, lava, and smoke.

✔ **Earth (or soil):** This can include things blended to form soil, like clay, rocks, dust, sand, and even bone.

✔ **Metal:** This phase incorporates the various metals the early Chinese knew about — like gold, silver, copper, and bronze — but it also includes their properties like magnetism and conductivity.

✔ **Water:** Liquid comes in many different forms, including vapor, the oceans, precipitation, and condensation.

Again, the significance of these phases is not that they represent separate components of reality, but that they interact with one another through a set of predictable cycles and relationships. In this section, I talk about the two different cycles that coordinate the five phases, and explain how Tsou You integrated *yin-yang* theory with the five elements theory.

Production and generation

The first type of interaction among the five phases is what the Chinese identify as a *generative* or *productive cycle,* the specific ways that the phases continually give rise to (and are dependent on) one another. Here's the most common synopsis of that type of cycle:

- ✔ **Water generates wood.** Water doesn't really turn into wood, but you can certainly see how trees (wood) depend on water to grow.

- ✔ **Wood generates fire.** Well, you can watch a tree for days and it probably won't spontaneously burst into flames, but fire requires fuel (wood) in order to burn.

- ✔ **Fire generates Earth.** When fire consumes a substance, it produces ashes, which settle back into the soil.

- ✔ **Earth generates metal.** Okay, this one's not really obvious, until you consider how, in much of the ancient world, people believed that metal grew in the ground. Got it?

- ✔ **Metal generates water.** This one may not be obvious either, until you pick up a cold tin cup on a humid day. It must have certainly looked to a lot of people like the metal actually produced the liquid.

Conquest and overwhelming

One of the things that makes the five-phase cycle so interesting, and gives it so much potential for variation and application to different circumstances, is the way the Chinese also imagine a *conquering* or *overwhelming cycle.* When they jog the sequence of phases, you get the following relationships:

- ✔ **Water conquers fire.** And it's a good thing it does. If we didn't have easy access to an abundant substance to control fire, things would get pretty hot, pretty fast.

- ✔ **Fire conquers metal.** At first glance, metals seem fairly solid and permanent. That is, until you apply some heat to them. Use enough fire, and the metal melts.

- ✔ **Metal conquers wood.** Implements made of metal are your best bet for felling trees or fashioning things out of wood.

- ✔ **Wood conquers Earth.** This refers to how wooden implements can dig up soil. Just don't tell Tsou Yen about the problems for homeowners of Earth-to-wood contact!

- ✔ **Earth conquers water.** Water can be a furious force that's difficult to maintain, but the natural banks of a river or an earthen dam can rein it in and even redirect it.

The Chinese sometimes illustrate the two directions of influence through a circle containing a five-pointed star, with each of the stars' vertices representing one of the five agents. Arrows on the circle pointing in a clockwise direction illustrate the generative cycle, while arrows on the star indicate the directions of the conquest cycle. Like the *yin-yang* symbol, this diagram indicates a dynamic, constantly moving, and internally complete system.

Yin-yang and five phases

So, how does this all connect with *yin-yang?* By identifying the phase of lesser *yang* with wood, greater *yang* with fire, *yin-yang* balance with Earth, lesser *yin* with metal, and greater *yin* with water. Some of this may seem intuitively obvious. The *Tao Te Ching* says that nothing is more yielding than water, so it makes sense to identify that with a preponderance of *yin.* Fire can be blindingly bright and is so frenetic that you can't even make out its borders, a natural match with *yang.* And the Earth is where you can be, quite literally, *grounded,* a place of balance between *yin* and *yang* (and perhaps) other dualities as well.

When Tsou Yen (or whoever) first started making connections between cycles of *yin-yang* with the five-phase cycles, he may have started speculating about how these progressions related to other things he studied, like history, ethics, and science. In particular, he may have associated the phases of generation and destruction with the rise and fall of successive dynasties.

A Whole System of Correspondence and Correlation

Whether or not Tsou Yen was truly the architect of this basic scheme, it expanded fairly quickly — in Huang-Lao Taoism and the Confucianism of that same period — into a much more elaborate system of correspondences. Because these correspondences covered everything from colors and numbers to planets and units of time, some scholars have taken to identifying this way of ordering the universe as *correlative cosmology* or sometimes the more descriptive (but really cumbersome) *correlative anthropocosmology.*

The governing principle — or at least one of the governing principles — of this system is the idea of "impulse and response," the observation that the motion or transformation of any agent in the cosmic scheme of things is necessarily related to every other participant in that cosmos. This doesn't really mean that everything is "one" as much as it means that they're interrelated parts of one organic network. Your hand and your nose aren't really the *same,* but what happens to one of them can't ever be completely separated from the other.

It may seem that *impulse and response* refers simply to cause and effect, but you'll probably get a better handle on this principle if you think of it as something more like *resonance* or *synchronicity.* The system describes a kind of "cosmic Internet" of mutual influence and interpenetration. In order to understand something, it's necessary to understand the web of connections and relationships in which it participates.

In this section, I talk about the specifics of this system of correlative cosmology and relate it to the foundations of Taoist self-cultivation.

Everything resonates with everything else

You may not make an intuitive connection between how a particular food tastes and the tone of a specific note in a musical scale, but the correlative system lays out an entire system of correspondences where, quite literally, just about everything resonates with everything else. The logic isn't always immediately clear — remember, it doesn't follow standard Western methods of scientific inquiry — but that's why the Chinese have traditionally needed experts to interpret and apply the system.

Table 10-1 lays out how the five phases relate to many different processes. You may want to cover some of the rows, to see if you guess what goes where. Do you have any idea what planet corresponds to fire, or which relative corresponds to wood?

Table 10-1	The Five Phases and Their Correspondences				
	Wood	*Fire*	*Earth*	*Metal*	*Water*
Phase	Lesser yang	Greater yang	Balance	Lesser yin	Greater yin
Direction	East	South	Center	West	North
Color	Green	Red	Yellow	White	Black
Animal	Green dragon	Red bird	Yellow dragon	White tiger	Black tortoise
Number	3 or 8	2 or 7	5 or 10	4 or 9	1 o 6
Planet	Jupiter	Mars	Saturn	Venus	Mercury
Solid organ	Liver	Heart	Spleen	Lungs	Kidneys
Hollow organ	Gallbladder	Small intestine	Stomach	Large intestine	Bladder
Sensory organ	Eyes	Tongue	Lips	Nose	Ears
Emotion	Anger	Joy	Pensiveness	Sorrow	Fear
Taste	Sour	Bitter	Sweet	Pungent	Salty
Climate	Windy	Hot	Damp	Dry	Cold
Relation	Father	Daughter	Ancestors	Mother	Son

Got a headache? No big deal — I'll just stick some needles in your arms and legs

While reading this chapter, you may have started making the connection between *yin-yang* or five elements theory and Chinese forms of holistic medicine, especially acupuncture. Even without knowing all the correlative details, you can probably see how the overall acupuncture approach reflects the Chinese understandings of resonance and a body composed of circulating *ch'i*. Think of it this way: You go to the acupuncturist complaining of a headache. The doctor, it seems to you, examines just about everything *except* your head. He checks your pulse (in your wrists and elsewhere), inspects your tongue, and maybe even asks about the regular color of your urine. Then, the doctor may tell you that the problem is that you have weak kidneys or liver, and then treats you by inserting needles in your arms, back, and legs. In other words, you may have symptom A, which the doctor diagnoses by examining locations B, C, D, and E, tells you that the problem is in organ F, and then inserts needles in your G, H, I, J, K, L, M, and N spots. Pretty different from Western medicine, no?

That's because traditional Chinese medicine maps the human body not only in terms of the obvious organs and appendages, but also in terms flowing channels of *ch'i* called *meridians,* which can be either *yin* or *yang*. The maps indicate how weakness or dysfunction of one spot may disturb the flow of *ch'i,* which produce symptoms you feel in other parts of your body and signs that the specialist can detect in your pulse and elsewhere. Along these same lines, a proper diagnosis should indicate which specific regions — the "acupuncture points," usually calculated by specific distance from key organs and located near muscles — need stimulation to strengthen or rectify the flow of *ch'i* to the troubled organ or organs. And yes, the five elements theory apparently influenced why acupuncturists originally understood the *ch'i* meridians as they did and how they constructed their maps of the body.

Like the *yin-yang* and five elements theories, acupuncture is not uniquely Taoist, but the Taoist Canon does include medical texts that draw on the same principles, and some medical texts unearthed in Ma-wang-tui — during the same archaeological dig that uncovered ancient versions of the *Tao Te Ching* — talk about the circulation of *ch'i* through early versions of acupuncture meridians. In the West, some modern practitioners of what's becoming known as "integrative medicine" borrow in different degrees from Chinese traditional medicine, though the discipline is still fairly new and there's considerable variation from professional to professional.

This table doesn't by any means exhaust all the correspondences that this system identifies. Some versions of this chart may include things like stage of life, hours of the day, scents, other emotions or body parts, bodily fluids, moral virtues, musical notes, and *calendric units* (which the Chinese traditionally understood in terms of 60-year cycles, based not on weeks and months, but on a system of 10 heavenly "stems" and 12 earthly "branches"). In short, there's nothing under the sun that doesn't somehow get swept up in this comprehensive and holistic way of making sense of the world.

The cultivation of body and spirit

At this point, you've probably gotten the idea that balancing *yin* and *yang* in a Taoist context is a lot more complicated than breaking out of gender stereotypes through women getting in touch with their "masculine sides" or men, learning to bake cookies. The all-purpose *yin-yang* balance really refers to a cultivation or harmonization of the *ch'i,* which Taoists understand as involving intricate networks of psychophysical stuff that function in complex but ultimately intelligible cycles of generation and conquest.

So, what does all this mean for things like Taoist ritual and self-cultivation? Here are a few important themes that show up in many different practices:

- ✔ **The person as a simultaneously biological and psychological entity:** Just as the concept of *ch'i* blurs the boundaries between the physical and the psychological (or the "spiritual"), the Taoist person is a holistic, integrated entity. So, the cultivation of your *ch'i,* whether through *ch'i-kung* or more advanced Taoist practices, is what one Taoism scholar labels "biospiritual" training.

- ✔ **A multiplicity of interpretations of cultivation or harmonizing *ch'i:*** The tidy label of cultivating or harmonizing *ch'i* doesn't really do justice to the truly *vast* range of Taoist practices that have historically fallen into this category. Some accounts of the early Way of the Celestial Masters, for instance, indicate that one way they tried to harmonize *ch'i* was through sexual rituals, though there's considerable debate about how accurate those reports were. And some later longevity practices attempted to interfere with the natural cycles, by expelling *yin ch'i* from the body — cultivating the *ch'i* by subverting the harmony.

- ✔ **The body as a microcosm of the cosmos:** Because of the dynamic, continuous fluctuations of *ch'i,* the individual person's body is connected to the entire cosmos through the mechanism of impulse and response. But some Taoist texts and practices take this even further, suggesting that the structure and motion of the cosmos is somehow replicated in society, sacred space (like a ritual altar), and the human body — think of it as a series of concentric circles, with the outer ring representing the entire cosmos and the central core representing the individual. And so, the ritual training of the body — the holistic biospiritual body, that is — can influence, set right, or even *renew* the entire cosmos.

When Taoist adepts talk about "achieving balance" or "cultivating *yin* and *yang,*" those deceptively simple phrases actually plug into an entire system of resonant, synchronous correspondences, which include a complex understanding of the human body and its relationship to the cosmos.

Chapter 11

Blue Heaven, Yellow Heaven: The Belief in a New Age

I'll bet you dollars to doughnuts that when you first think of Taoism, you'll probably come up with things like returning to simplicity or balancing *yin* and *yang* before you finally get around to the end of the world and an apocalyptic vision of a new age. And that's quite understandable. When you read the *Tao Te Ching* and *Chuang Tzu,* you have no way of knowing that when the first Taoist communities arose several hundred years after those texts were written, they were organized around a common belief that they'd be leading humankind into a new cosmic era. And even modern Chinese people who visit Taoist temples, hire Taoist priests to preside over family funerals, and attend dramatic public Taoist rituals may not know (or have readily in mind) the utopian, new age roots of the tradition.

Chang Tao-ling's Way of the Celestial Masters and the kindred Way of Great Peace exemplified a kind of religious movement called *millenarianism,* which you can actually find in many different traditions all over the world. In this chapter, I discuss "new age" religion in general, and give you a sense of how Taoism fits into the overall "new age" picture. I fill you in on the basic features of millenarian movements, the unique qualities of Taoist millenarianism, and the coincidental adoption of Taoism by the modern Western New Age Movement.

Millenarian movements are not unique to Taoism. In fact, almost all the major world religions have undergone periods of what you might call "millenarian fervor" or given rise to specific sects that held strongly millennial beliefs.

Millenarian Religious Movements

Before we talk about Taoist millenarianism, it would help to have something of a global perspective on the subject. You may see some similarities between Taoist millenarianism and your own tradition or traditions you know well. On the other hand, you may see some significant differences, too.

In this section, I set the stage by talking about millenarianism as a recurring theme in the history of religion. You hear a more precise definition of millenarianism and get to know some of its basic features, learn to recognize millennial traditions that have popped up in the West, and discover the "new age" roots of the modern New Age Movement.

What is millenarianism?

A *millennium* is a period of a thousand years. You may remember a lot of excitement when the new millennium started in 2000 (even though technically it didn't really start until 2001!). But in some ways, it doesn't really matter how long a millennium is and when it starts — if humans only had eight fingers, we'd be less than 30 years away from the fifth millennium C.E. — because when we use the term *millennium* religiously, it really refers to any extended period of cosmic or divine time. In other words, a religious millennium is a significant era, age, or epoch in the turning of human history.

A *millenarian* (or *millennial*) organization (or philosopher or theologian, for that matter) is one that has some version of the belief that a new millennium is about to replace (or has just replaced) an old one, and that its followers have some important role to play in the new era. Millennial beliefs can take a lot of different forms, because what these groups actually mean when they say one age is ending and a new age is coming can have several variations. Here are some of the most common ways of understanding the new millennium:

✔ **A literal end of the world:** Some traditions teach that the physical world is coming to an end, which they expect will be foreshadowed by major physical catastrophes (like earthquakes or floods) and social upheavals. In many Western traditions, they call this the *eschaton* or *apocalypse.* If you watch movies about a "zombie apocalypse," the description is a good one. They portray an era when the world we know no longer exists and has been replaced by an age of flesh-eating reanimated humans. All zombies aside, apocalyptic millenarians usually believe a new cosmos will eventually be created or that the faithful will experience Rapture and be rewarded in Heaven or some other type of paradise-like existence.

✔ **A figurative "end of the world" and a beginning of a new cosmic age:** Some traditions teach that the world is about to undergo (or has undergone) a change of such major cosmic significance that the "world as we know it" is, in effect, coming to an end and being replaced by a new cosmic era. They may understand this as precipitated by the second coming of a deity, a transformation of the elements, or even a realignment of the stars. Did you ever hear someone sing that "this is the dawning of the Age of Aquarius"? That was actually a pop version of a common millenarian belief at that time: that a new astrological era was about to begin.

✔ **A major social transformation that figuratively creates a "new world":** Some traditions don't believe that the world is coming to a literal end or that the cosmos is shifting in some earthshaking way, but they do believe that humankind — perhaps because of divine decree, perhaps out of its own natural evolution — is collectively undergoing a transformation of consciousness so momentous that what lies ahead will mark a radical shift from what came before. Sometimes what separates a millennial from a more generic radical reformer is the gravity of the change he imagines and the enthusiasm he brings to that change.

Familiar (and unfamiliar) millenary traditions in the West

One way to help get a handle on Taoist millenarianism is to keep an eye out for millennial tendencies in traditions you already know something about. In its most basic sense, Christianity is a millenary tradition through and through; in fact, any messianic religion, any tradition that is awaiting the arrival or return of a savior, is an example of millenarianism. And then, there are different variants of Christian millenarianism. For example, *premillennials* believe that the second coming of Jesus will occur before the new age; his presence may serve as a sign that the apocalypse is imminent. On the other hand, *postmillennials* believe that humans have a divine mandate to transform and reform the world, to prepare it for the second coming. What's more, some postmillennials call themselves "optimillennialists," reflecting their optimism that humans will inevitably defeat the forces of evil and prepare the world for the second coming — they view the supposedly pessimistic premillennials as "pessimillennials." There are even Christian *amillennials,* who believe that we're already in the new millennium — it began with the gift of the Holy Spirit at the first Pentecost — and so there's no need to *wait* for any new age. Obviously, there can be plenty of competition for the same audience.

And because Christianity picked up its messianism from Judaism — Jews originally imagined a messiah not as a son of God, but as a descendant of King David who would restore the kingdom of Israel — you can also think of Judaism as a millennial tradition, though many Jews have departed significantly from the messianic aspects in recent centuries. Although some branches, like Hasidism, maintain more literal interpretations of the messiah, others think more symbolically about the idea of a "messianic age." Jewish messianism shows up in some unexpected and creative places, too. For instance, an innovative New York–based Jewish playwright and performance artist, Deb Margolin, performed a touching and funny one-woman monologue titled *O Wholly Night and Other Jewish Solecisms,* where she related the concept of "waiting for the messiah" to a range of ordinary (but somehow extra-ordinary) life events, from an exhausted couple experiencing an intimate New Year's moment with a tender jazz dance, to a distraught mother anxiously anticipating her newborn child's first smile.

There are lots of different types of millenarianism. Broadly speaking, any messianic or "new age" movement falls into that category.

As you may imagine or already know, some Christians and Jews are more millennial than others. Here's a list of some denominations that have an especially millenarian outlook:

- **Seventh Day Adventists:** Non-Adventists know little about this group, which began in the 19th century, beyond that their dietary restrictions and recognized Sabbath day look very Jewish. But Adventists also believe that most of the prophecies about Christ's "Second Advent" have already come true, which means that his return must also be happening soon.

- **Jehovah's Witnesses:** Another late 19th-century denomination, the Witnesses believe that the "final days" began about 100 years ago (because of Satan's presence on Earth), that the world faces imminent destruction, and that God will eventually restore it to a kind of paradise for those who worship correctly.

- **Unification Church:** Known pejoratively for many years as "Moonies," the Holy Spirit Association for the Unification of World Christianity has gotten more attention for its missionary activity and widely reported group marriages than for any of its particular beliefs. Regardless, they believe that Christ's second coming will occur during the current era, and that he and his human bride will become parents for all humankind, which will eliminate all traces of original sin.

- **The People's Temple:** Founded in the 1950s by religious leader and political activist Jim Jones, the People's Temple was a multiracial community that formed an agricultural commune in Guyana, which was supposed to be the beginning of a new utopian world. The People's Temple ended tragically in 1978, with mass suicides killing more than 900 people, including many children. The followers swallowed poison mixed with a sweet instant drink — since then, "drinking the Kool-Aid" has become a popular metaphor for being deluded by a charismatic leader.

You say to-may-to, I say to-mah-to, you say cult, I say new religious movement

It may have crossed your mind that some of the millenarian groups you've heard of are actually examples of "cults," not "real" religious denominations. However, experts in religious studies are usually not too comfortable with that term because it implies more of a negative judgment of the group than a concrete description of it. In other words, people often apply the label *cult* to religious movements they simply don't like. And even when they try to come up with a more neutral definition of the term, they'll usually just list a lot of qualities — like complete trust in a charismatic leader, or rigid indoctrination and control of followers — that they just don't like in a religion (or don't even recognize in their own tradition!). It can be a powerful tool in public debate, too. What better way to argue that a religious group doesn't deserve certain religious freedoms (like practicing rituals that may otherwise be against the law) or tax exemptions than to argue that it's simply a cult?

A less judgmental, more descriptive term is *new religious movement* (NRM). This term levels the playing field, so to speak, in that you may be more likely to take the group seriously and learn something accurate about it without prejudice. This doesn't say that you can't eventually make your own moral judgments — people do that all the time, and no one's going to stop you. It just encourages you to get better informed before you do so. First, find out what they believe — not just about the end of the world, but about the "big picture," *including* millenarianism. And then find out *why* they believe these things, and how that influences the ways they live. After all, every established religion was an NRM once, and many of them (like Christianity) also encountered a lot of hostility in their early days. But in one way, the fact that people frequently do use the term *cult* is quite instructive. It reminds us that one reality almost any NRM faces is that, regardless of whether it's profound or dysfunctional, whether it deals with gods or flying saucers, you can be sure at least some people somewhere will greet it with suspicion. For one colorful example, members of an unusual, but intelligent Unitarian Universalist offshoot — the tiny First Existentialist Congregation of Atlanta — good-naturedly report that they sometimes have to explain to neighbors that they don't engage in any cultish activities, even though most of their practices are pretty down to Earth.

And you can bet that even before the Way of Great Peace began the Yellow Turbans rebellion, plenty of Chinese were nervous about the Way of Great Peace and the Way of the Celestial Masters, two new millennial religious movements that promised to shake up the way people saw the world.

✔ **The Branch Davidians:** This small group is primarily known for its nearly two-month standoff with the federal government in 1993, which ultimately left more than 80 people dead, including their leader, David Koresh. What people don't usually remember is that the group was a breakaway sect from the Seventh Day Adventists, and shared the Adventists' millennial beliefs. The Davidians still exist today, though they're still a small group, and there have been repeated struggles over leadership and control of property.

✔ **Christian Identity:** This is an umbrella term for several American white supremacist groups, whose understanding of *armageddon* (the final battle between good and evil that will occur during the "end times") is that it will be a "race war" for control of the United States.

As you may have noticed, many millenarian groups are controversial in the broader community. This actually makes a lot of sense, because such groups usually emerge during trying times, interpret the times as unstable, prophesy the coming of difficult times, or long to return to an imagined golden age of the past, all of which can pose a serious challenge to those who are more invested in the status quo and finding stability in their lives. And although it's certainly not true of all of them, many millenarian groups do anticipate some type of violent struggle, which also has a tendency to make others get a little nervous. As a result, millenarian groups sometimes try to separate themselves from the mainstream, developing independent, closely knit communities. On the other hand, most millenarians simply don't last too long or develop ways to "domesticate" their teachings so they can adapt themselves to mainstream culture, perhaps thinking of the new age more as coming sometime in the indefinite future.

More than crystals, incense, and aromatherapy

Because we're talking about new age movements, maybe we ought to talk for a minute about something in the modern West called the New Age Movement. Perhaps you've been to a new age bookstore, or have some friends you think of as kind of "new age-y," or like to listen to those repetitive (or hypnotic) new age musicians like Enya or the Paul Winter Consort. Mention the New Age Movement to your friends, and they'll probably think about any or all of the following:

✔ **Eclectic spiritual beliefs,** perhaps drawn from Native American or Asian traditions, mysticism, goddess worship, astrology, and so forth

✔ **Holistic health techniques,** like acupuncture, massage, aromatherapy, homeopathy, reflexology, and macrobiotics, among others

✔ **Asian-based physical-spiritual practices,** like yoga, transcendental meditation, Buddhist Zen or Insight Meditation, *t'ai-chi,* and *ch'i-kung*

✔ **Exotic objects,** like crystals, incense, rock gardens, sand sculpture, glass hummingbirds, and so on

✔ **General nonconformity,** like alternative dress, liberal (especially feminist) politics, vegetarianism, and suspicion of organized religion

From *The Outer Limits* to the New Age

If you'd like to take a look at an early New Age Movement document that really develops the millenarian vision, try a book called *est: The Steersman Handbook,* which was published in 1970 with the subtitle *Charts of the Coming Decade of Conflict.* This quasi-fictional, quasi-prophetic narrative describes how a coterie of visionary, compassionate, technologically adept, and computer-literate leaders — remember, this was more than two decades before the Internet — would soon usher in an era of a radically transformed humanity. These leaders, the "steersmen" of the book's title, would possess the unusual quality of "simulsense," a "nonlinear" way of thought and perception, which they could use to guide people to become "est people," participants in the coming "electronic social transformation" (though *est* stood for other things as well, including "eco-strategy-tactics"). The book envisioned a 50-year transformation from 1950 to 2000, with the 1976 presidential election — occurring at roughly the halfway point and identified as "Transit Zero" — marking a pivotal moment in human development. Pretty avant-garde stuff.

So, what New Age thinker came up with this vision of est? The author is listed as one L. Clark Stevens, but that was just so no one in the New Age Movement would know that it was really a man named Leslie Stevens, who had spent the last several years working in (gasp!) television, which certainly would've earned widespread suspicion (or scorn) from early New Agers! Stevens's best-known TV creation was the cult favorite *The Outer Limits,* which ran from 1963 through 1965 (though he quit after the first year) and invited its viewers to "experience the awe and mystery which reaches from the inner mind to the outer limits." With its over-the-top monsters, gothic cinematography, and futuristic morality plays, *The Outer Limits* presented a feverish vision of a world ricocheting through cosmic crises but ultimately veering toward some type of creative resolution in the world ahead. Watch it now, and you'll find that many of the gritty black-and-white episodes are laced with a surreal millenarianism, like when the alien visitor in the pilot episode rhapsodizes on a young Cliff Robertson's request for theological edification: "Electromagnetic forces underlying all; electromagnetic force is intelligent. Matter, space, time — all the same. Infinity is God . . . God, infinity . . . all the same."

But if you look at this list, there doesn't seem to be anything really "new age" about it. What most people don't know is that what we call the New Age Movement actually *began* in the early 1960s (though its roots go back substantially earlier) as an explicitly millenarian movement, with lots of literature discussing some imminent transformation of human consciousness, sometimes linked to anticipated technological breakthroughs. Some thinkers who are deeply steeped in the movement still think in terms of a coming new age, but most people who have a passing familiarity with the movement — or even dabble in it from time to time — never think of it as millenarian. That's really quite the irony; the New Age Movement is barely a "new age" movement these days.

Some religious traditions or denominations are pretty much defined by their millenarianism, but others reinterpret their millennial qualities over time. So not only are there different types of millenarianism, but the traditions themselves may change from one type to another. And some traditions that begin as millenarian movements eventually let the "new age" aspect slip away altogether. The New Age Movement is one such new age movement.

The Peaks and Valleys of Taoist Millenarianism

As is the case with many Western traditions, Taoism goes through periods where the millenarian element dominates, and others where you'd scarcely know it was ever a new age movement. So, does that mean that Taoism is or is not a millenarian religion? That's hard to say. If you talk about the early Way of the Celestial Masters and the Way of Great Peace, you'll never really understand their social organizations or trademark practices — the healing techniques, the public confession of sins, the priestly hierarchy, the military rebellions — unless you consider the millenarian motivations behind it all. On the other hand, when you look today at monks practicing variations of inner alchemy or priests performing rituals to cajole the protection of a particular spirit, it's hard to find how those fit with new age ideas. But to some extent, it doesn't really matter. Just as the idea of the uncarved block might apply to classical Taoist philosophy but not to later Taoist liturgical practices, millenarianism permeates some aspects of religious Taoism but not others (and certainly not the classical texts).

In this section, I take you through the peaks and valleys of Taoist millenarianism, keeping an eye out for moments when it really defined the tradition, but also noting when its role and influence were more subtle. You'll get a feel for the basic characteristics of Taoist millenarianism, the messianic aspects of that millenarianism, and the marks that it eventually left on Chinese religion in general.

The earmarks of Taoist new age beliefs

The Way of the Celestial Masters and the Way of Great Peace (also known as the Yellow Turbans) shared a basic belief that the prevailing Han Dynasty was beyond moral repair and that the entire social structure needed to be replaced with a radically new one. They didn't have exactly the same vision — the Celestial Masters imagined the new world as governed by the Covenant of Orthodox Unity, while the Way of Great Peace conceived of it as the human parallel to the cosmic transition from the old "Blue Heaven" period to the new "Yellow Heaven" period — but their general ideas about the new age's causes, timing, and communal organizations had much in common.

Though the original Celestial Masters community lasted only a couple of generations, and the Yellow Turbans Rebellion ultimately failed (after causing turmoil in much of China), for several hundred years, millenarian ideas and literature still influenced the scattered and regrouped Taoist remnants (occasionally popping up in short-lived rebellions), as well as some of the newly formed self-cultivation cliques. The following themes seem to be the most important and recur most often:

- **A millenarian calendar:** Taoist millennial thinkers envisioned a cycle of eons, each one rising, falling, and giving way to the next in line. Texts from the Highest Purity and Numinous Treasure revelations even give names to the earlier cosmic eras: Draconian Magnificence, Extended Vigor, Vermilion Brilliance, Opening Luminary, and Higher Luminary. Of course, they thought the current one was about to end.

- **Natural disasters:** Taoist millenarian texts warned that the beginning of the end would be marked by disruptions in the weather, floods, massive fires, drought and famine, and widespread illness. The *Tao Te Ching* may sound may sound like a peaceful plea for returning to simpler times, but the later Taoist millennials really imagined an apocalypse.

- **Political and social disasters:** The millenarians imagined that all the natural disasters would be accompanied by human disasters as well. For every flood or fire, there would also be family collapse, crime, government oppression of the people, unfair trials and punishments, war, and invasions by barbarians.

- **Dangerous spirits:** Taoist millenarians didn't think all these disasters just happened to spring up out of the blue. They thought that the moral decline of humankind triggered restless, violent actions from spirits of the dead and titanic armies of malevolent demons. This may have been the medieval Taoist equivalent of a zombie apocalypse!

- **The Kingdom of Great Peace:** Most of the Taoist millenarian literature spends more time warning of the apocalypse than describing the new age, but the texts do use the "Great Peace" terminology (that both the Celestial Masters and Yellow Turbans used) to describe the new world. The bits and pieces they offer is that it will contain an egalitarian community of healthy people who had followed the appropriate liturgies, rejected corrupt unorthodox cults, and recruited followers to join the cause.

Traces of Taoist messianism

One aspect of Taoist millenarianism that you probably didn't anticipate — or maybe you did by this point — is the belief in a messiah, a saving figure who will emerge either just before or at the beginning of the age of Great Peace, to lead the new earthly kingdom. And who was the messiah described in the millenarian literature and awaited by various and sundry Taoists? The name you hear most often is one Li Hung (or Li Chen-chün, Perfected Lord Li). Doesn't sound familiar? His mythology may or may not have started out this way, but fairly early on, the Taoists identified him with — you guessed it — another form of the deified Lao Tzu. Or more accurately, they equated him with Lord Lao, the personification of the Tao, creator god, and source of many revealed scriptures.

As a messianic figure, Li Hung takes on many of Lao Tzu's and Lord Lao's qualities, but it's especially interesting how some Taoist texts imagine him as having undergone a series of incarnations for the purpose of imparting a sequence of revelations, all of which are supposed to lead up to the final appearance and new age. Though this doesn't match up particularly well with actual chronology, some texts specify that Li Hung — that is, the upgraded deified Lao Tzu — not only facilitated the beginnings of the universe, but also manifested on Earth at the following times and for the following reasons:

- At the end of the Chou Dynasty, in the late 3rd century B.C.E., he appeared on Earth to reveal the *Scripture of Great Peace.* It's not clear if the text they meant is the same one (actually two) that exists in the Taoist Canon, but it was almost certainly a new age manifesto.

- Sometime after this, he appeared again to reveal the *Tao Te Ching.* Because we know most of the *Tao Te Ching* goes back at least a bit earlier, this is one place where we know the chronology to be a little mangled.

- In the middle of the 2nd century C.E., he revealed the Orthodox Unity covenant to Chang Tao-ling, officially kicking off the Way of the Celestial Masters Movement.

- After this, he became the Buddha, but explained through the Taoist language of postmortem immortality. This didn't seem to do much for the story, except to take a dig at Buddhism at a time when the two traditions were in competition. Some versions of this story have Li Hung instructing the gatekeeper (the guy who urged him to write the *Tao Te Ching*) to become the Buddha.

The next rebirth of Li Hung is supposed to occur at the beginning of the new era, in the aftermath of all the disasters (which he himself had supposedly prophesied). And how will Li Hung rule the theocracy, as the manifest *Tao* and reincarnation of Lao Tzu? Well, they don't talk much about that. But just when you think this Taoist millenarianism couldn't be farther from classical

Taoism, records seem to indicate that people expecting the Taoist apocalypse believed that Li would govern by non-doing *(wu-wei),* and that the people would be able to follow through a kind of effortless naturalness, regardless of whatever rules they had to observe and rituals they had to perform.

The figure of Lao Tzu underwent several transitions, first from historical author of the *Tao Te Ching* to personification of the *Tao* and revealer of sacred scriptures, and then to a Taoist messiah referred to as Li Hung.

The legacy of Taoist millenarianism

I think you'd be hard-pressed to say that either of the two existing branches of Chinese Taoism — Orthodox Unity and Complete Perfection — has especially pronounced millenarian aspects. Part of that is that you really need a whole *community* of followers for any millenarian beliefs to matter much. And with Chinese syncretism, most people simply pick and choose which Taoist resources they find helpful, and that doesn't usually entail digging into the Canon and pulling out millenarian scriptures! But Taoist millenarianism left its mark on Chinese religion more broadly — some scholars even think that the Chinese have such a natural penchant for thinking in those terms that it will keep coming back in one form or another sooner or later. Regardless, there are some specific ways that you can see the Taoist millenarian or messianic legacy over time:

- ✔ **Imperial legitimacy:** Some Chinese dynasties, or individual emperors, justified their rule by claiming messianic authority. Some of them capitalized on having the surname Li, which they could use to assert that they were themselves living incarnations (or descendants) of Li Hong.

- ✔ **Millenarian societies and rebellions:** Several later secret societies and rebellions may not have been Taoist per se, but they made some use of ideas from Taoist millenarian texts. Although something like Sun En's 4th-century rebellion is an obvious example, you may also want to take a look at the 19th-century T'ai-p'ing Rebellion, which actually espoused a garbled version of Christian doctrine and took a highly anti-Taoist (and anti-Buddhist) posture. And yet, they yanked the name Great Peace *(t'ai-p'ing)* and the whole idea of a new age from Taoism.

- ✔ **Popular (or false) messiahs:** Just as Christianity and Judaism have had several times in their respective histories when people claimed to be the messiah, sometimes with the support of many followers (but always rejected by the religious authority at the time), Taoism had its share of Li Hungs showing up within grassroots movements. Many of these self-proclaimed prophets earned both mistrust from the government and scorn from the Celestial Masters leadership, which together could result in execution. Most of these self-styled Li Hungs arose during the first millennium C.E., but one was executed as recently as about 900 years ago.

✔ **Absorption into Buddhism millenarianism:** In some ways, Taoist millenarianism found expression in Buddhist beliefs and movements, which already had a ready-made messiah built into their doctrine. The Buddhists believed in the coming of the "future Buddha," a Buddha named Maitreya (Mi-lo, in Chinese) who would come to Earth at a time of moral decline when the Buddha's wisdom wasn't being well transmitted. The image of Mi-lo combines with another folk figure, to form an image you've probably seen countless times in Chinese restaurants: the pot-bellied laughing Buddha!

From Millenarian Movements to the New Age Movement

Taoism often influenced and was influenced by other Chinese religious traditions, but it hasn't quite played that same role in America. Although Taoism has prompted Western fascination for at least a century, it's hard to make a case that it's had any noticeable influence on the major Western religious traditions. Truth be told, you don't find many Taoist deities influencing the representations of angels and Catholic saints, or the Taoist concept of *Tao* changing the way Christian theologians understand God, or much reading of the *Tao Te Ching* in a Muslim mosque. But if there's one tradition — using the term loosely — that has been hospitable to Taoism, it would have to be the New Age Movement, which has eagerly gobbled up all sorts of Eastern wisdom, often mixing the ingredients together into a lively spiritual stew. One really fascinating coincidence, which you may not pick up on at first glance, is that the New Age Movement embraced a tradition that began in China as — what else? — a new age movement.

In this section, I talk about Taoism's place in the contemporary New Age Movement, explaining which Taoist features and practices have (and haven't) become popular in New Age circles and pointing out an amusing irony about this particular meeting of different traditions.

The place of Taoism and Taoist millenarianism in New Age thought

Because the New Age Movement is more an umbrella catch-all than a specific organized tradition, there isn't one New Age creed, practice, or service that we can check out to look for Taoist influences. A better approach would simply be to "follow the money" — that is, to look at popular New Age literature or New Age retreat centers and communities (like the Esalen Institute and Breitenbush Hot Springs), and see what sorts of Taoist elements show up with any regularity. Here's a list of some common New Age Taoist (not Taoist New Age!) themes:

- **Philosophy of *Tao*:** Many New Age sources embrace the notion of the *Tao,* though they'll usually interchange it pretty easily with other "big" ideas like Buddha or brahman (from Hinduism) or "ultimate concern." They especially seem to like the vague, wordless quality of the *Tao,* and the way that knowing the *Tao* translates into a kind of humble simplicity. Gia-fu Feng and Jane English's popular translation of the *Tao Te Ching* reflects a New Age reading of the text.

- ***T'ai-chi, chi-kung,* and similar practices:** If you're lucky, you can probably find someone at your local church, synagogue, or recreation center to teach you *t'ai-chi,* but you can pretty much guarantee success if you look at a bulletin board at a New Age bookstore or check the event schedule at a New Age retreat center.

- **Other vaguely Taoist health practices:** Many New Age-ers find the basic philosophy and health-based practice simpatico with a range of Chinese practices that aren't necessarily (or particularly) Taoist, like acupuncture, *feng-shui,* and herbalism. They tend to understand all these practices as bound up in a Taoist worldview.

- **Taoist self-help:** New Age workshops often repackage Taoist (and other) teachings into various self-help programs, often borrowing resources from disciplines as far afield as Jungian psychology and physics. One West Coast teacher markets this combination under the name "process work."

- **Taoist sex:** Well, if not exactly sexual encounter groups, some workshops have a kind of touchy-feely approach, integrating massage and other body work with theories of *ch'i* or inner alchemy.

In short, the New Age embraces much of what passes as Taoism in the West, mainly a mix of spiritualized classical philosophy, health practices, and variants of *t'ai-chi* or meditation. It pretty much ignores the more "ethnic" aspects of Taoism, like deities in the Taoist pantheon, rituals on behalf of the dead, and most of the thousand-plus texts in the Taoist Canon. If New Age thinkers know about Taoist millenarian beliefs and cults, those don't seem to have penetrated into the New Age Taoist consciousness at all.

Two New Age movements without any new age

So why are we even talking about Taoist millenarianism and the New Age Movement if they have nothing to do with each other? Not a bad question. It's really because the irony is quite delicious. On the one hand, the New Age Movement began as a new age movement, a millenarian philosophy that anticipated a radical transformation of human consciousness, which perhaps might be expressed or symbolized by all the crystals, goddesses, and astrological imagery. But most people, probably even most New Age dabblers and enthusiasts, have no idea — or don't really care — about the new age history of the movement. Instead, they know the spiritual philosophy, the literature, and the trappings.

And on the other hand, the social history of Taoism in China also began as a new age movement. The successful spread of both the Celestial Masters and the Way of Great Peace owed mainly to their millenarian appeal (and also to their track record on healing, to be fair), and they understood both Lao Tzu and the *Tao Te Ching* in purely millenarian terms. But similarly, few Chinese, and even fewer Americans, know about these communities and the millennial legacies they left behind.

But somehow, these two *de-millennialized* (if that's even a word) phenomena found each other. A loose Western alliance of spiritual thinkers and seekers with largely forgotten millenarian roots has taken an extensive interest in a Chinese tradition with millenarian roots, without knowing about those roots. The New Age Movement and religious Taoism both began as millennialists, but both have mostly left their millennialism behind.

The Taoist empire strikes back

Because the New Age Movement draws freely from multiple religious traditions and sources, you occasionally see some pushback from people who claim "ownership" of those traditions and don't feel particularly flattered that stuff from their bailiwick gets lifted without permission, taken apart, and put back together in a sometimes unrecognizable form. You've probably heard from time to time about some Native Americans who express dismay when other people appropriate (or misappropriate) their art, music, or religious rituals.

For the most part, practicing Taoists in China and other Asian countries haven't paid much attention to how Taoism has been transformed in the West, but once in a while you'll hear from someone who's protective of Taoism and critical of the New Age Movement. For example, Mak Jo Si, the co-owner of the Chi in Nature Taoist Temple in Markham, Ontario — which offers services in martial arts, exorcism, and "Taoist magic" — has publically dismissed the New Age Movement as a glorified self-help movement that makes shallow and superficial use of Taoism. He cautions enthusiasts that if they really want Taoism, they're not going to find it in the New Age Movement, which will only lead to disaster . . . though he doesn't specify if that disaster will be anything like what millenarians have in mind!

Chapter 12

Writing What Can't Be Spoken: The Many Texts of Taoism

*E*ven people who don't know much about religion have a pretty good idea that just about every tradition has to have some kind of sacred scripture. I mean, what kind of religion can it be if it doesn't have an authoritative account of its own history, a list of divine commandments, and so forth? What's more, many people can probably tick off each major tradition's sacred texts. It's a basic tidbit from any introductory class in world religion that Jews read the Hebrew Bible, Christians read the Old and New Testaments, Muslims read the Qur'an, and Taoists read the *Tao Te Ching,* right?

What's more, you may have some expectations about what sort of things appear in such texts and how participants in the specific traditions use them. After all, Jews, Christians, and Muslims all seem to look to their respective texts to try to understand God's will on any of a number of moral issues. They read the books for inspiration and comfort, they employ them during worship services, and people elected to Congress take the oath of office with their hands on their chosen texts. And they take seriously — though sometimes with considerable interpretation — what those texts say about God, creation, and the divine plan for the universe.

But when you dig more deeply into any one tradition, you start to discover that the matter of scripture can be a little more complicated. There may be more than just the one text you already know, or the contents may sound almost nothing like those of the Bible, or participants in the tradition may use the texts in ways you'd never imagined. In this chapter, I take you on a tour through Taoist sacred literature. You get a sense of what sorts of writings the Taoists consider sacred, how they compiled their canon, and how they use the texts in that canon.

The Tangled World of Taoist Literature

Just say the words *Taoist* and *text* in the same sentence, and many people put them together and immediately think of the *Tao Te Ching*. They may even come up with the *Chuang Tzu*, too. And — who knows? — maybe the *Lieh Tzu* or the *Huai Nan Tzu*. I suppose there could be a ringer who mentions something really obscure, like *Hsi K'ang and His Poetic Essay on the Lute*. Or perhaps *The Tao of Pooh* and *The Te of Piglet*, or any of the dozens of other "*Tao of*" books that pop up as reliably as spring daffodils.

Because the *Tao Te Ching* and the *Chuang Tzu* are easily the best known Taoist texts in the West, it's tempting to imagine that they are also the most *important* Taoist texts. And because you don't hear too much about many other Taoist texts — when was the last time you heard someone mention the *Obscure Essays on the Supreme Cultivation of the True* or *Requisite Knowledge for the Alchemical Laboratory?* — you may also think that Taoists work with a fairly small and manageable pool of scripture. As it turns out, both assumptions don't hold water.

In this section, I set straight some of these basic misconceptions about Taoist literature. You'll find out some surprising details about the role of the *Tao Te Ching* and the *Chuang Tzu,* and get a glimpse into the *enormity* of the Taoist literary corpus.

Setting the record straight on Lao Tzu and Chuang Tzu

The *Tao Te Ching* and *Chuang Tzu* are, indeed, important Taoist texts, but the Chinese have traditionally read and employed them in ways different from the individualistic, spiritualized interpretations that dominate Western readings of Taoism. First, just as Jews and Christians have historically relied heavily on commentaries to figure out how to interpret the Bible and apply it to their lives — the amusing recent book *The Year of Living Biblically,* by A. J. Jacobs (Simon & Schuster), points out how no one, *absolutely no one,* actually follows the "uninterpreted" Bible — Taoists also have their books linked to a rich and varied commentarial tradition. In fact, dozens of authoritative commentaries on the *Tao Te Ching* and *Chuang Tzu* exist, and they sometimes say some surprising things and don't always agree with one another. Here's a random sampling:

✔ **Hsiang-er Commentary on the Lao Tzu:** This treats the *Tao Te Ching* mainly as a text on cultivating the body. It talks about the *Tao* that lives in the human body, a Heavenly bureaucracy that records human acts of immorality, and the preservation of sexual energy.

✔ ***Straightforward Explication of the True Scripture of the Way and Its Power:*** This text sees Lao Tzu as advocating austere practices similar to those in Buddhism, leading to a "great emptiness" that transcends the distinctions between "being" and "non-being."

✔ ***General Purport of the Anthology of Commentaries on the True Scripture of the Way and Its Power:*** This text contains, among other things, charts and diagrams that illustrate the cosmic and physical locations of spirits of the human body. It offers a kind of translator's guide, which matches up key phrases in the *Tao Te Ching* to different organs, like relating the "mysterious female" to the kidneys.

✔ ***Collected Subtleties from the Sea of Meanings of the True Scripture of Southern Fluorescence:*** This text collects several different readings of the *Chuang Tzu*, including some that portray the ultimate goal as dissolving all beings into an undifferentiated unity, and that take special time to trash internal alchemy and physical exercises directed toward the cultivation of *ch'i.*

In short, Taoist "insiders" never really read the *Tao Te Ching* and *Chuang Tzu* in isolation — they almost always tied them to a much more extensive set of literature and practices, usually involving highly specialized language and coded exercises. That is, they function as *ingredients,* not "gospel," in the complicated process of transmitting and realizing the *Tao.* What's more — and this is the real shocker — although Taoists officially acknowledge more than 200 works of philosophy and commentary, those actually make up a relatively small fraction of their sacred scripture. In speaking about religion in general, the important 19th-century scholar Max Müller once said, "He who knows one, knows none." More than a century later, he may as well have been talking about Taoism and Taoist texts. As far as Taoist practitioners are concerned, if you know only one Taoist text, you don't really know any.

The *Tao Te Ching* and *Chuang Tzu,* the Taoist texts known best in the West, are not representative of the broader spectrum of Taoist texts.

Picking through a mysterious and unwieldy body of scriptures

As you may be starting to figure out by now, there are *lots* of Taoist sacred texts, and understanding any one of them probably requires familiarity with technical language, fluency in the intellectual background, experience with particular practices, and training or initiation from a qualified teacher. Perhaps more than the missionary bias against superstition and ritual, this helps explain why so little Taoist material has actually been translated into English.

In short, if you were to look at some random Taoist text — without explanations of its context and detailed, step-by-step annotations of the various historical, theological, liturgical, alchemical, and physiological references — you just wouldn't have a clue what it's talking about. But don't feel too bad about it. Even China experts who don't specialize in that particular aspect of Taoism probably wouldn't understand it either. And come to think of it, even *with* all those expert explanations and annotations, it wouldn't be a piece of cake.

Taoist texts number in the hundreds — actually, well over a thousand — and they cover an enormous range of subjects, including alchemy (see Chapter 5) and *physical cultivation* (the training of the body for biological and spiritual benefits), medicine and diet, *cosmological diagrams and speculation* (describing and mapping the structure of the universe), and biographies of sages and immortals. But far and away, the majority of Taoist texts, around 800 of them, reflect the priorities of two millennia of Taoist practitioners and don't really describe or communicate data for the reader; that is, they're not mainly explanations or interpretations of ideas or histories. Mostly, they're what you could call *operative* or *instrumental texts;* they're texts that adepts employ in specific ritual or liturgical situations with the understanding that they possess some kind of performative power. That's why you need to be properly initiated to have access to ritual secrets — this can be serious, even dangerous stuff, and the guardians of the tradition don't usually treat such matters lightly. So, what kinds of instrumental texts are they, and how do Taoists use them? Here are the main types:

- ✔ **Ritual formulas** to be recited as part of specific rituals
- ✔ **Hymns** to be chanted during specific rituals
- ✔ **Petitions** to be read and "delivered" to Heaven or specific deities
- ✔ **Instructions** on how to meditate or what to visualize during rituals

Most Taoist scripture isn't like the Bible, as much as it's like the contents of a prayer book, or a catalogue of Wiccan spells, or even an operator's manual for negotiating with spirits. These texts are important for what they can do, not exclusively what they say.

The Development of the Taoist Canon

All the recognized Taoist scriptures are assembled in a vast collection called the Taoist Canon *(Tao-tsang). Canon* is the term that people frequently use to describe a body of literature that a tradition recognizes as authoritative. Along these same lines, traditions establish the texts that belong in the canon by *canonizing* them, they regard works in the canon as *canonical,* and they regard works not in the canon (which may still be important) as *extracanonical.*

As you may expect, Taoism has its own idiosyncratic story when it comes to its canon. In this section, I bring you up to speed on that story. You get to know how the many Taoist texts came to be part of the Taoist Canon, what systems have been used for classifying those texts, how the Ming Dynasty established a more or less permanent canon, and what type of progress modern scholars have made in the truly daunting task of sorting the texts, translating them into English, and making them available and accessible to a Western audience.

The process of canonization

Some traditions may passively encourage a general understanding that their sacred scripture suddenly materialized all at once, like a fully written (and fully bound) text handed to the people directly from God, but almost all religious canons have actually taken shape through elaborate and lengthy historical circumstances. For example, during the first few centuries after the death of Jesus, quite literally *hundreds* of different gospel accounts were in circulation, some in particular regions, some among particular sectarian groups, and some offering very different representations of Jesus. It was well into the 4th century before church leaders — the equivalent of a college of cardinals — convened a council largely for the purpose of deciding which texts qualified as authoritative, and which were inaccurate or even heretical. From their findings, they established the collection of short histories and letters we now know as the New Testament. In Buddhism, monks and nuns, who preserved and transmitted the Buddha's teachings orally for a few hundred years, held several councils where they debated, among other things, the authenticity of competing versions of those teachings. Even in Islam, which views the Qur'an as nothing less than a divinely revealed text, Muslims understand that God didn't deliver the book overnight, but that Muhammad received revelations for decades.

In other words, each canon has a particular history, and each tradition had its own cast of specific historical figures who were recognized for one reason or another as having authority to determine the makeup of that canon. The Taoist Canon also has its own unique story, but it is (of course) a lot different from the Christian, Buddhist, and Muslim stories. Here are a few of the most important things to keep in mind:

- ✔ There have actually been several Taoist Canons, compiled at different times over Chinese history, sometimes several hundred years apart.
- ✔ Almost every version of the Canon was commissioned by the emperor, usually for the purpose of cataloguing a comprehensive list of Taoist texts in use and reinforcing imperial sponsorship of (and authority over) the tradition.

✔ Because there have been numerous collections, it may be helpful to think of the Taoist Canon as an *open* canon, kind of a like a textual amoeba with fluid contents and borders.

✔ Sometimes, the decision about what made it in or what got kicked out could be traced to sectarian differences or even competition with other traditions. One time, they tossed several dozen anti-Buddhist texts.

✔ Because the Canons represented comprehensive lists of Taoist texts in use, the materials ultimately came from different sources, lineages, and regions. So, it's extraordinarily unlikely that any single Taoist has ever employed every text in the Canon. In fact, apart from the person or persons doing the compiling and review, probably very few Taoists have ever read the whole thing from cover to cover.

Try to think of the Taoist Canon more as a diverse collection than a unified work. When you read any text in the Canon, you can't really make sense of it until you first identify its source, what kind of text it is, who originally used it and how, why it's in the Canon, and so on. And try not to get too frustrated — it really is an overwhelming body of material.

The Three Caverns compilation

The most important of the early Taoist compilations, which began in the 5th century, involved sorting the existing Taoist texts into three categories, called *caverns,* a division that would last through pretty much all later versions of the Canon. The use of the term *caverns* — some scholars prefer to translate it as *arcana* — captures the sense of unearthing some mysterious repository of power and wisdom through an inward journey, though some texts also suggest that the caverns corresponded to Heavenly layers or realms. Either way, there's also a good chance that the Taoists took a cue from the Buddhists, who already had a well-defined three-part textual canon, though the contents of the respective caverns didn't really correspond in any way to those of the Buddhist divisions.

So, how did these Three Caverns work? Here's a summary of the divisions and the basic contents of each:

✔ **The Cavern of Perfection:** This section included texts from the Highest Purity *(Shang-ch'ing)* revelations, mostly on alchemy, meditation, and visualization. Although the Complete Perfection lineage would not come into existence for another several hundred years, it's interesting to notice that the Chinese term translated as "perfection" is the same for both the cavern and the lineage.

✔ **The Cavern of Mystery:** This section included texts from the Numinous Treasure *(Ling-pao)* revelations, mostly instructions on how to perform public rituals, as well as liturgical formulas to be read during the actual ceremonies.

✔ **The Cavern of Spirit:** This section included texts from a tradition called the "Three Sovereigns," which didn't survive much beyond the formation of the Three Caverns. It probably involved things like talismans for calling on or drawing power from various deities.

If this seems relatively easy to keep track of, you may as well enjoy the feeling while it lasts. A century or two after Taoists established the Three Caverns, they added what they called "Four Supplements" or "Four Auxiliaries," possibly corresponding to stages of ordination and ritual transmission in the Way of the Celestial Masters, to create a seven-part canonical structure, where each part still corresponded to a different historical lineage. Here are the Four Supplements and their contents:

✔ **Great Mystery:** This section included (hooray!) the *Tao Te Ching,* later philosophical works, and various commentaries.

✔ **Great Peace:** This section included the Scripture of Great Peace, or at least one version of it, which had been one of the blueprints for the first millenarian Taoist groups.

✔ **Great Purity:** This section included texts from the Great Purity *(T'ai-ch'ing)* revelations, mostly on alchemy and other physical cultivation practices.

✔ **Orthodox Unity:** This section included scriptures on the precepts and rituals of the Way of the Celestial Masters. Much of this material may have been relatively new at the time, but it was attributed to Chang Tao-ling's original revelations.

And just in case you're still managing to keep all these straight, the Taoists then added a dozen subdivisions that they called "categories" within each Cavern and Supplement. So, every individual text was catalogued within a category, and that category fell within either a cavern or a supplement. The Twelve Categories are as follows:

✔ Basic Writings

✔ Spiritual Talismans

✔ Secret Instructions

✔ Numinous Charts

✔ Genealogies and Registers

✔ Precepts and Regulations

✔ Ceremonial Liturgies

✔ Techniques and Methods

✔ Miscellaneous Arts

✔ Records and Biographies

✔ Praises and Eulogies

✔ Memorials and Announcements

Finally, this is as good a time as any to point out how the Taoists eventually identified the Three Caverns as corresponding to the primary triad of Taoist deities. Though the various Canons wouldn't always agree on the exact details, they did understand that the Three Pure Ones — Heavenly Worthy of the Primordial Beginning, Heavenly Worthy of Numinous Treasure, and Heavenly Worthy of the Way and Its Power — presided over three Heavens and had been responsible for revealing the scriptures in the respective Caverns.

The importance of the Ming Canon

When people refer to "the Taoist Canon," they're almost always thinking of the canon produced during the early part of the Ming Dynasty, the second-to-last historic Chinese dynasty. The Ming Canon was the last of the various Taoist Canons, and it's the only one to survive intact. So, in that sense, it's the *existing* Taoist Canon, the canon of the living Taoist traditions. It's also likely to maintain its distinction as the *final* canon, although the future of China is always unpredictable, so there's really no certainty that circumstances won't conspire to add more texts to it, shave off a few, or produce a whole new compilation project. But at least for now, this is it.

History records that in the early 15th century, the third Ming emperor commissioned Chang Yü-ch'u, who was both the 43rd Celestial Master and the Chinese version of a renaissance man, to gather and edit an exhaustive collection of all Taoist books in circulation. Chang located books from various sources, edited them as he saw fit, and then presented them to an imperial panel that reviewed the submissions and gave them either a thumbs up or a thumbs down. Although both the emperor and Chang died before he could complete the project — which continued on and off for nearly four decades — a subsequent Ming emperor eventually approved a final version of the canon, had multiple copies printed, and circulated them among important Taoist temples, centers, and training facilities.

A century or so later, yet another Ming emperor commissioned Chang Kuo-hsiang, the 50th Celestial Master, to locate texts not currently in the Canon that he felt should be added (or should have been there in the first place). After 20-odd years, this Chang came up with several dozen more documents, which are now part of the Canon and sometimes identified separately as the Ming Canon Supplement. In short, the Ming Canon and Supplement basically defined what would remain the Taoist literary corpus up to this day.

Here are some basic facts and figures about the Ming Canon:

- Chang Yü-ch'u maintained the basic structure of the Three Caverns, Four Supplements, and Twelve Categories, though he noodled quite a bit with what went where, probably for ideological reasons. As a result, the internal organization doesn't always make sense to non-Taoists.

- The Ming Canon totaled about 1,487 texts in all. Do I say "about" because no one has ever actually counted them? No, it's actually that it's just not always clear where one text officially ends and the next one begins. So, you may as well round it up to "about 1,500" texts. Either way, it's one *ginormous* collection.

- Among those nearly 1,500 texts, the Canon includes materials from some of the short-lived Taoist lineages that popped up in the 12th through 14th centuries. If not for this compilation, we'd probably know even less than we do about obscure groups like the Pure Tenuousness *(Ch'ing-wei)*, Pure Brightness *(Ch'ing-ming)*, and Spiritual Firmament *(Shen-hsiao)* sects.

The Taoist Canon almost certainly excluded many texts that a number of practitioners must have regarded as authentic. Because of this, you may come across independent, unaffiliated teachers who claim to possess "unknown" Taoist texts that have been in their family for generations. So, are these the "real deal"? Unfortunately, there isn't one answer. Many of these texts have genuine connections to canonical texts and historic Taoist practices, and some may have really been passed down for centuries, and some no doubt are inventions of people interested in profit or self-promotion. It would be nice if there were some Taoist litmus test, but for the time being no one has invented one.

Reclamation projects: Cataloguing the Canon

The Ming Taoist Canon *almost* joined all its predecessors as a lost collection. The last Chinese Dynasty, the Manchu-run Ch'ing, was generally hostile to

Taoism. The Confucian literati — the same ones who fed so much misinformation about Taoism to the European missionary scholars — didn't hold back their contempt for Taoist institutions and practices as perpetuating backward superstition. The death knell nearly sounded during the Boxer Rebellion in 1900, when the Great Radiant Light Pavilion — the Taoist temple that contained the printing blocks for the Ming Canon — was destroyed by gunfire. This very well could have been it for Taoist scripture.

Fortunately, not long after the demise of the Ch'ing Dynasty and the founding of the Republic of China in 1912, the Chinese government took steps to reproduce and preserve the Canon. Working from copies of texts in the White Cloud Monastery, it produced a miniaturized version of the Canon through a process called *photolithography,* and published a thread-bound version of it in 1926. Since then, other editions have been published in both China and Taiwan, including a 49-volume version by the Chinese Taoist Association. Of course, all these versions have been in Chinese and include no helpful explanations of historical context. For at least a while, they've remained pretty impenetrable to Western audiences and to Chinese non-specialists.

One hugely important step in making this material more accessible to the English-speaking world is the monumental publication in 2004 of *The Taoist Canon.* Edited by top-flight scholars Kristofer Schipper and Franciscus Verellen, and involving nearly 30 other scholars for nearly 30 years, this three-volume collection testifies to the sheer enormity of the volume of textual material — it's only an annotated index to the Taoist Canon, not a translation of it. Yes, you heard right! This 1,637-page collection is not an actual translation of the Canon, but a scholarly guide to each and every text. Still, don't be disappointed — this work represents a giant step for anyone who wants to try to begin navigating a truly intimidating body of scripture.

The Taoist Canon is itself pretty intimidating, but when you figure out the general organization, you can use it *encyclopedically* — that is, not as a book to read from front to back, but as a reference book when you want to know about particular texts, periods, sects, and so forth. In the interest of intelligibility and continuity, the editors don't follow the traditional Cavern-Supplement-Category structure; instead, they develop their own system, though not every Taoism scholar today will agree with the way they've sliced and diced the cataloguing of texts. The most important distinction they make is to divide all the texts into two categories, in part because the scholars employed different research tools to study them:

- ✔ **Books in general circulation:** These include texts written for a general audience, many of which may have circulated independently outside the Canon. Most of the materials written by historians, philosophers, doctors, diviners, geographers, and so forth fall into this category.

✓ **Books in internal circulation:** These include texts restricted to those with privileged "insider" access through initiation and ordination in a Taoist lineage. These texts, dealing with things like ritual, talismans, and registers, make up the majority of texts in the Canon. The irony is that now that the Canon has been published, the insider texts are available to everyone, but that doesn't make them any more understandable, and ordained Taoists aren't usually in any hurry to explain them.

When you're clear on this distinction, you'll have an easier time following the structure of the volumes. You may also want to keep in mind that although the title *The Taoist Canon* seems to use the same system as this book for transliterating Chinese names, the collection itself actually uses the *pinyin* system, so the names may not be immediately familiar to you. For example, Chang Tao-ling is suddenly going to appear as Zhang Daoling, and Ch'üan-chen (Complete Perfection) Taoism as Quanzhen — the kinds of changes that will really keep you on your Taoist toes. In any event, here's more or less what you can expect when you poke your nose into its pages:

✓ The first volume begins with a 50-page general introduction, not to Taoism, but to the history of the Taoist Canon and the project that produced this set.

✓ Most of the first two volumes contain text-by-text descriptions of each entry in the Canon. These are organized chronologically, with each period divided into texts in general circulation and texts in internal circulation. What's more, each of those categories is divided into several headings and subheadings, including such titles as "Didactic and Doctrinal Treatises, "Cosmogony and the Pantheon," "Lamp Rituals," and "Hymnology." These entries are really the "meat" of the work.

✓ The third volume begins with brief biographies of Taoists whose names show up frequently in earlier parts of the book. These aren't your basic classical philosophers like Lao Tzu and Chuang Tzu; they're Taoist adepts who authored commentaries or received revealed texts that appear in the Canon.

✓ The third volume also contains a bibliography running about 40 pages. Most of the references are in Chinese or Japanese, or come from pretty technical scholarly journals, but you may find some of them helpful if you want to trace the research on a particular topic.

✓ Finally, the third volume includes several indices, mostly listing all the texts in the Canon through several different methods: in line with the order in the previous two volumes, according to the order in the originally published Ming Canon, in alphabetical order (again, using the *pinyin* system), and cross-referenced to other editions of the Canon.

Firing off the canon: Scriptures and zucchini

If it seems a little too ethereal or touchy-feely to think of a canon as a body of sacred scripture, then maybe you can get a better handle on it if you think of it like food. That's right, food! One imaginative contemporary religious studies scholar suggested that a canon is like a community's basic diet, in that they both represent examples of cultural limitation.

What does this mean? If you think about it, when you look at all the different foods that an ethnic or regional group eats, you'll see that they actually make up a very small portion of edible foods. Americans eat cucumbers and sea scallops, but they don't generally eat sea cucumbers, a popular Chinese dish that actually looks a lot like an underwater slug. The same Americans who have no trouble eating pigs' ribs aren't usually wild about pigs' intestines. Likewise, the books in a canon represent a small percentage of all the books out there. In this way, limiting yourself to a small canon of authoritative texts is very similar to limiting yourself to a diet of edible foods. Both represent a community's voluntary act of limitation or restriction.

But on the other hand, the interpretation and application of canonical texts have a lot in common not with diet, but with cuisine — both represent forms of cultural variation. Again, if you think about it, good cooks and chefs work with a limited pool of foods to produce an almost infinite array of combinations and variations. Zucchini may be the most boring food in the world, but you can grill it, stuff it, marinate it, mix it with tomatoes and eggplant for ratatouille, or shred it to make bread. Similarly, practitioners of a particular tradition often insist that they can apply their limited textual resources to any changing social situation. The authors of the Bible may not have known about embryonic stem cells, but that doesn't stop Jews and Christians from looking in the book for guidance on how to negotiate that thorny issue. In short, both the application of canon and the preparation of cuisine represent a community's act of variation or ingenuity, often requiring an expert — either clerical or culinary — to facilitate that expansion.

Canon is like food, and canon application is like cuisine? You may want to try chewing on that for a while.

Materials Found in the Taoist Canon

Obviously, with nearly 1,500 texts in the Taoist Canon, most of which are coded to be intelligible only to those trained and initiated into a specific lineage, and with even the English index to the Canon running more than 1,600 pages in length, it's probably not such a hot idea to try to do justice to all the contents in this single chapter. But on the other hand, it *is* possible to take some modest steps toward untangling those complicated scriptures.

In this section, I outline some of the main types of texts in the Taoist Canon, give a few examples of each, and offer up some interesting tidbits about their contents, function, or history.

Philosophies and commentaries

Even though the general thrust of the Taoist Canon is *liturgical* (that is, relating to rituals and ceremonies) rather than philosophical, it does include many philosophical texts from all periods of Chinese history. The foundational classical Taoist texts and their respective commentaries are all there, but you may also be a bit surprised to find that some unlikely outliers have found their way into the collection as well. Here's a sampling of some of the items in this category, including both the obvious entries and the "aliens":

- The main classical Taoist texts from the Hundred Schools Period through the Huang-Lao era of the Han Dynasty — the *Tao Te Ching, Chuang Tzu, Lieh Tzu, Huai Nan Tzu* — and dozens of commentaries on them.

- Other texts from the Hundred Schools Period that few people consider Taoist, like the self-titled works by Mo Tzu, the legalist Han Fei Tzu, the dialectician Kung-sun Lung-tzu, the political strategist Kuei Ku Tzu, and the syncretist Yü Tzu. In some cases, there are plausible connections between the texts and Taoism — for example, the *Han Fei Tzu* includes commentary chapters on the *Tao Te Ching* — but more often than not it's hard to figure out why Taoists included them.

- Independent later philosophical works, some of which are presented as companion pieces to earlier classical texts. One such text is the 8th-century *Arcane Principles of Master Tsung-hsüan*, which discusses the *Tao* and how it manifests in the universe, while advocating purification and concentration as ways to understand it. Another example is the *Scripture of Western Ascent*, a 5th-century document that represents itself as instructions that the historic Lao Tzu passed on to the gatekeeper before he disappeared off to the West.

- Commentaries on materials from different periods of Taoist revelations, like Highest Clarity, Numinous Treasure, and later Orthodox Unity texts. A bunch of these commentaries address the very first text to appear in the Ming Canon, the Numinous Treasure *Scripture on Salvation*.

Talismans and registers

Of all the scriptures in the Taoist Canon, instrumental texts like talismans and registers have probably drawn the least interest from Westerners who like their Taoist philosophy spiritualized and don't really get how a contemplative vision of spontaneity and returning to the *Tao* can have anything to do with texts meant to control, cajole, or ward off spirits. But texts like these often provide hints as to what's going on in Taoist esoteric practice and show just how much the West still has to learn about the living Taoist tradition.

Talismans are probably the hardest texts to read, because they often contain diagrams, symbols, or patterns that look like graphs, rather than literal text; when they do contain what appear to be regular Chinese characters, it's understood that their true meaning is accessible only to the deities who were believed to have bestowed the talismans sometime in the distant past. One of the most important historical talismans, the *Preface to the Five Numinous Treasure Talismans,* included recipes for longevity and other instructions, but it was mostly employed as an important ingredient in the performance of ritual. Here are some of the many functions of the various Taoist talismans:

- Conduits to Physical Healing
- Marking off Sacred Space
- Protection from Evil Spirits or General Dangers
- Assisting Safe Passage of the Dead
- Aids to Meditation
- Blueprints for Ritual Gestures

Registers are a lot like talismans, in that they deal with controlling deities, may contain symbols and drawings rather than words, and are intelligible only to initiated insiders. They also represent some of the earliest Taoist texts after the Classical Period, which go back to the original Way of the Celestial Masters. For the most part, they list deities that those possessing them can summon, and are conferred upon initiates in their stages of ordination. One typical register, *The Highest Purity Register of the Three Hundred and Sixty Five True and Divine Forces from the Nine Heavens in the Upper Origin of the Golden True Jade Emperor,* gives a sense of what territory they can cover.

Ritual texts and alchemical manuals

Although these should technically fall into two different categories — ritual texts relate to public ceremonies, and alchemical manuals relate to personal cultivation — both reflect the emphasis in the Taoist Canon on achieving some kinds of concrete, though cosmically significant, results through proper forms of practice. Some of these texts offer specific instructions on executing rituals or performing alchemical transformations, some are meant to be chanted or recited, and some contain mechanisms for directly petitioning deities. A number of these texts may come off as fairly straightforward, but most resemble talismans and registers, in that they employ language that's not easily understood by those who aren't Taoist adepts.

Most of the texts in the Canon relate to ritual or cultivation practices, and much of the material survives today, even if the actual texts aren't always employed in their entirety. To give you a taste for the range of practices these texts cover, here's a brief romp through some of the more interesting ones:

- ✔ **The Ten Islands and Three Isles of the Immortals Liturgies for the Yellow Register Ceremony:** In tandem with three other ritual texts, this scripture contributes to a ceremony conducted to remove sin and facilitate safe passage for up to nine generations of ancestors. Several other texts offer variations of the "Yellow Register" theme.

- ✔ **The Great Complete Collection of Ritual Protocols of the *Tao:*** This text serves as a ritual handbook for at least 20 different Taoist rituals, covering subjects like rainmaking and having male children. Most of the rituals have an astrological bent to them, designed to honor stars that control one's fate.

- ✔ **Secret Instructions for Prolonging Life, of the Purple Court of the Northern Emperor's Seven Primordia:** This text describes a colorful ritual involving the burning of ceremonial paper money and lighting seven lamps in a prescribed space. The purpose of the ritual is to present offerings to deities associated with the Big Dipper, on behalf of oneself and one's ancestors.

- ✔ **The Cavern of Perfection's Most High Perfect Scripture of Wisdom That Destroys Demons:** This text sort of combines alchemy with exorcism — it presents hymns and lists drugs that can be used to drive away evil spirits that cause illness.

Morality books

A genre of text called *morality books* or *virtue books (shan-shu)* circulated in China for many years both inside and outside the Taoist Canon. Some incorporated technical Taoist language and sophisticated cosmology, but many contained basic moral formulas that could be recited orally and transmitted to the masses, even those who were illiterate. By and large, these texts encouraged specific moral actions, enumerated lengthy lists of transgressions to avoid, and indicated the rewards or punishments that would follow from those actions.

Probably the best known — and best loved — of the morality books is the *Treatise of the Most High on Impulse and Response*, which is often translated as something like the *Book of Rewards and Punishments* or the *Tractate on Actions and Their Retributions*. The title alludes to the ancient *yin-yang* notions of resonance and correlation among different configurations of *ch'i*, but in the text itself, "impulse and response" is pretty clearly talking about the good or bad results of respective moral or immoral actions. This short text has been published in everything from rinky-dink pamphlets to illustrated multivolume coffee-table editions, and it's not all that uncommon to come across Chinese people today who fondly recall their grandmothers reciting the text to them at bedtime. If you have your heart set on finding a popular Taoist Bible, this just might be it.

When you browse the *Impulse and Response* text — it's a pretty quick and easy read — you'll probably notice that it's absolutely saturated with Chinese syncretism. That is, the text is a wonderful hodgepodge of Taoist, Buddhist, and Confucian ideas, mixed together into a totally digestible stew. Here's some of what you'll find there:

- **Attribution to Lao Tzu:** The entire text, though obviously a much later work, is supposedly spoken by the "Most High," whom the readers traditionally understand as Lao Tzu. This gives it a kind of Taoist *imprimatur* (mark of approval) from the very beginning.

- **The Buddhist idea of karma:** Though the text doesn't identify the idea as Buddhist, it's clearly using the standard Buddhist notion that all actions produce effects, based entirely on the moral disposition of those actions. In short, good actions produce rewards and bad actions produce punishments, mainly lengthening or shortening your overall life expectancy.

- **Popular understandings of deities:** Unlike Buddhism, which views the karmic process as automatic (much like gravity), this text depicts spirits of Heaven and Earth as the ones who pass judgment and dispense rewards and punishments.

- **Confucian morality:** Even though it's a Taoist book employing Buddhist notions of karma, the prescribed morality is Confucian through and through. The text encourages such things as loyalty to the ruler, obedience to parents, kindness to orphans and widows, modesty, and ritual propriety.

- **Dashes of Buddhist morality:** A handful of Buddhist ideas glom onto the Confucian morals, so it's forbidden to harm not only other people, but also animals, insects, plants, and trees.

- **Taoist deities and immortality:** The text also describes the Taoist idea of spirits inhabiting the human body, who are nurtured by good acts and poisoned by bad ones. Those who follow the right ways and serve the spirits correctly can be rewarded by becoming Taoist immortals.

- **Common-sense customs:** Many of the admonitions allude to basic folk customs that may seem kind of odd to a modern Western audience. For example, you're not allowed to lounge naked at night, feel lust at the sight of a beautiful woman, hope your creditors die before they can collect what you owe them, sing and dance on sacred days, cook food with dirty firewood, or take a whiz while facing north!

From medicine to numerology

While philosophy, talismans, registers, ritual, alchemy, and morality all figure prominently in the Taoist Canon, a number of other subjects — medicine, pharmacology, divination, breathing methods, biography, sacred geography, mythology, meteorology and numerology — all show up there as well. Just to make sure you don't ever *really* think you've got the entire Canon under control, here are a few more titles to whet your appetite:

- *Diagram of the Chou Dynasty Book of Changes:* This is a series of more than a hundred diagrams used to interpret the ancient divination manual, the *I Ching*.

- *Enlarged and illustrated Materia Medica (Pharmacology):* This extensive medical handbook catalogues hundreds of animals, insects, vegetables, herbs, and so forth, describing each in terms of taste, toxicity, and application to healing.

- *Comprehensive Mirror of Perfected Immortals and Those Who Embodied the Tao through the Ages:* This text attempts, not always successfully, to present a complete chronological record of Taoist immortals and "saints," tracing back to incarnations of Lao Tzu and legendary immortals of antiquity, and stretching forward to patriarchs of the Complete Perfection Lineage.

- *The August Ultimate through the Ages:* Written (or compiled) by an 11th-century Confucian scholar — which goes to show you just how diverse the Canon texts can be — this odd numerological text combines mathematics and delineation of historical cycles with metaphysical speculation.

Part IV
Exploring Taoist Practices

The 5th Wave   By Rich Tennant

"We've been playing motivational tapes about seeing the world from a different perspective."

In this part . . .

*T*aoism is much more than philosophical speculation about the Way — it's also a complex tradition with all sorts of different practices, most of which require years of training in order to do them right. Some of these are, quite literally, matters of life and death, or necessary to the health and well-being of the entire universe.

In this part, you find out about practices that teach you how to forget, techniques for cultivating your physical and spiritual body, popular martial arts like *t'ai-chi,* and rituals of purification and cosmic renewal. Which of these can you try at home? Read on.

Chapter 13

Remembering to Keep Forgetting

. . . .

In This Chapter

▶ Unlearning what you already know

▶ Fasting your mind and learning to forget

▶ Following the stages of forgetting

▶ Forgetting in the modern West

. . . .

*W*hen you look at the sheer diversity of specific practices in the many religious traditions of the world, you've probably noticed that they range from the explosively dramatic to the quietly contemplative. In short, religious practices can include everything from fire rituals, acrobatic parades, and snake handling, to silent prayer and meditative visualizations. If you're looking from the outside at practices from traditions other than your own, you can often get a pretty good sense of what's going on, although sometimes superficial similarities may make it harder to notice important differences. For instance, Hindu temple *puja* (hospitality rites for images of a deity) varies considerably from Christian church prayer. On the other hand, there are some practices, especially those that are open only to initiates or priests, where even followers of the particular tradition may not fully understand exactly what the ritual participants are hoping to accomplish through the ceremony.

And every once in a while, you come across some practices that simply boggle the mind, not because they're offensive or dangerous or anything like that, but because they just seem completely antithetical to everything you've ever heard about religion. In this case, I'm talking about the Taoist practice of "sitting and forgetting," an idea that first appears in the *Chuang Tzu* and still shows up in some Taoist circles today.

On the surface, it may sound a lot like daydreaming, developing dementia, or simply spacing out, but "sitting and forgetting" refers to a meditation that involves the systematic deconditioning and removal of what you already know. And if you stop to think about it, that's certainly not easy. How can you actually let go of something that's already found a comfortable resting place in your memory and working knowledge?

In this chapter, I talk about the Taoist practice of sitting and forgetting. You get to see its philosophical background, its development in the classical texts, its formalization in an important later scripture, and some of its unexpected applications in modern Western interpretations of Taoism.

Return, Reversal, and the Idea of Unlearning

One recurring theme in the classical Taoist literature is that attaining or experiencing the *Tao* involves a backward movement, a return or reversal to the original source of existence. In several texts, especially the *Tao Te Ching*, the authors connect this explicitly to a process of unlearning — mainly, the unlearning of the dominant Confucian (and sometimes Mohist) virtues of the day. This creates an odd kind of literary device, which basically denigrates knowledge, cultural literacy, and educated people — in short, the widely accepted image of the wise, virtuous sage-king — and presents an alternative picture of the sage as one who appears simple, confused, or (in many of Chuang Tzu's stories) grotesque and outcast.

In this section, I talk about the way Lao Tzu develops the theme of unlearning. You see just how consistently he attacks ordinary knowledge and provides hints that people do have the capacity to undo all this burdensome and unproductive learning.

The farther you go, the less you know

Lao Tzu begins one chapter with a counterintuitive admonition:

> Don't exit your doorways, and by this know the entire world. Don't peer through your windows, and by this know Heaven's Way. The farther you go, the less you know.

And similarly, "those who work at learning increase daily, while those who hear the Tao decrease daily." Obviously, this flies in the face of conventional wisdom, whether it's speaking to ancient China, which valued hard work and cultural refinement, or the contemporary West, which holds "progress" as a high ideal. On the other hand, it may provide some solace to unmotivated couch potatoes, who like the idea that their own lack of intellectual curiosity and drive ultimately works for the good of humanity!

Lao Tzu isn't just bashing intellectuals and eggheads for the fun of it — he's genuinely concerned that conscious, directed, affected learning drives one farther from the Tao, and he comes up with lots of ways to drive home this point:

- When knowledge and wisdom arise, there is then great artificiality.

- To use knowledge to order the state, is to be its thief; to use a lack of knowledge to order the state, is to be its benefactor.

- Those who know are not educated; those who are educated do not know.

- Too much learning produces frequent exhaustion and is no match for holding to the center.

In a typical Taoist paradox, Lao Tzu reiterates that you can't "learn" the Way through "learning." Routine learning not only misses the point, but also can drain you, produce artifice, and harm the community.

Learning not to learn

Because Lao Tzu has such low regard for learning, it makes sense that he tasks the reader with figuring out some way to "love the people," to "revive the state," and to "illuminate the four directions," all without the benefit of knowledge. But if this gives you the idea that he's proposing an easier, less-rigorous way of getting to where you want to go, you may want to take a closer look. It's not enough for Lao Tzu that you simply stop learning; you also need somehow to undo all the learning you've already done. That's why the *Tao Te Ching* says that only by "eliminating sagehood" and "discarding knowledge" can someone truly bring benefit to the people.

So, how do you unlearn everything you've learned? The almost comically puzzling answer is that you have to "learn not to learn." In other words, you can't just sit around waiting for all your intellectual apparatus simply to dissolve on its own accord — you actually need to take part in some specific practice that enables your mind to operate completely differently. In effect, you need to *retrain* the cognitive faculties of your own mind so that you are, in a sense, perceiving and processing the world completely differently from the way you did before.

The funny thing here is that while Lao Tzu and Chuang Tzu warn us that our regular learning is somehow not "natural," the more natural experience of the Tao doesn't actually come naturally. Or at least, we've gotten ourselves to such a place — so far from the *Tao* — that it no longer seems to come naturally. And so, we have to take active, conscious steps to return to the *Tao* — we need to learn how to reclaim the quality of naturalness that we've lost!

Try not to get too hung up on asking whether learning not to learn is still a type of learning and, therefore, contradictory. The point is not really that there's something wrong with "learning" — that is, in the broadest sense of understanding the world and discerning how to act in it — but that what we ordinarily think of as "learning" is not the right way (and may actually inhibit our ability) to accomplish those ends. It may be more helpful to think of the classical Taoist approach as a different *kind* of learning.

The Goal of Unlearning and the Task of Forgetting

It's often difficult to tell if the classical Taoist authors themselves really engaged in directed practices, or even had any secondhand knowledge of others engaged in such practices, but Chuang Tzu especially seems to offer the best testimony that at least a handful of practices meant to facilitate the task of unlearning were probably circulating during his time. And at least some of them continue, or resurface, considerably later on, providing one thematic thread that connects the classical texts to the later religious practices.

In this section, I talk about two particular (though related) practices that initially show up in the *Chuang Tzu* and that form the basis for later methods of meditation. You get an up-close look at the memorable vignettes that describe "sitting and forgetting" *(tso-wang)* and the "fasting of the mind and heart" *(hsin-chai)*.

Forgetting virtue and forgetting everything

In one of Chuang Tzu's short but utterly delightful dialogues, he concocts an intriguing sequence of conversations between Confucius and Yen Hui, who is remembered historically as Confucius's favorite disciple. The dialogue takes place over several days, with Yen Hui initiating each day's encounter with the claim that he's "progressing." In each case, Confucius asks about the nature of the progress, Yen Hui responds, and Confucius offers some modest encouragement but judges that his student hasn't quite hit the nail on the head and needs to try again. As this Confucian version of the Socratic method (repeatedly peppering someone with questions in order to stimulate critical thinking) unfolds, Yen Hui reports the following three distinct stages as indicators of his progress:

Meeting #1: I've forgotten humaneness *(jen)* and rightness *(yi)*.

Meeting #2: I've forgotten ritual propriety *(li)* and ceremonial music.

Meeting #3: I just sit and forget *(tso-wang)*.

When Confucius pushes Yen Hui further about what he means by sitting and forgetting, the latter replies that he lets go of his body, physical form, sense perceptions, and knowledge, and by this "comes into accord with the great thoroughfare," which is likely a metaphor for following the *Tao* (or working harmoniously with the transformations of Heaven and Earth). At this point Confucius recognizes that Yen Hui has moved beyond ordinary cognitive habits and humbly asks if he can switch roles and become Yen Hui's disciple.

Even with such a brief back and forth, it's possible to glean a few features of what this sitting and forgetting entails:

- **Gradual process:** The fact that it takes Yen Hui several tries suggests that the process of unlearning is not simply one massive "memory dump" — like the way a *Star Trek* starship ejects the entire reactor to avoid a "warp core breech" or some such thing — but involves undoing successive layers of cognitive misdirection, like peeling away the concentric layers of an onion.

- **Confronting conventional norms:** It's certainly no coincidence that Yen Hui's first successful "data dumps" are the most often cited Confucian virtues. The process of forgetting seems to begin not with some arbitrary or inconsequential detail to try to forget, but with the dominant public standards toward which most people aspire. For people of Chuang Tzu's era, to forget humaneness and ritual propriety was tantamount to letting go of a shared reality.

- **Contemplative practice:** Perhaps it's obvious to point out that one part of sitting and forgetting is the "sitting" part, but this places the practice as one variety of those introspective techniques we often identify as meditation or contemplation. That means that the process is, more likely than not, specifically structured and directed, even if the first people to employ it may have discovered it through trial and error.

- **Peak experience:** It would be premature (and probably projecting other religious sensibilities where they may not belong) to conclude that the process culminates with anything like an ecstatic union or dissolution of one's self, but the final lines do suggest that the successful practitioner is conscious of moving beyond conventional perception and knowledge and achieving some kind of heightened experience of the Way.

Based on one brief passage, Chuang Tzu's "sitting and forgetting" appears to be a contemplative practice that gradually unravels conventional norms and cognitive points of reference, ultimately returning the practitioner to the *Tao,* which allows for a dramatically different experience of and orientation toward reality.

The fasting of the mind and heart

Chuang Tzu also describes another technique that seems to have much in common with sitting and forgetting. In another one of his concocted conservations between Confucius and Yen Hui — this one much longer — Confucius continually berates his student for planning to meet with an immature, irresponsible local ruler, without having settled on an appropriate strategy for swaying him ethically. He eventually admonishes him to engage in "fasting," not the fasting from certain food or drink in preparation for a religious ceremony, but what he calls the "fasting of the mind and heart," for which he must first "unify" his will. As with sitting and forgetting, the fasting of the mind and heart also entails a sequence of steps, though this time they come in the form of specific (if not particularly easy) instruction from Chuang Tzu to Yen Hui:

- ✔ Don't listen with the ears, listen with the mind and heart.
- ✔ Don't listen with the mind and heart, listen with the *ch'i*.

The problem with the ears, Chuang Tzu explains, is that they can do little more than (literally) listen; likewise, the mind and heart (conceived of as one single organ) can do little more than calculate. But your *ch'i* can *attenuate* (that is, become empty), and the basis of the *Tao* is emptiness, so it is by "listening" with your *ch'i* (however that works) that you can become attentive to the *Tao*.

In other words, your mind and heart — that is, your cognitive and emotional faculties — follow particular habits, in the way they translate the world to you and orient you to that world. But "fasting" your mind and heart shuts down those ordinary habits and allows you to do develop new ones. If this strikes you as kind of a cryptic explanation, think about the various reasons that people ordinarily engage in religious fasting:

- ✔ **Purification:** People sometimes fast before religious rituals, or fast *as* a religious ritual, in order to attain a more *pure* state. The idea is usually that abstaining from ordinary stuff like food and drink can create the sense of being clean, fresh, or renewed, but also being in a proper or worthy state for a particular function.

- ✔ **Purgation:** Some religious fasts serve to *purge* you of something, perhaps as concrete as evil spirits, or as abstract as sin or negative feelings. Whether you think of it as a form of penance or as a spiritual cleansing, the goal is to expel something unwanted from your physical body or holistic self.

- ✔ **Focus:** In some cases, people fast simply to redirect their attention away from stuff that's distracting or less significant, and toward matters of greater spiritual interest. Christian monks would sometimes practice austerities not for reasons of atonement or ritual purity, but simply because they wanted to get out of the habit of thinking about food, and into the habit of thinking about God.

It may help you make sense of mind-heart fasting if you take all three of these into account. First, fasting helps *return* your mind-heart to its original, pure state, before it lapsed into the unhealthy mental habits that make it so hard for you to follow the Way. Second, it *ejects* all the clutter and bogus knowledge that have accumulated since you first began to think and feel. And finally, it *redirects* the mind-heart to pay attention in a totally different way — what Chuang Tzu calls "listening with the *ch'i.*"

The Chinese character *chai*, translated here as "fasting," also refers to the specific purification rituals and community retreats practiced by the later Taoist communities like the Way of the Celestial Masters (see Chapter 17). At some points in history, it also acted more or less as the generic term for Taoist ritual. Because of this, mind-heart fasting eventually evolves into one type of ritual practice, albeit an advanced one that followed more "concrete" fasting practices used to atone for sins and confer physical health benefits.

Mind-heart fasting: Redux

The place of Taoism in Chinese religious *syncretism* — the blending of practices from multiple sources (see Chapter 3) — can sometimes be difficult to untangle, especially when an idea or practice develops in one Taoist context, enters the "public domain" of raw materials and methods in the general Chinese religious "toolbox," and then reemerges some time later in a different form and with different ingredients added to the mix.

A fascinating case in point involves a late 19th-, early 20th-century figure named Ch'en Ying-ning, who put forward a modern spin on mind-heart fasting. Ch'en had a diverse scholarly background, studied extensively in the Complete Perfection Taoist linage, and was involved in founding the Chinese Taoist Association. But mostly, he identified with many of Chuang Tzu's teachings and devoted himself to learning various alchemical techniques, with the intention of making the search for immortality a national priority, presumably because of his lifelong battle with poor physical health.

Ch'en saw mind-heart fasting as an addendum to *ch'i-kung* practice, with a few dashes of Buddhist philosophy thrown in for good measure. Quoting the key passage in the *Chuang Tzu,* Ch'en recast the practice as a five-step process:

1. **Unify the will.**

   The first step involves focusing the mind-heart and letting go of distracting thoughts.

2. **Don't listen with the ears, listen with the mind-heart.**

   Perhaps taking a cue from Buddhism, this stage refers to "listening" to your own breath, which is silent and, therefore, can't be "heard" through the ears alone.

3. **Don't listen with the mind-heart, listen with the *ch'i.***

   At this point, the function of the mind-heart is identical to the movement of your *ch'i.*

4. **Your ears are limited to listening, your mind-heart is limited to calculating.**

   In the fourth stage, the practitioner does not feel as though she has any distinct cognitive identity.

5. **The attenuation is the fasting of the mind-heart.**

   The process concludes with a Buddhist-style elimination of individual self and an all-consuming experience of emptiness.

The Treatise on Sitting and Forgetting

Of the 1,400-odd texts in the Taoist Canon, many of them present commentaries on the *Chuang Tzu,* and many of those specifically address the practice of sitting and forgetting. Because many of the commentators were writing at a time when Buddhism first started making significant headway in China and Taoism was still developing its own institutional identity, they often grafted Buddhist ideas onto the theory and interpreted the practice in terms resembling Buddhist meditation. Because of this, it's sometimes difficult to separate Chuang Tzu's sitting and forgetting from the "Buddha-fied" version of it.

The most important later Taoist to write about this practice was Ssu-ma Ch'eng-chen, a 7th- and 8th-century Taoist priest in the Highest Purity tradition. Like other Highest Purity adepts, Ssu-ma engaged in alchemy and other esoteric practices with the hopes of achieving postmortem immortality, so he pretty much viewed sitting and forgetting (and just about everything else in the entire body of Taoist literature) as connected to that end. He eventually recorded his interpretation — or perhaps, his students recorded his lectures — in the *Treatise on Sitting and Forgetting,* which provides an important glimpse into at least one aspect of medieval Taoist practice.

In this section, I summarize some of the essential points of Ssu-ma Ch'eng-chen's *Treatise on Sitting and Forgetting.* You see how Ssu-ma explains the process of forgetting in terms of seven specific stages, what he understands is waiting for us at the end of the process, and how a kindred text from the same period contextualizes sitting and forgetting as only one stage in a longer path to "liberation."

The seven stages of forgetting

Now that you've gotten used to relating sitting and forgetting to the classical Taoist understandings of the *Tao,* returning, and unlearning, you may have some trouble buying Ssu-ma's interpretations of it, particularly his goals of leaving your corporeal body behind and roaming in the Heavens with various spirits. Some of the language does echo that of other Highest Purity scriptures, but it's also so Buddhist in places that it would be pretty hard to justify any claims that this represents the original meaning of the practice that first appeared in Chuang's Tzu dialogue. But, of course, that's part of the fun of studying Taoist history, which teems with these types of twists and turns in the development and reinterpretation of tradition. In any event, Ssu-ma's version of forgetting is a little more complicated than Chuang Tzu's.

Here's a summary of Ssu-ma's seven stages of forgetting, which chronicles a gradual process of realizing the *Tao.* Keep an eye out for ways the terminology means something different from what you would've expected.

1. **Respect and faithfulness:** Though the language sounds like a title for one of the popular "morality books," this stage actually refers to building self-confidence in your ability to know the Way (and presumably become a Taoist immortal) and trust in the teachers and texts that are there to guide you.

2. **Cutting off karma:** If you don't remember Chuang Tzu talking about the Buddhist concept of karma, that's because Buddhism wouldn't enter China for several hundred more years, though Ssu-ma doesn't seem to have been bothered by that fact. In this stage, you try to block off your own willfulness and intentionality — Buddhists generally define karma as willful (or volitional) action — which the author also explains using the traditional Taoist idea of non-doing *(wu-wei).*

3. **Collecting the mind-heart:** Though it isn't obvious, this, too, borrows a Buddhist idea: the aspect of meditation that involves concentration. This stage can occur most easily in a secluded setting, where you develop *one-pointedness,* the ability to gather your mind to a single object of attention and sever any distractions.

4. **Simplifying affairs:** At this point, having developed an ability to concentrate your mind, you can divest yourself of the ordinary affairs of the world (including things like career and social relationships) and begin to identify your own destiny as in harmony with the movements of the *Tao.*

5. **Perfect observation:** This is the stage that probably most resembles Buddhist "insight meditation," where the goal is to develop an ability to observe carefully the affairs from which you've already divested (and are continuing to divest) with complete detachment. When you're in this stage — and this is actually straight from Ssu-ma's text — you can walk into a fish market and not have any sense that it stinks!

6. **Utmost steadfastness:** When you look at the last couple stages, the descriptions start to get increasingly more jargon filled and difficult to sort out. At this point, it seems like you're so in tune with the *Tao,* that you effectively experience the processes of your own mind as indistinguishable from those of the *Tao.*

7. **Grasping the Way:** The last stage is the final realization of the *Tao,* which Ssu-ma describes with just about everything exciting in the Highest Purity Taoist cookbook: longevity, the attainment of magical powers, direct communication with spirits, and so forth.

As you can see, the *Treatise on Sitting and Forgetting* departs from the fairly vague bare bones of Chuang Tzu's fasting of the mind and heart — like the language of unlearning and returning, or the critique of Confucian virtue — and adapts the process to a more elaborate (and considerably more esoteric) set of practices more in tune with Ssu-ma Ch'eng-chen's Highest Purity Taoist sensibilities. But he also rewrites the story in terms that often look surprisingly Buddhist, including aspects of Buddhist meditation (like single-pointed concentration and detached observation) and stages that almost resemble the selfless bliss of a Buddha. Here, sitting and forgetting is not a universal technique of just gradually forgetting things you've learned, but a practice deeply embedded within a particular medieval Taoist religious context.

You may enjoy reading the *Treatise on Sitting and Forgetting,* and you may even feel that doing so enhances your sense of spiritual well-being or inspires you to try out some different meditation techniques. But more important, it's really a perfect example of how the vast majority of texts in the Taoist Canon were written with a very particular audience in mind, and were mainly employed by people with extensive (and often secretive) training in specific ritualistic contexts. Texts like this are usually pretty hard to penetrate, and you're often at the mercy of translators who may inadvertently embed their own interpretations into the translation.

From forgetting to spirit liberation

Sitting and forgetting began as the subject of one passing reference in the *Chuang Tzu* (a nearly identical passage also appeared in the *Huai Nan Tzu*), but it eventually took on a life of its own, as evidenced by Ssu-ma Ch'eng-chen's *Treatise on Sitting and Forgetting.* It also drew considerable interest from other authors of the Highest Purity era, including one anonymous writer who composed a short but intriguing text called the *T'ien Yin Tzu,* the *Master of Heavenly Seclusion.* In this text, instead of identifying specific stages of sitting and forgetting, the author identified sitting and forgetting as one specific stage of an even more comprehensive process. Once again, the procedure has gotten still more complicated.

Ssu-ma Ch'eng-chen must have found this text congenial with his own thinking about the subject, because he wrote an enthusiastic introduction (which is now officially part of the text) where he explains that the teachings go back to Lao Tzu and Chuang Tzu (and even the *I Ching*), deal with such things as the harmony of *yin* and *yang* and the nourishment of *ch'i,* and point toward the Highest Purity concerns for longevity and the path to immortality. Here are the five stages, according to the *T'ien Yin Tzu:*

1. **Fasting and abstaining:** This basically uses the five elements theory to explain proper dietary habits, which includes avoiding foods that are uncooked, overly spiced, fermented, or spoiled. It also talks about properly cleaning and massaging your body.

2. **Dwelling peacefully:** Perhaps because of associations people had about monastic life, the author explains that he's less interested in *where* you dwell than in *how* you dwell, including which directions you face when you sit or sleep, how to arrange furniture and allow the right balance of light and dark, and where to place windows and curtains.

3. **Visualizing and contemplating:** This is the most obvious meditation stage of the process. It includes closing your eyes and calming the mind in order to visualize your own "spiritual" essence. The author relates this stage to the classical Taoist ideas of returning to the original source and discovering the "gateway of all subtleties."

4. **Sitting and forgetting:** The author describes this stage as one where you perfect your visualizing and contemplating by — what else? — forgetting visualizing and contemplating. Like Ssu-ma's *Treatise,* it also spins in the Buddhist ideas of letting go of self, and of the distinction between self and other.

5. **Liberating the spirit:** After the adept completes the previous four steps, he's ready to free his spirit to enjoy an immortal existence, independent of the affairs of the world and the bondage of life and death.

Chuang Tzu appears to have related sitting and forgetting to the more basic task of unlearning and returning, but Highest Purity practitioners like Ssu-ma Ch'eng-chen and the author of the *T'ien Yin Tzu* understood it as part of a broader process of Taoist self-cultivation.

Contemporary Forgetfulness

As you can see, the Taoist theme of sitting and forgetting has undergone some pretty interesting transformations over time, and it's still showing up in new guises and new venues, particularly in the West. This may strike you as a little strange, because when most Westerners think of Taoism, they probably tick off a lengthy list of more common talking points — the *Tao, wu-wei, yin* and *yang,* the uncarved block — before they ever get anywhere near sitting and forgetting. But, in fact, interest in this fairly obscure Taoist practice has recently created something of a cottage industry, and you don't have to do too much looking around online to locate several small but enthusiastic networks of private teachers, multimedia resources, quasi-official Taoist organizations, and online discussion groups devoted to 21st-century forgetfulness.

Certainly, many people first come to sitting and forgetting through recent English translations of Ssu-ma Ch'eng-chen's *Treatise,* but it's safe to say that most modern *tso-wang* enthusiasts don't know much about the history of the practice in China (including its role in Highest Purity Taoism and the assimilation of Buddhist ideas) and instead take cues from the *Chuang Tzu* passage, *ch'i-kung* and *t'ai-chi* classes, and perhaps even New Age literature and generic discussions of meditation.

In this section, I sample some of the many examples of contemporary forgetfulness, and call your attention to each one's particular spin on the practice.

You see how various versions of sitting and forgetting have made it into practice groups and retreat centers, as well as how do-it-yourself *tso-wang* resources — some of which have little direct connection to Taoism — have begun to pepper the Internet.

Modern Taoism and the practice of forgetting

A recent issue of *Dragon's Mouth Magazine,* the journal of the British Taoist Association (BTA), featured an article on sitting and forgetting, written by one of the founders of the BTA. Although the author was an ordained Taoist priest, he presented the material in highly universalistic, spiritualized terms, almost completely downplaying Taoist technical language — certainly a far cry from the *Treatise on Sitting and Forgetting.* He also did everything he could to make it seem incredibly easy for anyone to do — you don't need to do any of the usual hard work like counting breaths or taking inventory of your own wandering mind. But that seems to be the trajectory of contemporary forgetting — finding aspects of the practice that can be easily related to other forms of meditation, that can apply concretely to today's problems, and that aren't bound up in Taoist jargon or ritual.

Here's a handful of Western outlets for sitting and forgetting, each of which spins it in a slightly different way:

- ✔ **Black Rock Wellness (**www.blackrockwellness.org**):** This Ontario center for acupuncture and holistic medicine teaches sitting and forgetting as a "non-dualistic" and "non-conceptual" form of meditation. Their main interest in the practice is for its physical and mental health benefits, including treatment of depression, decreasing stress, improving cognitive function, lengthening lifespan, and leading to overall happiness.

- ✔ **EnerQi Healing Arts Center (**www.enerqihealing.com**):** This California school of "healing energy" teaches classes in *ch'i-kung, reiki,* and yoga — but it also includes on its website a primer on sitting and forgetting, explaining it with a mix of language drawn from classical Taoism, Taoist physiology, and modern astronomy, and identifying the goal as elimination of the ego and participation in the "fabric of Tao."

- ✔ **Old Oak Taiji School (**www.oldoakdao.org**):** This California practice center also offers an online primer, but it spends a little less time on the Taoist philosophy behind the practice and more on the specific posture you need to do it right. This includes instructions for how you should orient your tailbone, *perineum* (the general area between your butt and genitals), belly, chest, spine, arms, shoulders, arms, eyes, tongue, and *occiput* (the back of your skull).

✔ **Instituto Qigong Chikung de Barcelona (Barcelona Institute of Ch'i-kung;** www.institutoqigong.com**):** Not all modern Western purveyors of sitting and forgetting are American; some of them are Western European. This Spanish center teaches *tso-wang* as one of seven "static" (that is, motionless) types of *ch'i-kung*. They understand it as an utterly down-to-earth teaching, explicitly rejecting that it leads to any "transcendent" experience, and instead emphasizing how it leads to intuition and creativity.

Most of the Western sources on sitting and forgetting use the *pinyin* system of Anglicizing Chinese characters. So, if you're looking for *tso-wang,* you'll probably have to look for *zuowang*.

Electronic forgetting

You can find instructions online for just about everything from making homemade ice cream to raising chickens in the city, so it's really not such a huge leap to discover that there are plenty of electronic sitting and forgetting resources, too. Some of these materials go well beyond explaining the philosophy behind the practice or explaining the proper steps of meditation, though. Some of them come up with remarkably creative and incongruous aids to self-directed *tso-wang*. Of course, websites don't always last very long, and what's here today may be gone tomorrow, but it's worth taking a chance and talking about one of these cyber-oddities.

I'm talking here about The Conscious Life (www.theconsciouslife.com), a commercial, interactive website designed by Wee Peng Ho, a self-described "wellness enthusiast," who overcame chronic health problems and dissatisfaction with the rat race through alternative methods of physical and spiritual healing. His website includes many posts and links related to meditation and alternative medicine, but his page on sitting and forgetting takes an especially unusual turn. Although his explanation of sitting and forgetting is rudimentary — he makes it sound an awful lot like Zen meditation in some places, forgetting about both past and future and concentrating on the present — he does provide access to the "Free Online *Zuowang* Meditation Timer"! If you follow this link, you come to a page that times you for a meditation session of any length from 1 to 99 minutes.

But wait, there's more. You can also choose the "alarm" that will accompany you in your meditation, the tone that announces the beginning and end of the session. For this, you've got four options:

✔ **Singing bowl:** This is the one you'll normally hear at meditation centers — that deep, reverberating sound of a metal object struck against a standing bell, sometimes called a rin gong.

✔ **Meditation bell:** Though this is called a bell, it's actually so high that it sounds more like a whistle. It also lasts several seconds before the sound completely fades out.

✔ **Gong:** This one has a less metallic, less bell-like sound, almost more of a throbbing, hollow (but sustaining) thud.

✔ **Nightingale:** And a lovely sound it is. Not exactly traditional for Taoist temples, but it does conjure up images of people gathering in a Beijing park at daybreak to do their *t'ai-chi* exercises.

There's actually one more interactive feature on the *Zuowang* Timer, though it's not clear why it's there, given that the instructions on the website say you should close your eyes during meditation. You can actually adjust the background behind the digital timer, perhaps to set the mood before you close your eyes, perhaps to have a memorable image for when you open them. Here are your visual possibilities:

✔ **Minimalist:** This recalls the Zen habit of meditating while facing a wall. Basically, there's just a white background, although it also has a couple links and the Facebook and Twitter icons.

✔ **Deep space:** This is a bright, colorful, galactic cluster, a perfect companion for someone trying to achieve cosmic consciousness.

✔ **Incense/fire:** Like the singing bowl, this image of a burning incense stick makes you feel "monastic."

✔ **Dandelion:** This is a fluffy white dandelion against an electric green background, making the mood a little bit pastoral, a little bit spacy.

And when the gong or the nightingale signals the end of your meditation, you get an inspirational meditative message. Here are a few that came up for me:

✔ Whatever you believe in rules your life.

✔ May mindfulness permeate everything you touch today.

✔ May deep inner peace be with you.

✔ The difference between an angel and a devil begins from a thought.

Chapter 14

Seeking the Path to Immortality

In This Chapter

▶ Accepting or overcoming death

▶ Engaging in longevity practices

▶ Tracing the origins of immortality cults

▶ Exploring Taoist images of immortal beings

*E*nthusiastic readers of texts like the *Tao Te Ching* and *Chuang Tzu* are often baffled (and justifiably so) when they first discover that the pursuit of "immortality" occupied an important place in a great deal of later Taoist practice. Because the classical Taoist texts generally seem to express a sort of *que sera sera* attitude toward death (and just about everything else, for that matter), this apparent incongruity often played right into the much-repeated trope that "religious Taoism" corrupted the wise original philosophy with a bunch of silly superstitions. But explaining something away doesn't actually explain it, and the Taoist attitudes toward life and death are diverse and interesting enough to deserve a little more careful attention.

As you can probably imagine, the things that your own religious tradition (or even Western thinking in general) say about death may shape the types of questions you ask of Taoists on the subject. For instance, do Taoists believe in Heaven and Hell? Do they believe that some souls are saved and some aren't? What are the respective roles of faith and grace? Of course, all these questions build in certain Western assumptions, like about a single monotheistic deity or the idea of an immortal soul that's somehow different from the corporeal body. Not that there's anything wrong with this type of thinking — it's just that Taoists have tended to answer a different set of questions and haven't always agreed among themselves about the answers.

Be prepared to encounter a range of Taoist attitudes toward life and death. Some of this will simply have to do with historical changes in the tradition, but as is the case with many other subjects, Taoists don't always speak with one voice about questions of death and immortality. And if you think about it, Christians, Jews, and followers of other traditions usually don't either.

In this chapter, I talk about Taoist understandings of life and death, and the related pursuits of longevity and immortality. You see how the classical authors sometimes lobbied for a *dispassionate* treatment of death, but sometimes depicted sages or perfected persons who seemed to know some tricks for doing an end run around it. You also get your first look at some of the Chinese cults of immortality and how some of those eventually found their way into mainstream Taoism.

Acceptance of Life and Death in Classical Taoism

Lao Tzu and Chuang Tzu, as well other classical writers retroactively labeled as Taoists, had plenty to say about life and death. To put it in a nutshell, they generally didn't seem to be all that worried about dying. Or more accurately, they gave the impression that when you reach a sagely, enlightened state of mind, you won't let a little thing like death — either your own or someone else's — ruin your day. In one passage, where Lao Tzu is setting the record straight on what makes up real wisdom and strength, he cavalierly brushes off the significance of death. True long life, he says, is simply dying but not being forgotten.

In one sense, this laissez-faire attitude toward death fits nicely into the broader classical Taoist themes like *wu-wei* (non-action) or returning to the source. As Chuang Tzu describes him, the "perfect man" (or "true man") of ancient times seems the very picture of equanimity: one who sleeps without dreams, wakes without cares, and knows nothing of either loving life or hating death. What's more, although the perfect man would never forget where he began, he'd never even contemplate where he might come to an end.

In this section, I explain how the classical Taoist authors explain their indifference to matters of life and death and chide their audience to question why they shouldn't share that indifference. You get to wander through a sampler of memorable passages (and characters) that represent death as just one run-of-the-mill stage of the cosmic process, or that plant a seed of the bizarre thought that maybe death is a better, more enjoyable state than life.

Recognizing death as part of the cosmic process

In one of classical Taoism's most unforgettable vignettes, Chuang Tzu sits cross-legged, pounds on a drum, and sings, which is not normally any big deal, except that this time he's engaging in these shenanigans shortly after his own wife has died. When his buddy, the logician Hui Tzu, expresses consternation about this turn of events, Chuang Tzu acknowledges his initial grief but then calmly gives his friend a primer on the great transformations that make up the ongoing processes of creation. There was a time, Chuang Tzu says, before his wife existed. But then, some patterns of *ch'i* emerged from chaos, and then form emerged from that *ch'i,* and eventually what we know as her life emerged from that form. Mysterious perhaps, but nothing particularly remarkable. And then, this same cosmic process brought her from life to death, which is no more unusual, no more tragic, than the cycle of the four seasons. Had Chuang Tzu continued to mourn her loss, he explains, he would have shown that he simply didn't understand fate.

This story underscores the recurring theme that the rhythms of existence, all the fluctuations and stages of *ch'i,* while not fulfilling any divine plan, are still perfectly sound and reflect a fundamentally healthy universe. These ongoing transformations certainly don't require our intervention or deserve our lamentation any more than do other natural transitions, like the passage from day to night or the revolution of planets around the sun. As Chuang says elsewhere, life and death may be great affairs, but they don't rattle the sage's heart and mind.

Several other classical Taoist accounts reiterate the same principle, often by reciting lyrical aphorisms or introducing a roster of colorful oddballs. Here are a few of the more striking examples from the *Chuang Tzu:*

- ✔ **The death of Lao Tzu:** In this brief account of Lao Tzu's death, his disciples get miffed by a man who offers a few perfunctory wails at his grave and then leaves, apparently unperturbed. When the disciples confront him over his haughtiness, he responds that crying over death is like rejecting our own natures or "hiding from Heaven." He admonishes them to be content with the passage of time and settle comfortably with whatever course life takes.

- ✔ **The four masters:** This vignette describes four ostensive masters, who cement their friendship by agreeing that the living and the dead make up a single body, and that you should view nothingness as the head of that body, life as the spine, and death as the derriere — a metaphor that matches up nicely with the traditional Chinese concept of time, which equates the future with what comes behind. When Master Lai develops an exotic illness blamed on some weird dysfunction of *yin* and *yang* — it causes his chin to stick in his navel and his shoulders to reach above his head — he shoos away anyone who would disturb the process of change, choosing instead simply to watch it with a kind of ironic fascination. If his left arm happens to transform into a rooster, he says, he may as well just crow at the crack of dawn!

✔ **The death of Meng-sun Ts'ai's mother:** Much like Chuang Tzu after the loss of his wife, Meng-sun Ts'ai seems remarkably unshaken after his mother's death, conducting her funeral without any look of sorrow on his face, and going through the motions of mourning without any sadness in his heart. The story slides into a reflection on the sometimes inscrutable process of change, comparing life and death to dreaming and wakefulness.

✔ **The imminent death of Chuang Tzu:** Here, Chuang Tzu's disciples gather at his deathbed, all pumped up to give him a lavish funeral, but Chuang Tzu couldn't care less, preferring instead to have Heaven and Earth serve as his coffin; the sun, moon, and stars as his adornments; and the 10,000 things as his parting gifts. When his disciples express concern that he'll get eaten by vultures and crows if left like that, Chuang Tzu simply chides them for favoritism. Why, he asks, would they prefer that he get eaten by the ants and mole crickets in the ground? Is it that they like the ants better than the vultures?

All these passages reinforce the idea of death as natural, just one transition in a universe full of constant transitions. As Chuang Tzu puts it, all the complementary motions — life and death, survival and loss, success and failure, wealth and poverty, worthiness and unworthiness, fame and slander, hunger and thirst — are alternations of affairs, the course of fate. You should actually delight in these oscillations, never letting them undercut your innate harmony. Matters of life and death, he says, have no effect on the sage.

Questioning the fear of death

But wait, there's more! Often, the classical Taoist authors ratchet up this tranquility in the face of death to something a little more dramatic, counterintuitive, and even over the top. In these stories, they tell you not only that you shouldn't fear death, but that you should actually *embrace* it because it's so much more enjoyable than dull, old life! If one vision of the Taoist sage is someone who's cool, calm, and collected in the face of life *or* death — that is, willingly letting go of what that most people clutch and accepting what most people fear — this flip-side approach depicts the sage who turns up his nose at life and wholeheartedly charges into death. Death awaits us all — and what's more, isn't that great!

Admittedly, these "pro-death" passages are the exception rather than rule, but they're just too bold to ignore. Here are a few doozies from the *Chuang Tzu* and *Lieh Tzu:*

✔ **Sang-hu and his friends:** Much like the anecdote about the Master Lai and his friends celebrating his bizarre physical transformation, this story portrays Master Sang-hu's friends laughing and singing at his funeral, celebrating that he's returned to his "true state," even as they're stuck in the world of humanity As the story moves forward, we learn that men such as these think of life as a tumor or carbuncle, and of death as the lancing of a boil and letting out the pus. This image definitely isn't subtle, but it sure is memorable.

✔ **Chuang Tzu and the skull:** In this story Chuang Tzu actually learns a lesson from a human skull he finds on the road and then uses as a pillow when he turns in for the night. His initial reaction is to wonder what sorts of evils led this one-time human to this fate, but the skull comes to him in a dream and lectures him on the wonders of the world of death, where there's no divide between subjects and rulers, no need for seasonal labors, only a kind of eternal spring and autumn. When asked if he would rather be alive again with his family, friends, and neighbors, the skull declines, saying that his present happiness exceeds that of a king on his throne.

✔ **Lin Lei and Confucius:** In this *Lieh Tzu* passage, the nonagenarian Lin Lei lectures Confucius and one of his disciples, who wonder why he's noodling along with such a devil-may-care attitude despite being so close to death. He explains that death is simply a return to the beginning, and that he has no way of knowing that he won't be born again after his death, or that life and death aren't equally good or that attachment to life itself isn't an illusion. Confucius isn't quite convinced by this line of reasoning, and it's not entirely clear exactly who's supposed to have "won" this exchange.

At first glance, it's kind of hard to know exactly what to make of passages like these and similar ones where characters express their delight in the prospect of early death. I mean, I don't really think Chuang Tzu is trying to encourage his readers to off themselves! But they make a lot more sense when you consider that Chuang Tzu and the author of the *Lieh Tzu* are probably combining their reflections on life and death with the skepticism that they consistently bring to other subjects, especially moral ones. Just as they question whether the Confucian and Mohist ethical positions only make sense from their narrow perspectives, they also ask if our only basis for preferring life over death is that we're making that determination from the perspective of someone who's living.

The classical Taoist texts, especially the *Chuang Tzu*, offer (at least) two reasons why we shouldn't fear death:

✔ We should willingly accept the various transformations of existence.

✔ We should be skeptical about preferences for any one stage of the transformations over any other.

Sagehood, Longevity, and Imperviousness to Harm

The classical Taoist texts often put forth an ideal of blissful indifference to death, or even one of bold eagerness to plunge into it headfirst, but almost as often they suggest a very different attitude toward the Grim Reaper. In many cases, the texts portray sages who don't have to come to terms with death at all, simply because they've developed the kinds of abilities that make it more or less irrelevant. Some of these figures have discovered ways to lengthen their lives, while others demonstrate various types of unearthly powers. In short, the texts describe them as having magical or super-human abilities.

Unless the authors intend all these narratives as allegorical accounts of those who've achieved extraordinary mental discipline, it's fair to say that this model of the "perfect man" reflects an alternative vision of sagehood and his treatment of death. While figures like Master Lai and Meng-sun Ts'ai exemplify enlightened understandings of or feelings toward death — that is, the achievement of some type of heightened cognitive and emotional state — others seem to illustrate how dramatic transformations of the person's physical body can turn death into kind of a moot point. The passages don't usually ascribe actual immortality to these transformed figures, but it's pretty clear that their powers have something to do with their getting to a place where death is no big deal.

Many of the selective, spiritualized Western renderings of Taoism have great affection for the calm and dispassionate sage, though they don't always know quite what to make of the biologically enhanced version. In this section, I dig a little more deeply into this alternative classical Taoist understanding of death. You get to see some attention-grabbing examples from the classical texts of the Taoist "super-sage," and also some indication that these sages may have come by their abilities through some specific processes of training or self-cultivation.

Images of the super-sage

One passage from the *Tao Te Ching* begins with a confusing discussion of the "companions of life" and the "companions of death" — there are 13 of each — and a typically paradoxical statement that how you regard life will determine your movement from one set of "companions" to the other. The payoff comes when Lao Tzu describes those who are good at "holding on to life" and who have "no place for death." Such people don't bother avoiding tigers and rhinoceroses, because the animals can "find no place" to stab with their claws or horns. Likewise, they don't wear armor or carry shields when they go into battle, because the enemy's weapons are equally ineffectual.

Similar passages are scattered throughout the *Tao Te Ching,* including one that says a man who "embraces the fullness of virtue" can't be stung by wasps or scorpions, or bitten by snakes, and can't be captured by wild animals or birds of prey. It's not really clear what role this reference plays here, though the image of a sexually excited newborn baby certainly captures the mood of someone whose physical capacities are considerably beyond what you may expect.

And here are summaries of a few passages from *Chuang Tzu* and *Lieh Tzu,* all of which depict a sage who possesses unusual powers, and which specifically relate those powers to questions of life and death:

- ✔ **Wang Ni's vision of the perfect man:** In responding to a question from the delightfully named Gaptooth about whether all humans can agree on any single proposition, Wang Ni reiterates Chuang Tzu's basic talking point that all affirmations and denials — even those about what is moral or beneficial — are limited by the specific perspectives and contexts of the people who hold them. And so, the "spiritual" (or spirit-like) perfect man "roams beyond the four seas," unaffected by the mundane details of profit and loss, untouched by matters of life and death. Such a person can't be burned by raging fires, can't be chilled by frozen rivers, and won't be scared of lightning that can split apart hills, or winds that can shake the oceans.

- ✔ **The Yellow Emperor's dream:** After deciding to direct his attention away from political affairs and toward the utmost *Tao,* the Yellow Emperor dreams of a place that can be reached only by a "journey of the spirit." There, the residents all follow their natural course, free from cravings and arbitrary preferences. Water can't drown them, fire can't burn them (this one seems pretty common), and anything that can normally wound the body — hacking, flogging, poking, scratching — doesn't even leave a mark. Lieh Tzu describes them as dying at their appropriate times — thanks to having no attachment to life or fear of death — but his concluding comment that the Yellow Emperor ascended to the heavens decades later may be invoking the idea of some kind of immortal Heavenly existence after death.

- ✔ **Woman Crookback's teaching of Pu-liang Yi:** In this interesting passage from *Chuang Tzu,* Woman Crookback explains how she tutored one Pu-liang Yi — a man who had had sagely "talents" that she lacked — in the *Tao.* The process took several days, but by the end, Pu-liang Yi could "externalize life" and "penetrate morning." This passage doesn't actually describe Pu-liang Yi as having attained any special powers, but it does say that he arrived at an advanced state (or perhaps a physical place) that was beyond past and present, without life or death.

Indications of cultivation practices in Classical Taoism

One of the most intriguing aspects of these super-sage passages — and several others that don't necessarily depict sages with special physical powers — is how they hint that these individuals achieved their states of perfection through the performance of actual physical practices, or of meditation-like practices you could call simultaneously physical and spiritual. Most of the descriptions aren't terribly specific, and they're often applied to fictional or mythic characters, but they occur regularly enough and employ similar-enough language that the authors must have heard at least *some* scuttlebutt about such practices.

Here are a handful of the more provocative passages:

- **The spirit-like man of the mountain:** Chieh Yü and Lien Shu describe this enigmatic figure who not only has the usual invulnerabilities (like resistance to heat and drowning) and supernatural abilities (riding a flying dragon), but can somehow harmonize and unify the 10,000 things. He lives not on the "five grains," but on wind and dew, and he accomplishes this through the "concentration of his spirit." This could suggest breathing practices, dietary regimens, or perhaps meditation.

- **The perfected man of antiquity:** Chuang Tzu's lengthy essay on the unnamed perfect man of the remote past mostly lists all the ways that he exemplifies complete peace and equanimity, dispassionately awaiting whatever comes (including life and death). But this passage also suggests that the perfect man may have practiced some type of breathing exercises, as ordinary people breathe from their throats, but he somehow breathes from deep down in his heels. It's not clear how someone could pull that off, but it could easily be coded language for some kind of refined respiratory technique.

- **Lieh Tzu's conversation with the gatekeeper:** In this passage, Lieh Tzu plays the straight man as Lao Tzu's supposed gatekeeper explains how the perfect man comes about his imperviousness to harm and general fearlessness. Such a person holds onto the "pure *ch'i*" and unifies his nature and virtue, which somehow allows him to interact with the forces involved in the process of creation. Again, the passage doesn't really give any clue as to what kind of *ch'i* is more pure than other *ch'i,* or how to purify it, or how to hold onto it once it's pure, and Lieh Tzu's naiveté suggests that if there really are people engaged in such practices, they're probably traveling in pretty esoteric circles.

The main classical Taoist texts sometimes give indications that the adept's physical powers, longevity, or (perhaps) resistance to death may follow from specific holistic physical and spiritual practices, though they provide few hints as to what these "nourishing life" practices might be and even fewer specific testimonies as to who may be practicing them.

Reconstructing a lineage of interior cultivation

So, can we put together all the passages in the Classical Taoist texts that allude to physical-spiritual cultivation and determine whether people actually engaged in such practices? If so, can we figure out who they were and what types of techniques they practiced? And is it possible that such practitioners could've thought of themselves as members or followers of a distinct lineage, one that tied in directly to the various texts and authors that get lumped into the amorphous heading of "Classical Taoism"? The right answers could indicate that some kind of self-conscious "Taoist identity" really did exist long before the organizations that grew out of the Way of the Celestial Masters. And the right answers could suggest some significant continuity between Classical Taoism and the last 2,000 years of Taoist religious history.

And the answer is, well, *maybe*. Just maybe.

In order to talk about this, I need to bring another text into the conversation, one that most people — probably including Orthodox Unity and Complete Perfection Taoists in China today — have never even heard of. The text, actually a single book chapter, is called "Inward Training" *(Nei-yeh),* and it's been sort of "rediscovered" (actually, rescued from simple neglect) in recent years. The brief document — it's less than a third the length of the *Tao Te Ching* — makes up one chapter of the Hundred Schools Period text *Kuan Tzu,* a heterogeneous work consisting chiefly of political and legalistic essays. Oddly enough, because most of that text was probably written during the 4th century B.C.E., but was named for a historical figure from several hundred years earlier, people generally treated it as a forgery or apocryphal and didn't pay it much attention. Now that some scholars have finally dusted it off, they're finding some really important stuff, including the "Inward Training" chapter, which is drawing interest for several reasons:

- The text probably slightly predates both the *Tao Te Ching* and the earliest portions of the *Chuang Tzu,* making it possibly the oldest source of Taoist literature.

- The text is written in verse form, much of it rhyming, which makes it the structural and stylistic ancestor of the *Tao Te Ching.*

- Its shared language and thematic continuities with the *Tao Te Ching* and *Chuang Tzu* suggest the possibility that all the authors were familiar with or participated in some of the same practices.

- It introduces terminology that figures prominently in both traditional Chinese medicine and later Taoist practices, possibly providing an important "missing link" between the Classical Taoist texts and later traditions of religious Taoism.

The "Inward Training" chapter seems to be describing a regimen that involves engaging in a series of "alignments" or "rectifications" (of the body, limbs, *ch'i,* and mind), for the purpose of "maintaining the One," where the "One" is almost certainly a reference to the *Tao.* This allows you to function with a fully cultivated mind and heart and demonstrate the various characteristics of a perfected person, including equanimity, longevity, and a transformative effect on those you encounter. The cultivation practices clearly cut across the basic Western division of physical and spiritual, as they stress the preservation of *ch'i* in order to maintain your *vital essence* (an innate reservoir of life-giving *ch'i*), and develop your *spirit (shen),* a more vaguely defined quality that seems to provide some direct conduit to the *Tao* (Chuang Tzu describes one of his sages as "concentrating his spirit"). The triad of *ch'i,* vital essence, and spirit will eventually play a crucial role in later Taoist practices, especially internal alchemy (see Chapter 15 for more on alchemy).

Some scholars have suggested, a few more strongly than others, that the "Inward Training" chapter provides the thread — one of holistic cultivation — that weaves through all the Classical Taoist texts, and may even continue into Huang-Lao Taoist texts like the *Huai Nan Tzu.* This then produces a revised picture of Classical Taoism not as simply one loosely affiliated cluster of participants in the Hundred Schools debates on morality and governance, but as a distinct lineage (or handful of related lineages) of teachers and students who seek the *Tao* through a specific set of contemplative and physiological practices.

It may be quite appealing to consider interior cultivation as the "essence" of early Taoism, the "holy grail" that unites disparate Taoist elements into one coherent tradition. But it's probably more likely that interior cultivation represents just one strand of a number of overlapping philosophical, religious, and hygienic currents. Before you start equating Taoism with inward training, you may want to remember the following:

- ✔ **There's still really no substantial historical evidence of a lineage of practitioners during the Classical Period.** At this point, some scholars are picking up the breadcrumbs of similar language in a few texts and then coming up with imaginative reconstructions of who might have written and used them, as well as how they interacted socially and transmitted their teachings. It's terrific work, but at the moment it's still speculative.

- ✔ **Other classical Taoist texts develop many other themes that don't appear in "Inward Training" and are more often than not presented without any reference to cultivation techniques.** These themes include logical skepticism, criticism of Confucian and Mohist morality, government by non-doing, suspicion of language, and ongoing creation of order from chaos.

> ✔ Even if a case can be made that variants of "Inward Training" tech-
> niques persist in different Taoist contexts, there are simply so many
> other central Taoist concerns and practices — millenarianism, healing
> and public confession of sin, the pantheon of deities, priestly ordina-
> tion ranks, and esoteric rituals of offering and purification — that it
> would be prudent not to exaggerate the importance of any one recur-
> ring theme or practice.

The Immortality Cults

It's not entirely clear how closely the Classical Taoist authors affiliated themselves with hygienic, longevity, or immortality practices, but there's really
very little doubt that various non-Taoist characters explicitly sought those
things in earnest. In other words, ancient China immortality cults flourished
quite independent of the emerging Taoist traditions, and probably figured
in folklore and mythology well before the *Tao Te Ching* and *Chuang Tzu*. So,
there's really nothing inherently Taoist about those particular pursuits. But
such practices — like so many others that originated outside of Taoism —
do eventually work their way into the Taoist "family tree," and it's helpful to
trace their origins before plunging right into the Taoist assimilation of them.

In this section, I fill you in on the pre-Taoist background of the Chinese
immortality cults. You get to know a few of the earliest legends concerning
immortal beings and far-off places that hold the secrets of immortality, as
well as the story of how the notorious (and truly sociopathic) first emperor
of a unified China acted on his obsessions to seek this elusive immortality.

Legendary tales of immortals

The ancient Chinese may never have actually found their fountain of youth,
but that never prevented ordinary people from searching for it, self-styled
experts from claiming to know all about it, or storytellers from passing on
fables about it. Some stories became especially popular, and many of these
endured for centuries in Chinese literature and popular culture. Here are
some of the more memorable images:

> ✔ **The island of P'eng-lai:** This was supposedly an island paradise — one
> of several "spirit mountains" — that people believed they could find
> somewhere off the eastern coast of China. Chinese rulers all the way
> back to the 4th century B.C.E. made efforts to locate it, so they could eat
> the native magical herbs that conferred immortality. But no one ever
> seemed to find it, probably because the giant turtles that carry the

island on their backs would move it away any time they saw someone coming. Eventually, the Palace of P'eng-lai became synonymous with a dwelling place for immortals.

Don't confuse the mythic island with the port town in modern Shan-tung that has the same name.

✔ **Mount K'un-lun:** This is a mythic mountain described in folklore as located somewhere off to the west, perhaps even deep in central Asia. The peak gradually takes on an association with the Queen Mother of the West, a popular goddess who also originated outside of Taoism. In addition to housing the goddess and various immortal beings, Mount K'un-lun also grows special peaches — the "fruits of immortality" — once every 3,000 years, which explains why there was once a temple in Beijing called the Palace of the Peaches of Immortality. The mountain makes a couple of cameo appearances in *Chuang Tzu,* and the Highest Purity Taoists adopted both the goddess and the mountain, giving both a permanent place in Taoism.

✔ **The far-off journeys:** This referred to a technique of engaging in ecstatic, otherworldly excursions. One ancient poem describes a traveler who journeys into the heavens and encounters both terrifying beasts and immortal deities, eventually transforming into a celestial emperor who commands the gods and reaches the "great beginning." Although these practices probably originated with "freelance" shamans, Taoist texts eventually adapt these to their own techniques and identified destinations as sacred islands and mountains.

These places and practices associated with immortals probably originated in non-Taoist circles, but eventually blended into the broader Taoist tradition.

The first emperor's obsessions

Of all the ancient Chinese who pursued the secrets of immortality, no one did so more dramatically, and at greater expense, than Ch'in Shih Huang-ti, the man who unified China through a Legalist ideology at the end of the Hundred Schools Period. To accomplish this, he frequently consulted a class of adepts known as *fang-shih,* a term that translates literally as "methods specialists," but which covers a whole range of quasi-scientific arts like divination, exorcism, and astrology. He sent several of them on expeditions to locate the island of P'eng-lai — many of them claimed to know where to go and how to find the immortality potions — and he had no reservations about executing those that he thought were frauds.

The best-documented (and most mind-boggling) of these expeditions involved a *fang-shih* named Hsü Fu, who communicated to the emperor that with the right crew, he could reach P'eng-lai, connect with the thousand-year-old immortal who lived there, and return with the magical herbs that grew there. Historical accounts record that the emperor dispatched Hsü Fu with hundreds, perhaps thousands, of children and young men and women to help him complete his quest. Most versions of the story say that Hsü Fu's ships neither found the island nor returned to China — perhaps finding Japan instead — but some versions say that a huge fish blocked the entry, which the emperor subsequently went out to try to slay, also unsuccessfully.

Although Ch'in Shih Huang-ti never found the immortality potions he had sought, he did take pains to make sure that he was well tended in the afterlife, arranging for an elaborate burial in what amounted to a vast underground city, with palaces, precious objects, elaborate crossbows (to stop thieves from looting the place), and candles made of whale oil. But of course, the most breathtaking feature of Ch'in Shih Huang-ti's tomb was the terracotta army, a statue battalion of thousands of soldiers and hundreds of horses and chariots, which any tourist in Xi'an can visit today. So, perhaps he didn't live forever, but how many people who lived 2,200 years ago still have such majestic tombs that are so exquisitely preserved?

Taoism and So-Called Immortality

By the time Taoism began to take shape as an established religious tradition, it had pretty much incorporated many of the various immortality practices that had floated around up to that point, eventually giving rise in China to the widespread impression that immortality was a "Taoist thing," even though the actual historical roots were a little more complicated. Certainly, immortality does make up an important part of later Taoism, but many people have either misunderstood or exaggerated the exact role. In fact, as you'll see here, even the words *immortal* and *immortality* don't really do justice to exactly what the Taoists have in mind.

In this section, I untangle some of the details of the part that so-called "immortality" has played in Taoism. You discover how the Taoists understood immortal or transcendent beings, as well as who some of the best-known immortals are in the Taoist pantheon and popular folklore.

The idea of postmortem immortality

If you can remember only one thing about Taoist immortals, it's that they're *not* people who live forever here on Earth. If you think about it, that makes a lot of sense, because if there were even *one* person who had accomplished that goal, we'd probably all know about him or her — not to mention all the attention that scientists, theologians, and advertising executives would be paying. But up to this point, apart from Mel Brooks's "2,000-year-old man," the world has yet to see any real Earthly immortals.

So, what do the Taoists mean by "immortals"? What kind of "immortality" are they talking about? The Chinese term *hsien* refers to people who, when they die, don't simply become ordinary "ancestral spirits" or "ghosts," who are in some ways dependent on the veneration and ritual offerings of the living. Instead, they achieve the status of what you could call "postmortem immortals," powerful and autonomous beings who, depending on their post-humous ranks, could reside in the heavens, on sacred mountains, or even in the underworld. It would be an exaggeration to say that every ordained Taoist priest or member of a Taoist community (like the original Way of the Celestial Masters) was actively pursuing postmortem immortality as a final goal, but there's no denying just how much Taoist practice did involve some variation on that theme. Individual practices like alchemy (both the internal and external varieties) were traditionally directed toward the attainment of postmortem immortality, and even some contemporary Taoists use rituals to transform "ordinary" spirits of the dead into *hsien*.

Fairly early in the era of organized Taoism, a number of biographies — or, more accurately, legendary accounts — of immortal figures began to circulate, and they often depicted immortals as having extraordinary powers to accompany their otherworldly status. Here are just a few of the qualities that immortals may possess:

- **The power of transformation:** Some immortals could change their own shape or transmute physical objects from one form to another. They could also appear in more than one place at the same time.

- **The powers of healing and exorcism:** Immortals may have the power to look inside your body in order to see which organs need healing, which they can take care of because they know how to do a sort of spiritual acupuncture or herbalism, a kind that doesn't involved actual needles or medicinal substances.

- **Extraordinary physical appearance:** If you're going to be an immortal for the rest of your postmortem "life," you may as well be nice looking. Immortals look young (but without the pimples) and have all their teeth, though some have exaggerated physical features.

- **Superhuman powers:** Immortals seem to have the usual Taoist imper-viousness to fire and cold, but some have unlimited strength or can do other things like walk through walls, levitate, or travel spontaneously through space and time.

- **Telepathic or telekinetic powers:** Some immortals can read minds or move objects through psychic energy. Along these same lines, some can use their minds to control animals or even other lower-ranking spirits.

Taoist immortality is not living forever here on Earth, but enjoying an eternal, super-powerful existence in a non-Earthly afterlife. Distinguishing how much of this is part of actual Taoist doctrine and how much is from the folklore and fantastic stories about Taoist practices is sometimes difficult.

The Eight (and other) Immortals

Several biographical texts in the Taoist Canon tell the stories of various immortals, ranging from idealized historical figures to purely mythic characters. For example, some accounts describe how when the first Celestial Master Chang Tao-ling died, his body took on a luminous glow and he then ascended to Heaven to become an immortal in broad daylight. Other important figures in Taoist history — Lao Tzu, Chuang Tzu, the Yellow Emperor, Liu An (the prince who commissioned the *Huai Nan Tzu*), T'ao Hung-ching (the architect of the Highest Purity lineage) —— also become "promoted" to that status in later texts. And a whole bunch of figures you've never heard of — like Kui Ku-tzu, Fei Chang-fang, and Ko Hsüan — also end up somehow earning that status long after they actually died.

Taoist scriptures and folklore attest to many other *hsien,* but no figures in the entire pantheon have as much star power as the Eight Immortals, an octet of (mostly) mythic adepts with colorful personal narratives. Apparently, the idea of Eight Immortals goes back to at least the 8th century, and because it carried so much religious and aesthetic cachet, several different groups may have competed for the title. The group that endures to this day emerged sometime around the 12th or 13th century, originally as characters in theatrical performances, and gradually working their way into the official pantheon. In fact, they're now so much a part of the mainstream tradition that the major Taoist temple in the terra-cotta army city of Xi'an, the Temple of the Eight Immortals (actually, the Eight Immortals Hut, as it's a smallish temple), is dedicated to them. The temple is affiliated with Complete Perfection Taoism, and the present-day Eight Immortals are mostly venerated in that lineage.

So, who are (or were) these Eight Immortals? Here they are — the actual order sometimes varies — with a little quasi-biographical tidbit on each one:

> ✔ **Chung-li Ch'üan:** Supposedly a one-time Han Dynasty general who received instructions from an immortal after escaping from an unsuccessful battle, Chung-li Ch'üan carries the title of second Complete Perfection patriarch, even though he would've lived about a thousand years before the lineage began. Most images show him with a bulging belly (a la the Laughing Buddha) and carrying a magic fan that can transform stones into special metals (alluding to alchemy) or revive the deceased.

✔ **Chang Kuo-lao:** A *fang-shih* and hermit from the 7th century, Chang Kuo comes across as a shape-shifting, wine-drinking eccentric. Images usually depict him with a long white beard — he's regarded as kind of an elder immortal — and riding a donkey backward, which is how he would supposedly travel the country.

✔ **Lü Tung-pin:** The most popular of the Eight Immortals, and supposedly taught by Chung-li Ch'üan himself, this 8th-century figure earns accolades from Complete Perfection Taoists as one of the forefathers of internal alchemy. He seems to be the Renaissance man of the bunch, with skills in poetry, calligraphy, healing, and swordsmanship. Folklore surrounding him includes the "Yellow Millet Dream" (a profound dream he had where he lived for some 18 years, even though in actuality he was only asleep for the time it took his millet to cook) and a series of ten ordeals he had to endure before he could achieve immortality.

✔ **Li T'ieh-kuai:** A figure of dubious historicity, Iron-Crutch Li (as he was known) frequently took "far-reaching journeys," where he would roam the heavens while leaving his (apparent) corpse behind on Earth. Of course, on one such journey, his disciples missed a memo and cremated his body, leaving him with no other option upon his return than to inhabit the body of a recently deceased beggar with a crippled leg and — you guessed it — an iron crutch.

✔ **Ts'ao Kuo-chiu:** A supposed relative of a Song Dynasty emperor (which explains why he's usually depicted dressed like a government official), Ts'ao Kuo-ch'iu fled the corruption of the world to become a hermit, eventually receiving instruction from Lü Tung-pin.

✔ **Ho Hsian-ku:** The only female of the bunch, Ho Hsian-ku supposedly lived in the late 7th or early 8th century. While she was in her teens, a deity instructed her during a dream on how to concoct an alchemical mixture, which she promptly ate and then gained immortality, making the promise that she would remain an eternal virgin.

✔ **Han Hsiang-tzu:** Sometimes identified as the nephew of a famous (though hot-headed) 9th-century Confucian scholar, Han Hsiang-tzu was a musician and magician who could make flowers grow. Because he's usually depicted holding a magic flute, he's also sort of a patron saint of flute players.

✔ **Lan Ts'ai-ho:** The most ambiguous character of the immortals, Lan Ts'ai-ho comes off as another oddball, wearing a single boot, sleeping in snow, and frequently getting loaded. Though generally regarded as a male, Lan sometimes showed up in female form in popular theater.

The Eight Immortals: Here, there, and everywhere

Western depictions of Taoism can't get enough of Lao Tzu and Chuang Tzu, but Chinese pop culture has embraced the Eight Immortals with relish, inserting them just about everywhere from postcards to comic books. And some of that has even spilled over into American pop culture. You may not have recognized these as the Taoist Eight Immortals, but here they are:

✔ *Drunken Master:* In this cheesy Hong Kong Jackie Chan movie, Chan's mischievous character learns a form of "drunken boxing" called "the eight drunken immortals," which supposedly copies the martial arts movements of the real Taoist Eight Immortals.

✔ **X-Men comics:** In several issues, the Eight Immortals appear as superheroes (what else?) charged with protecting China from evil mutants. In one issue, they team up (after some initial mutual mistrust) with the Collective Man to take on the villainous Xorn.

✔ **Feng Shui role-playing game:** In the role-playing game Feng Shui, the Eight Immortals appear in the "sourcebook" for one of the factions in the "secret war." Wow.

✔ **8 Immortals Restaurant:** If you happen to be wandering through San Francisco's Chinatown, you can try the sliced pork with dry mustard greens in a clay pot, or the sea cucumber and black mushrooms. It's not clear were the Immortals come in, but if the food's good, so what?

Chapter 15

Internal Cultivation through the Discipline of Alchemy

Chinese alchemy and various related practices involving meditation and visualization almost certainly make up the most difficult and impenetrable layers of Taoism. Of the world religions textbooks that do include a chapter on Taoism or Chinese religion, most make only passing reference to alchemy, provide little in the way of historical context, or simply skip the subject altogether. And it's easy to see why, at least according to Otis Redding:

✔ **Been Loving You Too Long:** The classical texts that have so captured the Western imagination make no mention of alchemy. What's more, the seemingly quietist, natural philosophy of the *Tao Te Ching* and *Chuang Tzu* genuinely appears to be at odds with the deliberate, gritty, and sometimes dangerous world of alchemical pursuits. It's just easier to stick with Lao Tzu, and leave alchemy for another day.

✔ **Too Hard to Handle:** The few Chinese alchemical texts that have been translated into English generally include dense technical language, references to unfamiliar historical figures, and coded directions that you probably couldn't follow if you wanted to. Even among specialists in Chinese religion, the fraternity of scholars who understand Taoist alchemy really well makes up a pretty small subset.

✔ **A Waste of Time:** Many people vaguely know the European alchemical legacy as a hodgepodge of pre-scientific, occult, and quackish ideas that would eventually be discredited and replaced by legitimate disciplines like chemistry and modern medicine. If we don't pay much attention to Western alchemy, why bother with the Taoist version?

But if you want to understand the actual practice of Taoism, you really have to confront alchemy sooner or later. Even though alchemy may have initially begun as an obscure, peripheral part of the tradition, it did eventually integrate considerably into the Taoist mainstream. True, you won't actually find many garden-variety alchemists mixing potions in China (or anywhere else for that matter) today, but you will find a range of contemporary practices — meditation techniques, physical health regimens, and rituals on behalf of the dead — that incorporate alchemical theory and language.

In this chapter, I discuss alchemy and alchemically based practices, introducing both the subject itself and explaining its role in Taoism. You get a feel for alchemy as a global phenomenon, its origins in China, the ways it became integrated into Taoist practice, and how the nature of alchemy transformed over time in some fascinating ways.

A Global Perspective on Alchemy

Perhaps you already know something about alchemical traditions in Europe and other parts of the world, or maybe you've only encountered a few random snippets of it here and there, or maybe you'd never even heard the term until someone played a CD by the eclectic and prolific quasi-jazz band called Acoustic Alchemy. Either way, I think it may be helpful to consider the subject first in a more global context, if only to provide a frame of reference for the conversation about Chinese and Taoist alchemy. Alchemy can be a pretty big subject, so I develop it from the general to the specific.

In this section, I set the stage by talking about alchemy as a recurring theme in world history. You come away with a working definition of alchemy, as well as some basics on the extent of its place in Western culture.

What is alchemy?

In its most basic sense, *alchemy* refers to the transmutation of one substance, or a combination of substances, into another substance, especially one that's more valuable, powerful, or imbued with paranormal properties. Historically, this often meant turning ordinary metals into gold, but it also referred to creating potions that could cure diseases, prevent aging and death, or confer supernatural powers. Today, our knowledge of scientific method and chemical reactions may render a lot of alchemical thinking dated and obsolete, but there's no arguing how much the theorists and practitioners believed was at stake.

In its more extended sense, *alchemy* can also refer to any dramatic transformation of something into something else, especially through the mixing of incongruous elements in unexpected ways. And so, the band Acoustic Alchemy "transmutes" ordinary, contemporary acoustic or folk instrumentation into an inspired hybrid of multiple genres.

Importantly, many of the most memorable practitioners of alchemy didn't usually see it as just a set of isolated adventures in the laboratory. Instead, they linked it to broader philosophical, religious, and scientific pursuits, even as many of them historically operated on or near the fringes of their respective intellectual communities. The following are all disciplines that someone, at one time or another, tried to link to alchemical practices:

- **Astronomy:** The 16th-century alchemist Edward Kelly published a treatise that's usually translated as *The Theatre of Terrestrial Astronomy,* where he related alchemical practice to, among other things, the "copulation" of the sun and moon.

- **Astrology:** Also in the 16th century, Valentin Weigel — though less an alchemist himself than philosophical heir to the tradition — wrote *Astrology Theologised: The Spiritual Hermeneutics of Astrology and Holy Writ.* For a modern spin, the contemporary Scottish writer Adam McLean has compiled many "alchemical emblems" that employ astrological symbolism. Check out his website at `www.alchemywebsite.com/amcldraw.html`.

- **Psychology:** Though common use of the word *psychology* comes well after the heyday of European alchemy, many alchemists discussed what we can recognize now as psychological themes, and thinkers like Carl Jung were especially interested in relating alchemical imagery to his theories of the collective unconscious.

- **Medicine:** Paracelsus, the quite literal "Renaissance man" physician, had elaborate theories that combined pharmacology, toxicology, theology, and chemistry. He explicitly rejected alchemy for the purpose of refining precious metals, instead embracing it for the "power and virtue" that could be catalyzed medicinally.

Try to think of alchemy not as one thing, but as a general name given to a variety of practices involving the physical (sometimes chemical) transformation of substances, that usually tie in to broader religious or philosophical goals.

The presence of alchemy in the West

As you've probably figured out by now, Western alchemy is actually a huge subject, one that evolves and mutates for centuries, and that crosses into a number of different fields. There's really almost no way to boil it all down into a fistful of a few main themes, but it is feasible to give you a feel for just how pervasive alchemical practices have been in Western history.

Here are some key moments and places of alchemy's historical development in the West:

- **The Greco-Roman world:** During the period scholars generally refer to as Late Antiquity, which stretches from about the 2nd through 8th centuries, the city of Alexandria (in Egypt) was a hotbed of alchemical experimentation, which may have traced its roots to ancient Egyptian technological advancements (like metallurgy). One important figure was the 4th-century dabbler in Gnosticism, Zosimos of Panopolis, who saw the transformation of lead and copper into silver and gold as mirroring an internal process of purification and redemption of the individual person.

- **The Islamic world:** Piggybacking on the collapse of the Roman Empire, the Islamic Middle East harbored many alchemists, though not always without hostility from Muslim authorities. One fascinating Persian figure from the 8th century, Abu Mūsā Jābir ibn Hayyān, not only intended literally to create life in the laboratory, but also established an early system of classifying elements. The Latinized version of his name, Geber, may be the root of the word *gibberish,* in reference to the veiled language — which was unintelligible to outsiders — that he used for describing his theories.

- **The Medieval European world:** Beginning in the 12th century, English, Spanish, and French philosophers began translating Arab and Persian alchemical works, and found them congenial with their own attempts to construct holistic sciences. One important figure was Roger Bacon, a 13th-century Franciscan friar, who connected his search for the "elixir of life" with theological reflections on Adam and Eve and the ultimate goal of Christian salvation.

- **The Renaissance world:** During the period from the 14th through the 17th centuries, many different types of alchemy flourished in Europe, drawing from an eclectic swath of pharmaceutical, philosophical, and occult sources. Often, the titles of alchemical and related works from this period are especially provocative: John Dee's *Hieroglyphic Monad,* Johann Ambrosius Siebmacher's *Waterstone of the Wise,* and the anonymous Rosicrucian (a nominally Christian secret society) *Chymical Wedding of Christian Rosenkreutz.*

- **The modern world:** Though alchemy doesn't really exist as a distinct discipline or practice any longer, the interest in alchemy and its philosophical application is very much alive. Various recent movements — including the Theosophical Society, Western Esotericism, and Jungian psychology — have all embraced different aspects of it at one time or another. The contemporary New Age Movement also draws freely from alchemical theory.

The study and practice of alchemy has occurred in many places around the world, and for many different reasons. Some of these occurrences have influenced one another, but some developed independently. The forms of alchemy in the West took a completely different trajectory from those that developed in China.

Your one-stop for contemporary alchemy

Despite the decline of alchemy as an established practice in the West, a number of people still maintain a proprietary interest in it and have established online networks for enthusiasts to communicate with one another and make use of historical sources. In some ways, this is only fitting; just as alchemists often operated on the philosophical and scientific fringe, many of today's would-be alchemists indulge their interests not through organized classes and retreats (some versions of which are actually available in New Age circles), but through a cottage industry of virtual associations.

One of the most extensive of these virtual alchemy one-stops is The Alchemy Web Site (www.levity.com/alchemy), which was founded in 1995 by Scottish author and text compiler Adam McLean, who has in some ways been singlehandedly responsible for spreading alchemy to a contemporary Western audience. The site contains tens of thousands of pages of text, and thousands of alchemical images, so you need far more than a half-hour coffee break to dig into it in any depth. Here are some of the main resources you can find there:

✔ **Historical timelines:** Alongside lots of other historical data, the site includes a pair of legible timelines, one tracking various alchemists all the way back to about the 12th century, the other tracking known alchemical works during the same period.

✔ **Personal blog:** McLean's blog goes back to 2006, and it's still active. He periodically posts images, passages from texts, and his own autobiographical chronicles of reading and translating alchemical texts.

✔ **Primary sources:** The site includes hundreds of translated chapters from the original texts, including those dealing with philosophy, poetry, and yes, actual practical applications of the formulas.

✔ **Images:** You can find numerous images from alchemical sources, everything ranging from the ancient Egyptian symbols for metals, graphic signs for alchemical substances, images of laboratories and pharmacies, and "alchemical iconography."

✔ **Online discussions:** The site links to an online discussion forum, where only alchemy scholars can post materials (though others can eavesdrop). There's also an ordinary guestbook, which in the year after it opened, had posts by people from the United States, Canada, Germany, Uruguay, and Malta, commenting on such things as personal diet and graphic novels.

✔ **Global alchemy:** McLean includes resources on not only European and Chinese alchemy (including Fabrizio Pregadio's www.golden elixir.com, a Taoist alchemy one-stop in its own right), but also Indian, Islamic, and Burmese alchemy, with texts appearing in several different languages.

✔ **Miscellaneous links:** The Alchemy Web Site includes some links that are tangential to alchemy, but fit nicely with the overall fascination with medieval *esoterica* (obscure and impenetrable materials). You can follow the links to information about Dutch painter Hieronymus Bosch, a subsidiary one-stop on tarot art, and a separate blog just on tarot.

Early Alchemy in China

There's really no way to tell exactly how far back alchemy goes in China, but historical records do suggest that at least some versions of it had been lurking in the shadows for quite some time. In the early 2nd century B.C.E., a ritual specialist of some kind advised the emperor that the production of a potion transmuted from *cinnabar* (toxic mercury sulfide) before an imperial sacrifice would remedy his physical ailments. Not much later, a few texts began making references to ingesting such substances and relating the practice to the pursuit of immortality, and some of these texts may have attracted some imperial interest. For example, some fragmentary records indicate that the eclectic sponsors of the *Huai-nan Tzu* may have compiled texts at least partially concerned with alchemy.

In this section, I flesh out the details of the earliest alchemy groups in China. I discuss exactly what alchemy does (or doesn't) have to do with Taoism, as well as a pair of important figures and texts that were instrumental to the development and spread of Taoist alchemy.

The relationship between Taoism and alchemy

The short version of the story is that there's nothing inherently Taoist about Chinese alchemy, although they eventually became closely identified with each other. This doesn't mean that alchemy doesn't have certain thematic resonances with Taoism, or that they don't fit together well. What it does mean is that Chinese alchemy didn't initially have any historical connection to Taoism, that it evolved as an independent tradition (or several independent traditions) for a few hundred years before they began to come together. But because they did, in fact, come together eventually, Taoists more or less retroactively wrote the earlier alchemy into their own history, much the same way Neo-Platonist Christian theologians would retroactively write classical Greek thought into theirs.

The earliest documented alchemical tradition in China probably dates to around the 2nd or early 3rd century, in a southern part of the country before the migration of the original followers of the Way of the Celestial Masters into that region. The fledgling alchemists there had a belief in postmortem immortals, which they linked to the worship of the Queen Mother of the West, the goddess who inhabited Mount K'un-lun, which was the source of the legendary peaches of immortality. In this region, the practitioners received and compiled the Great Purity revelations, what may contain the oldest known source of alchemical literature.

So, why shouldn't you think of these early practitioners as Taoists? Who am I to tell you that they can't be "real" Taoists if they want to be? Both of those questions really come from the assumption that alchemy is a specifically Taoist practice, and that there needs to be some good reason to exclude any

Chinese alchemists from the Taoist "club." But that assumption only occurs in the first place because hindsight gives us the benefit of 1,500 years of Taoist alchemical history. At the time, it doesn't appear that they understood anything they were doing as related to any specifically Taoist lineage. They didn't attach their teachings to the classical Taoist texts, made no mention (that we know of) of any typically Taoist notions of following the *Tao,* and had no relationship (yet) with the Celestial Masters community. It really does seem to have been an independent tradition.

The origins of alchemy in China almost certainly weren't Taoist. They were probably tied in most closely with a southern immortality cult that had not yet cross-pollinated with Taoist influences.

The Master Who Embraces Simplicity

As you probably expect by now, the unambiguously historical person who arguably did more than anyone else to legitimize the practice of alchemy wasn't a Taoist and was actually at times hostile to the Taoist legacy. His name was Ko Hung, a low-level public official who came from an aristocratic southern family, received a solid education in Confucian cultural and literary traditions, and to this day casts a long shadow over Taoist history. His surviving writings from the early 4th century constitute the most important and comprehensive existing glimpse into China's dim alchemical past.

Unlike most other Confucian scholars of his time, Ko Hung was fixated on the search for immortality — either Earthly or Heavenly — and he compiled numerous texts not only to aid in his own quest, but also to convince other members of the intelligentsia and social elite that such a pursuit was, indeed, a worthy, dignified way for an educated scholar-official to spend his time. During his years of research and travel, Ko supposedly authored dozens of books, but he pretty much owes his alchemical legacy to two of them:

- *Biographies of Spirit Immortals:* Ko wrote (or collected) this book, which includes accounts of many figures who would later be revered by generations of Taoists. It even includes the first known biographical record of Chang Tao-ling.

- *Master Who Embraces Simplicity (Pao-p'u Tzu):* More important, Ko wrote this book, the "Inner Chapters" of which provide instructions — albeit sometimes obscure ones — in a range of alchemically based immortality techniques. More a collector than an inventor, Ko didn't just come up with all the recipes himself, and he was kind enough to include a bibliography of his sources, which included more than 200 texts and dozens of talismans. Though most of these original sources haven't survived, the records provide crucial details for anyone trying to reconstruct the early history of Chinese alchemy.

In the *Master Who Embraces Simplicity,* Ko demonstrates familiarity with a number of physical cultivation practices — respiratory, gymnastic, sexual — but he gives only qualified praise to any method that doesn't go directly after the big enchilada of immortality. To help the reader achieve that ultimate end, Ko provides a series of complicated steps, which look far more like the performance of religious ritual than simply flinging a bunch of ingredients into a pot and cranking up the fire:

- ✔ **Selection of laboratory space:** This involves divination, similar to *feng-shui,* to identify a location that has the proper configurations and flow of *ch'i,* and that's sufficiently isolated so as not to be contaminated by people who are immoral or not sufficiently purified.

- ✔ **Preparation of laboratory space:** Alchemy is dangerous work, and it may involve summoning spirits, so you need to make sure the wrong ones don't come and gum everything up. This involves protective measures, like hanging talismans, wearing registers, making sacrificial offerings, suspending a mirror and sword over the entrance to the lab, and installation of a multi-tiered brick oven.

- ✔ **Preparation of the practitioner:** Keeping in line with the ritual aspect of this performance, the aspiring alchemist can't officially begin the process until he's in a state of ritual purity. This may involve cleansing, fasting, sexual abstinence, and no contact with human or animal blood.

- ✔ **Creation of the elixir:** Actually, the text includes several different recipes, involving a number of exotic (and often toxic) substances –things like deer antler, arsenic, mushrooms, *nacre* (mother of pearl), sulfur, and, of course, mercury — all of which you need to cook, stir, cool, and bury according to exact stipulations.

- ✔ **Post-production rituals:** Once the elixir is completed, you don't just scarf it all down. Because this product is tapping into an awesome power not normally accessible by humans, you first need to make thanksgiving offerings to appropriate spirits, and then take a portion of the substance into a public place where it can be shared with those less alchemically adept, though it's not clear whether this part of the practice really happened and how keen people were on ingesting glowing substances offered to them by strangers who probably looked like they hadn't slept for several nights.

Depending on the particular recipe, the quality of the hard-to-find substances in the mix, and the moral constitution of the person consuming it, the adept could attain various levels of immortality, including an indefinite Earthly existence, an immediate transformation of the body into refined *ch'i* and subsequent resolution in the Great Purity Heaven or the "deliverance from the corpse" after an apparently conventional death, which is what Ko's followers believe happened to him. Before the final transformation, he could also develop special powers like an ability to control wild animals or evil spirits, to fly or become invisible, or to appear in several places simultaneously.

The Seal of the Unity of the Three

A critical link in the development of alchemy is a single text that provides us with a throbbing headache of mysteries — even by Taoist standards. In this case, there's widespread disagreement about the authorship of the document, its exact dates of composition, and even how its five-character title should be best translated. For that matter, more than one subsequent alchemical lineage would claim "ownership" of the text. I'm talking here about a rich reservoir of alchemical reveries called the *Chou I Ts'an T'ung Ch'i,* which in its most recent English version translates into *The Seal of the Unity of the Three, in Accordance with the Book of Changes (Chou I* is literally the *Changes of Chou,* another name for the *I Ching* or *Book of Change).*

According to traditional histories, *The Seal of the Unity of the Three* came from the pen of a quasi-historical alchemist named Wei Po-yang, who actually would've predated Ko Hung by nearly a century. Still, it's almost certain that the text evolved over the next several hundred years, taking on many different authors who spliced into it their own language and interests. And so, the text seems to speak with many different "voices," which may or may not actually coalesce around a single, consistent line of thought. What's more, the text is packed with metaphors and allusions to other documents. It's not an easy read, by any stretch of the imagination.

That said, it does appear that *The Seal of the Unity of the Three* develops at least three distinct (but intertwined) motifs, which may reflect different authorial strains. Here's a quick summary of them:

- **Correlative cosmology:** Using repeated references to *I Ching* hexagrams, the text relates divination and movements of *yin* and *yang* (and the five elements) to the actions of ghosts and spirits, the interactions of sun and moon, the power of the emperor, and so forth. Most of this isn't intelligible if you're not already fluent in the *I Ching* and the legacy of commentaries on it.

- **Alchemy:** The text constantly talks about all the stuff of alchemy, like the "essential radiance" of gold in an intense fire, the "wooden essence of cinnabar," the consumption of a "reverted elixir," and the construction of metallic dikes and embankments, but very little of it looks like actual "instructions" in the conventional sense of the word. This no doubt presumes that only someone with extensive prior training in alchemical methods will have a clue as to how to apply it.

- **Classical Taoist terminology:** It's probably premature to think of this as a book of "Taoist alchemy," because it doesn't seem to assert any connection to a Taoist lineage and probably wasn't composed in a Taoist context, but it does employ some traditional Taoist language — particularly from the *Tao Te Ching* — in a number of places. For the most part, this language is divorced from its Hundred Schools Period parentage and juxtaposed with possible alchemical meanings, like when the dyad of being and non-being is related to the respective "cavities" of metal and breath, or when the admonition to "know the white, but keep to the black" refers to the "essence of metal" and the "foundation of water." The term *true man* may echo Chuang Tzu's labels for his airy and whimsical sages, but in this text it clearly refers to an alchemical adept.

The *Seal of the Unity of the Three* combines alchemy with a number of other influences, including the divination patterns from the *Book of Change* and the correlative cosmology of the "five elements" theories. It also drew on some Classical Taoist terminology, foreshadowing the much more intimate relationship between Taoism and alchemy that was just ahead.

The Taoist Integration of Alchemy

As *The Seal of the Unity of the Three,* the works of Ko Hung, and other sources began to circulate more widely, alchemy continued to pick up steam in China, achieving something of a heyday during the period between the 5th and 9th centuries. It's also around this time when alchemy became a clear-cut part of Taoism, mainly through its role in the Highest Purity cultivation groups, which integrated their own wide-ranging practices with various features from the fragmented Celestial Masters tradition. At this point, many streams began to converge, including the rituals and deities from the Way of the Celestial Masters, the southern cult of immortality, the practice of alchemy, and the expansive worldview (and associated practices) of the Highest Purity revelations. From this point on, the sense of a distinct Taoist identity would grow more pronounced.

In this section, I talk about the impact that alchemy had on the development of Taoism. I unpack some of the details of the synthesis of Taoism and alchemy in the early cultivation groups like Highest Purity, explain how this gave rise to a new understanding of the human body, and introduce you to some visualization practices that the Taoists taught during this period.

Alchemy in the Taoist cultivation groups

If Chinese alchemy began as a literal search for wealth through the production of metals or for immortality through the concoction of a magical potion, the alchemical methods in Highest Purity Taoism made up just one piece of a much more comprehensive regimen of physical and spiritual self-cultivation. In other words, alchemy and postmortem immortality came to augment, rather than define, an elaborate Taoist process of individual cultivation. You'll sometimes hear scholars refer to the overall aim as "cosmicizing" the individual practitioners — granting them a new status as elevated beings existing in harmony with the cosmos, putting some slightly different spins on the concept of immortality. Highest Purity practitioners alternately understood this process as unifying with spirits or perfected beings, undertaking ecstatic journeys, or having your name inscribed in a cosmic register.

One example of a newly transformed Highest Purity alchemical practice is the preparation, meditation on, and ingestion of an "efflorescent elixir" named for either a rare gem or a tree that supposedly grows on Mount K'un-lun. As always, the process is pretty elaborate, though now it takes an extraordinary length of time to complete and incorporates numerous ritual practices that take place both inside and outside the laboratory:

1. **The practitioner purges himself or herself of impurities through 40 days of cleansing rituals.**

2. **The practitioner fashions a *crucible* (laboratory vessel for heating substances) from a special mud.**

   The mud is made from things you might expect (like red clay) and a handful of odd surprises (like sheep's hair and worm poop).

3. **After divination has identified the appropriate day to start the adventure, the practitioner must engage in another 30 days of purgation rituals.**

   At this point, it's already been more than two months, and you haven't lit a single match or swallowed a single metal.

4. **The practitioner mixes 14 different exotic ingredients.**

   The ingredients include *malachite* (a copper carbonite hydroxide), *actinolite* (a complex silicate), and *orpiment* (an arsenic sulfide), with mercury added last. Not stuff you find at the grocery store.

5. **The practitioner seals the crucible (with another inverted crucible made of the same substance as the first one) and heats the concoction for 100 days.**

   At this point, we're talking about close to six months into the process.

6. **After completing the previous stages (which technically make up only one "official" stage of the process), the practitioner engages in three distinct periods of meditation.**

7. **The practitioner swallows the completed substance on a prescribed day.**

   This causes a change in the practitioner's complexion and the emanation of multicolored vapors from his or her head. Depending on what the practitioner does next, he or she can summon chariots, flying dragons, immortals, or even deities known as the Three Pure Ladies.

8. **The practitioner buries remaining portions of the completed substance in the ground.**

   A tree should grow in this place over the next three years. The fruits of that tree confer — what else? — immortality, just like the peaches of Mount K'un-lun.

Don't try this at home! Just in case you're thinking that it may be cool to give some of this stuff a whirl, I'd like to warn you that it's really not a good idea. Aside from the fact that Taoist texts repeatedly warn that this is big-time *dangerous* for an uninitiated person to try, modern science and medicine corroborate that most of these substances are seriously toxic and will get you really sick, or worse.

The changing map of the human body

Taoism employed alchemy less for a single-minded quest for immortality than as one component of a considerably more complex and holistic vision of self-cultivation. This accompanied a changing, ever-expanding application of correlative cosmology's correspondence theories, which related every aspect of the alchemical enterprise — the ritual steps, the physical ingredients, the process of transmutation, the transformation of the person after ingesting the substance — to configurations of *ch'i,* spiritual beings, the alignment of the stars, and various other cosmic agents or processes. And given the utter physicality of the practices, it makes sense that they would subject the human body to much the same kind of analysis.

The idea of the body as microcosm extends to many different areas, including geographical regions (often in Heavenly locations), so it's not unusual to see Taoist texts or art depicting the body as, for example, a celestial mountain or palace. One of the most significant features of this rethinking of the human body is how the Taoists began to imagine it as the dwelling place for deities who simultaneously live in Heaven (or elsewhere). As a result, the physical cultivation of the body becomes equated with the spiritual maintenance of the gods and, by extension, the stewardship of the universe. Personal cultivation takes on very high stakes indeed.

Although the new map of the body depicts deities in the various organs and a number of general locations, much of the attention goes to deities who are concentrated in three specific regions, which the Taoists identify (using overtly alchemical language) as "cinnabar fields" or "elixir fields." A trio of deities called the "Three Ones" (not to be confused with the "Three Pure Ones" or the "Three Pure Ladies"), who were created in the original transformations of *ch'i,* reside in these fields, one in each. Working from bottom to top (which is the appropriate direction for cultivation and visualization), the three cinnabar fields and their respective main deities are as follows:

- **The lower field:** Located in the abdomen (slightly below the navel), and later sometimes called the Gate of Destiny, this field houses the Lower One (or the Masculine One). His attending deity takes care of stuff like blood and intestines.

- **The middle field:** Located in the heart (or upper solar plexus), and also called the Mysterious Female (a term from the *Tao Te Ching*) or the Yellow Court, this field houses the Middle One (or the Feminine One). Even though this deity possesses a talisman identified with femininity, it is still seen as a male being.

- **The upper field:** Located in the head (or brain), and also called the Muddy Pellet, this field houses the Upper One (or the Emperor One). Because the human brain is such a complex organ, adepts further divide this field into a number of chambers they refer to as "palaces."

Taoist teaching will continue to refer to these regions of the body as cinnabar fields, even when no specifically alchemical practice is involved. This is an example of how Taoism integrated alchemical theory and language, as part of a more comprehensive understanding of cosmology and personal cultivation.

The role of visualization

As Taoists integrated alchemical principles with other established Taoist ideas and practices, and came to understand deities as internalized within the body, they soon began to accomplish the joint processes of cultivating the person and maintaining the deities through various types of visualization, performed in a meditative setting. This practice involves not only sitting and visualizing internal deities themselves, but going through the types of ritual preparations associated with alchemy (like fasting and preparation of the meditation chamber as though it were an alchemical laboratory), following directions in order to generate and hold specific mental images (like a burning sun, which then resolves into the image of a deity), and perhaps experiencing psychic encounters with the deities or journeys to other parts of the cosmos.

The Taoists developed many types of visualization techniques, or forms of meditation that involve visualization. Here are few of the more interesting ones, all developed in Highest Purity Taoism:

- **Whirling wind:** The practitioner is supposed to visualize a white concentration of *ch'i,* which circulates through the entire body, changes color, and, upon exhalation, transforms into an androgynous child, a form of the Upper One of the upper cinnabar field.

   ✔ **Triple harmony:** This visualization of the Three Ones includes confession
      of sins, with the intention of driving out of the body a trio of disease-causing
      parasites called the "Three Corpses," and their buddies the "Nine Worms."

   ✔ **Untying embryonic knots:** By visualizing primal *ch'i,* you can literally
      untie a dozen "knots" that formed in your organs during gestation and
      make you susceptible to illness, aging, and death. Successfully untying
      them all can result in the formation of an "immortal embryo."

From External to Internal Alchemy

As alchemy's popularity grew in China, so did the number of chemical
poisonings, whether through accidental ingestion of toxic substances or
intentional ritual suicides where the adept fully expected to be reborn as a
postmortem immortal. In fact, a few emperors in the early 9th century apparently died from alchemical poisoning while hoping for something better.
Although it's hard to know for sure how responsible these deaths were for
changing people's attitudes, it was right around that time when Taoists
began to rethink completely what they even meant by *alchemy.*

The new understanding was to view alchemical instructions as metaphorical,
to interpret all the talk of ritual purification, preparing the laboratory, finding
substances, firing furnaces, and eating concoctions as symbolic illustrations
of meditational and visualization techniques, all without employing any actual
equipment or playing with any actual physical substances. Because this didn't
involve the use of any *external* trappings, the Taoists who adopted this practice started calling the original, more conventional, and literal alchemy by the
name "external alchemy" *(wai-tan),* which they viewed as an inferior or merely
preparatory practice. They called the new model — which involved only introspective practices, attention to energies inside the body, and transmutations
of the person (as opposed to the metals) — "internal (or inner) alchemy" *(nei-
tan).* The Complete Perfection Taoists especially adopted this form of alchemical practice, eventually coming to understand that it had replaced the earlier
types. And over time, the external alchemy did, indeed, disappear in favor of
the safer, more spiritualized version of chemical transmutation.

The use of the terms *internal alchemy* and *external alchemy* may actually imply
a subtle polemic — that is, a contentious argument — against those who still
practiced the less "advanced" forms of alchemy. Practitioners of internal
alchemy also reinterpreted external alchemy texts (like *The Seal of the Unity of
the Three*), effectively claiming them as part of the *nei-tan* tradition.

In this section, I take you on a tour of some of the new features of this new
kind of symbolic alchemy. You'll become familiar with still another Taoist
interpretation of the human body, a new model of self-cultivation that persists in some circles to this day, and a type of structured Complete Perfection
meditation that utilizes the principles of internal alchemy.

Religious and linguistic supersession

Before the internal alchemists came along, there wasn't any reason to call alchemy "external alchemy" — alchemy was just alchemy. And so the irony here is that the expression *external alchemy* is only used by people who don't practice it. In effect, the internal alchemists claimed to supersede the earlier alchemists, so they created "external alchemy" to characterize what they rejected.

This strategy is actually fairly common when one religious tradition positions itself as moving beyond and superseding another one. Perhaps you've noticed that most Jews don't call their holy book the "Old Testament," because that's a label invented by Christians to recast a book they believe has been superseded by a new one. And the type of Buddhism that you find in China, Japan, Korea, and Tibet describes itself as the "Greater Vehicle" (Mahayana), while casting the earlier, traditional Buddhism in Southeast Asian the "Lesser Vehicle" (Hinayana). But sometimes, these new labels on old wine have pejorative connotations; if you meet a Sri Lankan monk or a Buddhist from Thailand, you may not want to ask him if he's a Hinayana Buddhist.

By the way, this method of changing something's name when a "replacement" comes along happens all the time in matters far more mundane than religion. Here's a list of a few words that didn't exist in the recent past, but now they're standard, thanks to changes the world has undergone lately:

- **Landlines:** We used to just call them "telephones." But now in the era of cellphones, we needed a name for those things you can't take out of the house and that won't bother people in movie theaters or cause auto accidents.

- **Snail mail:** Thanks to e-mail, we have a name for the literal mail that someone has to fly or walk from one place to another. I'm not sure postal workers particularly like this term.

- **Acoustic guitar:** There once was a time when all music was unamplified, where the only way someone could sing the national anthem at a ballgame loud enough for anyone to hear was to croon loudly into a huge megaphone. The pervasiveness of electric instruments has even forced multiple genres — rural blues, bluegrass, traditional Irish dance — into the single category of "acoustic music."

The body as the crucible

By reforming the entire alchemical enterprise as they did, internal alchemists managed to accomplish two goals simultaneously, goals that are necessary for any successful implementation of a reform movement:

- **They maintained continuity with the Taoist alchemical legacy.** That is to say, they didn't just toss out alchemy as dated or too dangerous, and they didn't just develop new forms of meditation and then try to convince everyone that those were still somehow forms of alchemy. Instead, they kept the terminology, the underlying theories, and the fundamental patterns of practice.

✔ **They adapted to the changing times and interests, perhaps even accommodating criticisms from the scholar-officials of the government by domesticating a dangerous practice and making it less threatening.** So, they had it both ways. As far as internal alchemists were concerned, it was still alchemy, but they managed to toss out whatever they regarded as the bathwater.

Once they undertake this synthesis, the internal alchemists give a spiritual interpretation to the alchemy vocabulary — a kind "interpretive alchemy." For instance, they now read references to a lab or a crucible as metaphors for the human body, raw chemicals as the basic internal energies of the body, and the refined elixir as the internal results of transformation.

The following five stages come from traditional external alchemy, but now refer to exclusively internal processes:

1. Laying the foundation

2. Union of *yin* and *yang*

3. Gathering the ingredients

4. Nourishing the embryo

5. Renewal of self

At the conclusion, the adept has returned to the *Tao,* understood as a harmonizing of his or her spirit with the original *Tao.* Yes, it's still a kind of postmortem immortality, but even this has a symbolic flavor to it.

Transformation from essence to emptiness

So, what's actually occurring during this internal alchemical process? What symbolic alchemical transformation occurs in the practitioner's body? To answer these questions, you need to know still another refinement of the Taoist view of the body. In internal alchemy, the three cinnabar fields don't just house important deities, they also contain different configurations of physical energies, and it's those energies that the meditation and visualization practices transform.

Here's a summary, again from bottom to top, of this even newer map of the body:

✔ **Vital essence *(ching):*** This is an unrefined reservoir of matter and energy that collects in the lowest cinnabar field, the one in the abdomen. Concretely, it can be identified with reproductive fluids.

- ✔ *Ch'i:* This is the more "generic" *ch'i* that collects in the middle cinnabar field, in the chest. It can be identified with air and breath, but also with emotional states.

- ✔ **Spirit** *(shen):* These are the most refined configurations of physical-spiritual "stuff" that collect in the upper cinnabar field. It's associated with mind, personhood, and access to spiritual beings.

You may recognize that all three of these terms had been knocking around Taoism in one form or another, for perhaps a thousand years before this system finally settled into place. They were key ingredients in the *Inward Training* text from the classical period — providing still another thread to connect the ancient and later forms of Taoism — although they were vaguely defined and hadn't yet taken on the associations that they acquired in internal alchemy. If you've dabbled in acupuncture or Chinese medicine, you may recognize these as the "three treasures," which make up an important triad in the underlying theory.

In internal alchemy, the starting point is the presumption — a la Lao Tzu's idea about the gradual departure from the *Tao* — that our living has effected an ongoing downward movement of these energies, a gradual diminishing of the person's vitality and life force. The ultimate goal, therefore, is to reverse that flow, to engage in a progressive refinement of these three quantities, moving in an upward direction from one cinnabar field to the next. So, the first stage consists of "refining vital essence and transforming into *ch'i*," which is basically cultivating the gross substance below and moving it upward in a more refined configuration. Then, the second step is "refining *ch'i* and transforming into spirit." But it doesn't end there — there's a final step of "refining the spirit and returning to emptiness," where they identify emptiness as nothing other than the *Tao,* just as Lao Tzu had done centuries earlier. And this reversion to the *Tao* is identical with the physical-spiritual cultivation of the person and attainment of immortality in harmony with the cosmic flow.

All internal alchemical practices have this theory and process at their base, and they do get translated into some unexpected forms. For example, the initial stage is often equated with males intentionally becoming sexually stimulated, avoiding orgasm, and "meditationally" redirecting the flow of semen upward, a process called "taming the white tiger." Sometimes, on late-night cable TV shows, you can hear testimony from people who claim to practice a more literal version of this.

Internal alchemy for women

Many Taoist practices are theoretically open to both sexes, but there's actually a technical term for women's internal alchemy *(nü-tan),* and the general process involves one or two significant changes. Women also follow a three-step spiritualized alchemical program, but because they don't possess semen (obviously), their movement from vital essence to *ch'i* works a little differently. Where the male tries to suppress the flow of semen, the woman tries to stanch the production of blood, which depletes the woman's energies (and distances her from the origin) each month. In the lexicon of women's alchemy, this is called "beheading the red dragon."

The other important difference involves the physical location of where this practice begins. The Chinese identified the source of the male "white tiger" in the testicles, which explains why they focus initial attention "down there" in the production and redirection of semen. However, they placed the female "red dragon" in the breasts, so they imagined that concentrating in that area — literally, massaging the breasts — would direct the flow of blood down to the lowest cinnabar field, from where it could only then could be redirected upward. And since blood is the focus, the ideal time to do this is shortly before menstruation.

Alchemical meditation

To some extent all forms of inner alchemy qualify as types of "alchemical meditation," because they basically operate as contemplative, internally oriented practices. But the Complete Perfection Taoists developed some specific forms of communal practices that made internal alchemy start to look a lot like another practice that was getting a lot of good press at that time in China: Buddhist sitting meditation. Eventually, Taoist monks and nuns would engage in seated meditation practices, which made them start to look a lot like Buddhist monks and nuns doing the same thing.

Probably the first such collective meditation in Complete Perfection circles was a practice called "sitting around the bowl," which was occasionally the centerpiece of study retreats lasting more than three months. The "bowl" in this practice was a device called a "water-clock," an ingenious little contraption where an inverted bowl with a hole in it gradually sinks into a larger bowl filled with water, a period which lasts for a predetermined increment (usually an hour). Having that as the object of meditation supposedly elicits a renewed attention to and awareness of time; it also visually embodies certain pieces of correlative cosmological theory, namely the meeting of wood and metal giving rise to the movement of water.

Chapter 16

Martial, Gymnastic, and Healing Arts: T'ai-chi and Ch'i-kung

*W*ere it not for the tremendous popularity in North America of *t'ai-chi, ch'i-kung,* and various other martial and gymnastic practices, it would be hard to justify putting a chapter like this one in an introductory book on Taoism. This is because of two undeniable pieces of background:

✔ **The vast majority of Chinese martial arts and physical health exercises aren't (and never were) Taoist.** Even *t'ai-chi* and *ch'i-kung* aren't necessarily Taoist — there are actually more forms of *ch'i-kung* that *aren't* Taoist than are.

✔ **When such practices do occur (or have occurred) in a Taoist context, they tend to inhabit a relatively small piece of the overall landscape.** If you look at the primary religious functions that practitioners from either major lineage perform today, you won't see either *t'ai-chi* or *ch'i-kung* at the top of the list.

In short, when the Chinese think of martial and gymnastic techniques, they don't particularly think of Taoism (except in some strains of popular fiction). And when they do think of Taoism, they don't particularly think of martial and gymnastic techniques. In terms of actual Chinese Taoist history, these practices occupy a relatively small corner, and it's important not to exaggerate their role.

But — and it's a big but — if you were to ask your friends — at least the ones who know anything about Taoism — to name some Taoist practices, they would probably be hard-pressed to name anything other than either *t'ai-chi* or *ch'i-kung*. And that's not including the ones who would insist that Taoism is all about *wu-wei* and that there's actually no such thing as Taoist practice! Of course, a big piece of this is simply, to put it bluntly, the market. Many teachers, recognizing that the Taoist "brand" carries a bit of a mystique — especially for the kind of audience that would be interested in pursuing holistic, Eastern-based physical-spiritual practices — have learned to play up, amplify, or even make up the Taoist connections. As a result, *t'ai-chi, ch'i-kung,* and similar practices have largely become the face of North American Taoism, recast to suit the spiritual needs of the modern West.

Ironically, American Taoism is more closely connected to *t'ai-chi* and *ch'i-kung* than Chinese Taoism is. And the reverse is true, too — American *t'ai-chi* and *ch'i-kung* are probably more consciously Taoist than Chinese *t'ai-chi* and *ch'i-kung* are.

But what are these practices with Chinese roots that have made such a splash in the United States and Canada? And how did they transform after they were transplanted into a new context. In this chapter, I help you find your way around some of these practices, sorting out *t'ai-chi, ch'i-kung,* and one controversial contemporary offshoot of *ch'i-kung,* all of which have had a major impact on the West.

T'ai-chi Ch'üan: The Boxing of the Great Ultimate

As you've no doubt gathered, China has produced a great number of personal practices that employ complicated maps of the body, combine the pursuits of physical and spiritual health, and cut across different religious traditions. Of all these, the one that is probably the best known worldwide is officially called *t'ai-chi ch'üan,* though it's often abbreviated in the West simply as *t'ai-chi.*

The often-ignored *ch'üan* part translates literally as "fist," which is important because, by extension, "*t'ai-chi* fist" refers to a particular type of boxing (there are others, like "eight extremities boxing" or "chop-hanging boxing"). No matter how much people employ it for health, spiritual wholeness, or fun, the name certainly suggests that it's a *martial* art.

So, what type of boxing is *t'ai-chi ch'üan?* It's an "inner boxing" — that is, one that is driven more by the internal circulation of *ch'i* than brute strength where the practitioner tries to tap into, align oneself with, or replicate the movement of *t'ai-chi,* the "Great Ultimate." And what's the Great Ultimate? The concept appears in many Chinese traditions (though it possibly originated in Taoism), and it refers to a kind of metaphorical cosmic ridgepole that binds and orients the universe. So, to practice *t'ai-chi* is to perform the boxing of the Great Ultimate, to engage in the stylized physical movements that are characterized by fidelity to the cosmos itself.

In this section, I talk about the history and practice of *t'ai-chi ch'üan*. You find out about its Taoist (or not Taoist) roots, the basic components of the practice, the way "ordinary" people in China tend to employ it, and the way it has become mixed and matched with other martial arts in the West.

The roots of t'ai-chi

Many people in China who teach *t'ai-chi* understand themselves to be heirs to and transmitters of a distinct training lineage that goes back to a 14th- or 15th-century figure named Chang San-feng. Like many Taoist "founding fathers," Chang may or may not have really existed, though he was actually already a legend in his own time, and more than one Chinese emperor unsuccessfully sent emissaries out to find him. Different popular accounts portray him as blind, funny looking, and adept at internal alchemy, Taoist sexual practices, and ordinary feats of magic. After these stories had circulated for some time, he achieved widespread recognition as a Taoist immortal, and you can find images of him at mainstream Taoist temples today.

The only problem with this version of the story is that there's no historical evidence that *t'ai-chi ch'üan* actually goes back that far, and the welding of the practice to a Taoist lineage seems to be a somewhat later invention. The earliest credible evidence of an actual *t'ai-chi* practitioner was a 17th-century former military officer named Ch'en Wang-t'ing, who may have learned from a teacher but also may have synthesized the various gymnastic methods popular at the time with his own military sensibilities. Ch'en passed the teaching down in his own family for several generations, and to this day "Ch'en style" endures as a popular form of *t'ai-chi*.

Several other styles of *t'ai-chi* also flourish today, and they, too, can be traced either directly or indirectly to Ch'en Wang-t'ing. Here are the most common styles and their lineages:

- ✔ **Yang Style:** This style descends from Yang Lu-ch'an, an employee of the Ch'en family who, depending on which version you believe, either learned or stole the practice from Ch'en's great-great-great-grandson. The Yang Style is the most common style today.

- ✔ **Wu Style:** As these things typically work, one of Yang's sons transmitted the teachings to the Wu family, who within a couple generations had put their own mark on it. This is another very common style, though not as popular as Yang Style.

- ✔ **Li Style:** One of the Wu family passed the teaching on to someone in the Li family, who established his own style, which is not particularly well known today. This is different from the Lee Style that you sometimes see, which claims a different, older ancestry but is hard to trace more than a few decades back.

- ✔ **Hao Style:** Continuing the transmission, one of the Li family taught members of the Hao family, who put their own stamp on it. Probably the least widely circulated of the active styles, the Hao Style is often called the Wu-Hao Style, because the Wu name carries more cachet than either the Li or Hao name does.

- ✔ **Sun Style:** Finally, the Hao family passed it on to Sun Lu-t'ang, who lived well into the 20th century. The Sun Style has noticeably slow and fluid movements, which makes it especially popular among older audiences.

The steps of t'ai-chi

Practitioners of *t'ai-chi ch'üan* learn several postures and movements called *forms,* each of which unfolds like a carefully choreographed cross between dance and gymnastics, which then combine into more complicated *routines.* Because there are so many different styles and sub-styles (which are still undergoing considerable change), there's really no one fixed "master list" of all the *t'ai-chi* forms and routines, and most students learn only a handful, at least for starters. Some styles have supposedly boasted routines with well more than 200 forms, but as the practice has grown more popular and more mass marketed, it's become pretty common for teachers to pare it down to a much smaller number. You can almost certainly buy videos online that will teach you a half-dozen or so forms, spelled out in easy steps.

Many of the forms vaguely resemble pantomime of particular actions, and their names describe them nicely: pounding the ground, needle at sea bottom, step up to seven stars, tornado kick, and playing the lute (sometimes called playing the guitar). Probably the best-known forms allude to animals in motion, or to the human interaction with animals, and their names conjure up some truly delightful images:

- ✔ White crane spreads its wings

- ✔ Step back and repulse the monkey

- ✔ Parting the wild horse's mane

- ✔ Golden rooster stands on one leg

- ✔ Tiger and leopard spring to the mountain

- ✔ Snake creeps down

- ✔ Green dragon shoots out pearl

Tigers crouching and dragons hiding in the Klingon home world

When Ang Lee's artsy film *Crouching Tiger, Hidden Dragon* somehow made the transition from low-budget Chinese fantasy to international success story, many American filmgoers suddenly caught their first glimpse of Chinese martial arts portrayed as a romantic, almost supernatural dance form. Many of the steps came from — or at least looked a lot like — *t'ai-chi ch'üan,* but this is by no means the only place where you can find *t'ai-chi* in the world of popular culture. As you'd probably expect, different versions of it permeate martial arts movies, books, and video games, and it also shows up in places neither specifically Chinese nor specifically martial artsy.

For example, in the 2000 film *Remember the Titans,* a half-true, half-fictionalized account of a Virginia high-school football team (and the community) coming to grips with racial integration in 1971, one scene shows a handful of girls swooning over the hippy backup quarterback Ronnie Bass while he does *t'ai-chi* in the yard. On two other occasions in the film, Bass puts his martial arts to use — once while preventing a teammate from laying a hand on him during a locker room fracas, and once while ducking on the field and effectively forcing a rusher to tackle himself. Of course, the especially funny thing about this is that in 1971, Richard Nixon hadn't yet made his diplomatic trip to China, the country was still pretty much closed to the West, and virtually no one in the United States — including the students at T. C. Williams High School, among them Ronnie Bass — had ever even heard of *t'ai-chi!* It's like they say: Art exaggerates life, or something like that.

But of all the pop-culture places where *t'ai-chi* has taken on a life of its own, probably none has a more interesting backstory than the long-running TV show, *Star Trek: The Next Generation.* As Trekkies can doubtless narrate in their sleep, the edgy, human-raised Klingon character Worf regularly practices (and teaches) a martial arts form called *mok'bara,* which is supposed to prepare body and mind for the rigors of personal combat, though some of the more milquetoast members of the crew are among his students. Of course, *mok'bara* looks an awful lot like a more aggressive and over-caffeinated *t'ai-chi,* which is not so surprising when you figure out that Dan Curry, the *Star Trek* visual-effects supervisor who developed and choreographed the techniques, was himself a longtime *t'ai-chi* enthusiast. Curry also came up with some of the Klingon weaponry and paraphernalia that were crucial in remaking the Klingons from generically evil space pirates into honorable space samurai, complete with their own versions of mystical vision quests and the Zen tea ceremony.

 Depending on who's doing the talking, the goal of learning these *t'ai-chi* forms can range from achieving a sense of "oneness" with the universe, to cultivating the body's *ch'i,* to obtaining a harmony of *yin* and *yang,* to improved balance, flexibility, and circulation. In the West, some people participate in *t'ai-chi* because they already engage in a range of holistic physical practices, like yoga and meditation. Others do so because they appreciate the resonances between the practices and Taoist philosophy. And I'm sure others pick it up simply because they have heard good things about it, have come across an inexpensive course at the local YMCA, and have a few hours a week to kill.

Sunrise in the park

You can practice *t'ai-chi* just about anywhere, indoors or outdoors, in front of the TV with one of the late David Carradine's instructional videos, or in your backyard with your friends and the family dog at your side. But many visitors to China are quick to report that some of their most charming experiences there took place near daybreak in a public park, where groups of people gathered for their morning exercise regimen. From Beijing in the north to Guangdong in the south, wherever your studies, business, or leisure travel takes you, chances are good that you can find a similar scene in a park near where you're staying.

These gatherings can be surprisingly diverse, including small practice groups, solo practitioners, and larger classes run by well-respected local teachers. You may find groups of all men, or all women, or both together, with some people wearing traditional martial arts outfits and others wearing ordinary street clothes. By and large, the practitioners tend to be a little older, though *t'ai-chi* has definitely begun appealing to increasingly younger audiences over the years. It's especially cool how, as the folks go through their motions, activity in the park proceeds as usual. Some people stop to watch for a few minutes, and others walk by without a glance. Just another morning at Ditan or Zhongshan Park!

There was a time not too long ago when Chinese kids and teenagers pretty much associated *t'ai-chi* — with its sometimes excruciatingly slow movements — as something only "old people" did, and they couldn't quite understand why so many younger Westerners gravitated to this "exotic" mystical practice. Back when *t'ai-chi* was still fairly new to America, many Chinese students studying here just kind of scratched their heads when their classmates got all excited about guests on campus conducting *t'ai-chi* workshops. It would probably be like an American teenager going to China for a student exchange program, and then learning that Chinese teenagers had all recently discovered water aerobics or bingo and thought it was the coolest thing!

The cement mixer of American Taoist martial arts

If you go shopping for a martial arts class for yourself or one of your kids, you may quickly find yourself overwhelmed by all the options. There are literally dozens of traditional Chinese styles, dozens more modern versions, dozens of Japanese styles, and, of course, styles from other countries as well. And although some martial arts centers and schools specialize in just a few types, it's not unusual to find many styles from many different places side-by-side in the same establishment, or different styles cross-pollinating with one another to form a new, "genetically engineered" hybrid. Of course, some of these are described as Taoist, and some of them have more obvious Taoist historical roots than others.

T'ai-chi for becoming healthy, wealthy, and wise

Irrespective of the quasi-religious background of *t'ai-chi,* some American research studies have demonstrated that *t'ai-chi* and similar practices may, indeed, have beneficial effects, including increasing energy and agility, decreasing stress, allowing for more restful sleep, and perhaps even bolstering the immune system. In fact, the Mayo Clinic, which is hardly an outlier when it comes to matters of public health, actually recommends *t'ai-chi* practice on its website. Apart from listing the possible benefits, it also emphasizes that *t'ai-chi* is easy to try and carries minimal risk (though Mayo does advise you to consult a healthcare professional first if you're pregnant or have certain medical problems). Here's a quick summary of Mayo's "soft sell":

✔ It has a low physical impact on your body.

✔ It puts minimal stress on your joints and muscles.

✔ It's adaptable to most ages and fitness levels.

✔ It's inexpensive to practice.

✔ It doesn't require you to obtain special equipment.

✔ It can be done in any location, alone or with others.

Actually, Mayo doesn't really say much of anything about *t'ai-chi* making you wealthy or wise, but it does say that the gentle and fluid movements can help promote a feeling of serenity, a general sense of well-being, and maybe even an ability to stay calm during a traffic jam. Now, who couldn't use a little of that?

One name that may bubble up to the top of the cement mixer of styles is *Wu-tang ch'üan* or simply Wu-tang (or Wudang) Style, which sometimes seems to be almost a synonym for *t'ai-chi ch'üan* but can also be identified more with straight-ahead, martially oriented *kung-fu.* Wu-tang is actually the name of a mountain in China, which, not so coincidentally, is one of the most important Taoist sacred sites. The mountain first came to fame nearly eight centuries ago as the seat of a deity associated with Taoist exorcism, and then a couple hundred years later as the home of the mysterious Chang San-feng, the same Chang San-feng who a few hundred years later still would take on the persona as the legendary founder of *t'ai-chi.* Since then, Mount Wu-tang has become the unofficial *t'ai-chi* capital of China, though Wudang Style martial arts can include many other even more marginally Taoist forms, like the "eight trigrams palm" or "Wu-tang sword."

Ch'i-kung: The Efficiency of the Psychophysical Stuff

Although in America, *ch'i-kung* and *t'ai-chi* tend to appeal to much the same audience and tend to show up in many of the same Taoist and non-Taoist practice centers, websites, and mail-order marketplaces, the two actually have very different origins, histories, and applications. The *ch'i* of *ch'i-kung* is indeed the *ch'i* that keeps showing up in Taoist philosophy and practice, the psychophysical stuff of existence that cuts across the usual Western dichotomies of matter and energy, body and mind, and substance and spirit. The *kung* part usually means "skill" or "accomplishment" — it's the same *kung* that shows up in *kung-fu* — though, in this case, it really translates better as either "exercise" or "efficiency." So, the practice of *ch'i-kung* is the practice of the efficiency of the psychophysical stuff.

T'ai-chi, despite its many different styles, basically involves learning specific gymnastic routines for some combination of spiritual and physical benefit. *Ch'i-kung,* on the other hand, includes (or can include) a more complicated regimen of movements, breath control, meditation, dietary restrictions, and healing practices, all based in some way on the principle of circulating the *ch'i* through the body. In this section, I orient you to this fascinating set of practices, tracing their historical roots, explaining the rise and fall of *ch'i-kung* in contemporary China, and discussing some of the variations you may encounter if you ever consider picking up the tradition.

The roots of ch'i-kung

Various types of gymnastic and therapeutic movements called *ch'i-kung* go back in China more than a thousand years, but the coherent systems that exist today are barely a century old.

Interestingly, the earliest important figure in the development of modern *ch'i-kung* was neither a medical professional nor a religious figure, but an early 20th-century educator and politician who eventually turned to religious texts on physical cultivation in order to address his own recurring illnesses, including a nasty bout with tuberculosis and stomach ulcers. His name was Chiang Wei-ch'iao, and he apparently healed himself by following programs described in an internal alchemy text — it's pretty much this connection that places at least some types of *ch'i-kung* into the Taoist family tree, even though Chiang eventually became a lay Buddhist and wrote or translated several books on Buddhism.

Chiang's major contribution to *ch'i-kung* was a book he wrote or compiled around 1914 called *Master Yin-shih's Method of Quiet Sitting,* in which he spelled out the details and background philosophy of a self-healing regimen, which combined inner alchemy with Western science and, possibly, Japanese interpretations of "quiet sitting," which had at one time been a mainly Neo-Confucian practice. The gist of Chiang's book was to advocate the cultivation of a breathing technique, which would retrain the body's flow of *ch'i* so that it would continually dispel toxins and replenish itself with pristine, curative energies.

Chiang's text didn't exactly create an immediate rush of enthusiasm for this type of healing, but it did start the ball rolling. The first real breakthrough occurred in the 1950s, when a political activist and confidante of Mao Tse-tung named Liu Kuei-chen — who was trying to deal with his own health problems —received some private instruction from a Taoist teacher, noodled with Chiang's writings, and became something of a public missionary for the practice. He eventually opened up a pair of institutes in northeastern China devoted to this therapeutic healing method, which was then for the first time being touted as a coherent system with the name *ch'i-kung*. This may have been the start of something big, had the Cultural Revolution not derailed it — and just about everything else remotely Taoist or religious in China — in the mid-1960s. For a while, anyway, *ch'i-kung* stopped dead in its tracks.

The term *ch'i-kung* circulated as a generic name for a wide variety of physical practices long before the system we now know as *ch'i-kung* came into existence. The *ch'i-kung* that's so prevalent in North America today is largely a child of specific 20th-century developments.

The ch'i-kung explosion

After Mao's death in 1976 and the subsequent easing of Cultural Revolution restrictions, *ch'i-kung* made a huge public comeback in China in the 1980s and early 1990s. This was triggered, in part, by a woman named Kuo Lin, a cancer survivor who claimed to have cured herself through a form of walking *ch'i-kung* that she developed and went on to teach in public parks. It would really be an understatement if you were to think of this surge in popularity as a "fad," "boom," "craze," or even "mania" (a la Beatlemania), in that there wasn't just a spike in sales of *ch'i-kung* literature or a sudden appearance of *ch'i-kung* T-shirts and posters. Instead, *ch'i-kung* reemerged in a somewhat more permissive China with the coordinated intensity of a religious revival or populist political movement, rapidly generating institutional support, charismatic public icons, and millions of enthusiastic followers. Suddenly, it seemed like *ch'i-kung* was just about everywhere, growing in ways that would've been unimaginable only a few years earlier.

Here's a basic summary of what sorts of things were happening:

- ✔ **Government sponsorship:** Many people in the Chinese government felt that the country had a lot to gain from the *ch'i-kung* explosion, whether for the prestige that it brought as a cultural heirloom or the financial benefits it brought by cutting down on healthcare costs. At one point, they were sponsoring research on it, having it taught in clinics and public schools, and touting it as a fundamental expression of Chinese identity.

- ✔ **Influential *ch'i-kung* teachers:** Many people who had (or professed to have) expertise in *ch'i-kung* began to appear on the scene, some claiming descent from antiquated lineages and identifying themselves as "masters." Although most *ch'i-kung* teachers attracted small groups of disciples whom they instructed in parks and similar places, some actively recruited followers for breakaway organizations or took on the public persona of self-help gurus, filling stadiums for massive group sessions. One such teacher, Yen Hsin (or Yan Xin, as he is better known), at one point became something of an international celebrity, and you can even see apparently authentic photos of him online with two different U.S. presidents. Though he has since all but disappeared from public view, his International Yan Xin Qigong Association is still going strong.

✔ **New techniques and applications:** Responding to the burgeoning interest in *ch'i-kung*, teachers began both reinterpreting older practices and creating new ones. Some also began advertising more than just personal healing methods, claiming to be able to heal others with a touch of their own hands, or transmit magical powers like superhuman strength and the ability to read minds.

After a sustained period of growth, *ch'i-kung* in China did encounter some damaging public scandals over such things as recurring reports that certain physical patterns induced seizures, inconsistent scientific research on its value, and accusations that teachers may have physically abused their followers. The government gradually became more ambivalent about the practices, and some controversial teachers left China under a public cloud, like Chang Hung-pao, whose legacy is still vigorously debated. Although some describe him as criminal and leader of a "heretical teaching," others see him as a visionary who was victimized by a government eager to silence him. Chang lived in the United States for several years, at one point dealing with charges of domestic violence, and then died (or was murdered, depending on whom you believe) in an auto accident in Arizona.

The popularity of *ch'i-kung* in America is an outgrowth of the Chinese *ch'i-kung* explosion of the 1980s and early 1990s. Although a similar development in China would've had little international impact two generations ago, Chinese immigration, European and North American tourism, and student exchange programs all facilitated the transformation of *ch'i-kung* from a uniquely Chinese popular vogue into a global quasi-religious practice.

Hard and soft ch'i-kung

As you've probably noticed by now, *ch'i-kung,* like *t'ai-chi,* doesn't refer to just one thing and comes in many different flavors, including specifically Buddhist or Confucian *ch'i-kung.* But in general, the different types all fall under two main headings, neither of which comes off as inherently religious: soft (or flexible) *ch'i-kung* and hard (or strong) *ch'i-kung.* Technically, practitioners usually understand the latter as an advanced application of the former for those who've undergone years of training, but it doesn't always work out that way.

The soft varieties, which are also sometimes called "medical *ch'i-kung*" or "healing *ch'i-kung,*" are what you're most likely to find offered in holistic wellness centers, New Age or other "spiritual" outlets, and American Taoist temples and retreat centers. These usually include some combination of "quiet" practices, like meditation and breathing techniques, and "active" practices, like regulating posture and performing gymnastic routines.

The hard variety, which is also sometimes called "martial *ch'i-kung*" often seems less overtly Taoist, though it may be informed by some elements of Taoist physiology (like the three cinnabar fields, or the refinement of essence, *ch'i,* and spirit). For the most part, it involves developing the kinds of abilities that might serve you well in hand-to-hand combat, like superhuman strength, tolerance of physical pain, and resistance to injury. During the height of the *ch'i-kung* boom in China, practitioners of this style would sometimes perform extraordinary feats for paying audiences, supposedly manipulating *ch'i* in such a way that they could throw other people several feet by barely touching them, or by touching another person who was touching them! If this sounds to you like the stuff of *kung-fu* movies, you wouldn't be too far off.

As you go searching the Internet for *ch'i-kung*, you may encounter websites that organize it into several other varieties, including "musical *ch'i-kung,*" "art *ch'i-kung,*" "dance *ch'i-kung,*" "business *ch'i-kung,*" or "spiritual *ch'i-kung.*" Though these varieties don't reflect the traditional historical divisions, they may, in fact, be used by specific lineages.

Fa-lun Kung: The Skills of the Wheel of the Law

The *ch'i-kung* movement in China gave rise to numerous sub-groups that forged their own identities, maintained distinct practices, and enlisted followers who professed loyalties specifically to them. Many such sectarian groups owed their existence and continuation to the teachers who founded them, and often their fortunes rose and fell with the fortunes of their founders. One of the best known, most successful, and most hotly debated of these comparatively new *ch'i-kung* organizations is the Fa-lun Kung or Fa-lun Ta-fa (usually spelled Falun Gong or Falun Dafa), which currently has followers in dozens of countries all over the world.

The *Fa-lun* of Fa-lun Kung is a technical Buddhist term for "*dharma* wheel," where *dharma* means the ultimate truth (or law) that the Buddha experienced and taught. The *Kung* of Fa-lun Kung is the same *Kung* from *ch'i-kung* ("exercise," "skill," or "efficiency"). So, *Fa-lun Kung* translates as the skills of the *dharma*

wheel (or wheel of the law). The official name Fa-lun Ta-fa translates similarly, as the great methods of the *dharma* wheel. As you can tell from the translation, Fa-lun Kung is actually a Buddhist (rather than Taoist) lineage, but it's such an important *ch'i-kung* offshoot that a chapter like this isn't really complete without some discussion of it.

In this section, I introduce you to this emerging tradition, bringing you up to speed on its beginnings in China and basic teachings. I also flesh out the controversies that have soured relations between the movement and the Chinese government, which at the same time has made it something of a cause célèbre among human-rights organizations around the world.

Origins and practices of Fa-lun Kung

The Fa-lun Ta-fa was founded in 1992 by Li Hung-chih (Li Hongzhi), who claimed to have had extensive training in both Taoist and Buddhist teachings, while somehow managing to avoid the excesses of the Cultural Revolution. He grafted the *ch'i-kung* emphasis on healing and gymnastic practices onto Buddhist terminology and moral values and a somewhat vague interpretation of Buddhism's ultimate goal (variously translated as "consummation" or "spiritual perfection"). Li taught his methods with a missionary fervor — spreading the *dharma* is a trademark of Buddhism — and he quickly attracted throngs of followers (thanks, in part, to relatively low costs), earned government praise, and went on numerous speaking tours.

Li has written extensively on the philosophy that informs his practice, and both locally and internationally sponsored Fa-lun Kung websites will link anyone interested to texts, lectures, instructional videos, and even therapeutic music. Here are some of their key teachings in a nutshell:

- **Moral goodness, degeneration, and recovery:** Li teaches that human beings are morally good by nature, but that the *dharma* has been in a lengthy period of decline — a common tenet of some Buddhist denominations, which gives Fa-lun Kung a quasi-millenarian flavor. The human task is to put things back together morally, so to speak, by pursing a triad of virtues — truthfulness, compassion, and forbearance — qualities that are reflected in the very structure and flow of the cosmos.

- **Cultivation of the *dharma*-wheel:** The process of recovering our nature comes not only from moral action (which is, indeed, necessary), but from engaging in physical cultivation exercises. The point of these is to set in motion a *dharma*-wheel (understood as a microcosm of cosmic forces) in a spot in your abdomen corresponding to the Taoist lower cinnabar field. This motion circulates your *ch'i* and, depending on the direction of that motion, either helps renew your physical body and moral-spiritual disposition or extends those healing energies for the benefit of others.

✔ **Attaining the *dharma*-wheel:** The problem is that in order for this process to occur, you actually need to have this *dharma*-wheel implanted in your body, and the one who has the authority and capacity to do that is Li Hung-chih, the leader of Fa-lun Kung. But not everyone has easy access to Li, and official movement literature does note that those who are serious and sincere in their cultivation can attain the *dharma*-wheel through more indirect means, like reading Li's books, watching his lecture videos, or studying with other members of the tradition.

✔ **Community relationships:** Applying fairly conservative interpretations of Buddhist morality and the doctrine of *karma,* Li expects Fa-lun Kung practitioners to live as responsible householders, abstaining from things like alcohol, violence, and sexual misconduct. (The current doctrine is not particularly tolerant toward homosexuality.) And while explicit restrictions on social or political activism don't seem to exist, the leaders tend to discourage such things.

Because of the centrality of Li Hung-chih, a set of unifying social values, the emphasis on group practice, and the place for mutual healing, Fa-lun Kung practitioners tend to form tightly knit pockets, something that doesn't usually hold true for *t'ai-chi* and *ch'i-kung* groups. Overall, Fa-lun Kung really does start to look a lot like a religious denomination.

Controversies and persecution

Chances are pretty good that even if you don't know much about Fa-lun Kung, you've heard something about it being caught up in public controversies of one kind or another. Things started getting hot around 1997, when the Chinese government began investigating the movement, initially trying to knock it out through propaganda alone. The watershed moment occurred in 1999, when the government officially labeled Fa-lun Kung a "heretical teaching," a term historically reserved for a hodgepodge of religious outliers, political dissidents, and, sometimes, millenarian groups that may have their eyes on establishing a "new age" sooner rather than later. Since then, the denomination has been officially banned in China, and members have reported various methods of government harassment, ranging from social coercion to arrest and torture, many of which seem to have been corroborated by human-rights organizations.

On the surface, it's difficult to see why the government would have such a difficult time with Fa-lun Kung, because the teachings don't seem any more farfetched than the beliefs common to more mainstream traditions, and the practices don't in any obvious way seem unhealthy, violent, or *seditious* (having to do with inciting resistance to authority). But despite the language of "heresy," official Chinese antipathy toward specific religious denominations doesn't usually come from any investment in religious orthodoxy or concerns about beliefs that members hold privately or practices they do in their own homes. Instead, it follows from perceiving certain organized groups as threats to political or social stability, as either subverting national loyalties or breaking down traditional relationships and community responsibilities. So, certain things that may have easily passed as the simple exercise of religious freedom elsewhere presented serious "red flags" to the Chinese government. Here are a couple of them:

- ✓ **Tensions over government oversight:** Having never developed an idea of a "wall of separation" between church and state (while technically permitting religious freedom), the Chinese government has insisted on exercising oversight on the practice of religion, determining which traditions deserve official recognition, monitoring the bureaucratic structures of those traditions, and having a say over matters of leadership and personnel. The 1996 withdrawal of Fa-lun Kung from a state-sanctioned *ch'i-kung* association may have indicated a desire for more autonomy over internal matters.

- ✓ **An emerging personality cult:** Although it may be an exaggeration to say that followers of Fa-lun Kung "worship" Li Hung-chih, it is fair to say that Li commands fierce loyalty from his followers, and you could make an argument that the necessity for Li either directly or indirectly to install your *dharma*-wheel personally creates a situation where followers feel dependent on him. When Fa-lun Kung practitioners started (apparently with Li's encouragement) pushing back against the initial signs of government hostility — writing letters en masse to state-run media and organizing well-attended demonstrations — that revealed exactly how much sway Li had in the lives of his followers.

In the years since these opening salvos, China and Fa-lun Kung have been waging war in the media, with each side telling vastly different versions of the story. The Chinese government paints a picture of Li (now living in the United States) as a huckster who has deceived or brainwashed the ignorant masses (a portrayal sometimes reinforced by conservative Christians and Western "anti-cult" organizations). At the same time, representatives of Fa-lun Kung insist their teachings are peaceful and publicize testimonies of people who have allegedly been unfairly persecuted, imprisoned, or tortured because of their commitments.

Chapter 17

Cosmic Renewal and Other Rituals

Many Taoist concepts — the Tao, *wu-wei,* unlearning, the tension between being and non-being — present philosophical paradoxes, the kind that really make your head hurt when you try to make some kind of intellectual sense out of them. But Taoist ritual presents a different kind of paradox, what you might call a paradox of perception and interpretation. On the one hand, ritual constitutes a crucial aspect of Taoist practice. The vast majority of texts in the Taoist Canon have (or had) at least *some* ritual function or application, and you could even make a case that ritual is the single most important feature for defining Taoism as a living religious tradition. On the other hand, Taoist ritual remains obscure or unknown to Western audiences, and it will almost certainly remain that way, no matter how many books are written about it or how exciting I can make it sound in this chapter. In fact, you'll probably find no shortage of people who will still insist that "Taoist ritual" is an oxymoron, that there's not really any such thing as Taoist ritual, and that the stuff you find Taoist priests doing today isn't "real" Taoism.

What's going on here? Why is it that for all the Westerners dying to plunge deeper into Taoism, for all the scholars trying to set the record straight on Taoist practice, and for all the Taoists going about their business performing rituals every day in China, Taoist ritual just hasn't translated into the Western consciousness, either as a popular topic of "spiritual" conversation or as common religious practice? The answers to these questions have a lot to do with the dominant Western myths about Taoism, but even more to do with the nitty-gritty details of Taoist ritual itself.

In this chapter, I get into some of those details, which probably come with the usual batch of surprises. I talk about the basic relationship between Taoism and ritual, as well as some of the most common (and dramatic) forms of Taoist ritual you could be lucky enough to see if you happen to be in China at the right place and time.

The Truth about Taoism and Ritual

So, what is the truth about Taoism and ritual? As always, there's not always one answer to a question like this. A big part of the answer depends on which types of Taoism you mean, and what definition you have in mind for *ritual*. This is an easy place to get confused if you think someone's talking about one kind of Taoism, or has one understanding of ritual, when that person actually has something very different in mind.

In this section, I lay out once and for all the role of ritual practice in Taoism, explaining why this particular phenomenon has such a hard time translating for the Western mind-set. Along the way, I give you a set of guidelines for thinking about ritual, discuss the attitudes toward ritual in the classical Taoist texts, identify some of the recurring ritual forms that show up in later incarnations of Taoism, and introduce you to some of the typical "stuff" that shows up in Taoist ritual today.

What is ritual?

It seems like ritual is one of those "you know it when you see it" ideas. Just about everyone has some intuitive idea of what a ritual is, but they may get a little wobbly when they try to come up with an exact definition or list its specific qualities. Most people would probably say it refers to some kind of repeated, orchestrated religious act, like taking communion in church, or kneeling in prayer in a mosque. But would you also call it a ritual when you stand up for the national anthem or receive your diploma at a graduation ceremony? For that matter, how about some uncomfortable but equally formalized processes, like performing the public execution of a prisoner? When does something qualify as a ritual, and when is it simply a "custom" or a "tradition"?

Sometimes, people refer to their daily habits — like doing morning exercises or drinking coffee while listening to their favorite radio show — as rituals, and psychiatrists are quick to identify certain obsessive-compulsive behaviors as ritualistic. Is a ritual, then, the same thing as a "routine"? If not, what would be the difference? Does there have to be something "sacred" about a ritual, and how do we judge what qualifies as sacred? Suddenly, knowing it when you see it gets a little fuzzier.

As it turns out, sociologists, anthropologists, psychologists, theologians, and religion scholars have been debating the nature and functions of ritual for a long time, sometimes coming to dramatically different conclusions. Some zero in on how ritual ties into the participants' established mythology, while others focus on the emotional and experiential aspects of participating in a ritual. That said, it may not be so easy to settle on one definition that will make everyone happy, but it's still very possible to tease out some general, recurring qualities that can serve as kind of a framework for thinking about ritual actions and their consequences.

Here are a few of the more important ones to keep in mind:

- ✔ **Participant roles:** In order for people to perceive that a ritual is being done right, that it will accomplish whatever it's supposed to do or even just have the appropriate effect on the mood and personal imagination, it's necessary for ritual *functionaries* to play their prescribed roles. These functionaries could be people with special recognized religious status — like priests, monks, or rabbis — but people undergoing rites of passage or just laypeople participating in a ceremony also need to "follow the rules." If you have any doubts about this, see what happens when rituals don't go according to plan, and how shaken up some of the participants may get.

- ✔ **Materials and objects:** There's a reason why you place a ring — and not a rubber band, a cigar band, or a finger-puppet — on your spouse's finger during a wedding ceremony. Or why the Hanukkah menorah must have a certain number of candles lit on the right day. Or even something as simple as how the officiant of a ceremony dresses. The sense that you're using "the right stuff" (the *rite* stuff?) adds to the feeling and importance of the experience.

- ✔ **The right place at the right time:** Religious rituals often depend quite a bit on time and space — it matters both *when* and *where* you perform them. The most obvious cases concern ceremonies associated with a particular holiday, performed in a neighborhood temple or church. But some rituals depend on the exact moment — like an evening vigil anticipating the midnight arrival of the baby Jesus, or may be held in more exotic places, like on mountaintops or sites where religious heroes or martyrs left their historic marks.

- ✔ **Language, gestures, and movements:** Very often, the communities that utilize rituals expect that those carrying them out should use specific language — either through a language not native to the participant (like

Latin in a Catholic Mass, or Hebrew in a Jewish prayer) or customary choice of words in the participant's own language (like beginning a wedding ceremony with "dearly beloved"). The same is true for hand gestures and physical body movements, like when the pope offers a blessing or when observant Muslims prostrate themselves during prayer.

✔ **Shared understanding of the meanings or results:** This can include a collective understanding that

- Someone has changed official status through a rite of passage (like a boy becoming recognized as a man, or a bachelor transforming into a married man)

- Sharing a Passover Seder at the family dinner table establishes a connection to the Israelites liberated from Egyptian slavery more than 3,000 years earlier

- Burying a beloved relative through prescribed methods both expresses feeling toward that relative and offers hope for the future

Not every participant necessarily interprets every ritual or ceremony the exact same way, but the key is that they're generally on the same page and can "speak the same ritual language" with one another.

In general, it may be helpful to think about a ritual as a routinized action or set of actions that

✔ Assigns specific roles to those who participate in it

✔ Makes use of a broad "vocabulary" of tools — objects, language, gestures, physical movements, and so on

✔ Is attentive to proper time and location

✔ Points toward some concrete or symbolic meaning that can be understood by the participants and members of the community in which it occurs

Attitudes toward ritual in the classical texts

One funny thing about classical Taoism and ritual is that for all the general impressions people may have about Lao Tzu and Chuang Tzu being anti-ritualistic, their texts don't really take that explicit position all that often. Yes, Lao Tzu calls the Confucian ideal of ritual propriety the "thinnest husk of loyalty and sincerity," and Chuang Tzu praises the character who forgets ritual propriety (along with all the other standard Confucian virtues), but those are both in the context of a larger, more general indictment of Confucian morality, without really targeting the concrete stuff of ritual performances. Still, Chuang Tzu's turtle would rather drag its tail in the mud than assume some honored place in a court ceremony, and the texts do give the general impression that they've got bigger fish to fry than conducting or taking part in rituals.

It's probably fair to say that the classical Taoist rejection of ritual comes not from any inherent distaste for specific ritual acts, but from a sense that Confucian ritual propriety can serve as a convenient stand-in for many of the world's ills. By (sort of) trashing ritual, Lao Tzu and Chuang Tzu can go after the real "villains":

- **Conformity:** If you want a symbol of something that's the opposite of healthy, critical skepticism, you probably can't find anything that fits the job description better than ritual. People often accept and perform rituals blindly and uncritically — to those who don't share in the ritual's language or reject its significance, ritual participants must look like the original zombies.

- **Artificiality:** If you're trying to encourage genuine, spontaneous actions and responses to given situations, you certainly don't want anything that smacks at all of being "pre-programmed." By its very nature, ritual is the reenactment of an already established form.

- **Superficiality:** You must have encountered situations where you felt like you were (or sensed that someone else was) "only going through the motions," or where a prescribed act became "only a symbol" rather than something truly substantial. And rituals, especially those that incorporate micromanagement of minutia, seem to be inviting that.

- **Publicity:** Because the classical Taoist authors generally identified ritual as the ceremonial activities of government and other public figures, they no doubt equated it with the desires for reputation and power, and especially with the personal presumption of thinking oneself deserving to rule the country. If ritual carries a sense of urgency, of gravity, and of self-importance, Lao Tzu and Chuang Tzu want none of it.

The bare facts of Taoist ritual

Before plunging into the somewhat daunting task of describing the various types of Taoist ritual, I think it would be helpful to consider the subject a bit more generally, in terms of who the basic players are, when and why they perform ritual functions, and what elementary characteristics appear most often. This way, even if you're not quite sure exactly what's going on in a particular ritual, the overall rhythm and texture won't feel quite so unfamiliar.

The rituals of the anti-ritualistic

Religious traditions, or sects within traditions, sometimes distinguish themselves by maintaining a public position that they reject certain trappings of "ordinary" traditions, like language, scripture, priesthood, or — you guessed it — ritual. More often than not, these "anti-dogma dogmas" don't really reject completely all the stuff they say they do, as much as they force a different way of imaging those things. For instance, the *Tao Te Ching* may make a big fuss about the limits of language (as do many other supposed mystical texts) and excoriate those who presume to talk about what can't be spoken, but that didn't stop the anonymous authors of the text (and subsequent generations of Taoists) from using an awful lot of words and spilling an awful lot of ink. Ironically (and obviously, once you think about it) using language to make a point about the limitations of language is a wonderfully strategic use of language.

There's probably no single tradition more identified with this kind of iconoclasm than Zen Buddhism, which talks about the direct personal transmission of an intuitive, experiential insight outside of scriptures, outside of rituals. What's so striking is just how convincing this "official" line has been. It's extraordinary how often you'll see people reading Zen texts, and then claiming that Zen Buddhists don't use scripture, or observing monks enter a meditation hall in ritual fashion, or ritualistically approach a teacher for a personal interview, but then claim that Zen Buddhists don't practice any rituals. In fact, you'd probably be pretty hard-pressed to come up with any religious tradition that doesn't have some kind of ritual component, however clear the participants are that what they're doing doesn't "count" as ritual, whether it's the silent waiting of Quakers for the spirit to come upon them, or the gathering of a regional Baha'i community in order to elect a new Local Spiritual Assembly.

If it seems like there's a huge jump from Lao Tzu and Chuang Tzu rejecting ritual propriety to members of the Way of the Celestial Masters participating in public confessions of sins and consumption of talisman water, to the various colorful rituals that Taoist priests preside over today, it may be helpful to make a quick note that the ritual propriety that gets trashed in the classical texts isn't quite the same operative ritual that shows up in later Taoism. When the classical Taoists talk about letting go of ritual propriety, they're invoking the Chinese term *li*, which refers specifically to ritual acts associated with dynastic functions, aristocratic social relationships, and Confucian values more generally.

But the later Taoists don't normally label their performances as *li;* instead, they use a variety of different terms that describe the specific operations, like *chiao*, which translates (sort of) as "offering," or *chai*, which translates as "purification" (or "retreat"). You'll also hear the more generic term *fa* (the same *fa* from Fa-lung Kung) translated as "ritual," but that may be a little bit of a misnomer, because it really means something more like "way" or "method," which underscores the *operative* and *instrumental* purpose of Taoist ritual. This term for method, *fa*, shows up in a lot of ritual places.

Ritual specialists, whether Taoist, Buddhist, or "redhead Taoist," are sometimes called *fa-shih*, ceremonial objects are *fa-ch'i* (ritual-method tools), and certain exorcisms are called *lei-fa* (thunder ritual-methods).

In any event, no matter which ritual functions we're talking about, you'll probably see some combination of the following:

✔ **Altars:** Some ceremonies are performed at elaborate, sometimes multi-level altars, with intricate symbolism that's usually intelligible only to those with specific training. Symbols can include *yin-yang* cosmology trigrams, images of animals (often the dragon and tiger), various high or regional deities, and implicit divisions that mirror things like Heavenly compartments, cinnabar fields in the body, and so on.

✔ **Officiants:** Depending on the ceremony and the lineage, there may be anything from a small group to a huge entourage taking part, where each person occupies a different priestly rank. They all wear ritual vestments, enact specific movements, and possibly play musical instruments (with distinct *yin* and *yang* tones) or speak or chant in dialects specific to the ritual. The different functionaries may have the authority to play particular roles by virtue of the registers that have been conferred on them.

✔ **Channeling:** All rituals involve some type of communication with Taoist deities, and many of these involve summoning specific deities to the ceremony, with a priest or assistant acting as the spirit medium. Priests only have the authority to summon specific deities, so they sometimes have to summon *other* deities to do the summoning. It's not all that common, but priests occasionally have to kick out a wrong spirit who shows up by mistake!

You may be noticing by now that just about every aspect of the ritual requires some kind of special authorization even to participate and some kind of "insider knowledge" to understand what's going on, whether it's the symbolism on the altars, registers possessed by the priests, or the interior conversations between a medium and a channeled spirit. And that's not an accident. Taoists have always protected their lore and rituals, demanding years of esoteric training before extending the privilege of ritual access. For this reason, the *laypeople* — that is, the "ordinary" people who attend such events — usually have a sketchy (at best) idea of what's going on during the ceremonies. They may attend out of a vested interest in the anticipated effects of the rituals, respect for the officiants doing the work, a sense that something "big" is happening, or even just to witness a colorful spectacle.

Because of all this — as well as the fact that a great many of these practices are closely tied to regional geography and history, local gods and spirits, and specific family and community interests — you probably don't want to hold your breath waiting for these to show up in your hometown. However fascinating these Taoist rituals may be, their esoteric quality and regional particularity make them an unlikely fit for Western audiences. If Chinese laypeople don't really understand them, the many Westerners who appreciate Taoism as a *spiritual* resource understandably have a hard time making heads or tails of them.

Swords and plaques and implements of petition

Even if you don't really follow the *yin* and *yang* (so to speak) of Taoist ritual, the performances are seldom less than intriguing to watch, if only for the music, decorations, and ceremonial objects, which can be quite the feast for the senses. Here's a quick inventory of some of the auditory and visual effects you're likely to encounter:

- ✔ **Music:** This often includes sophisticated ensembles of bells, stone chimes, hollow wood blocks (usually shaped like fish), gongs, cymbals, drums, bamboo flutes, and various exotic reed instruments. Sometimes a single priest will play a buffalo or ox horn (though called a dragon horn) to call for good spirits or drive away evil ones.

- ✔ **Mood:** Some rituals are adorned by objects that have a kind of background symbolic function, in that they're necessary for the ceremony even if priests don't actually do anything with them during the performance. This can include paintings, banners, plaques, mirrors, lamps, and copies of scriptures and texts.

- ✔ **Tools:** These are a variety of basic objects — which often have symbols or inscriptions on them — that the priests move and employ in various ways. These may include a measuring stick for exorcizing spirits, a seal for stamping documents, a wooden-handled whip (styled to look like a snake), a bowl of purified water, an incense burner, and gizmos used for divination.

Rituals of Purification and Offering

In line with basic Chinese religious sensibilities, Taoist rituals are never merely decorative, never just to make you feel good or give you a sense that you're carrying on a tradition for its own sake. Taoist specialists perform rituals for the same overall reasons they venerate spirits or engage in personal cultivation: to accomplish concrete, tangible ends (or at least what they perceive as concrete, tangible ends), though this may be quite high-minded, like the health of the community or even the entire cosmos. In very broad strokes, most rituals involve some kind of transactional quality, where participants are petitioning or in some other way asking something of the deities, in exchange for veneration or offerings they give to the deities. The rituals may be esoteric and require years of training to perform optimally, but they still pretty much replicate some version of a cosmic "you scratch my back and I'll scratch yours" religious drama.

Specifically Taoist (as opposed to generically Chinese) ritual probably traces back to the practices of the earliest Way of the Celestial Master community, which involved

- ✔ Ordinations and advancement in the priestly hierarchy
- ✔ The employment of registers and talismans for healing and the safe passage of the dead
- ✔ The meditation on and confession of sins
- ✔ Participation in public feasts

All these things influenced the forms that later rituals would take. As the tradition expanded over the next several centuries, it took on ritual forms developed within the Highest Purity and Numinous Treasure cultivation groups, as well as those related to both external and internal alchemy.

Nearly two millennia of historical growth have produced a dazzling variety of Taoist rituals, but Chinese Taoists have generally sorted them into two distinct categories: rituals of purification *(chai),* and rituals of offering *(chiao).* In this section, I differentiate these two types of ritual, give examples of each, and introduce you to a spectacular ritual of offering that only occurs once every several years.

Rituals of fasting, purification, purgation, and retreat

The rituals referred to as *chai* normally translate as purification, purgation, or fasting — it's the same *chai* from Chuang Tzu's "fasting of the mind and heart" — but they can also refer to retreats, where groups of people withdraw to specific ritually pure places to practice abstinence and purification of the body, always in the hope of a tangible benefit. It was probably within the Numinous Treasure cultivation group that they adapted the older Celestial Masters rituals of repentance and created newer formalized practices.

Here are a handful of typical retreat rituals:

- **The Mud and Soot Retreat:** Just like it sounds, this extended ritual involved smearing mud on your face and rolling around on the ground (and possibly some more disgusting punishments), presumably to atone for the sins you've committed and to dispel the unhappy fate that could await you. A priest performing the ritual could do so on behalf of those who are already dead, a motif that will persist in Taoist ritual.

- **The Three "Register" Retreats:** This trio of retreats — the Yellow Register Retreat, the Jade Register Retreat, and the Golden Register Retreat — lasted several days and were performed at specified times during the year. Priests performed the Yellow Register Retreat for the well-being of the dead, the Jade Register Retreat for the well-being of dynastic officials and the wife of the emperor, and the Golden Register Retreat for the well-being of the emperor (which would presumably protect the people and guarantee the stability of the community).

- **The Great One Retreat:** This performance of this purgation was limited to the emperor, who, as the son of Heaven, was supposed to perform this ritual on behalf of *T'ai-i,* a name given to the "oneness" of the cosmos or to the deity by that name who personifies this unity and serves as a kind of celestial overseer.

These types of Taoist rituals of purification don't really exist anymore as standalone retreats, though they haven't fizzled out altogether. Several components of *chai* have become absorbed into the most common types of rituals of offering that are still practiced today.

The rite of cosmic renewal

Technically, Taoist rituals of offering serve to cement the connection between a community and the deity or deities with whom the people have a special symbiotic relationship, though the best known and most important version of these are also called rites of cosmic renewal, because the elaborate, multi-day (or multi-week) events are designed to do just what the name suggests: to make the cosmos a newly fresh, harmonious organism that nurtures the well-being of the community. You may read somewhere that *chiao* rituals are only offered on a 60-year cycle and are, thus, quite rare, but it appears that the term now pretty much applies to many different types of offering-based rituals, and that even the special type supposedly offered every six decades shows up a little more often, and at odd intervals.

The major *chiao* rituals can have it all, like a boatload of priests taking part, the ceremonial marking off of sacred space, construction of temporary altars, performance of ceremonial music, presentation of petitions to Heaven, lighting ritual lamps and incense burners, reciting moral precepts, summoning deities to present them with offerings, and so forth. Often, these rituals are preceded by lengthy periods of repentance and purification — that's the *chai* piece — and conclude with an addendum straight out of Buddhism, a prayer for universal salvation.

The great offering for a peaceful world

The great-granddaddy of all the rituals of offering is the *Lo-t'ien Ta-chiao,* the Great Offering to All-Encompassing Heaven, which historically attracted the involvement of dozens of priests and supposedly addressed offerings to well over a thousand deities. The first of these extravaganzas could go back as far as the 8th century, but the modern history of it really begins when Chang En-p'u, the 63rd Celestial Master, presided over one in Shanghai in 1933, a decade or so before he escaped to Taiwan and revitalized Taoist practices there.

In the aftermath of the Cultural Revolution, as Taoism began to regroup in China, with the refurbishing of temples and ordination of new priests, the China Taoist Association (CTA) made efforts to revive the *Lo-t'ien Ta-chiao* as an ecumenical Taoist mega-event that would unite both major branches of modern Taoism — Orthodox Unity and Complete Perfection — and bring together representatives from the pan-Chinese Taoist world and the various local Taoist associations. In 1993, the White Cloud Monastery in Beijing — with the co-sponsorship of abbots from temples all over China, Taiwan, and Hong Kong — hosted the ten-day Great Offering, constructing ten new shrines where they installed some 1,200 deities. The CTA reported having raised the equivalent of nearly $125,000, mainly through donations, which it then passed on to a charitable educational organization for Chinese living in poor rural areas.

The CTA co-sponsored a second Great Offering in 2001, this time attracting more than 300 clerics from as far afield as Macao, Singapore, and Korea, and constructing 15 new altars. The ceremony was specifically dedicated to "praying for world peace, state prosperity, national reunion, and the people's happiness." The reunion motif no doubt referred to the recent transfer of Hong Kong back to Chinese rule, perhaps with an eye toward the sometimes uncomfortable relationship between China and Taiwan. But the Taoists pulled out all the stops for the biggest Great Offering yet, which occurred in Hong Kong in 2007. Commemorating the tenth anniversary of Chinese rule over Hong Kong, and with the overall goal of praying for world peace (as well as the elimination of natural disasters), this event topped out at more than 400 priests and acolytes (including many women), and coincided with various other cultural and educational activities. Fortunately, a Taoism scholar named James Miller videotaped many of the proceedings, and you can probably find some really spectacular, clear-as-a-bell footage online without too much trouble — try http://youtu.be/VaoFe3u5E7c.

The reemergence of the *Lo-t'ien Ta-chiao* may be the biggest and best indicator that Taoism really is in for a comeback in China. It will be interesting to see if the CTA's ecumenical undertakings continue to bear this kind of fruit, and if events like these inspire any widespread renewed interest in Taoism.

Taoist Funeral Rituals

Apart from the seasonal cycles of rituals of purification and offering, Orthodox Unity priests also preside over highly complex funeral rites, which are necessary for guaranteeing a peaceful afterlife for the recently deceased. Because the death of one's parents constitutes a major generational breach, the rituals reflect the seriousness and gravity of the situation. The services can be extravagant and expensive — employing talismans, exorcism, and the construction of large altars — but families usually consider it an important-enough investment that they may even go into debt to pay for it if necessary.

In this section, I discuss how Taoists employ funeral rituals in order to make merit for deceased loved ones and intercede on their behalf during the unpredictable period immediately after death. I also identify some unusual aspects of the ritual, including one that involves the emotional participation of immediate family members.

Negotiating a treacherous journey

You can never be sure how much of this is understood metaphorically, but Taoist funeral rituals portray the soul of the deceased person as in a kind postmortem limbo, stuck in a netherworld purgatory (some sources translate it as "Hell," but that's a little bit misleading). The purpose of the ritual is to make merit on behalf of the deceased, essentially earning him a spiritual "pardon" from the interim subterranean prison and safe passage to some kind of Heavenly paradise (or to a good rebirth, if the priest has had some Buddhist influences).

The narrative crux of the ritual is the symbolic dispatching through the netherworld of a horseman bearing a "writ of pardon," which the priest has procured through his own access to spirits. Often, the horseman is symbolized by a paper effigy carrying straw (for his horse), an alchemical elixir for the welfare of the deceased, or ceremonial paper money for bribing inhospitable spirits along the way. The ritual enactment of this journey involves the usual assortment of esoteric gestures, theatrical movements, and perhaps even acrobatics.

Crossing the bridge to Heaven

The process of releasing the soul of the deceased person from limbo and enabling the final exodus to Heaven involves several more dramatic steps, the most striking of which is called "attacking purgatory." During this part of the ceremony, the presiding priest engages in feverish, sometimes almost violent actions that symbolically break open the walls of purgatory and release the trapped soul.

In many performances of this ritual, family members actually take a small role — just about the only time laypeople actually participate in, rather than just watch, a Taoist ceremony — gathering in a circle around a paper model of the underworld fortress, and literally extending their hands to assist in the destruction of the walls. One ethnographer researching this ritual observed that of all the times during the extensive funeral and mourning ceremonies, this moment most inspires a sense of grief in the family members, whose physical actions literally facilitate the departure of the loved one and, in effect, force the family to say goodbye.

The final stage of the ceremony, at least the final stage before the actual burial, involves leading the newly liberated spirit of the deceased across a bridge to Heaven, which is also usually symbolized by a paper model. The ritual may also include paper models of a palatial estate, representing just how spectacular this Heavenly paradise will surely be. If the ritual is conducted properly, the dollars paid and the emotional efforts expended by the family prove to be well worth it!

Part V
The Part of Tens

The 5th Wave

By Rich Tennant

"You know how you're always saying we can learn a spiritual lesson when bad things happen to us? Well, you're about to get a spiritual lesson from Herb's Towing & Collision and the Able Auto Insurance Co."

In this part . . .

Here's everything you've wanted to know about Taoism, in bite-size snippets for today's man or woman on the go. What are the misconceptions about Taoism you most want to avoid? How can you bring a little Taoist wisdom into your life? Where can you find Taoism in action?

Lao Tzu said that simplest is best. You can't get any simpler than this, can you?

Chapter 18

Ten Common Misconceptions about Taoism

To Westerners, Taoism can seem like a huge mystery, in large part because most of us don't have Taoist classmates or neighbors to reality-check the stuff we hear about it. Someone may say something on a website, or in a conversation, or even in a world religions textbook, and the next thing you know that little anecdote or tidy generalization sprouts legs and starts to walk around. And as politicians say, it can be hard to change someone's opinion about something once a story already "has legs." So, people often have a whole bunch of vague impressions of Taoism, most of which actually have a kernel of truth to them, but which ultimately misrepresent Taoism more often than not.

These misconceptions come from lots of different places, including biased scholarship, general Western assumptions about how religious traditions are supposed to function, and sometimes even the sheer emotional appeal of the bogus interpretations. In this chapter, I take a look at the most stubborn of the common misconceptions about Taoism, identify (in some cases) where they probably came from, and set the record straight on those particular issues.

Taoism Is a Philosophy, Not a Religion

Many people tell me that Taoism is more like a philosophy than a religion, or that it's not a religion at all. They seem to mean that Taoism includes ideas, attitudes about the world, or just an overall way of approaching life. "I have a Taoist philosophy" someone says, when she grows organic vegetables or lets her pets (or kids) roam freely and unsupervised. They also seem to mean that Taoism doesn't have all the *stuff* — usually stuff they don't care for — that they associate with religious institutions, like lots of doctrines and rules, clergy telling people what to do, and ceremonies that have to be done a certain way.

This misconception, though probably brewing since the beginnings of the European Enlightenment, really originated more than a century ago when the first European scholars of China bought (and sold) the notion that the texts of Lao Tzu and Chuang Tzu made up "real" Taoism, that the philosophical legacy was the most important and sophisticated part of the tradition. And for "spiritual" seekers, this hit the bull's-eye. It portrayed a profound repository of wisdom that one could adopt without "joining" any organization, taking any leaps of faith, or dealing with burdensome regulations. If you have any misgivings about religion, what could be more perfect than a religion that doesn't act like a religion?

But of course, to find out otherwise, all you have to do is read up about the last 2,000 years of Taoist religious history, with all its priests and institutions and rituals and other recognizably "religious" stuff. If you don't buy that, just go to China and check out the life at a Taoist temple, or watch a Taoist priest and his entourage preside at a funeral, or talk to people making offerings to Taoist deities. Regardless of whether you want to call it a religion, it's about as religious as you can get.

Taoism Was Founded by Lao Tzu

The idea that Lao Tzu "started," "founded," or "began" Taoism comes from the same place where many of these other myths originated (that is, the old scholarship that told the story this way). But it also reflects a general way of thinking that makes the history of religion come off as much more orderly than it ever really was. Many people like to think of history as a series of distinct "events," where things happened at very clear and obvious times. And so, it's sometimes hard to grasp the idea that a text could take generations to reach its final form, or that a community could evolve for several hundred years before developing a clear-cut identity, or (as in this case) that a religion could slowly take shape without someone actually founding it. Taoist origins are less a single moment in time than an extended process of many currents coming together.

And even if we were going to talk about a founder, it would be kind of hard to give that title to someone who probably didn't really exist. And even if we could find out that there was one Lao Tzu who wrote the *Tao Te Ching,* he certainly didn't in any way "found" the millenarian groups that developed 500 years later, or the alchemy groups a few hundred years after that, or the monastic Taoism that's peppered all over China today. Perhaps he *inspired* these (even that's a big "perhaps"), perhaps he set something in motion that gave rise to the Taoist religion, but it's a big jump to parlay that into thinking of him as a founder. If anything, Lao Tzu belongs to the pre-history of Taoism, and Chang Tao-ling might be the most likely candidate for founder in that he actually organized a community and most Taoists today continue to trace their history to him. But even that interpretation sets up some technical problems — Chang Tao-ling is also a questionable historical figure — and you're probably just better off thinking of Taoism as a founder-less religion.

The Tao Te Ching Is the Taoist "Bible"

This misunderstanding follows from the idea that Taoism began when Lao Tzu wrote this text, which served as a blueprint for the entire tradition. But it also comes from an overgeneralization about the relationship between a religion and its canonized literature, one that was certainly reinforced by the publication of Max Müller's *Sacred Books of the East* series. In the Western monotheistic religions — Judaism, Christianity, and Islam — the Torah, or the Gospels, or the Qur'an each function as a single authoritative scripture. Followers of the respective traditions consider their text to be divinely revealed or inspired and the ultimate source for moral lessons and models. People often believe that if they consult scripture, they can arbitrate ethical issues, find a clear position on what should or shouldn't be against the law, or make important life decisions. And they might expect that when Taoists want to make similar determinations — whether about basic moral values or hot-button issues like abortion or homosexuality — they consult the *Tao Te Ching* and see what it says. But of course, it just doesn't work that way.

First, the *Tao Te Ching* is only one text in the Taoist Canon, one of well over a thousand different documents, many of which have the status as "revealed" scripture. What's more, it's even arguable whether the *Tao Te Ching* is the most important single text (if by "important" you mean how much it actually influences Taoist day-to-day life). The Chinese don't usually carry it around with them to read on buses and subways, they don't place a hand on it before making affirmation in court, and they don't read from it and hear sermons about it at weekly services. The texts in the Taoist Canon serve many different purposes — they can function as ritual guides, alchemical recipes, protective formulas, far more than just offering up sacred history and moral lessons. And even with morality texts, you probably won't find many people arguing that some behavior is unethical because it says so in a Taoist text. In short, the *Tao Te Ching* is not the only Taoist scripture, and Taoist scripture in general functions differently than the Bible does.

Taoists Don't Believe in Any Gods

Taoism is a lot like Buddhism, in that for most of the 20th century, Western textbooks presented both of them as individualistic, rational, and free of beliefs that you can't verify through your own experience. To be sure, when you read the Classical Taoist texts, you find a lot about modeling yourself on the emptiness of the *Tao,* unlearning all sorts of contrived and unnecessary virtues, and returning to a state of primal simplicity, but you don't find a whole lot about any deity creating the Earth, expecting you to worship it, or handing you a roster of commandments. And when you see the way Lao Tzu describes the sage, or the various freaks and misfits Chuang Tzu holds up as examples of a wise person, you really don't expect any of these figures to be spending a lot of time praying, asking deities for favors, or repenting sins.

But once you get into actual Taoist practice, you find not only that there are deities, but that there a whole army of them — sometimes literally an army, like the 60 celestial generals who assist in the maintenance of the world, each one putting in some time once every six decades. And what's more, the Taoists see their pantheon as having a special status, where the gods are somehow direct manifestations of the *Tao,* not just ordinary local spirits who get involved in mundane business. These include the Three Pure Ones (one of which is the deified Lao Tzu), the Jade Emperor, the Eight Immortals, and historical Celestial Masters and adepts, not to mention the various guardians associated with specific temples and regions. You want gods and goddesses? Taoism has gods and goddesses.

Taoism Rejects Religious Doctrine

At first glance, Taoism seems like it's almost *doctrinally* opposed to religious doctrine of any kind, and even some fairly well-respected scholars fall for this one. After all, doesn't Lao Tzu tell us that you have to *return* to the *Tao* because so much religious doctrine — Confucian and Mohist doctrines of virtue, benevolence, righteousness, and propriety — has mucked everything up? And doesn't Chuang Tzu say that any position presented with certainly is one that you can take apart, deconstruct, and show to be tied to a specific and temporary perspective? Taoism wants everyone to get rid of cleverness and knowledge and firm convictions, and even if you do "know" anything, you'd certainly better not talk about it, right? Based on the original Taoist philosophical texts, it certainly does look like you'd be skeptical if anyone started talking about Taoist doctrine. Can you imagine a "Taoist creed" or a "Taoist proclamation of faith"?

But if by "Taoist doctrine," we simply mean the systematic statement of principles and teachings that Taoists hold to be true, then the Taoist Canon is bursting with all kinds of doctrines. These thousand-plus texts include handbooks and encyclopedias of philosophy, physiology, numerology, pharmacology, and sacred history, exactly the types of things that you'd see as doctrine in other traditions. The image of the Taoist as detached skeptic matches nicely with the Lao-Chuang texts, but it dissolves pretty quickly when you try to apply it to the last 2,000 years of Taoism.

Still, there is one important reason why it may be a good idea to be a little bit careful when you think about Taoist "doctrine." In Western traditions, people frequently associate doctrine with "belief," the idea that it's important to make a conscious decision to "believe in" someone or something. That's why many Christians are quick to identify themselves as "believers" — there's a sense that the act of belief is itself an important one. But in Taoism, there's no reward for believing, no punishment for not believing. Believing in a doctrine is only important insofar as it gives you the motivation to take advantage of whatever insights or observations are expressed in that doctrine.

Taoists Don't Practice Rituals

Lao Tzu makes one memorable comment about ritual, and it's a doozy, something about how it's a rock-bottom degeneration of the *Tao,* the "thinnest husk" of sincerity and loyalty. And Chuang Tzu spins a sympathetic vignette about a sacred tortoise that would rather be "dragging its tail in the mud" than taking part in some silly old religious ceremony. Because Taoism so values the natural, the simple, and the genuine, how could it possibly have anything other than disdain for religious rituals, which often involve wearing special clothes, following the prescribed ceremonial structure, attaching great significance to various symbolic objects, and maybe even chanting in a language you don't understand? Taoists don't like what is artificial, and is there anything more artificial than a ritual?

Like most of the previous misconceptions, this one pretty much comes from reading Taoist classical texts instead of actually observing Taoists in action. From the very beginning of the Celestial Masters community, priests oversaw various rituals, including public confession ceremonies and the recitation of the *Tao Te Ching.* The Cheng-i Orthodox Unity sect of Taoism today is almost always described as the liturgical branch of Taoism, which means that it is known primarily for its ritual functions, like funerals, cosmic renewal ceremonies, and purification rites. In fact, Taoist rituals are among China's most dramatic and colorful, and you can find good video of them if you surf the Internet with just a little ingenuity.

Taoism Is All about Nature and Going with the Flow

In some ways, this is the one misconception that is pretty close to being true. Taoists do understand that the *Tao* is the source that underlies existence, and the human task is to try to harmonize with or follow the natural contours of the Way. And so, Taoism really is about going with the flow, about getting back to what is natural. But what really is "natural"? And what is the "flow"? Was Henry David Thoreau a Taoist sage because he left technology behind and lived in the woods near a pond? Are you being a Taoist if you eat granola and decorate your home with stones and wear seashells around your neck? Is it Taoistic to trust your instincts and follow whatever impulses seem natural? A lot of people seem to think so.

The Taoist understanding of the natural doesn't usually have a whole lot to do with getting back to nature, as in living with the flowers and trees. Taoist training for harmonizing with the *Tao* is not what a hippy or wilderness scout may imagine. More often than not, this involves harnessing the power of deities who embody the *Tao,* cultivating energies inside your own body, and performing obscure rituals to reestablish the harmony of the cosmos. And these particular skills are all things that Taoist adepts say you have to *learn,* not by reading a handful of texts or making a concerted effort to act spontaneously (which is kind of funny, if you think about it), but by undergoing a specific initiation and training. Believe it or not, it's *hard* to be natural!

But even if we forget for a minute about Taoist monastics and ritual experts and restrict Taoism to the texts of Lao Tzu and Chuang Tzu, naturalness is still not only a matter of choosing simple lifestyles. Both authors tell us repeatedly that getting a bead on the flow is not so easy, and that it may require some kind of mental and physical training to get our perception and intuition to that point. If anything, it's a kind of *enlightened* naturalness. ***Remember:*** Cook Ting didn't become a master ox-carver overnight (see Chapter 4).

Taoists and Confucians Are Exact Opposites

This misconception comes from two different places, but they fit together nicely:

> ✔ **The textbooks and even the Chinese histories portray a set of clean *yin-yang* opposites.** Confucianism is moral; Taoism is natural. Confucianism stresses learning and progressing forward; Taoism stresses unlearning and returning. Confucianism speaks to the public official; Taoism speaks to the private individual.

> ✔ **The general assumption in Western religion is that if you "belong" to one, you don't belong to another.** If you say you're Christian, you're also in some way saying that you're *not* Jewish or Muslim.

Together, these pieces combine to give the impression not only that the Chinese can be *either* Confucian or Taoist, but also that Confucians and Taoists are so different from one another that they probably wouldn't get along one bit.

But this formula falls apart once you remember that the Chinese have always been religiously *syncretic* (that is, drawing their religious practices from more than one tradition). The Chinese have historically utilized whichever practices have been customary in their families or communities, or whichever ones they understand will somehow take care of specific needs. Taoist priests may study Confucian classical texts; someone trained in Confucian calligraphy may make offerings at a Taoist temple. Taoism and Confucianism may sometimes appear to take opposite positions, but that doesn't usually provide any problem for the Chinese, who seldom take either one of them "whole." And because of the pervasiveness of Chinese syncretism, there really aren't a whole lot of people anymore who even identify themselves as Taoists or Confucians exclusively. If they don't really exist, it doesn't make a whole lot of sense to think of them as opposites.

Religious Taoism Is Just Silly Superstition

The idea that religious Taoism — the alchemy groups, the ritual experts, the organized monastic tradition today — is just a corruption of Lao Tzu's original genius goes back to the missionary scholars, who got it from conservative Confucian scholars in the late 19th century. Neither the Confucians nor the missionaries had much patience for successions of Celestial Masters, priestly hierarchies, colorful rituals, odd theories of deities inhabiting your body, or secretly transmitted doctrines, and they had no trouble writing it all off as superstition that somehow bubbled up from the "unenlightened" masses and infected Taoism. Even when texts and websites don't use such disparaging language to describe religious Taoism, they still don't usually pay it a whole lot of attention either.

So, we may know where the myth of a corrupted Taoism began, but once you really take a look at some of their unusual ideas and beliefs, could it still be accurate to say that these "other" types of Taoism are superstitious? That's actually an interesting question, not because it's debatable whether religious Taoism is superstitious, but because the word *superstition* is such a loaded term.

If you think about it, what's the difference between a religious belief and a superstitious belief? What's the difference between a practice you do religiously and one you do superstitiously? Technically, both religion and superstition are "unscientific," and both tend to consider forces that most people can't see, but people normally hold one of them (religion) in high esteem but have low regard for the other (superstition). And to some extent, that's the real difference between them! People often use the word *religious* simply to characterize beliefs and practices they find profound, and use the word *superstitious* to characterize beliefs and practices they find silly.

So, the word *superstition* is more a judgment than a description. And yes, that was the judgment that Confucian scholars and Christian missionaries pronounced on Taoism more than a hundred years ago. But it's probably a good idea to toss the word *superstition* altogether when we talk about religion today.

Anyone Can Be a Taoist

Let's say you read the *Tao Te Ching,* really like the philosophy, and decide you want to adopt it in your life. Or you take lessons in *t'ai-chi* and really like the teaching that seems to be behind it and the way it makes you feel. And so now you can consider yourself a Taoist. Why not? The *Tao Te Ching* doesn't have any membership rules — you don't have to have a "conversion" ceremony — and religion is a matter of choice anyway, right? You can choose to be a Christian, a Buddhist, a Wiccan, an agnostic, an atheist, or a worshiper of the spaghetti monster in the wall for all anyone cares, and who's going to stop you?

No one's going to stop you — I know that I certainly won't. Religious freedom is something that many of us value highly, and it seems ridiculous — maybe even offensive — to think that anyone could tell you that you can't be a Taoist.

The only problem here is what we mean by "can." Think of it this way: Any citizen of the United States *can* be president, but that doesn't mean that you can simply make that choice. Anyone *can* join a social club, but that doesn't mean that you can just declare yourself a member. There are circumstances in which you *can* be something, but not until you've undergone an election, or an initiation, or some other thing that actually changes your official status. Why? Because that's how everyone else understands the "rules." You're certainly free to identify yourself as a club member, and you may even live up to its ideals more than some of its official members do, but if you don't know the secret handshake, they won't even let you in the door.

Throughout most of Chinese history, a person became a Taoist not by accepting a body of doctrine or even attending a Taoist temple regularly; the modern Western model of "choosing" religious affiliation just doesn't apply to China and Taoism. Instead, a person did so by studying and training in a specific lineage and eventually earning recognition from those in authority in that lineage, and that route for becoming a Taoist is certainly available today, even to Westerners. But it probably requires more than leafing through the *Tao Te Ching* and taking a two-week study-tour.

All that said, if it doesn't matter to you whether you actually *join* any Taoist lineage and you just want to *learn* or grow spiritually from Taoist resources, then that's what Chapter 19 is for!

Chapter 19

Ten Bits of Advice for Acquiring Taoist Wisdom

In This Chapter

▶ Thinking about Taoism in your own life

▶ Taking specific steps to integrate Taoist ideas

▶ Looking honestly at things within your power to control

I wouldn't be surprised if this is the chapter that you came to first, even if you're a little nervous that anything I say about the *Tao* couldn't possibly be the "eternal *Tao*" (see Chapters 4 and 8). Taoist texts can sometimes seem so profound and elusive that it wouldn't hurt to try to get some of that wisdom in a few easy steps, would it?

But for most of its history, you can't really classify Taoism as much of a "wisdom tradition," unless by "wisdom" you mean such things as acquiring power over spirits, gaining access to esoteric rituals, and learning methods of cultivating the simultaneously biological and psycho-spiritual energies of your body. And for that, my best advice would be for you to learn Chinese, go to China, find some Orthodox Unity priest who will take you on as an apprentice, or some Complete Reality monastery that will admit you as a novice, and spend the next decade or two training in the tradition.

Don't quite have the time, money, or motivation to do that? I can't say that I blame you. But in terms of more modest steps, of taking some helpful cues from the more easily spiritualized aspects of the tradition, there are plenty of things you can do that just might get you a little bit closer to the *Tao*. In this chapter, I offer ten hints for bringing some of that Taoist wisdom into your own life.

Become Educated

Wait a minute, don't Taoist texts say that you should *unlearn* all the supposed knowledge and morality that bring us so far from the *Tao?* Doesn't Lao Tzu tell us that the farther we go, the less we know, and that the ideal sage is muddled and confused? Didn't Chuang Tzu tell us just to sit and forget? And frankly, isn't part of the appeal of Taoist philosophy the idea that we can just tap into the Way spontaneously, without all sorts of silly training and education?

Aside from the fact that those training in Taoist monasteries or under Taoist priests actually do engage in what might look like ordinary textual study, the simple truth is that you can't unlearn anything until you've learned something first, you can't return unless you've actually gone somewhere. It's kind of like the old hippy ditty put it, "How can I miss you if you won't go away?"

Not all types of forgetting, not all types of unlearning, are exactly the same. To be able to forget requires not just simply dumping everything we know, but first recognizing what we know and identifying our mental habits, those intellectual and cognitive tendencies to see or order the world in a certain way. And believe it or not, the process of educating ourselves, of increasing the breadth and depth of our "conventional" understandings of the world, not only gives us something to forget, but helps us acquire the skills to examine critically our so-called knowledge. Yes, we're all products of modernity, and if you're reading this book in English, you're probably also a product of the modern, individualistic Western world. So, first, become educated in that world, and then go about the process of unlearning it.

Observe Nature

Now this is more like it. What could be more Taoist than observing nature, right? Yes, but this involves more than basking in the romantic glow of a majestic oak tree, or feeling dwarfed by the fury of ocean waves crashing on the rocks, or even pondering the infinity of the countless stars in the sky on a moonlit evening. If nature really is anything like Lao Tzu's understanding of the *Tao,* then yes, it is the home to the 10,000 things, but that home isn't necessarily a warm and fuzzy one. **Remember:** Heaven and Earth are not humane, and the natural flux and flow of the universe are utterly indifferent to our pleasures and desires. Sometimes that flux and flow can have a few bumps in the road.

In one of her famous autobiographical stories, Annie Dillard describes watching a frog in a pond that appeared to be resting peacefully . . . but in reality it had actually been paralyzed by a variety of water beetle that was literally sucking the life out of it. Sometimes the cosmos may appear hospitable, but it may also seem ruthless. Nature is gentle breezes, but it's also tropical storms. It's ripples of cool streams, but it's also searing desert heat. So, which is it: Is nature beneficent or is it brutal? It's tempting to say both, but it's really neither. Ideas of beneficence and brutality come from our mentally and socially constructed stuff, and it's just not kosher to project those onto a universe that is ultimately unconcerned about such things. It's simply the great transformations of *yin* and *yang,* the spontaneous flow of existence that we can choose to accept, or choose to fight, or choose to travel with to the best of our abilities.

Several years ago, I was outside walking when I heard a peculiar sound, like the flapping of an anemic helicopter, a small sputtering motor that was trying desperately to engage but couldn't. I looked down and saw a huge, beautiful dragonfly hobbling around on the ground, unable to rev up its wings because they were gunked up by an ill-advised trip through a spider web. So, *this* was nature. The poor thing probably would've died soon, or met the bottom of someone's shoe, or turned into some other creature's snack. So, I picked it up, and as gently as I've ever done anything in my life, I carefully picked all the goop off the gauzy rice-paper wings, until they started flapping furiously and my new friend flew away for parts unknown. Was I interfering with nature? Perhaps. Or maybe I was acting like Chuang Tzu's ox-carver Cook Ting (see Chapter 4), following the contours of those natural delicate wings until the insect could rejoin the cosmic network on its own spontaneous accord.

Learn to Play

Sometimes, it seems that humankind has the potential to come up with some really good ideas, but it somehow manages to miss the mark by just a hair. When many people contemplate what single act they can do to get connected to realities bigger than themselves, to address the mysteries of the universe in a sincere and faithful way, they come to the conclusion that they should pray. They say that prayer brings you closer to the presence of God, makes you receptive to God's presence, and inspires you to listen for God's will. And that's all well and good. But if you want to step into the Chuang Tzu mindset, you might want to think less about *praying* and more about *playing!*

The universe is what it is — a vibrant, shifting network of interconnections. But however confusing or crazy it may appear, if you look at it the right way, you can see that its natural rhythms pulse with a sometimes sublime, sometimes goofy irony. The challenge is to tune yourself to that same pulse and develop an instinctive ability to chuckle with the cosmic jokes, to feel like an integral player in the interplanetary prank we call existence. In short, learn to play, learn to laugh, learn that the only *real* way to take life seriously is not to take it too seriously. Like the line from another song says, "Treat your life like it's your favorite toy."

Seek the Simplest Way

If you hacksaw a piece of wood, slice a vegetable, or even tear a piece of paper, it's always easier when you don't cut against the grain. The principle is deceptively simple; the natural shape and consistency of the object almost seem to *want* you to work *with* them, rather than *against* them. The same thing is true on the cosmic level, whether we're talking about the orbits of planets or the passage of seasons. The universe has a secure place for you, but for whatever reason, it's not always easy to find the simplest way.

Let's try this out with an example. Are you any good at math? Take a shot at quickly adding up these numbers: 71, 56, 37, 44, 68, 29, 32. Can you do it? How long did it take? If you wrote them down and added them up the old-fashioned way, it probably took you a few minutes and you might even have gotten it right . . . if you carried all the right digits and didn't mess up on the computation. Or did you punch them into a calculator? That can get it right too, but I'll bet it took a little time and required you not to key in any of the numbers incorrectly. But there's a simpler way, a faster way, and a *better* way. Look at those numbers again. Try rearranging them a little. Without using pen and paper, how much is 71 plus 29? Right, it's 100 even, and it didn't require much work to see that. And 68 plus 32 is also 100, as is 56 plus 44. In other words, you've got three pairs that add up to 100, and the lonely 37 tossed in for good measure. So, the total is 337, without lifting a finger, tiring your brain, or risking a mistake.

And when you do something like this the simple way, it just *feels* right, as if all the cosmic tumblers have clicked into place. Now imagine increasing this simple perfection exponentially. Imagine if that quality of "rightness" could infuse every breath you take, every step you take, and let you glide along with effortless grace, never struggling, never draining your own precious energy, always doing less to accomplish more.

Practice at Music and Sports

The two places where you can most often find yourself in the "*Tao* zone" are music and sports. Both serve as wonderful metaphors for (and microcosms of) the rhythms of the universe. Making music and playing a sport don't come easily, and you really *know* it when you hit a bad note or mess up on a play. Negotiating them can leave you feeling baffled, frustrated, and helpless. And yet, when you're in the zone for those fleeting moments, you know that, too. Like when you roll the ball down the bowling alley and just know the minute it separates from your fingertips that it will make the pins absolutely explode.

Or when you swing the bat and the pitched ball rockets off into the ozone at the moment of contact, as though you had somehow channeled all the power of the universe into that one swing. Or when you play whatever instrument you've bonded with, either alone or with a band, and you almost feel like a stunned spectator sitting back and marveling at where the music is traveling on what seems to be its own inertia. During these lyrical *Tao*-zone interludes, you can catch a glimpse of a pervasive harmony, a sense of taking part in an utterly alive and dynamic kaleidoscope of existence.

But are music and sports natural? Aren't they skills you have to learn in order to do them well? Fair enough. One of the great Taoist ironies is that humanity has gotten to the point that what's natural doesn't feel natural anymore, and that we have to learn all over again how to do what should follow from our natures. When you practice *t'ai-chi* (which you also have to learn because it doesn't just come to you naturally), the teacher may tell you that a person in any given motion can mirror and even enact the movement of the universe. A perfectly executed athletic or musical moment can do that, too.

Eat Raw and Organic Fruits and Vegetables

Okay, there's really nothing Taoist about raw or organic fruits and vegetables. But still, the relationship between "pure" food and processed, factory-farmed, and overcooked food resonates nicely with Taoist philosophy. The latter has gradually become the "new normal," to the point that many people (especially children who have never seen otherwise) think that cakes and cookies come from boxes, have never eaten a green bean that didn't come from a can, and gag when they taste real maple syrup because they've become accustomed to the high-fructose substitute that fills supermarket shelves. Today's mass-produced, insecticide-covered, and hormone-infused foods bear about as much resemblance to real food as today's culture bears to the eternal *Tao*.

So, what good does it do to eat the real stuff? Does it bring you closer to the *Tao?* Probably not. But to make a conscious, intentional effort to put in your body only cleaner, more natural substances can be a first step in reorienting your entire approach to the world. A raw, organic piece of cauliflower can just *taste* like the *Tao,* and it can give you quite literally a taste of what's to come if you seek out the natural.

Ask Questions

No matter who you are or where you live, chances are that the community in general shares a set of assumptions and preferences that are so hard-wired that most people would never considering challenging them and probably aren't even aware of them. In other words, they share a "consensus" view of reality, the kind of locked-in perspective that Chuang Tzu spends so much time telling us to undo. Sometimes, these shared orientations don't seem to matter much or aren't particularly significant, but they accumulate to create a kind of "artificial" world, where we can't tell the difference between what's real and what we've just made up.

Take something pretty basic, like dressing up to go to church, or a Broadway show, or a job interview. Why do people have the impression that certain occasions or events are "higher" and require you to dress "up"? People don't usually have much patience for questions like this, and they often try to wrap them up with straightforward principles. "You dress up because these events are special," they might say. But is that really it? Visiting the Grand Canyon and watching a lunar eclipse are special, but most people don't dress up for them. Okay, well maybe it's that these events qualify as "serious"? But watching a presidential debate or attending therapy sounds pretty serious to me, and most people don't dress up to do either. Does it really have to do with expectations that other people have of you? Or do clothes carry some kind of statements about wealth or personal status? There isn't one answer to these questions, but Chuang Tzu thinks we should keep asking them.

Even these questions were just the tip of the iceberg. Even if we question why and when someone should "dress up," it's still important to ask why we consider certain clothing dressing "up." Why do we think of clothing in terms of height or altitude? What is "upward" about a tie and "downward" about a tie-dye shirt? Why is it that children "play" dress-up — does it involve an act of pretending? Why is *dressing down* a synonym for delivering someone a reprimand — are we rebuking ourselves when we dress down? If you find yourself losing patience with these types of questions, then I've got one more question for you: Why *shouldn't* we ask them?

Interrogate Your Own Preferences and Motivations

Of course, the most important questions to ask are the ones about yourself; the most important "consensus" reality to interrogate is your own. You don't have to go after the "big" theological or metaphysical issues either — before you start asking yourself why you believe in God or what the relationship is between language and the reality it describes, you might want to start a little smaller. If you have any firm convictions, or a strong sense of how moral people "ought" to behave — and most people do — then ask yourself why you feel that way. Did you arrive at these convictions all by yourself? Or did you get some of them from your parents, or a group of friends, or something you read or heard somewhere? Are you satisfied that you can justify every (or any) position you hold? What is at stake for you in holding those positions? What happens to you or the world if you no longer hold them?

But be careful. The point of this exercise is *not* to make you discard everything you hold dear, *not* to convince yourself that all preferences and motivations are equally valuable (or equally) worthless. The point is to become gradually aware of your own *situatedness* — to become aware of yourself as a complex social, historical, and biological being — and to take notice of how the complexities of your situation *shape* the sum total of who you are and how you view the world. The hardest part of discovering what is natural and authentic in the world sometimes lies in discovering the most natural and authentic part of yourself.

Think About When to Be Skeptical and When to Be Generous

If it sounds like all this questioning, of yourself and the world around you, is going to turn you into a cynical, detached skeptic, then don't forget to ask yourself one more question: When is it intellectually honest and spiritually healthy to be suspicious, and when is it intellectually honest and spiritually healthy to be charitable? This may be the hardest of all these bits of advice, mainly because the answer to this question never comes easily. There's no abstract principle you can apply so that "when Fred says such-and-such, I'll be skeptical, but when he says such-and-such, I'll be generous." But it may also be the most rewarding, because it zeroes right in on what can you bring to your day-to-day life. Really, what can you do with this questioning when you bring it back to your relationships to your friends and family? Yes, you might be able to slice apart any perspective and prove that any attitude or opinion rests on fairly shaky ground, but to what end?

The key here is not to think about this, come up with an answer, and then move on. The key is to keep thinking about this, to keep asking yourself what to do once you find you can deconstruct "consensus" reality and even deconstruct your own reality. If it only makes you a little more tentative, a little more cautious, a little more pragmatic, and a little less inclined to wind things down neatly before you've really thought them through and examined yourself carefully, then even that is one important step in the right direction.

Don't Pretend You Can Acquire Taoist Wisdom through Ten Easy Steps

To some extent, this just repeats the way this chapter began, by reminding you that the process of drawing "wisdom" lessons from Taoism doesn't really match up well with actual Taoist history. You may find it life-giving to spiritualize Taoist texts and pick up whatever you can from the lessons you find there — certainly no one's going to stop you from doing so! But it may also be helpful to remind yourself from time to time that what you've taken from them has probably universalized Lao Tzu and Chuang Tzu and read them out of context. And, of course, before you think of yourself as a Taoist, it wouldn't hurt to compare your brand of Taoism with that of the trained, practicing Taoists in China and other Asian countries.

So, why am I trying to spoil your fun? Am I trying to rub your nose in your own Western-ness, your own modern-ness, and make you feel crummy that you're not a "real Taoist"? I hope not! Believe it or not, I'm really just trying to get all Taoist on you. One important principle that Lao Tzu and Chuang Tzu seem to share is that if you have a confident belief that you know the *Tao*, you almost certainly have a *mistaken* belief that you know the *Tao*! **Remember:** Lao Tzu said that to "know you don't know" deserves praise, but that "not to know you don't know" should be recognized as a flaw. And to make things even crazier, Lao Tzu says that what makes a sage flawless is, well, that he recognizes his flaws as flaws!

So, do everything you can to try to acquire Taoist wisdom — just make sure you don't really think you've ever gotten it!

Chapter 20

Ten Places to See Taoist Stuff Happening Today

Chuang Tzu once commented that the *Tao* was everywhere — in insects, blades of grass, shards of glass, even piles of manure — and so you might expect Taoism to be everywhere, too! In a way, it is. You can find translations of the *Tao Te Ching* in almost any mainstream bookstore, the concept of *Tao* shows up regularly in newspaper crossword puzzles, and New Age storefronts teach everything from Taoist philosophy to Taoist sex. And with such an abundance of "*Tao* of" literature, we seem to be living in the "Age of *Tao*."

But on the other hand, actual Taoist stuff can seem as mysterious as the primordial *Tao* itself. How many Taoist classmates did you have in school? How often do you see Taoist holiday decorations in the town square? When was the last time you attended a Taoist wedding or naming ceremony? And even when you do find some Taoism here in the West, it's not always clear if it has much to do with the Taoism that's practiced in China. It may take a Taoist to say that "stuff happens," but you don't have to be Taoist to observe that "Taoist stuff happens." But where? And how Taoist is it really?

Actually, you *can* find Taoist stuff in many places, but it's always important to figure out what *kind* of Taoism it is, how it fits in to the whole Taoist picture, and how different Taoist "stuff" relates to one another. In this chapter, I take you on a tour of some accessible Taoist resources — some Chinese, some American or European — including not only places to go, but also films, websites, and books. In each case, I give you a sense of what you may find there, what interesting features to look for, and how to incorporate it all into your growing Taoist vocabulary of real Taoist stuff.

The White Cloud Monastery

Okay, not everyone can walk out the door and go to China, but if you do find yourself traveling there on business or on tour, chances are good that you'll eventually make your way to Beijing, the country's capital. And if you do, it shouldn't be hard to put the White Cloud Monastery on your itinerary. This temple — some people call it an "abbey" — goes back more than a thousand years and is almost certainly the most famous Taoist facility in China. It's now the institutional headquarters of Complete Perfection Taoism (the monastic branch of contemporary Taoism), the home of the Chinese Taoist Association, and a major training center for Taoist monks.

No two days at the White Cloud Monastery will feel exactly the same, but here are some things you can look for:

- ✔ **Priests and monks:** You can't miss them, with their grayish blue robes and long hair tied up in a bun. They might be tending particular shrines, offering guidance to lay visitors, or just milling around. If you speak some Chinese or have an interpreter, they might stop to answer some questions for you. Or, they might not!

- ✔ **Shrine halls:** Most of the day-to-day activity occurs inside the shrine halls, each of which is usually devoted to one deity or a handful of deities. You'll see visitors kneeling on small mats in front of statues, bowing and clasping their hands in a prescribed way, and perhaps making a financial offering in a collection box. A monk may be there to ring a bell when people pray. You can try it yourself, but expect lots of stares if you're not Asian.

- ✔ **Incense cauldrons:** You can't miss these huge, ornate cauldrons where visitors throw whole packages of incense. Don't worry if you forgot to bring your own bunch — vendors outside the temple will be happy to make sure you don't go in empty-handed.

- ✔ **Celebrations:** Time your visit so you're there around Chinese New Year, the Spring Festival, or other seasonal events, and you might get to witness some colorful public ritual or musical performances.

Dragon Tiger Mountain

In the interest of impartiality, it's only fair to give equal time to the official headquarters of Orthodox Unity Taoism (the liturgical branch of modern Taoism), which is located at the Dragon Tiger Mountain (Lung-hu Shan) complex in Yintan Kiangsi. Traditionally identified as the place where Chang Tao-ling received his revelations, the many temples (including the Palace of Highest Purity) here were bustling places until the Communist Revolution, when the 63rd Celestial Master and many of his followers fled to Taiwan. In recent years, Orthodox Unity Taoists have gradually regained control over the space and reestablished their presence.

Since the 1990s, the Chinese Taoist Associated facilitated ordination of several hundred priests at Dragon Tiger Mountain, and the current Orthodox Unity leadership presides over the Mansion of the Celestial Master. However, although this spot enjoys its status as Taoist sacred space and has again become a pilgrimage site, the decentralized nature of Orthodox Unity Taoism means that much of its significance is historical and ceremonial. In other words, you can sometimes see some Taoist pageantry there, but you'll still need to find a local Orthodox Unity priest, probably in the countryside, if you want to see any day-to-day practice.

A Question of Balance

Although this film is otherwise a little long in the tooth — it was made in the late 1970s — the last 15 minutes or so show some spectacular footage of an Orthodox Unity funeral in Taiwan, and you'll probably never get a closer look at this aspect of the tradition. The scenes include the final days of a nearly two-month-long series of services memorializing a late grandmother from a prestigious family and several other recently deceased people. The events are lavish and expensive, almost certainly sending a few families into hock.

Although the film shows clips of mourners, much of it looks very little like a traditional Christian, Jewish, or Muslim funeral, and if not for the affable (if somewhat goofy) narrator's voiceover, you could think you're watching a carnival rather than a religiously significant occasion. There's a lot going on, but make sure to notice the following:

- ✔ **The Orthodox Unity priest:** He's really the "brains of the outfit," so take note of all the different roles he plays here. At one point, he's wearing a Western business suit and rolling up scrolls needed for the ceremony. At another, he's changed into colorful vestments to direct a rite that symbolically traces the journey of a spirit charged with assuring safe passage of the deceased. The last time you see him, he signals his acolytes to perform dramatic acrobatics, symbolizing the final descent of the spirit.

- ✔ **Elaborate rituals:** Watch here for all kinds of ritual objects and actions, including wreaths, photographs, texts, food, ceremonial paper money, firecrackers, traditional music, and live animals. Notice how the priest and his acolytes engage in carefully choreographed hand gestures and physical movements, all of which have meanings accessible only to those with clerical training.

- ✔ **Funeral procession:** The climax of the ceremony is the actual funeral procession, which looks a lot like a parade, complete with full bands, dancers, and old-style sedan chairs. Make sure to catch the narrator's discussion of how the families used *feng-shui* (though he doesn't call it that) to determine the time and place of the burials.

At the very end of the film, the scene switches to a glimpse of several people doing *t'ai-chi* exercises in a Taipei park at dawn. The cool part is when the camera fixes on the leader of the group, while the narrator explains the movements by using passages from the *Tao Te Ching* and relating them to *wu-wei* (non-doing). He then goes off on a little riff about Taoism as a universal wisdom, which doesn't exactly qualify as good scholarship, but it does nicely express the standard Western spiritualization of the *Tao*.

The film was part of an educational series called *The Long Search,* which has many excellent entries (though some are quite dated as well). You can usually find these titles in college and university libraries, and you can purchase it at www.ambrosevideo.com/items.cfm?id=869, though you may be able to grab used copies at Amazon.com or other online marketplaces.

American Taoist Temples and Study Centers

If you poke around, especially in any major U.S. city, you can probably find someplace that identifies itself as a Taoist temple, study center, or retreat center, and you're sure to find plenty of Taoist stuff there. But just make sure to remember that these places usually represent the American version of Taoist institutions — these Taoist-flavored *t'ai-chi* and *ch'i-kung* training facilities seldom have any affiliation with either Complete Perfection or Orthodox Unity Taoism. Also, because many of these organizations are fairly small-scale operations, they could very well change their names, change hands, or cease to exist altogether, so you may want to call ahead before you plan a field trip.

Here's a cross-section of some of the more visible, and more durable, American Taoist institutions:

- **Taoist Sanctuary of San Diego** (www.taoistsanctuary.org)**:** The ancestor of the first Taoist temple in the United States, this institution emphasizes a specific strain of *t'ai-chi* called "old frame, first road."

- **Temple of the Celestial Cloud, Monterey, California** (www.daoist magic.com)**:** The founder of this temple boasts of ordination from a former Orthodox Unity Celestial Master, but the facility itself teaches martial arts and medical *ch'i-kung.*

- **Center of Traditional Taoist Studies, Weston, Massachusetts** (www. tao.org)**:** Founded by a Russian Taoist priest, this center claims somewhat ambiguous Complete Perfection ties, teaches "traditional Taoist theology" and meditation, and houses the Temple of Original Simplicity.

- **SunDo Mountain Taoist Center, West Hartford, Connecticut** (www. sundo.org)**:** This center has roots in a Korean lineage, which teaches a combination of Zen meditation and Taoist techniques for circulating *ch'i.* SunDo is the Korean pronunciation of *hsien-tao,* the way of the immortals.

✔ **Great River Taoist Center, Washington, D.C. (**www.grtc.org**):** Primarily a *t'ai-chi* training center, Great River also teaches traditional Chinese swordsmanship and offer an online forum on various Taoist or quasi-Taoist issues.

The Abode of the Eternal Tao

In the early 1990s, an Oregonian man named Solala Towler, a self-professed child of the '60s, built a small shrine dedicated to a handful of Taoist deities and patriarchs. Since then, the Abode of the Eternal Tao (www.abodetao. com) has evolved into something of an American Taoist one-stop, sponsoring literature, workshops, travel tours, and online resources. Towler's Taoism is noticeably American, in that it tends to spiritualize Taoist philosophy, emphasize wellness practices like *ch'i-kung* and Chinese herbalism, and self-consciously resist overtly "religious" aspects of Taoism.

If you check out the Eternal Tao's website, you can pick and choose from any of the following:

✔ *The Empty Vessel: The Journal of Daoist Philosophy and Practice:* This quarterly magazine includes articles by modern Taoist figures (like Ni Hua-ching), *ch'i-kung* instructions, chronicles of visits to Taoist locations, interpretations of Taoist texts, and so on.

✔ **Instructional books and videos:** You can purchase resources on most of the usual things — philosophy, *t'ai-chi, feng-shui,* and so on — but also more specialized stuff like Taoist exorcism, magic, talismans, and sexual cultivation.

✔ **China travel:** The Abode sponsors Taoist study tours of China, where participants visit Taoist temples and monasteries, trek to sacred mountains, and undergo direction for "inner journeys" while they practice *ch'i-kung* throughout the trip.

✔ **Online and in-person instruction:** Towler provides online discussions of Taoist philosophy (and quotations from Taoist texts and figures) and also coordinates live *ch'i-kung* seminars.

The Taoist Tai Chi Society

Sure, you can probably learn *t'ai-chi* at a local YMCA or neighborhood recreation center, but the Taoist Tai Chi Society (www.taoist.org) plugs you in to an international community of practitioners and a specific Taoist history.

Through its affiliation with the Fung Loy Kok Institute of Taoism (which began as an alliance of Canadian and U.S. temples), the Taoist Tai Chi Society presents itself as the practical arm of a Taoist movement — obviously a very Western one — directed toward internal cultivation, harmonization with oneself and the world, and the ecumenical bridging of all religious traditions and cultures.

The society has branches in dozens of countries, including the Taoist Tai Chi Society of the USA (http://usa.taoist.org), which operates in nearly 30 states and identifies itself as a charitable organization, though it doesn't seem to publicize which charities it supports. In any event, whether you live in New England, the Southwest, the Pacific Northwest, the Rocky Mountain states, the Deep South, the Upper Midwest, or even Alaska, there's no doubt one of these centers somewhere not too far from you.

Healing Tao USA

Like the Taoist Tai Chi Society, Healing Tao USA (www.healingtaousa.com) has successfully marketed semi-Taoist materials to an American audience in a way that's accessible, while preserving that necessary sense of Taoist mystery. Based in the New Age mecca of Asheville, North Carolina, and descended from Mantak Chia's lucrative Universal Healing Tao Center, Healing Tao USA could well be the nation's most extensive full-service Taoist provider.

Just snoop around its website and you'll encounter a dizzying barrage of Taoist supplies and opportunities. Depending on your mood, interests, or amount of free time, you can savor any of the following:

- ✔ **Healing ch'i retreats:** More than just the occasional workshop, Healing Tao offers an average of 30 different weeklong retreats in the spring and summer, on subjects ranging from *ch'i-kung* and *t'ai-chi* to sexual yoga and deep organ massage. It also sponsors an occasional trip to China, focused on Taoist sacred sites.

- ✔ **Multimedia resources:** Who can resist a CD on Taoist dream practice, a DVD on eight extraordinary vessels ch'i-kung, or a book about the multi-orgasmic man?

- ✔ **Wellness supplies:** You can purchase herbal mixes like the inner light flower essence, which protects you from negative emotions, or the inner smile flower essence, which "bathes" your cells with feelings of bliss.

The British Taoist Association

If there were any form of Western missionary Taoism, the British Taoist Association (BTA; www.taoists.co.uk) would probably be as close at it comes. Unlike many American and European Taoist institutions, whose ties to China are a little more tenuous, the BTA was founded by four British citizens who had previously traveled to China to study with (and receive ordination from) a Taoist monk. They also maintain connections with the Chinese Taoist Association and occasionally host Chinese monks to assist with their teaching. Although their training seems to have been in the Complete Perfection lineage, they insist that their approach is nonsectarian and that they embrace all forms of Taoism.

What most gives the BTA their almost missionary flavor is the way they have their fingers in a lot of pieces of the Taoist pie. Their stated goal is to establish a permanent practice center in the United Kingdom, but they also participate in the following activities:

- ✓ **Dragon's Mouth Magazine:** This quarterly publication includes essays by Chinese and Western Taoists, as well as updates on Taoist activities in China.

- ✓ **Workshops and retreats:** The BTA sponsors retreats taught by Chinese and British teachers, much of it focusing on a kind of internal cultivation that they trace back to Lao Tzu and a later text titled *The Classic of Purity and Tranquility.*

- ✓ **Temple restoration:** Much like the Chinese Taoist Association, the BTA has raised money to restore neglected temples, including a recent pair in or near Xi'an, which have transformed from abandoned relics to centers of religious life.

The Reform Taoist Congregation

No Taoism can be more modern and more Western than this virtual Taoist community, an online gathering place for like-minded individuals who fancy themselves members of "Reform Taoism" (www.reformtaoism.org). Founded by a disaffected Methodist named Michael Torley (who holds degrees in psychology and religious studies), this postmodern new religion has no deities, belief in an afterlife, actual physical space, clergy, rituals, holidays, or ethical demands of its adherents. Of course, this doesn't even remotely resemble anything in China that you could call Taoist, but it perfectly captures the individualistic, utterly nondogmatic spiritualization of Taoism that characterizes much of the Western Taoist ethos.

If you visit the Reform Taoist Congregation website, you can find most of the regular philosophical resources and links, but it also has the kinds of things you might expect from a group whose primary religious reference is Christianity but that has rejected that tradition:

✔ **A Taoist creed:** Loosely patterned on the Nicene Creed, the Taoist creed affirms belief in "the formless and eternal Tao," rejects both deities and a host of human evils (like intolerance and violence), and embraces love and harmony.

✔ **A catalog of Taoist beliefs:** While the congregation takes a generally tolerant posture toward just about everything, it does weigh on in many "loaded" issues, including abortion, animal rights, intoxication, extraterrestrial life, sexuality, and wealth.

✔ **A Taoist calendar:** Torley and his associates had no problem making up a whole religion from scratch, so it should come as no surprise that they also had no problem assembling a calendar of holidays. Some correspond to seasonal changes (like the spring equinox and summer solstice), while others — Day of Unity, Day of Sages, Day of Nature — were invented to celebrate different aspects of Taoist philosophy or history.

The Writings of Ursula K. Le Guin

Once you get out of China, it's hard to say exactly who *is* and who *isn't* a Taoist. True, most American Taoists haven't trained in either the Orthodox Unity or Complete Perfection lineage, don't know their way around the texts of the Taoist canon, and wouldn't recognize a Taoist talisman if their kids brought one home from school. But one of the whole points of this book is that Taoism has changed over time, from philosophical tradition, to millenarian community, to lineage of hereditary priests, to monastic practitioners of internal alchemy, and now to American wellness and martial arts centers. And every once in a while, the American transformation of Taoism — which has its own contours, idiosyncrasies, and peccadilloes — lights on something that's aesthetically compelling, philosophically astute, and morally engaging. One such transmitter of Taoist wisdom is the science-fiction and fantasy author Ursula K. Le Guin.

To some extent, it's fair to say that Le Guin was *raised* Taoist. Her father, a famous anthropologist, studied Taoist texts and asked that the *Tao Te Ching* be read at his funeral. And although she never laid claim to being a Taoist, her creative version of the *Tao Te Ching*, the body of her writings, and her public profile and various social issues put forth a wise and subtle vision that you could quite arguably call Taoist. If you're not sure, read *The Lathe of Heaven, Always Coming Home,* and other books, and decide for yourself.

Part VI
Appendixes

In this part . . .

*A*lthough I define terms when I use them in this book, sometimes it's handy to have all the Taoism-related terminology in one place. That's where the Glossary in this part comes in. Use it to look up terms you're unfamiliar with, in this book and beyond.

I also include an appendix full of resources — places you can turn for even more information on Taoism, from books and encyclopedias to websites. You can spend a lifetime learning about Taoism, and these resources will give you some places to continue your journey.

I close out this book with a pronunciation guide. After you get comfortable with the basic rules of pronunciation, you'll never again have trouble reading (or remembering) Chinese names and words! Well, almost never. . . .

Appendix A

Glossary

alchemy: The laboratory preparation of powerful elixirs, made from various metals, minerals, and herbs. The trained adept who swallowed these potions supposedly gained magical powers and transformed after death into an immortal spirit. *See also* internal alchemy *and* external alchemy.

blackhead Taoists: Priests who are ordained in an official Taoist lineage, usually Orthodox Unity. *See also* redhead Taoists *and* Orthodox Unity Taoism.

Celestial Master: Translation of *T'ien-shih*. The title given to the hereditary leader of Orthodox Unity Taoism. *See also* Orthodox Unity Taoism.

chai: Rituals of purification or purgation, which are currently combined with *chiao* rituals. *See also chiao.*

Chang Chin-t'ao: The short-lived 65th Celestial Master in the Orthodox Unity lineage, who willingly relinquished the title in 2009 after an internal power dispute. *See also* Celestial Master *and* Orthodox Unity Taoism.

Chang Chüeh: The charismatic leader of the Way of Great Peace, who led his followers in the Yellow Turbans Rebellion. Also known as Chang Chiao. *See also* Way of Great Peace *and* Yellow Turbans Rebellion.

Chang En-p'u: The 63rd Celestial Master in the Orthodox Unity lineage. He fled the Chinese mainland during the Communist Revolution, ending up in Taiwan and continuing the tradition there. *See also* Celestial Master *and* Orthodox Unity Taoism.

Chang Lu: The third Celestial Master and the grandson of Chang Tao-ling, he may have been most responsible for organizing the Five Pecks of Rice Sect and instituting the Orthodox Unity covenant. *See also* Celestial Master, Chang Tao-ling, Five Pecks of Rice Sect, *and* Orthodox Unity Taoism.

Chang San-feng: A legendary Taoist immortal, traditionally (though dubiously) identified as the founder of *t'ai-chi ch'üan*. *See also t'ai-chi ch'üan.*

Chang Tao-chen: The current (though not entirely undisputed) 64th Celestial Master in the Orthodox Unity lineage, whose ascension posthumously negated Chang Yuan-hsien's claim to the title. *See also* Celestial Master, Orthodox Unity Taoism, *and* Chang Yuan-hsien.

Chang Tao-ling: The founder and first Celestial Master of the movement that would become the first Taoist community. *See also* Celestial Master.

Chang Yuan-hsien: The Taiwanese-born 64th Celestial Master, whose title was posthumously revoked when Chang Tao-chen assumed the position in 2009. *See also* Celestial Master *and* Chang Tao-chen.

Cheng-i Tao: *See* Orthodox Unity Taoism.

ch'i: The "psychophysical stuff" of existence, including matter, energy, thought, and so on.

Chia, Mantak: Thailand-born teacher of *t'ai-chi ch'üan* and other Taoist-related practices, who founded the Universal Healing Tao Center in New York. *See also t'ai-chi ch'üan.*

chiao: Rituals of offering, including the dramatic rite of cosmic renewal, performed by Taoist priests. *See also chai.*

ch'i-kung: Literally, "the efficiency of the psychophysical stuff," a general name given to various gymnastic, breathing, and healing practices that became popular in late 20th-century China. See also *ch'i.*

Chinese Taoist Association: A bureaucratic organization that works to enhance Taoism's public profile in China, through educational, ecological, ecumenical, and philanthropic initiatives.

ching: See vital essence.

Ch'üan-chen Tao: *See* Complete Perfection Taoism.

Chuang Tzu: One of the earliest Classical Taoist authors, who may have lived around the 4th century B.C.E. and wrote the most important chapters of the book that bears his name. *See also* Classical Taoism.

cinnabar fields: Translation of *tan-t'ien.* Three regions of the body thought to house distinct deities and contain specific configurations of matter and energy. An important idea in Taoist physiology and alchemy. *See also* alchemy.

Classical Taoism: The general name given to Taoist texts and authors predating the Way of the Celestial Masters. *See also* Way of the Celestial Masters, Lao-Chuang Tradition, *and* School of *Tao.*

Complete Perfection Taoism: The *Ch'üan-chen Tao,* the newer and more monastic of the two Taoist lineages that are common in China today; the other is Orthodox Unity Taoism. This sect flourishes more in the northern part of the country, and has its base at the White Cloud Monastery in Beijing. *See also* Orthodox Unity Taoism *and* White Cloud Monastery.

Confucianism: A cultural and moral tradition dating back to the Hundred Schools Period, often the subject of criticism in Classical Taoist texts. *See also* Hundred Schools Period *and* Classical Taoism.

Confucius: The Latinized name Western scholars gave to K'ung Fu-tzu (or Master K'ung), the moral and cultural teacher who loosely founded what is now known as Confucianism. *See also* Confucianism.

Cook Ting: A character in the *Chuang Tzu* whose ability to carve oxen for 19 years without ever sharpening his blade makes him a perfect example of the Taoist sage who is capable of spontaneous, effortless, effective action. *See also Chuang Tzu.*

correlative cosmology: The general name given to the elaborate theory of how different elements and dynamic phases resonate and correspond with one another; associated with five elements theory and *yin-yang* theory. *See also* five elements theory *and yin-yang* theory.

Cultural Revolution: More familiar name for the Great Proletariat Cultural Revolution. An oppressive national movement instituted by Mao Tse-tung in the mid-1960s, officially intended to cleanse China of forces hostile to communism. During this period, Mao nearly eradicated all traces of Taoism from China.

Dickerson, Kenneth: Actor known by the name Khigh Dhiegh, who was perhaps the first American-born Taoist practitioner; studied under Share K. Lew and co-founded the Taoist Sanctuary. *See also* Lew, Share K. *and* Taoist Sanctuary.

Dispatching the Writ of Pardon: An important stage of Orthodox Unity funerals, in which a horseman is sent to the underworld to release the spirit of the deceased from purgatory limbo. *See also* Orthodox Unity Taoism.

divination: A general term for various practices, like *feng-shui,* devised to predict the future, learn the will of spirits, or otherwise figure out things we can't normally see. *See also feng-shui.*

Dragon Tiger Mountain: Lung-hu Shan, the official center of Orthodox Unity Taoism, in the southeastern province of Kiangsi, and the traditionally recognized ancestral home of Chang Tao-ling. *See also* Orthodox Unity Taoism *and* Chang Tao-ling.

Eight Immortals: An octet of mythic Taoist adepts, who are now in the Complete Perfection pantheon. *See also* Complete Perfection Taoism.

external alchemy: Translation of *wai-tan.* The process of literally transmuting metals and ingesting elixirs. *See also* alchemy *and* internal alchemy.

Fa-lun Kung: *See* Fa-lun Ta-fa.

Fa-lun Ta-fa: A controversial new religious movement, with roots in *ch'i-kung* and Buddhism. Also known as Fa-lun Kung. *See also* ch'i-kung.

fasting of the mind and heart: Translation of *hsin-chai*, a Taoist practice first referenced in the *Chuang Tzu*, that involves thinning and emptying ordinary cognitive processes to the point that you can "listen" with your *ch'i*. Related to sitting and forgetting. *See also* Chuang Tzu, *ch'i, and* sitting and forgetting.

feng-shui: Literally "wind and water," a form of divination that entails reading the physical environment in order to decide the best location to place a home, school, or cemetery. The Chinese also employ *feng-shui* to determine changes they should make to an existing dwelling, like where to place furniture or hang a mirror. *See also* divination.

five elements theory: An elaborate theory on the five phases of wood, fire, earth, metal, and water, which interact with one another in both generative and destructive cycles. Identified closely with *yin-yang* theory. *See also yin-yang* theory.

Five Pecks of Rice Sect: The original community organized by Chang Tao-ling, named for the tithe that each family paid for membership in the group. This community eventually grew into the Way of the Celestial Masers and the Orthodox Unity lineage. *See also* Chang Tao-ling, Way of the Celestial Masters, *and* Orthodox Unity Lineage.

Fung Loy Kok: Several different North American Taoist temples, founded by Moy Shin-lin. *See also* Moy Shin-lin *and* International Taoist T'ai-chi Society.

Great Peace: The name given to the "new age" that was eagerly awaited in Taoist millenarian traditions. *See also* millenarianism *and* Way of Great Peace.

Great Proletariat Cultural Revolution: *See* Cultural Revolution.

Great Purity: Translation of *T'ai-ch'ing*, a group of 3rd- and 4th-century revealed texts (originating from a Heavenly realm by the same name). Among the first Taoist writings to deal with alchemy. *See also* alchemy.

Han Fei Tzu: Architect of the Legalist school from the Hundred Schools Period, his text includes two chapters that may be the oldest existing commentaries on the *Tao Te Ching*, though it's unclear if he was actually the author of those chapters. *See also* Legalism, Hundred Schools Period, *and Tao Te Ching*.

Heaven: Translation of *T'ien*, a relatively impersonal "high god" of Chinese religion in general, associated with things like fate, cosmic order, and the protection of a righteous ruling regime.

Highest Purity: Translation of *Shang-ch'ing*, an extensive series of revealed texts from the 4th century (dealing with alchemy, meditation, descriptions of Heavenly realms, and so on), and of the self-cultivation groups that organized around them.

Hoff, Benjamin: The American author of whimsical quasi-Taoist texts called *The Tao of Pooh* and *The Te of Piglet.*

hsien: *See* immortal.

Huai-nan Tzu: A Han Dynasty text, commissioned by Prince Liu An (though actually written by many different hands), and an important source of Huang-Lao Taoism. *See also* Liu An *and* Huang-Lao Taoism.

Huang-Lao Taoism: A short-lived, syncretic form of Taoism, supposedly based on the teachings of the Yellow Emperor (Huang Ti) and Lao Tzu, which flourished during the early part of the Han Dynasty and had some influence on later Taoist philosophy. *See also* syncretism, Yellow Emperor, *and* Lao Tzu.

Huang Ti: *See* Yellow Emperor.

Hundred Schools Period: The period from about 600 to 200 B.C.E., when many strains of Chinese thought, including Taoism and Confucianism, first began to emerge.

immortal: Ordinary translation of *hsien,* one who has achieved postmortem immortality, a goal of many Taoist practitioners, and the status of many beings in Taoist pantheons.

impulse and response: Related to *yin-yang* theory and five elements theory, the observation that the motion or transformation of any agent in the cosmic scheme of things is necessarily related to every other participant in that cosmos, following regular, predictable patterns. *See also yin-yang and* five elements theory.

Integral Way: The general name for the teachings of American Taoist Ni Hua-ching. *See also* Ni Hua-ching.

internal alchemy: Translation of *nei-tan,* a later, spiritualized form of alchemy that understood the process of transmuting substances and consuming elixirs as a metaphor for cultivation occurring within the human body. Also called *inner alchemy* or *interior alchemy. See also* alchemy *and* external alchemy.

International Taoist T'ai-chi Society: Founded by Moy Shin-lin, an umbrella organization of affiliated *t'ai-chi ch'üan* teaching centers in dozens of different countries. *See also* Moy Shin-lin *and t'ai-chi ch'üan.*

Inward Training: The *Nei-yeh,* a brief, recently discovered document from the Hundred Schools Period that describes forms of physical-spiritual cultivation and has thematic and structural similarities with the *Tao Te Ching. See also* Hundred Schools Period *and Tao Te Ching.*

Ko Hung: A 4th-century Confucian scholar and alchemist, whose text *The Master Who Embraces Simplicity* would be embraced by later generations of Taoists. *See also The Master Who Embraces Simplicity.*

K'ou Ch'ien-chih: A 5th-century Taoist who attempted to revive the Way of the Celestial Masters lineage and helped established a short-lived Taoist theocracy. *See also* Way of the Celestial Masters *and* theocracy.

kuan: The most frequently used Chinese term for Taoist temple or monastery.

kuei: A malevolent spirit, ghost, or demon.

kung: A common term for a Taoist temple. Translates literally as "palace."

K'un-lun: A mythic mountain and frequent destination of those seeking the "fruits of immortality" that supposedly grow there.

Lao-Chuang Tradition: The teachings of Lao Tzu and Chuang Tzu. More or less another name for Classical Taoism. *See also* Classical Taoism.

Lao-chün: *See* Lord Lao.

Lao Tzu: The Old Master. A legendary figure identified as the founder of Taoism and supposed author of the *Tao Te Ching. See also Tao Te Ching.*

Legalism: An important philosophy during the Hundred Schools Period, emphasizing the rule of law and the mystique of political power, which briefly served as China's ruling ideology. *See also* Hundred Schools Period.

Legge, James: A 19th-century scholar-missionary whose understandings (and misunderstandings) of Chinese religion shaped a great deal of the modern Western impression of Taoism.

Le Guin, Ursula K.: A modern American fantasy and science-fiction author, occasional political and social commentator, and all-around Renaissance woman, whose stories often incorporate Classical Taoist ideas. *See also* Classical Taoism.

Lew, Share K.: A Chinese immigrant, teacher, and founder of the Taoist Sanctuary. *See also* Taoist Sanctuary.

Li Hung: The anticipated Taoist messiah, understood to be an incarnation of Lord Lao who would lead the world into an age of Great Peace. Also known as Li Chen-chün. *See also* Lord Lao *and* Great Peace.

Li Hung-chi: The controversial founder of the Fa-lun Ta-fa, currently living in the United States. *See also* Fa-lun Ta-fa.

libationer: Translation of *chi-chiu,* the highest priestly rank in the Way of the Celestial Masters, and forerunner of the married priesthood in the Way of Orthodox Unity. *See also* Way of the Celestial Masters *and* Way of the Orthodox Unity.

Lieh Tzu: An early Hundred Schools philosopher who may have had similar ideas to Chuang Tzu, but whose writings have been lost. A book that bears his name is a forgery from a much later period. *See also* Hundred Schools Period *and* Chuang Tzu.

ling: The "spiritual efficacy" of a ghost, spirit, or other non-obvious being. The special quality a spirit has so that its effects are felt in this world.

Ling-pao: *See* Numinous Treasure.

Liturgical Taoism: The general name given to lineages of Taoism, like Orthodox Unity, that primarily focus on rituals and ceremonies directed to various spirits and deities. *See also* Orthodox Unity Taoism.

Liu An: The Prince of Huai-nan, and sponsor of the Huang-Lao Taoist text, the *Huai-nan Tzu. See also* Huang-Lao Taoism *and Huai-nan Tzu.*

Lord Lao: Lao-chün, the deified Lao Tzu, object of worship and source of many revealed scriptures in the Taoist Canon. Also known as T'ai-shang Lao-chün. *See also* Taoist Canon.

Lo-t'ien Ta-chiao: The Great Offering to All-Encompassing Heaven, a spectacular Taoist ritual performed at irregular intervals, involving the participation of hundreds of priests from several countries and lineages.

Lou-kuan: The earliest known Taoist center for study and worship. The forerunner of contemporary Taoist temples.

Lung-hu Shan: *See* Dragon Tiger Mountain.

Master of Heavenly Seclusion: The *T'ien Yin Tzu,* an anonymous 7th- or 8th-century Taoist text, closely identified with the *Treatise on Sitting and Forgetting. See also Treatise on Sitting and Forgetting.*

The Master Who Embraces Simplicity: A 4th-century book of by Ko Hung. One of the earliest collections of alchemical instructions and sources. *See also* Ko Hung *and* alchemy.

Ma-wang-tui: The location of an archaeological site in Hunan province, where a 1973 excavation unearthed numerous important manuscripts, including what at that time were the two oldest extant versions of the *Tao Te Ching. See also Tao Te Ching.*

millenarianism: The belief in a coming "new age," a literal or figurative new era of cosmic time, which followers have an obligation to prepare for or perhaps help facilitate.

Ming Canon: The final version of the Taoist Canon, dating back to the 15th century and almost destroyed near the turn of the 20th century. *See also* Taoist Canon.

Mohism: An important philosophy from the Hundred Schools Period, founded by Mo Tzu and advocating utilitarianism and the moral practice of universal love. *See also* Hundred Schools Period *and* Mo Tzu.

Monastic Taoism: The general name given to lineages of Taoism, like Complete Perfection, that train priests and nuns in various types of self-cultivation, most often in temples and monasteries. *See also* Complete Perfection Taoism.

morality books: Translation of *shan-shu,* a type of text appearing in the Taoist Canon (and elsewhere) that teaches basics moral lessons through accessible vernacular language. *See also* Taoist Canon.

Mo Tzu: An important 5th-century B.C.E. philosopher from the Hundred Schools Period, who criticized the followers of Confucius and advocated his own alternative ethical principles. *See also* Hundred Schools Period *and* Mohism.

Moy Shin-lin: An important North American Taoist figure, founder of both the International Taoist T'ai-chi Society and the Fung Loy Kok Taoist temples. *See also* International Taoist T'ai-chi Society *and* Fung Loy Kok.

mysticism: A general term applied to various disciplines that a practitioner believes facilitate a direct experience of a higher reality or with the true character of reality

nei-tan: *See* internal alchemy.

Nei-yeh: *See Inward Training.*

New Age Movement: A largely unstructured, originally millenarian, spiritual "movement," that draws on eclectic resources ranging from holistic medicine to Jungian psychology to Eastern philosophy. *See also* millenarianism.

Ni, Daoshing: An acupuncturist and son of Ni Hua-ching. One of the directors (with his brother Mao Shing Ni) of the Tao of Wellness medical centers in California. *See also* Ni Hua-ching *and* Ni, Mao Shing.

Ni Hua-ching: Chinese-born American Taoist, founder of the Integral Way and the organizations that grew from it. Known as OmNi to his followers. *See also* Integral Way.

Ni, Mao Shing: An acupuncturist and son of Ni Hua-ching. One of the directors (with his brother Daoshing Ni) of the Tao of Wellness medical centers in California. *See also* Ni Hua-ching *and* Ni, Daoshing.

nine worms: *See* three corpses.

non-doing: Translation of *wu-wei,* a concept introduced in the Classical Taoist texts. It refers to the effective performance of action that doesn't spring from personal will, intention, or goal orientation, but rather harmonizes spontaneously with the *Tao. See* Classical Taoism.

Numinous Treasure: Translation of Ling-pao, an extensive series of revealed texts from the 4th and 5th centuries (dealing with meditation and visualization, use of talismans, descriptions of Heavenly realms, and so on) and of the self-cultivation groups that organized around them. *See also* talismans.

nurturing life: A general name applied to a wide spectrum of practices, ranging from ordinary care for the body to specifically Taoist physical cultivation techniques.

nü-tan: Literally "women's alchemy," forms of internal alchemy addressed specifically to women. *See also* alchemy *and* internal alchemy.

OmNi: *See* Ni Hua-ching.

Orthodox Unity Taoism: The Cheng-I Tao, the older, more liturgical and ritualistic of the two Taoist lineages that are common in China today. Priests in this lineage mostly flourish in the southern part of the country and Taiwan. *See also* Complete Perfection Taoism.

Pao-p'u Tzu: See The Master Who Embraces Simplicity.

P'eng-lai: A mythic island paradise and frequent destination of immortality seekers.

Philosophical Taoism: The somewhat misleading name given to the Classical Taoist texts of Lao Tzu, Chuang Tzu, and others from the Hundred Schools Period and shortly thereafter. *See also* Classical Taoism *and* Hundred Schools Period.

Primitivist: One strand of writings in the *Chuang Tzu,* which rejects society and longs for a simple utopia.

p'u: See uncarved block.

redhead Taoists: Distinguished from blackhead Taoists, these are local, usually hereditary priests who aren't ordained in any official Taoist lineage, but who perform many (but not all) of the same functions as ordained priests. *See also* blackhead Taoists.

registers: Protective texts, often attached to a practitioner's clothing during rituals, which identify the spirits or divine beings the initiate has the authority to summon or control.

Religious Taoism: A misleading name given to pretty much all Taoist history and practice, apart from the early texts of Classical Taoism. *See also* Classical Taoism *and* Teachings of the *Tao.*

School of Chuang Tzu: One strand of writings in the *Chuang Tzu* (rather than an organized school) that is philosophically and stylistically similar to the authentic chapters, though written during the subsequent generations by followers trying to emulate his work. *See also* Chuang Tzu.

School of *Tao:* Translation of *tao-chia,* the term scholars and librarians first used to refer to text by Lao Tzu, Chuang Tzu, and other similar thinkers from the Hundred Schools Period. Often translated, somewhat misleadingly, as Philosophical Taoism. *See also* Hundred Schools Period *and* Philosophical Taoism.

Scripture of Great Peace: Title of several Taoists texts, some of which are lost, explaining the ideology of early millenarian Taoist movements. *See also* millenarianism.

The Seal of the Unity of the Three: The *Chou I Ts'an T'ung Ch'i,* one of the earliest works of Taoist alchemy, probably composed over several centuries but traditionally attributed to a legendary alchemist named Wei Po-yang. *See also* alchemy *and* Wei Po-yang.

Seven Perfected: Early "founding fathers" of Complete Perfection Taoism, credited with spreading the tradition and organizing several subsects. *See also* Complete Perfection Taoism.

shan-shu: *See* morality books.

Shang-ch'ing: *See* Highest Purity.

shen: General term for benign or good spirits, but also the term for the "spiritual" aspect of the person, especially important in later Taoist theories of the human body.

sitting and forgetting: Translation of *tso-wang.* Taoist meditation, first referenced in the *Chuang Tzu,* which involves the systematic deconditioning of knowledge and cognitive habits. *See also* Chuang Tzu.

sitting around the bowl: A form of group meditation, once common in Complete Perfection Taoism. *See also* Complete Perfection Taoism.

spiritualization: The process of reinterpreting particular texts or traditions in order to extrapolate universal lessons or apply them to new contexts.

Ssu-ma Ch'eng-chen: A Highest Purity Taoist adept of the 7th and 8th centuries. Author of the *Treatise on Sitting and Forgetting. See also Treatise on Siting and Forgetting.*

syncretism: The tendency to make use of religious practices and resources from different traditions, regardless of whether their respective doctrines agree with one another.

Syncretists: One strand of writings in the *Chuang Tzu,* possibly representing the actual compilers and editors of the text, which attempted to integrate Taoist philosophy with other teachings. *See also* Chuang Tzu.

t'ai-chi ch'üan: Literally, the "boxing of the Great Ultimate," a set of stylized martial arts thought to promote physical and spiritual health.

T'ai-ch'ing: *See* Great Purity.

T'ai-ping Ching: *See Scripture of Great Peace.*

T'ai-p'ing Tao: *See* Way of Great Peace.

T'ai-shang Lao-chün: *See* Lord Lao.

talismans: Textual diagrams and symbols ritually employed by initiated Taoists for purposes of healing, marking off sacred space, interceding on behalf of the dead, and so forth.

tan-t'ien: *See* cinnabar fields.

Tao: Literally "the Way" or "Way." Refers in philosophy and religion to "ways" of ultimate truth and human obligations.

tao-chia: *See* School of *Tao.*

tao-chiao: *See* Teachings of the *Tao.*

T'ao Hung-ching: A late 5th-century figure, responsible for the assembly and propagation of Highest Purity texts.

Tao-tsang: *See* Taoist Canon.

Taoist Canon: The *Tao-tsang,* the recognized collection of Taoist scriptures, containing nearly 1,500 volumes.

Taoist Sanctuary: The first publically recognized Taoist institution in the United States to receive tax-exempt status.

The Tao of Pooh: An entertaining book by Benjamin Hoff, which adapts the *Winnie the Pooh* characters to quasi-Taoist philosophy. A prime example of the Western spiritualization of Taoism. *See also* Hoff, Benjamin *and* spiritualization.

Tao Te Ching: The Classic of the Way and Its Power. One of the foundational texts of Taoism, supposedly authored by Lao Tzu. *See also* Lao Tzu.

te: Usually translated as "power" or "virtue," the manifest quality of the *Tao.*

Teachings of the *Tao*: Translation of *tao-chiao,* a general term applied to all the liturgical and institutional Taoist developments from the Celestial Masters up through modern times. Often translated, a bit misleadingly, as "religious Taoism." *See also* Religious Taoism.

Three Caverns: The original threefold subdivision of texts that would eventually make up the Taoist Canon. *See also* Taoist Canon.

three corpses: A trio of spiritual parasites who, together with the nine worms, can be driven out of the human body through visualization and hygienic techniques. *See also* nine worms.

Three Ones: A trio of deities thought to inhabit the three cinnabar fields of the body. *See also* cinnabar fields.

Three Pure Ones: The three deities at the top of the Taoist pantheon, who grew from the Highest Purity and Numinous Treasure revelations. They include Heavenly Worthy of the Primordial Beginning, Heavenly Worthy of Numinous Treasure, and Heavenly Worthy of the Way and its Power. *See also* Highest Purity *and* Numinous Treasure.

T'ien: *See* Heaven.

***T'ien-shih*:** *See* Celestial Master.

T'ien-shih Tao: *See* Way of the Celestial Masters.

T'ien Yin Tzu: *See Master of Heavenly Seclusion.*

Treatise of the Most High on Impulse and Response: One of the most popular morality books in the Taoist Canon, characterized by a syncretic mix of Taoist, Buddhist, and Confucian ethics. *See also* morality books, Taoist Canon, *and* syncretism.

Treatise on Sitting and Forgetting: Translation of *Tso-wang lun,* a text by Ssu-ma Ch'eng-chen, which articulates a seven-step process of meditation. *See also* Ssu-ma Ch'eng-chen.

Tzu-jan: Translates literally as "self-so," though often rendered as "natural- ness" or "spontaneity." Describes both the pristine state of the *Tao* and the disposition of those who know and follow it..

uncarved block: Translation of *p'u.* Recurring image in the *Tao Te Ching.* Serves a metaphor for simplicity, authenticity, and unlimited potential. *See also Tao Te Ching.*

vital essence: Translation of *ching.* In Taoist spiritual physiology, identified as an unrefined reservoir of matter and energy that collects in the lowest cinnabar field, the one in the abdomen. Sometimes equated with sexual energy or reproductive fluids. *See also* cinnabar fields.

wai-tan: *See* external alchemy.

Way of the Celestial Masters: Translation of *T'ien-shih Tao.* An alternative name for the Way of Orthodox Unity. Usually refers to the first few centuries of historical development, especially after the dispersion of the original c ommunity. *See also* Way of Orthodox Unity.

Way of Great Peace: The T'ai-p'ing Tao, a millenarian movement contem- poraneous with the original Way of the Celestial Masters, responsible for the Yellow Turbans Rebellion. *See also* millenarianism, Way of the Celestial Masters, *and* Yellow Turbans Rebellion.

Way of Orthodox Unity: The liturgical, southern branch of modern Taoism, claiming descent from the Way of the Celestial Masters. *See also* Way of the Celestial Masters.

Wei Huan-ts'un: An important libationer from the early Way of the Celestial Masters, and an equally important channeled spirit in the Highest Purity rev- elations. *See also* libationer, Way of the Celestial Masters, *and* Highest Purity.

Wei Po-yang: A semi-legendary alchemist and the supposed author of *The Seal of the Unity of the Three. See also The Seal of the Unity of the Three.*

White Cloud Monastery: An important Taoist temple in Beijing, affiliated with the Complete Perfection lineage and the China Taoist Association. *See also* Complete Perfection Taoism *and* China Taoist Association.

Wu-tang: The name of a sacred Taoist mountain and of the martial arts traditions that have been based there for centuries.

wu-wei: See non-doing.

yang: Often defined as the "masculine principle." Refers to dark-active-expanding configurations of *ch'i*. *See also ch'i and yin-yang.*

Yang Chu: An early Hundred Schools philosopher sometimes classified as a Taoist, who taught that you should fulfill the desires of the physical body, a position that attracted accusations of hedonism or egoism. *See also* Hundred Schools Period.

Yangists: Anonymous followers of Yang Chu and likely authors of several chapters of the *Chuang Tzu*. *See also* Yang Chu *and* Chuang Tzu.

Yellow Emperor: Huang Ti, a mythical emperor and culture hero of ancient China. *See* Huang-Lao Taoism.

Yellow Turbans Rebellion: A far-reaching, but ultimately unsuccessful, military rebellion undertaken by members of the Way of Great Peace. *See also* Way of Great Peace.

yin: Often defined as the "feminine principle." Refers to light-passive-contracting configurations of *ch'i*. *See also ch'i* and *yin-yang.*

yin-yang: Concern for the interactions of *yin* and *yang*. Relevant for divination, physical cultivation, and correlative cosmology. Identified closely with five elements theory. *See also* correlative cosmology *and* five elements theory.

Appendix B

Resources

I f you start looking for other resources on Taoism, prepare yourself for walking in on a stand-up comic's bombardment of "good news, bad news" jokes. The good news is that bookstores and online booksellers have an abundance of Taoist materials — you may find yourself drowning amidst thousands of options. The bad news is that the vast majority of them are either inaccurate or misleading. The good news is that the 1979 publication, *Facets of Taoism,* by Holmes Welch and Anna Seidel, marked the unofficial beginning of a new era of responsible publications on Taoism, so you can pretty much narrow your search down to items no earlier than about 1980 (unless you plan on surfing through old scholarly journals). The bad news is that the more recent materials are usually either accessible or faithful to the subject, but not both; books published by popular presses tend to skip over historical context and rely on dated conceptions of Taoism, while books published by academic presses tend to linger on technical details and assume the reader's familiarity with all sorts of scholarly conversations. The good news is that there's a new invention called the Internet, and you don't have to rely so much on old-fashioned books made out of paper. The bad news is that online sources talking about Taoism have an even lower accuracy rate than books. And so on. . . .

But all is not lost. Amidst all the Taoistic chaos out there, you really can find a number of resources that do help you broaden your base of Taoist understanding without short-circuiting your neural net. I can't give you a list of absolutely every single website or book that falls into that category, but I can give you some places to start.

Websites You Can Trust

There aren't many websites you can count on, but here are a few of the most reliable ones:

- ✓ **Center for Daoist Studies** (www.daoistcenter.org): This handsome website is sponsored by the Daoist Foundation, a nonprofit organization designed to transmit Taoist teachings. The directors are a husband-and-wife team of American Taoist practitioners. He's a professor; she's a professional acupuncturist.

✔ **Daoist Studies** (www.daoiststudies.org): This informational site is run by Taoism scholar James Miller. It includes updates for scholars (like job postings and upcoming conferences), as well as interested non-specialists (like thematic essays and a basic Q&A).

✔ **The Golden Elixir** (www.goldenelixir.com): This site is run by Fabrizio Pregadio, the editor of *The Encyclopedia of Taoism*. It includes a blog, lists of new Taoism books and translations, and lots of information on Taoist alchemy.

General Introductions to Taoism

All the books in this section offer surveys of the Taoist tradition, though each with its own particular approach, interests, and interpretations. Some are more historical, others more thematic; some focus more on institutions, others more on popular practice. If you have time, you may want to try more than one:

✔ *Daoism: A Short Introduction,* **by James Miller (Oneworld):** This book is a thematic (as opposed to an historical) introduction to Taoism, with topics like "body," "light," "power," and "nature."

✔ *Daoism: An Introduction,* **by Ronnie Littlejohn (I. B. Tauris):** This book follows Taoism's historical development, using the "family tree" metaphor, including a wide range of "branches" and even some "withered vines."

✔ *Daoism and Chinese Culture,* **by Livia Kohn (Three Pines Press):** This book is organized historically, from the Classical to the Modern periods.

✔ *Daoism in China: An Introduction,* **by Wang Yi'e (Floating World Editions):** This book is written from the perspective of the China Taoist Association, with emphasis on deities, sacred space, and contemporary institutions. It's interesting to see how a modern Chinese association prefers to understand Taoist history.

✔ *Introducing Daoism,* **by Livia Kohn (Routledge):** This book takes a mainly historical, modular approach to the subject. It's intended as a classroom textbook for a survey course on Taoism.

✔ *Taoism,* **by Hsiao-lan Hu and William Cully Allen (Chelsea House Publications):** This book is a brief primer, emphasizing popular practice more than history, and including things like holiday and temple worship.

✔ *Taoism: Origins, Beliefs, Practices, Holy Texts, Sacred Places,* **by Jennifer Oldstone-Moore (Watkins):** This book is a much shorter treatment of Taoism, with thematic chapters on Taoist ethics, sacred persons, sacred time, death and the afterlife, and so forth.

✔ *Taoism: The Enduring Tradition,* **by Russell Kirkland (Routledge):** This book includes a mix of historical and thematic approaches, paying particular attention to social and political factors.

Translations of the Taoist Classics

There's no beating the old favorites, and most Taoism enthusiasts still want to read translations of the classical texts like the _Tao Te Ching_ and _Chuang Tzu,_ though you'd be well served to stay away from versions translated by people who don't know Chinese — at least most of them. Here are some recent, consistently reliable translations:

- _**The Book of Lieh-Tzu,**_ **by A. C. Graham (Columbia University Press):** This book is a dated but serviceable translation of this much- neglected text. The "Yang Chu" chapter may contain some material by that shadowy figure.

- _**Chuang Tzu: Basic Writings,**_ **by Burton Watson (Columbia University Press):** This is a readable translation of the seven "Inner Chapters" and a handful of thematically similar chapters from the rest of the text.

- _**Chuang Tzu: The Inner Chapters,**_ **by A. C. Graham (Hackett Publishing):** This is a challenging, but technically rich translation, using historical-critical analysis to divide the text into likely authors and time periods.

- _**The Complete Works of Chuang Tzu,**_ **by Burton Watson (Columbia University Press):** This is a solid, readable, though somewhat dated translation of the entire text. It often misses some philosophical subtlety, but it has stood up well over time.

- _**Dao De Jing: A Philosophical Translation,**_ **by Roger T. Ames and David L. Hall (Ballantine Books):** This book is a creative translation from the perspective of correlative cosmology, offering philosophical analysis with each chapter.

- _**Five Lost Classics: Tao, Huang-Lao, and Yin-Yang in Han China,**_ **by Robin D. S. Yates (Ballantine Books):** This book is a technically adept translation of five of the recovered Ma-wang-tui texts.

- _**The Huainanzi: A Guide to the Theory and Practice of Government in Early Han China,**_ **by John S. Major, Sarah Queen, Andrew Meyer, and Harold D. Roth (Columbia University Press):** This is a new translation of the most important text ever written for an audience of one. A quartet of first-rate scholars worked on this for years.

- _**Lao Tzu – Tao Te Ching: A Book about the Way and the Power of the Way,**_ **by Ursula K. Le Guin (Shambhala Publications):** This book isn't a scholarly translation of the text (though Le Guin was assisted by Chinese professor J. P. Seaton); instead, it's a thoughtful rendering with honest explanations of when and why she took the interpretive ball and ran with it.

- _**Original Tao: Inward Training (Nei-yeh) and the Foundations of Taoist Mysticism,**_ **by Harold D. Roth (Columbia University Press):** This translation and analysis of this important "discovered" text argues that it formed the basis of a practice-based Taoist lineage.

✔ *Tao Te Ching: The Classic Book of Integrity and the Way,* by Victor H. Mair (Bantam Books): This book is based on the Ma-wang-tui versions of the text, and reflects the translator's conviction that the text shows influences from Indian philosophy that hadn't been previously acknowledged.

✔ *Te-Tao Ching,* by Robert G. Henricks (Modern Library): Also based on the Ma-wang-tui versions, this straightforward translation also includes side-by-side comparisons of the Chinese characters in the excavated texts, which are especially helpful if you can read even a little Chinese.

✔ *Wandering on the Way: Early Taoist Tales and Parables of Chuang Tzu,* by Victor H. Mair (University of Hawaii Press): This is a colorful translation of the entire text, emphasizing more Chuang Tzu as literary stylist than skeptical philosopher.

Anthologies on Classical Taoism

All the books in this section contain collections of essays, written by different authors, which address the classical texts. These are especially useful because you can pick and choose the chapters you find most interesting or the authors whose work you most enjoy.

✔ *Experimental Essays on Chuang-tzu,* edited by Victor H. Mair (University of Hawaii Press): This book offers creative interpretations of the text, including Lee Yearley's explanation of Chuang Tzu as an "intraworldly mystic" and Michael Saso's report on the text as a meditation manual.

✔ *Hiding the World in the World: Uneven Discourses on the Zhuangzi,* edited by Scott Cook (State University of New York Press): This book offers fascinating, technically sophisticated analyses of the text, including Harold Roth's discussion of "bimodal mysticism" and Chad Hansen's essay on skepticism.

✔ *Lao-tzu and the Tao-te-ching,* edited by Livia Kohn and Michael LaFargue (State University of New York Press): This book includes a smorgasbord of essays on the text, including Julia Hardy's chronicle of influential Western readings, William Baxter's attempt to date the text, and LaFargue's own essay on the challenges of historical interpretation.

✔ *Religious and Philosophical Aspects of Laozi,* edited by Mark Csikszentmihalyi and Philip J. Ivanhoe (State University of New York Press): This book is composed mostly of fairly dense philosophical analysis, but the first few essays on mysticism are more accessible.

✔ *Riding the Wind with Liezi: New Perspectives on the Daoist Classic,* edited by Ronnie Littlejohn and Jeffrey Dippman (State University of

New York Press): The first modern collection of essays on this text, this book discusses subjects as wide ranging as life and death, the theme of chaos, and the role of the body.

✔ *Wandering at Ease in the Zhuangzi,* edited by Roger T. Ames (State University of New York Press): This book is an eclectic mix of essays, including Chris Jochim's excellent analysis of Chuang Tzu's implicit understanding of "self" and William Callahan's reflections on *wu-wei* as a legitimate ethical action-guide.

Thematic Approaches to Taoism

Each text in this section approaches Taoism with an emphasis on one particular theme. These can be especially useful if you want to put Taoism in a comparative framework and relate it to other subjects.

✔ *Daoism and Ecology: Ways Within a Cosmic Landscape,* edited by Norman J. Girardot, James Miller, and Liu Xiaogan (Harvard University Press, Center for the Study of World Religions): This book consists of essays taken from the Taoism and Ecology Conference held in 1998 at Harvard, including both analysis of Taoism's historical position on ecological matters and constructive suggestions for how to make use of Taoist resources in addressing contemporary ecological crises.

✔ *Daoism in the Twentieth Century: Between Eternity and Modernity,* edited by David Palmer and Xun Liu (University of California Press): This is a collection of essays on different aspects of modern Taoism, including ritual, meditation, new religious movements, and globalization.

✔ *Myth and Meaning in Early Taoism: The Theme of Chaos,* by Norman J. Girardot (University of California Press): This book discusses the role of chaos and creation in the Taoist classical texts, drawing heavily from the theories of the now-controversial Romanian scholar Mircea Eliade.

✔ *The Tao of the West: Western Transformations of Taoist Thought,* by J. J. Clarke (Routledge): This book is written more as a "history of ideas" than a study of China. It provides excellent insight into the many ways in which Taoism has influenced and been interpreted by the West.

✔ *Taoism and the Arts of China,* by Stephen Little et al (Art Institute of Chicago with University of California Press): This book includes a catalogue of a comprehensive exhibition of Taoist art covering many different periods of historical development, as well as several explanatory essays.

✔ *The Victorian Translation of China: James Legge's Oriental Pilgrimage,* by Norman J. Girardot (University of California Press): This book isn't really on Taoism per se, but it's a fascinating narrative account of the missionary-scholar whose translations and studies of Chinese texts defined the Western view of Taoism for more than a century.

✔ *Women in Daoism,* **by Catherine Despeux and Livia Kohn (Three Pines Press):** Just what it sounds like, this book surveys Taoist goddesses, nuns, and legendary figures, as well as teachings supposedly directed specifically to women.

Reference Volumes to Be Used Encyclopedically

The books in this section aren't ones you'll want to keep by your nightstand and read from cover to cover — they're encyclopedias, reference books, and collections of primary source material that you can use for information about particular people, texts, schools, periods, and so forth.

✔ *The Daoism Handbook,* **edited by Livia Kohn (Brill Academic Publishers):** This is a two-volume collection of sophisticated essays on Taoism, covering specific historical periods and selected themes, like immortality, ordination rituals, divination, cults to specific deities, and sacred sites.

✔ *Historical Dictionary of Taoism,* **by Julian Pas (Rowman & Littlefield):** This book is incomplete and a bit dated, but it's a relatively accessible listing of hundreds of important Taoist terms and names.

✔ *The Routledge Encyclopedia of Taoism,* **edited by Fabrizio Pregadio (Routledge):** This highly technical, two-volume magnum opus provides a wealth of knowledge on the historical legacy of Taoism in China. It's sometimes kind of frustrating, because it employs a lot of jargon and drops names the authors assume you should know, but the info here is invaluable.

✔ *The Taoist Canon: A Historical Companion to the Daozang,* **edited by Kristofer Schipper and Franciscus Verellen (University of Chicago Press):** This is a three-volume index to the unwieldy compendium of Taoist sacred texts, containing historical background to the development of the canon and synopses of each of its nearly 1,500 texts.

Appendix C

Pronunciation Guide

··

*T*his book uses the Wade–Giles system of Romanizing Chinese names and words, but you won't really know how to pronounce them until you become familiar with the rules I list in this appendix.

Be aware that many texts and websites on Taoism and Chinese religion use the *Hanyu Pinyin* system (which I explain in Chapter 1), so don't forget that certain terms appearing one way in this book may appear very different in other sources. In this appendix, I also show you how each Wade-Giles Romanization would be written in *pinyin*.

For the *first letters* of each syllable, many of them — *f, h, l, m, n, s, sh* — are pronounced just as they sound in both Wade–Giles and in *pinyin,* so you don't need any special help for those. Table C-1 outlines the ones you need to watch out for.

Table C-1	Pronouncing the First Letters of a Syllable	
Wade–Giles	*Pinyin*	*Pronunciation*
p'	*p*	*p*
p	*b*	*b*
t'	*t*	*t*
t	*d*	*d*
k'	*k*	*k*
k	*g*	Hard *g* (as in *go*)
ch'	*ch* or *q*	*ch*
ch	*zh* or *j*	*j*
ts'	*c*	*ts* (as in *guts*)
ts	*z*	*dz* (as in *bids*)
hs	*x*	*sh*
j	*r*	*r*

Got it? Good. But now it gets a little trickier. For the vowel sounds (see Table C-2), which almost always occur after an initial consonant or consonant combination, try to remember that these were originally designed as a kind of code for experts, so they don't always make the most sense. But give it a shot!

Table C-2		Pronouncing Vowel Sounds
Wade–Giles	*Pinyin*	*Pronunciation*
a	*a*	*ah* (so, *pan* rhymes with *con* rather than *can*, and *yang* rhymes with the first syllable of *bongo* rather than *bang*)
ai	*ai*	Long *i* (so, *pai* is pronounced like *buy*)
ao	*ao*	*ow* (so, *p'ao* is pronounced like *pow*)
e	*e* (when occurring in the middle of a syllable)	Short *u* (so, *p'eng* rhymes with *lung*)
eh	*e* (when occurring as the last letter of a syllable)	Short *e* (so, *yeh* rhymes with *meh*)
ei	*ei*	Long *a* (so, *wei* is pronounced like *way*)
i	*i*	Long *e* (so, *mi* is pronounced like *me*)
iang	*iang*	*ee-ahng*, with the accent on the second part
iao	*iao*	*ee-ow*, with the accent on the second part (so, *miao* sounds a lot like a cat's *meow*)
ieh	*ie*	*ee-eh*, with the accent on the second part
ien	*ian*	*ee-en*, with the accent on the second part
ih	*i*, when occurring in *ci, si, zi, shi, chi, or zhi*	*er* (so, *shih* rhymes with *her*)
iuh	*iu*	*ee-oh*, with the accent on the second part
iung	*iong*	*ee-oong*, with the accent on the second part
o	*o* or *uo*	*aw* (so, *mo* is pronounced like *maw*)
ou	*ou*	Long *o* (so, *chou* is pronounced like *Joe*)
u	*u*	Long *u* (so, *p'u* is pronounced like *pooh*)

Wade–Giles	Pinyin	Pronunciation
ü	*ü*	Sort of like the German *ü* (but if that's too hard to keep straight, just pronounce it like a long *u*)
ua	*ua*	*wah* (so, *hua* is pronounced like *hwah*)
üan	*uan*	*ü-en*, with the accent on the second syllable (so, *yüan* is pronounced a little like U.N.)
üeh	*ue*	*ü-eh*, with the accent on the second syllable (so, *yüeh* is pronounced a little like *you-eh*)
ung	*ong*	*oong*
uei or *ui*	*ui*	*way* (so, *kuei* is pronounced like *gway*)

Between the first list of opening consonant sounds and this longer list of vowel sounds, that just about covers any Chinese words you'll read in English. Just about. There are a couple more oddities that, again, only make sense to specialists, but you need to know them just because they're part of the system. The initial consonants *Tz* or *Tz'* sound identical to *Ts* and *Ts'* respectively, and the prefix *Ss* sounds like just *S*, but when those three starters — *Tz, Tz',* and *Ss* — are followed by a *u*, the vowel is a sound that doesn't really have an English equivalent, but the closest would probably be the schwa sound that you frequently find in American dictionaries as an upside-down *e*. This symbol is used for the *a* sound in *about* or the *e* sound in *item*. So, remember, Lao Tzu's *Tao Te Ching* is more like "Lao Dzuh's Dow Duh Jing" than "Lao Tzoo's Tao Tay Ching." And Chuang Tzu is "Jwahng Dzuh," not "Chwang Tzoo."

Index

• Q •

Queen, Sarah (author), 349
A Question of Balance (film), 325–326
questions, asking, 320

• R •

raw fruits/vegetables, eating, 319
Reagan, Ronald (president), 130
"real" Taoism, 32–34
Rebellion, 80–81
Records and Biographies category, 214
"redhead priests," 98–99
redhead Taoists, 297, 341. *See also* blackhead
    Taoists
Reform Taoist Congregation, 329–330
registers, 78, 219–220, 342
religion, 27–29, 307–308
Religions of the World and Ecology conference
    series (website), 132
religious, compared with spiritual, 113
Religious and Philosophical Aspects of Laozi
    (Cslkszentmihalyi and Ivanhoe), 350
religious doctrine, 310–311
religious quests, 116
religious supersession, 273
religious syncretism, 39–41
Religious Taoism, 27–29, 313–314, 342. *See also*
    Classical Taoism; Teachings of the *Tao*
Remember the Titans (film), 281
Renaissance world, alchemy in, 262
resources, 347–352. *See also specific resources*
respect and faithfulness stage, 35
response, 189–192
retreat, rituals of, 299–300
returning, 26, 150–151, 228–229
Riding the Wind with Liezi (Littlejohn and
    Dippman), 350–351
righteousness, 53
rightness, 53
rite of cosmic renewal, 300–301
rites of passage, 97
ritual formulas, 210
ritual texts, in Taoist Canon, 220–221
rituals
    about, 291–292, 311
    of anti-ritualistic, 296
    attitudes in classical texts, 294–295
    facts of, 295–298
    of fasting, 299–300
    funeral, 302–303
    Great Offering to All-Encompassing Heaven
        (Lo-t'ien Ta-chiao), 301–302
    implements of, 298
    of offerings, 98, 298–302
    process of, 18
    of purgation, 299–300
    of purification, 98, 298–302
    of retreat, 299–300
    rite of cosmic renewal, 300–301
    Tao-chiao, 87
    viewing, 325
    what are, 292–294
The Romance of the Three Kingdoms, 80
Romanized, 2
Romney, Mitt (presidential candidate), 129
rooms, as images of empty space, 147
Roth, Harold D. (author), 349
The Routledge Encyclopedia of Taoism
    (Pregadio), 352
ruling, 163–167

• S •

Sacred Books of the East series, 34–36, 309
sacred places, 29
sagehood, 246–247
sage-king, 165–166
Sang-hu, 244–245
Saso, Michael (scholar), 93
Schipper, Kristofer (scholar), 93, 216, 352
School of Alliances (The Diplomats), 50
School of Chuang Tzu, 342. *See also* Chuang Tzu
School of Chuang Tzu (SCT) strand, 66
School of Law (Legalism), 50, 72, 338
School of Miscellany (The Eclectics), 50
School of Mo (Mohism), 50, 52–53, 340
School of Names (The Logicians/Dialecticians), 50
School of Soldiers (The Militarists), 50
School of Tao (Taoism), 49
School of *Tao*, 25, 71, 342. *See also* Hundred
    Schools Period Taoism; Philosophical Taoism
School of the Scholars (Confucianism), 49–50,
    52–53, 72, 312–313, 335
School of Tillers (The Agriculturalists), 50
School of Yin-Yang (The Naturalists), 50, 72
Scripture of Great Peace (T'ai-p'ing Tao), 79, 202,
    342. *See also* millenarianism
Scripture on Salvation, 219
scriptures, 29, 88, 209–210
The Seal of the Unity of the Three, 267–268, 342.
    See also alchemy
second-order thinking, 54
Secret Instruction category, 213
*Secret Instructions for Prolonging Life, of the
    Purple Court of the Northern Emperor's
    Seven Primordia,* 221
sectarian gods/goddesses, 41